DARK
ENTRIES

D1016710

VERTIGO
CRIME

WRITER
IAN RANKIN

ART
WERTHER DELL'EDERA

LETTERS
CLEM ROBINS

DARK ENTRIES

DARK ENTRIES
VERTIGO CRIME

DARK ENTRIES Published by DC Comics, 1700 Broadway, New York, NY 10019. Copyright
© 2009 by DC Comics. All rights reserved. VERTIGO, VERTIGO CRIME and all characters,
the distinctive likenesses thereof and all related elements are trademarks of DC Comics.

The stories, characters and incidents mentioned in this book are entirely fictional.

DC Comics does not read or accept unsolicited submissions of ideas, stories or artwork.

Printed in the U.S.A. First Printing. DC Comics, a Warner Bros. Entertainment Company.

ISBN: 978-1-4012-2429-5

Certified Chain of Custody
80% Certified Fiber Sourcing and
40% Post Consumer Recycled
www.sfiprogram.org

NSF-SFICOC-C0001801

This label applies to the text stock

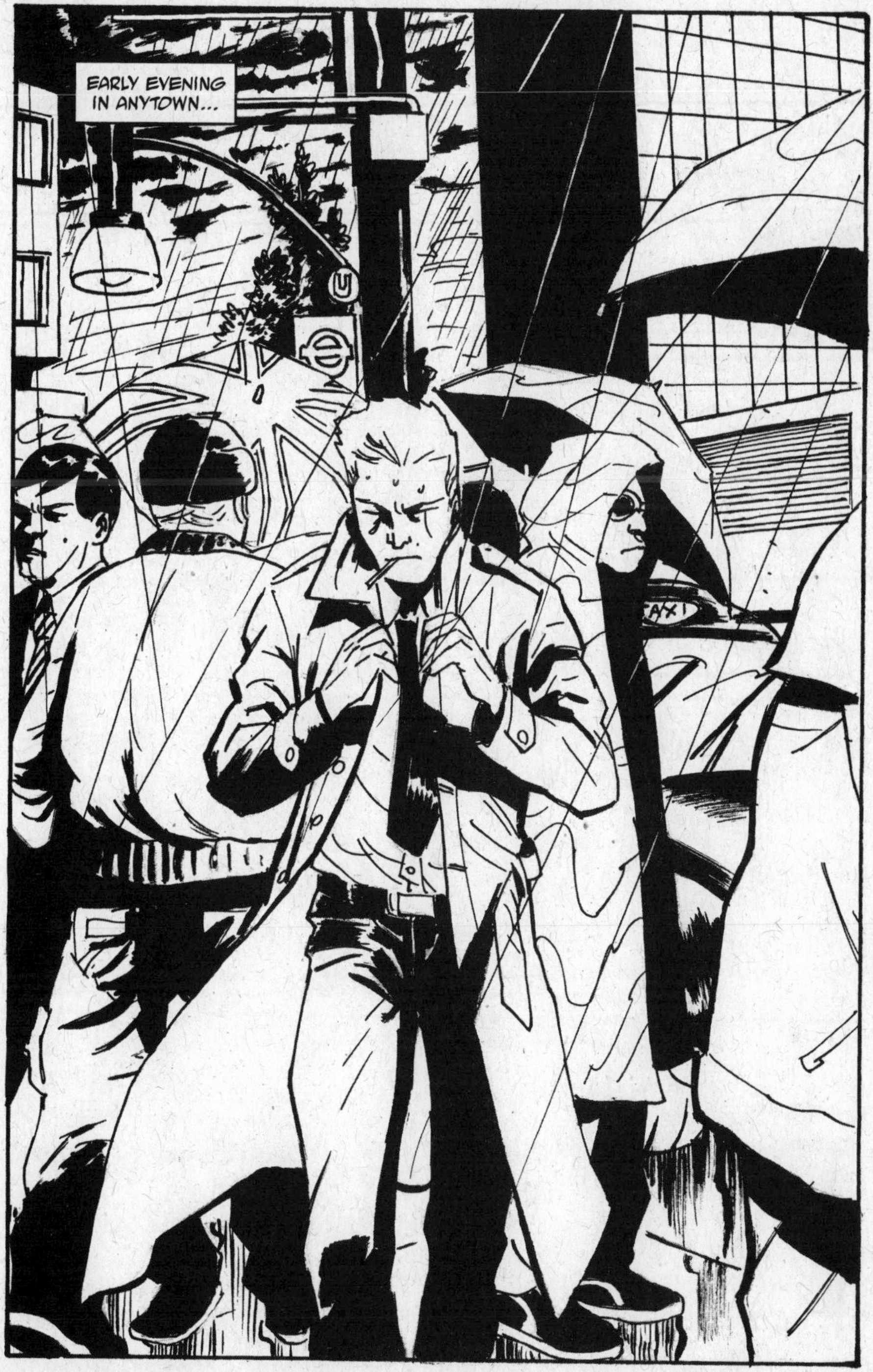
EARLY EVENING
IN ANYTOWN...
TAXI

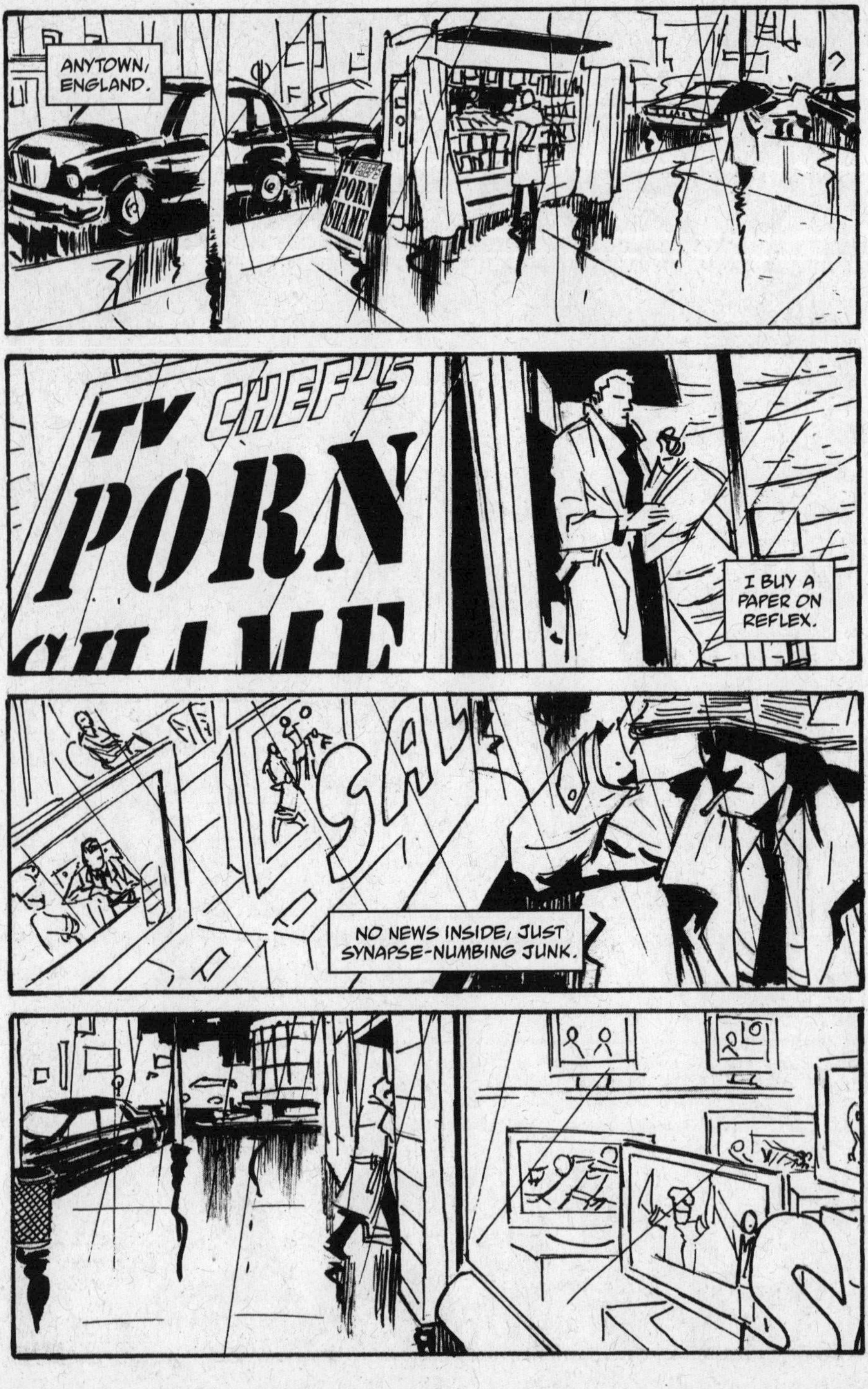
ANYTOWN, ENGLAND.
PORN SHAME
TV CHEF'S PORN SHAME
I BUY A PAPER ON REFLEX.
NO NEWS INSIDE, JUST SYNAPSE-NUMBING JUNK.

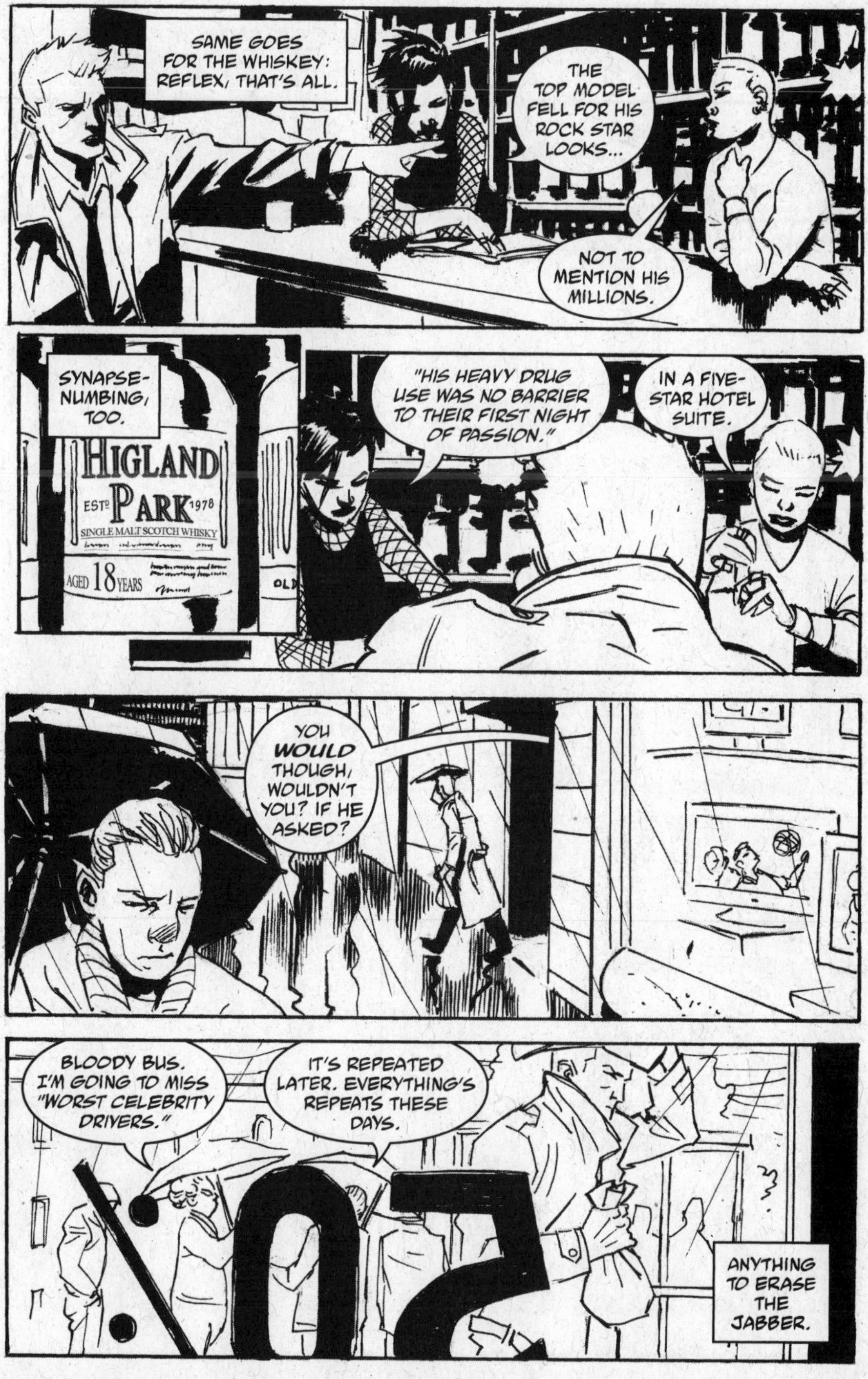
SAME GOES FOR THE WHISKEY: REFLEX, THAT'S ALL.
THE TOP MODEL FELL FOR HIS ROCK STAR LOOKS...
NOT TO MENTION HIS MILLIONS.
SYNAPSE-NUMBING, TOO.
HIGLAND PARK
ESTD 1978
SINGLE MALT SCOTCH WHISKY
AGED 18 YEARS
"HIS HEAVY DRUG USE WAS NO BARRIER TO THEIR FIRST NIGHT OF PASSION."
IN A FIVE-STAR HOTEL SUITE.
YOU **WOULD** THOUGH, WOULDN'T YOU? IF HE ASKED?
BLOODY BUS. I'M GOING TO MISS "WORST CELEBRITY DRIVERS."
IT'S REPEATED LATER. EVERYTHING'S REPEATS THESE DAYS.
ANYTHING TO ERASE THE JABBER.

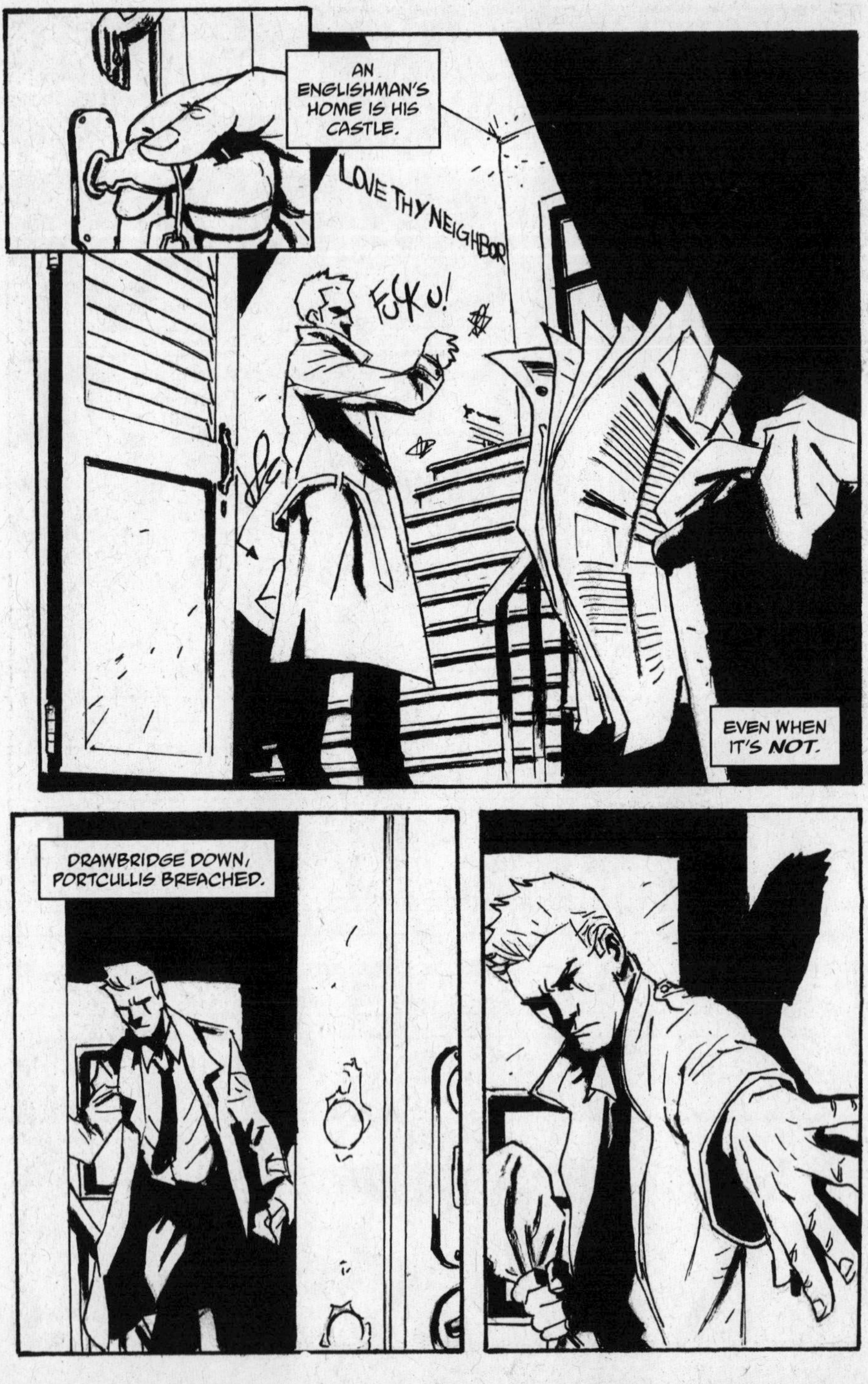
AN ENGLISHMAN'S HOME IS HIS CASTLE.
LOVE THY NEIGHBOR
FUCK U!
EVEN WHEN IT'S *NOT*.
DRAWBRIDGE DOWN, PORTCULLIS BREACHED.

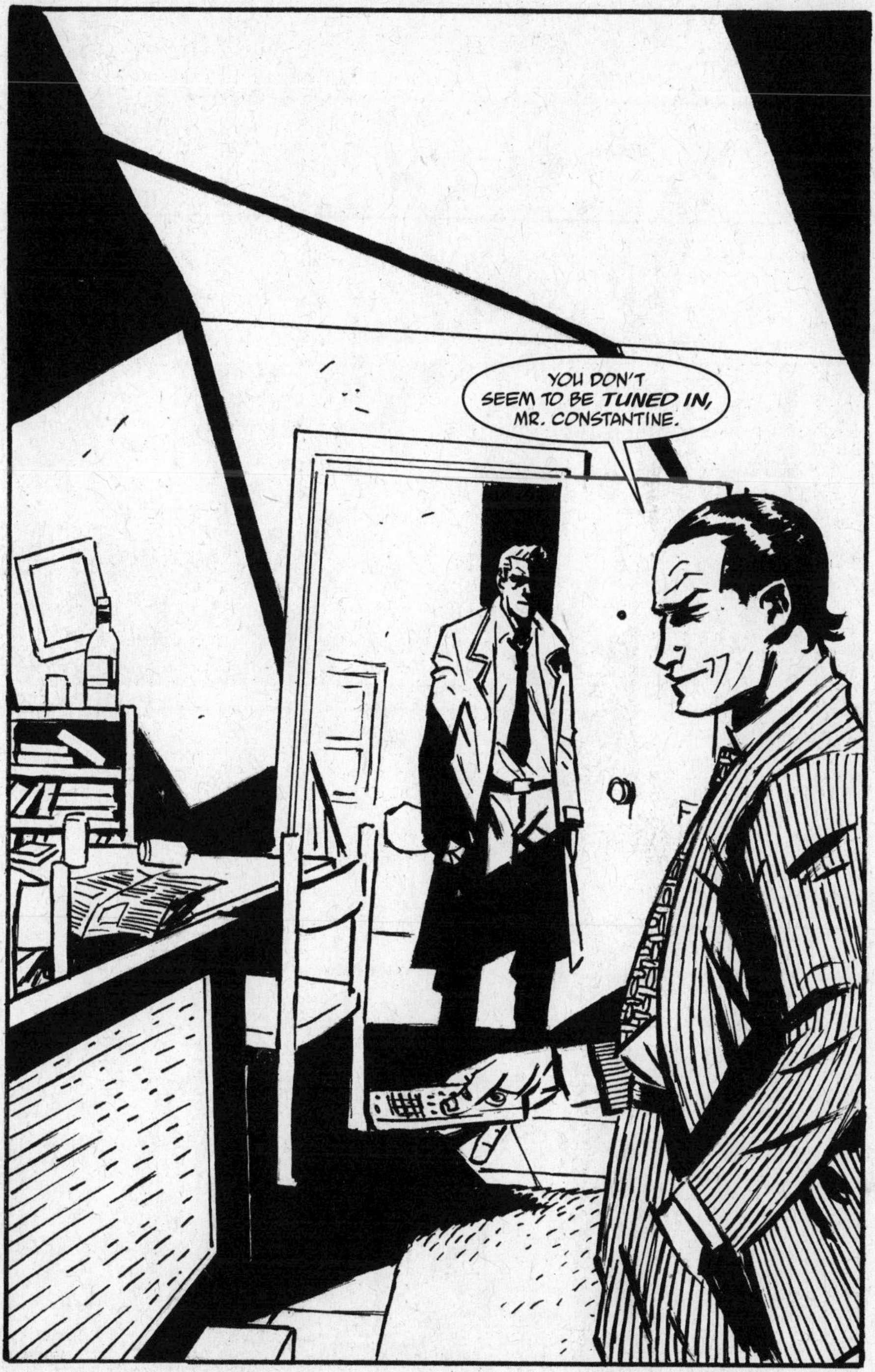
YOU DON'T SEEM TO BE TUNED IN, MR. CONSTANTINE.

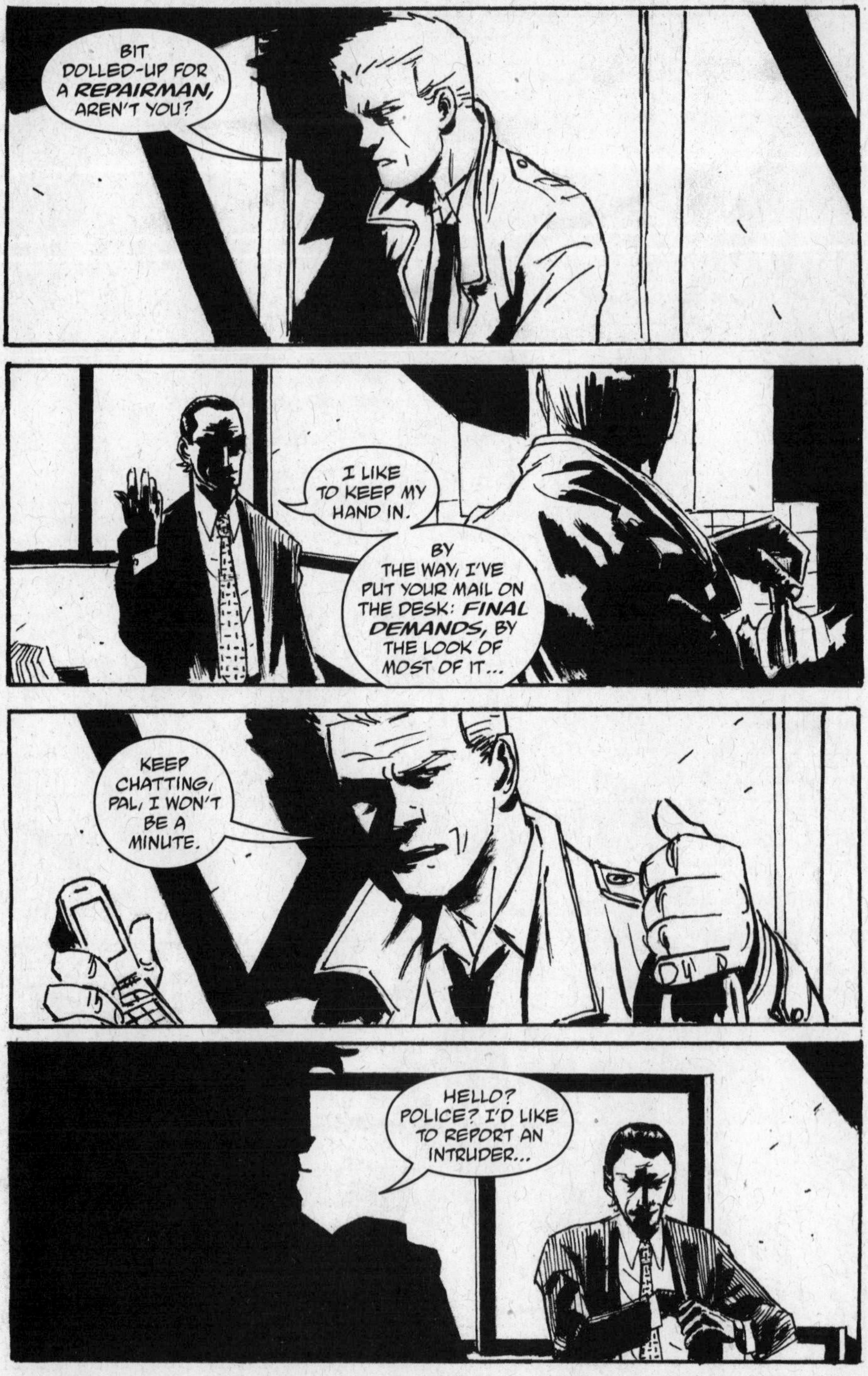
BIT DOLLED-UP FOR A REPAIRMAN, AREN'T YOU?
I LIKE TO KEEP MY HAND IN.
BY THE WAY, I'VE PUT YOUR MAIL ON THE DESK: FINAL DEMANDS, BY THE LOOK OF MOST OF IT...
KEEP CHATTING, PAL, I WON'T BE A MINUTE.
HELLO? POLICE? I'D LIKE TO REPORT AN INTRUDER...

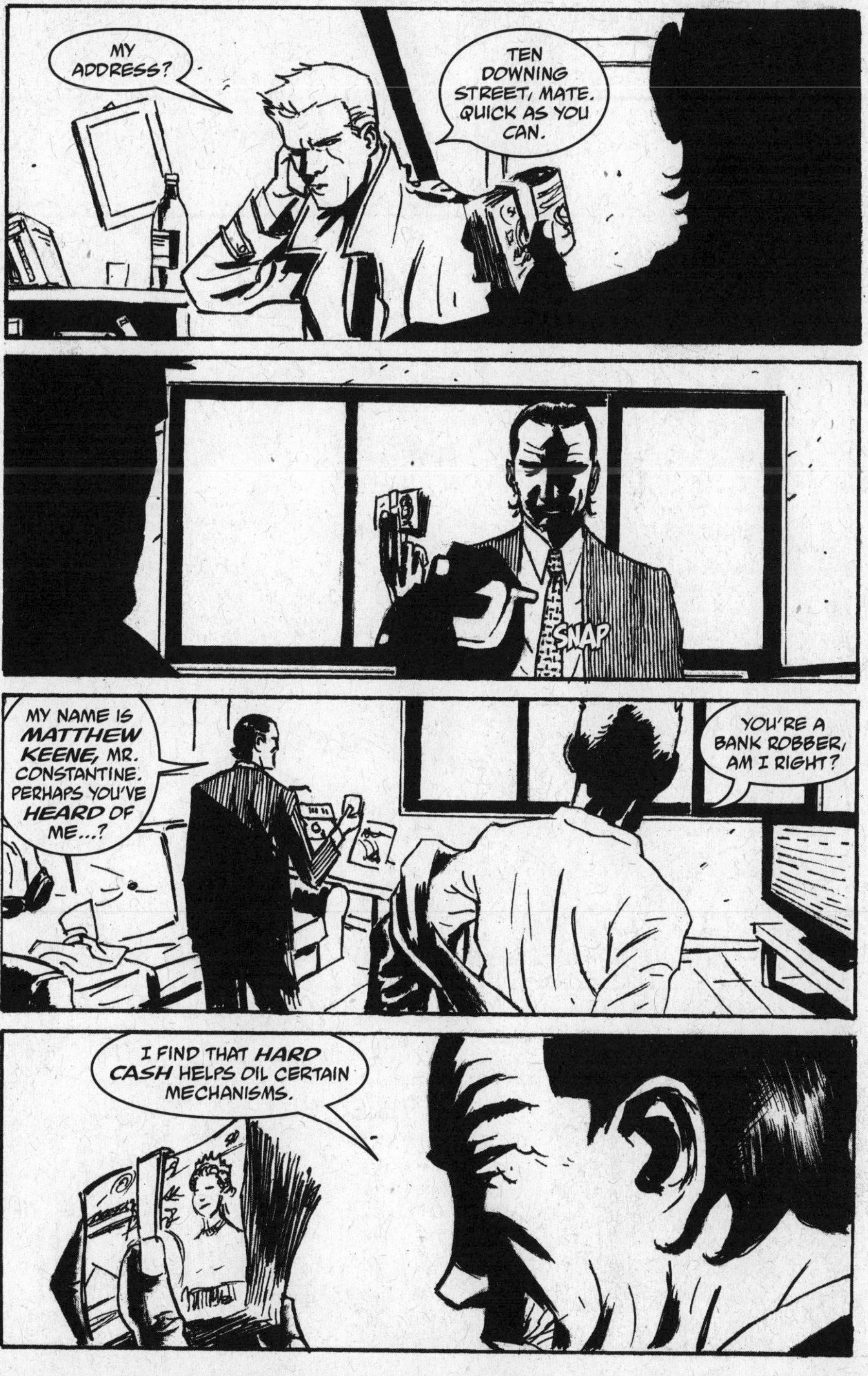
MY ADDRESS?
TEN DOWNING STREET, MATE. QUICK AS YOU CAN.
SNAP
MY NAME IS **MATTHEW KEENE,** MR. CONSTANTINE. PERHAPS YOU'VE **HEARD** OF ME...?
YOU'RE A BANK ROBBER, AM I RIGHT?
I FIND THAT **HARD CASH** HELPS OIL CERTAIN MECHANISMS.

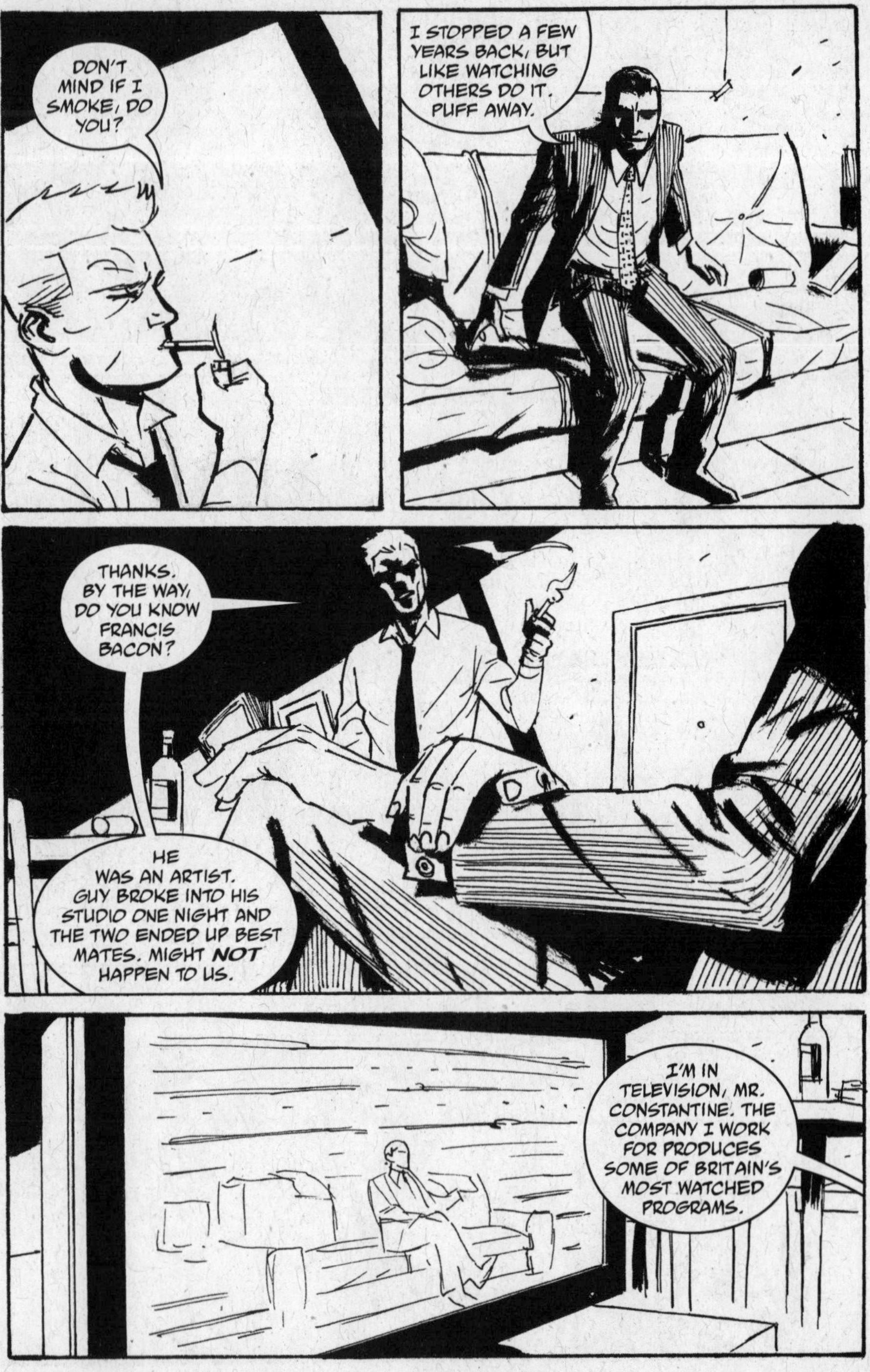
DON'T MIND IF I SMOKE, DO YOU?
I STOPPED A FEW YEARS BACK, BUT LIKE WATCHING OTHERS DO IT. PUFF AWAY.
THANKS. BY THE WAY, DO YOU KNOW FRANCIS BACON?
HE WAS AN ARTIST. GUY BROKE INTO HIS STUDIO ONE NIGHT AND THE TWO ENDED UP BEST MATES. MIGHT **NOT** HAPPEN TO US.
I'M IN TELEVISION, MR. CONSTANTINE. THE COMPANY I WORK FOR PRODUCES SOME OF BRITAIN'S MOST WATCHED PROGRAMS.

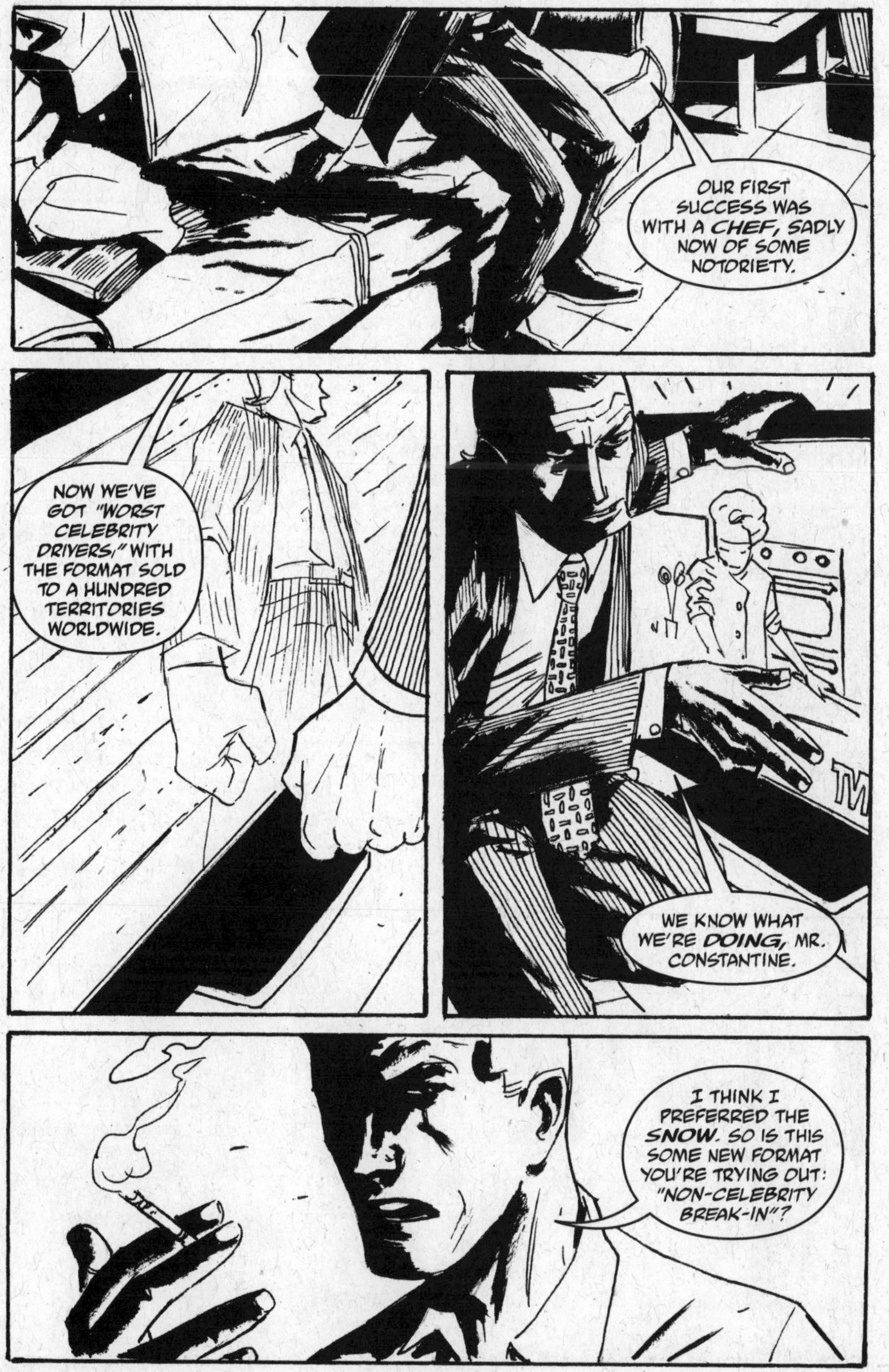
OUR FIRST SUCCESS WAS WITH A CHEF, SADLY NOW OF SOME NOTORIETY.
NOW WE'VE GOT "WORST CELEBRITY DRIVERS," WITH THE FORMAT SOLD TO A HUNDRED TERRITORIES WORLDWIDE.
WE KNOW WHAT WE'RE DOING, MR. CONSTANTINE.
I THINK I PREFERRED THE SNOW. SO IS THIS SOME NEW FORMAT YOU'RE TRYING OUT: "NON-CELEBRITY BREAK-IN"?

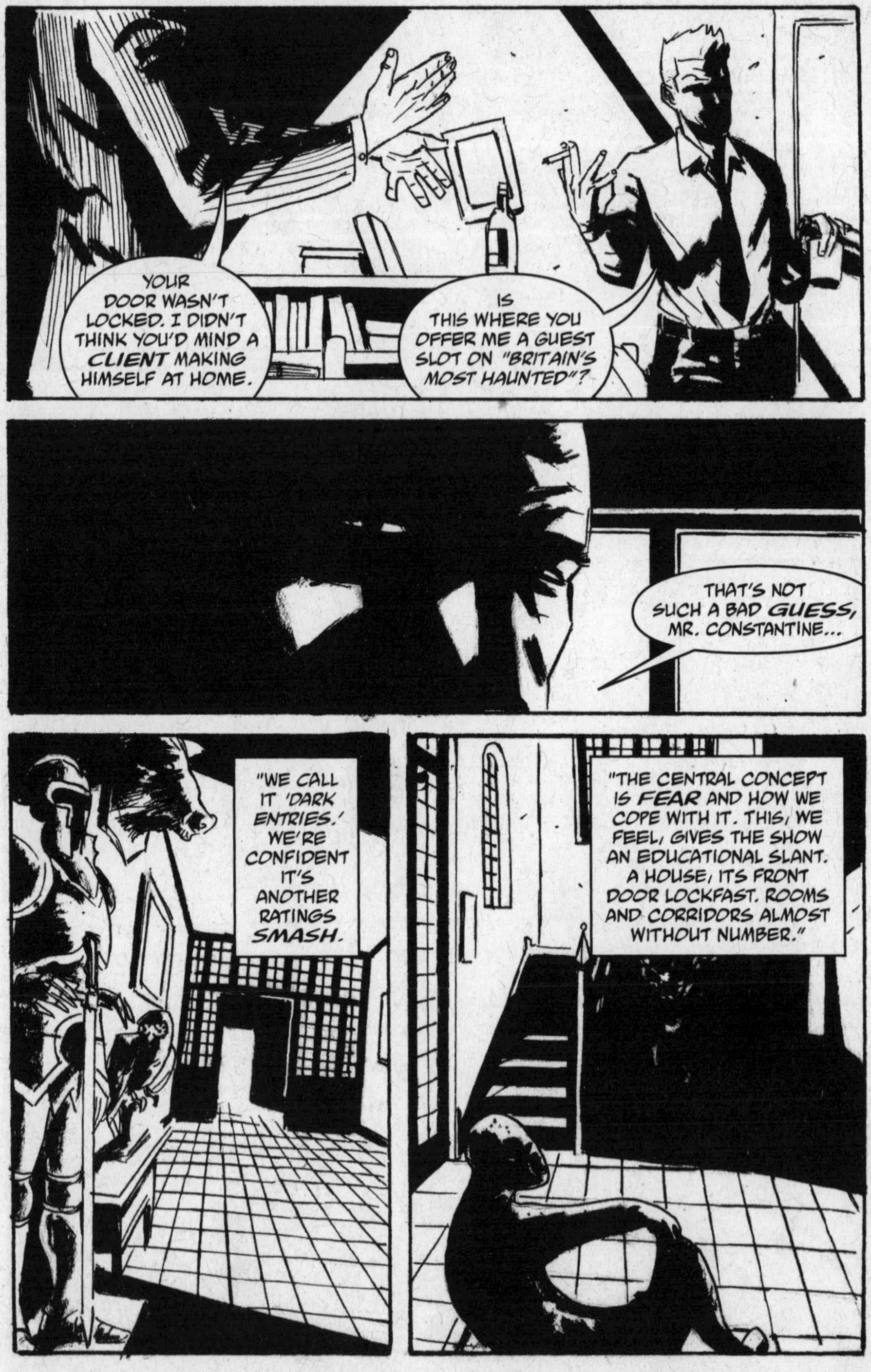
YOUR DOOR WASN'T LOCKED. I DIDN'T THINK YOU'D MIND A CLIENT MAKING HIMSELF AT HOME.
IS THIS WHERE YOU OFFER ME A GUEST SLOT ON "BRITAIN'S MOST HAUNTED"?
THAT'S NOT SUCH A BAD GUESS, MR. CONSTANTINE...
"WE CALL IT 'DARK ENTRIES.' WE'RE CONFIDENT IT'S ANOTHER RATINGS SMASH.
"THE CENTRAL CONCEPT IS FEAR AND HOW WE COPE WITH IT. THIS, WE FEEL, GIVES THE SHOW AN EDUCATIONAL SLANT. A HOUSE, ITS FRONT DOOR LOCKFAST. ROOMS AND CORRIDORS ALMOST WITHOUT NUMBER."

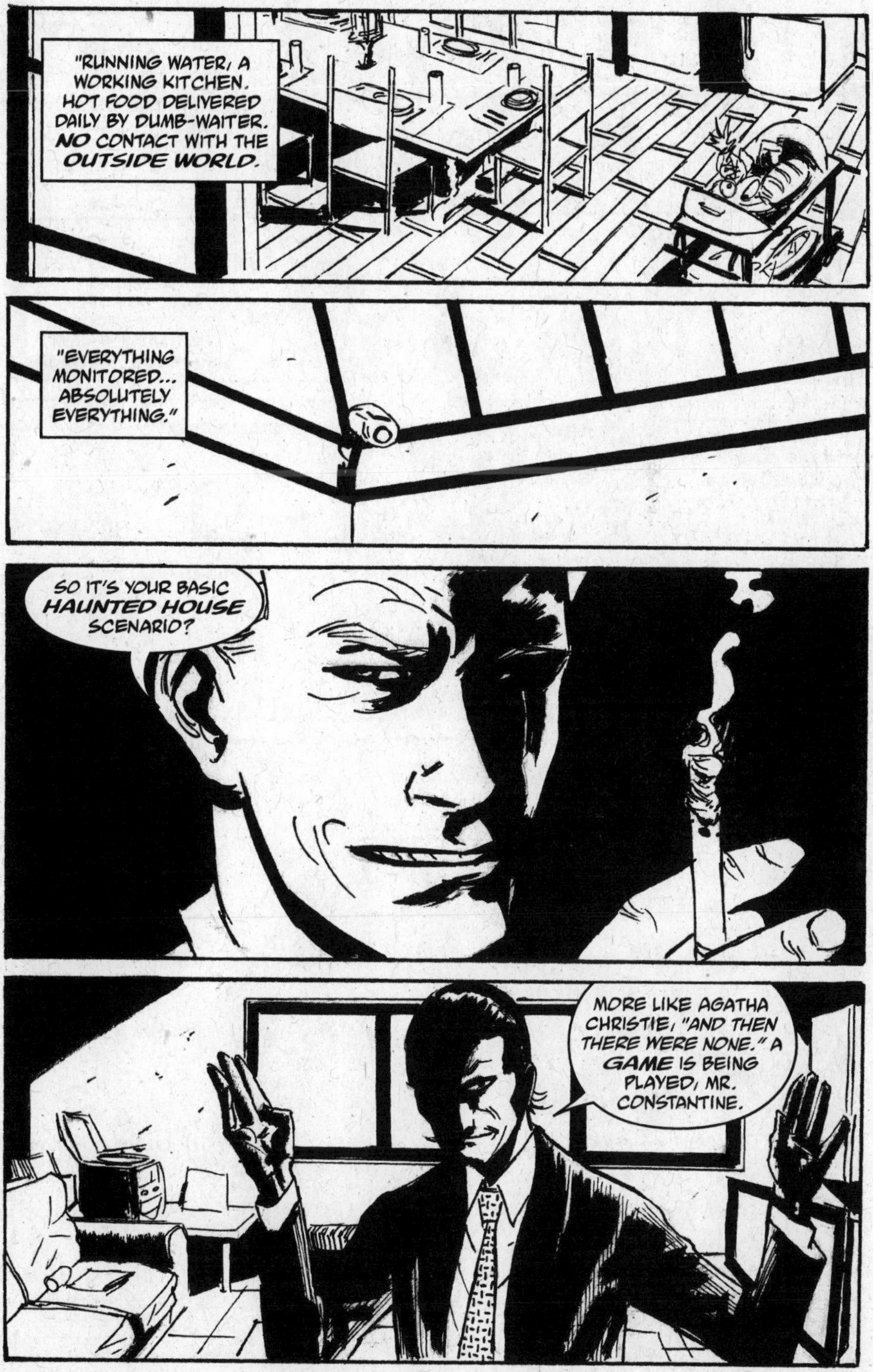
"RUNNING WATER, A WORKING KITCHEN. HOT FOOD DELIVERED DAILY BY DUMB-WAITER. NO CONTACT WITH THE OUTSIDE WORLD.
"EVERYTHING MONITORED... ABSOLUTELY EVERYTHING."
SO IT'S YOUR BASIC HAUNTED HOUSE SCENARIO?
MORE LIKE AGATHA CHRISTIE, "AND THEN THERE WERE NONE." A GAME IS BEING PLAYED, MR. CONSTANTINE.

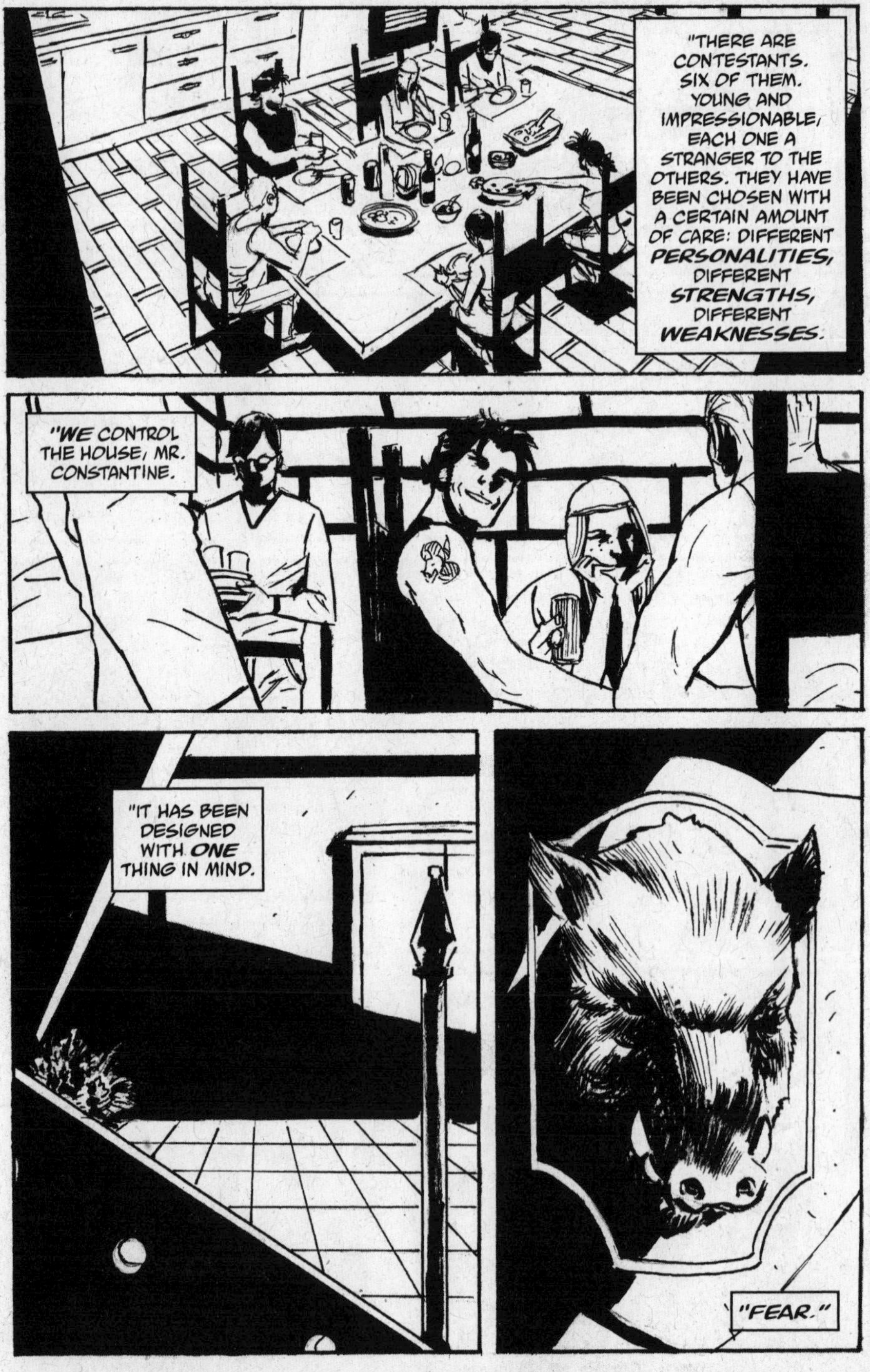
"THERE ARE CONTESTANTS. SIX OF THEM. YOUNG AND IMPRESSIONABLE, EACH ONE A STRANGER TO THE OTHERS. THEY HAVE BEEN CHOSEN WITH A CERTAIN AMOUNT OF CARE: DIFFERENT PERSONALITIES, DIFFERENT STRENGTHS, DIFFERENT WEAKNESSES.
"WE CONTROL THE HOUSE, MR. CONSTANTINE.
"IT HAS BEEN DESIGNED WITH ONE THING IN MIND.
"FEAR."

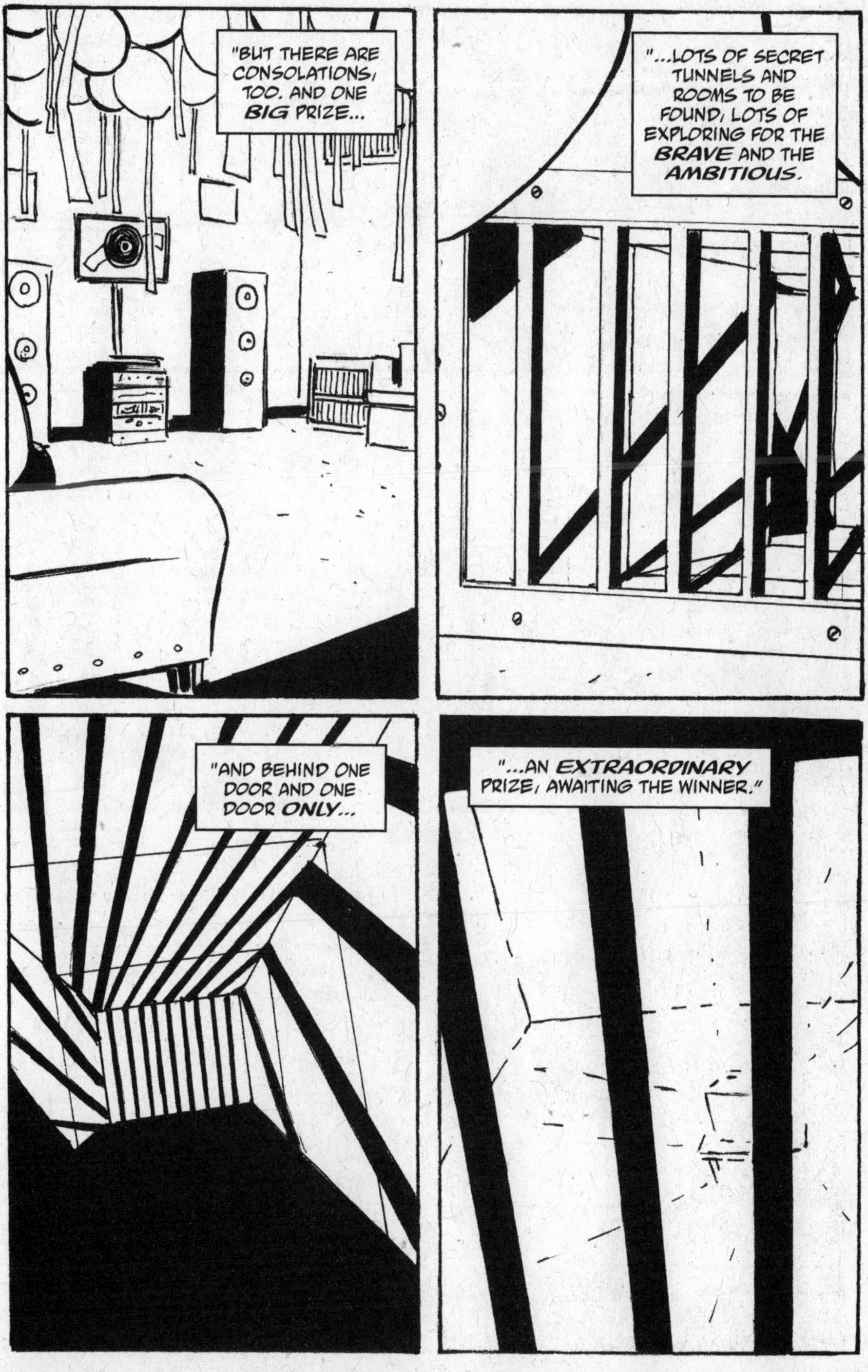
"BUT THERE ARE CONSOLATIONS, TOO. AND ONE BIG PRIZE...
"...LOTS OF SECRET TUNNELS AND ROOMS TO BE FOUND, LOTS OF EXPLORING FOR THE BRAVE AND THE AMBITIOUS.
"AND BEHIND ONE DOOR AND ONE DOOR ONLY...
"...AN EXTRAORDINARY PRIZE, AWAITING THE WINNER."

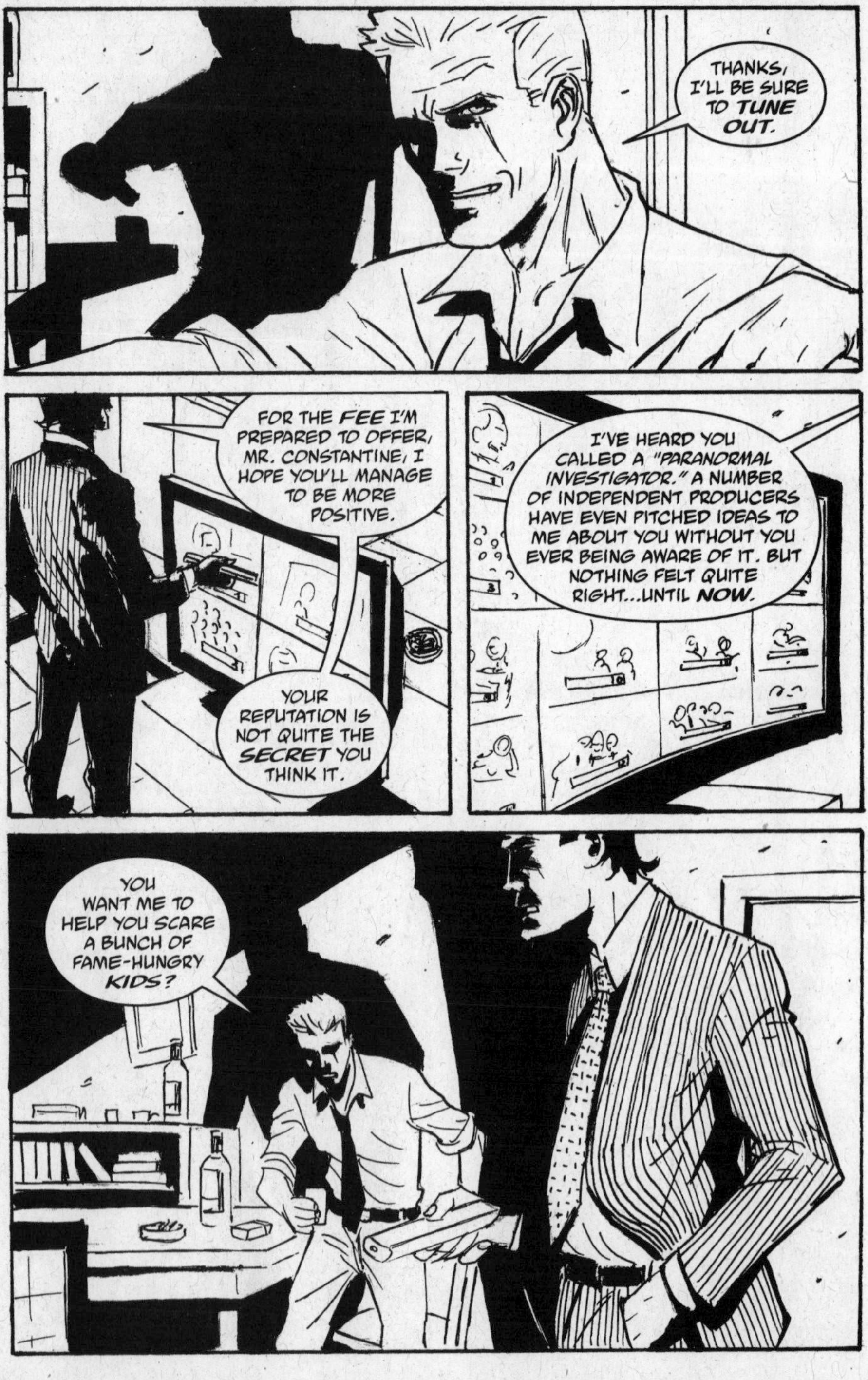
THANKS, I'LL BE SURE TO TUNE OUT.
FOR THE FEE I'M PREPARED TO OFFER, MR. CONSTANTINE, I HOPE YOU'LL MANAGE TO BE MORE POSITIVE.
YOUR REPUTATION IS NOT QUITE THE SECRET YOU THINK IT.
I'VE HEARD YOU CALLED A "PARANORMAL INVESTIGATOR." A NUMBER OF INDEPENDENT PRODUCERS HAVE EVEN PITCHED IDEAS TO ME ABOUT YOU WITHOUT YOU EVER BEING AWARE OF IT. BUT NOTHING FELT QUITE RIGHT...UNTIL NOW.
YOU WANT ME TO HELP YOU SCARE A BUNCH OF FAME-HUNGRY KIDS?

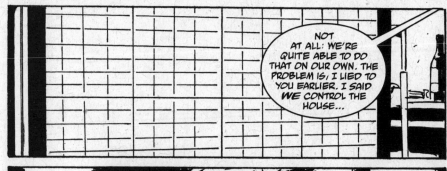

NOT AT ALL: WE'RE QUITE ABLE TO DO THAT ON OUR OWN. THE PROBLEM IS, I LIED TO YOU EARLIER. I SAID *WE* CONTROL THE HOUSE...

WE *DON'T.*

THE HOUSE... THE "SET"... SEEMS TO HAVE DEVELOPED A *MIND OF ITS OWN.*

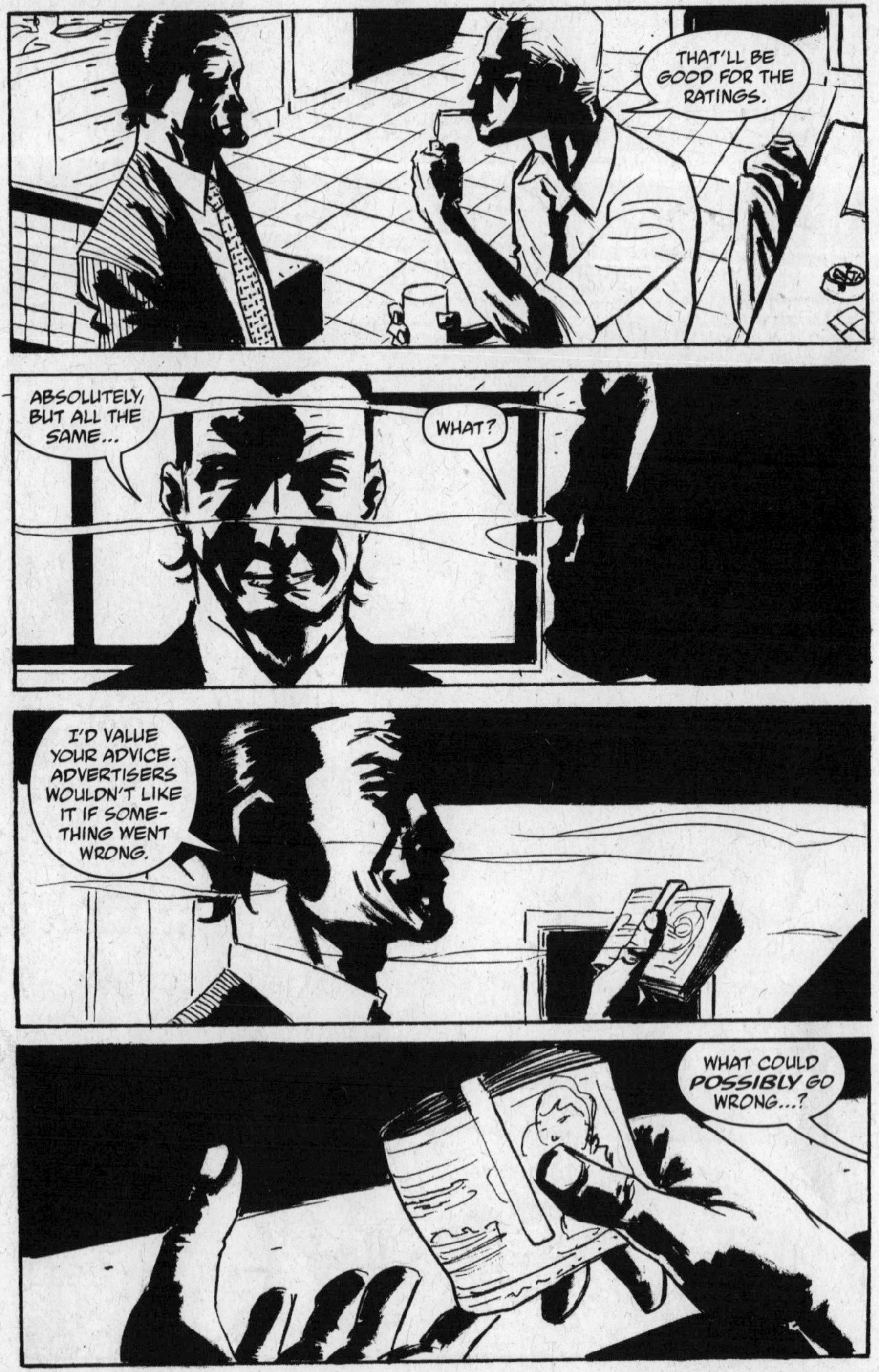
THAT'LL BE GOOD FOR THE RATINGS.
ABSOLUTELY, BUT ALL THE SAME...
WHAT?
I'D VALUE YOUR ADVICE. ADVERTISERS WOULDN'T LIKE IT IF SOME- THING WENT WRONG.
WHAT COULD *POSSIBLY* GO WRONG...?

This morning saw the burning man again.

BUT IS IT REALLY MORNING? NO WAY OF KNOWING. NO WINDOWS TO LOOK OUT OF. NO SUNSHINE, NO SOUNDS OF RAIN. WE SLEEP WHEN WE'RE TIRED, DAY OR NIGHT.

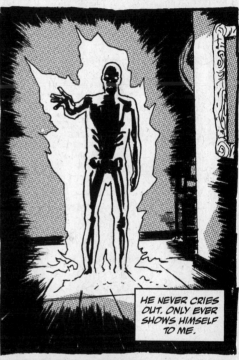

HE NEVER CRIES OUT. ONLY EVER SHOWS HIMSELF TO ME.

I THINK HE'S THE SCARIEST, BUT THEN I'M THE ONLY ONE WHO SEES HIM.

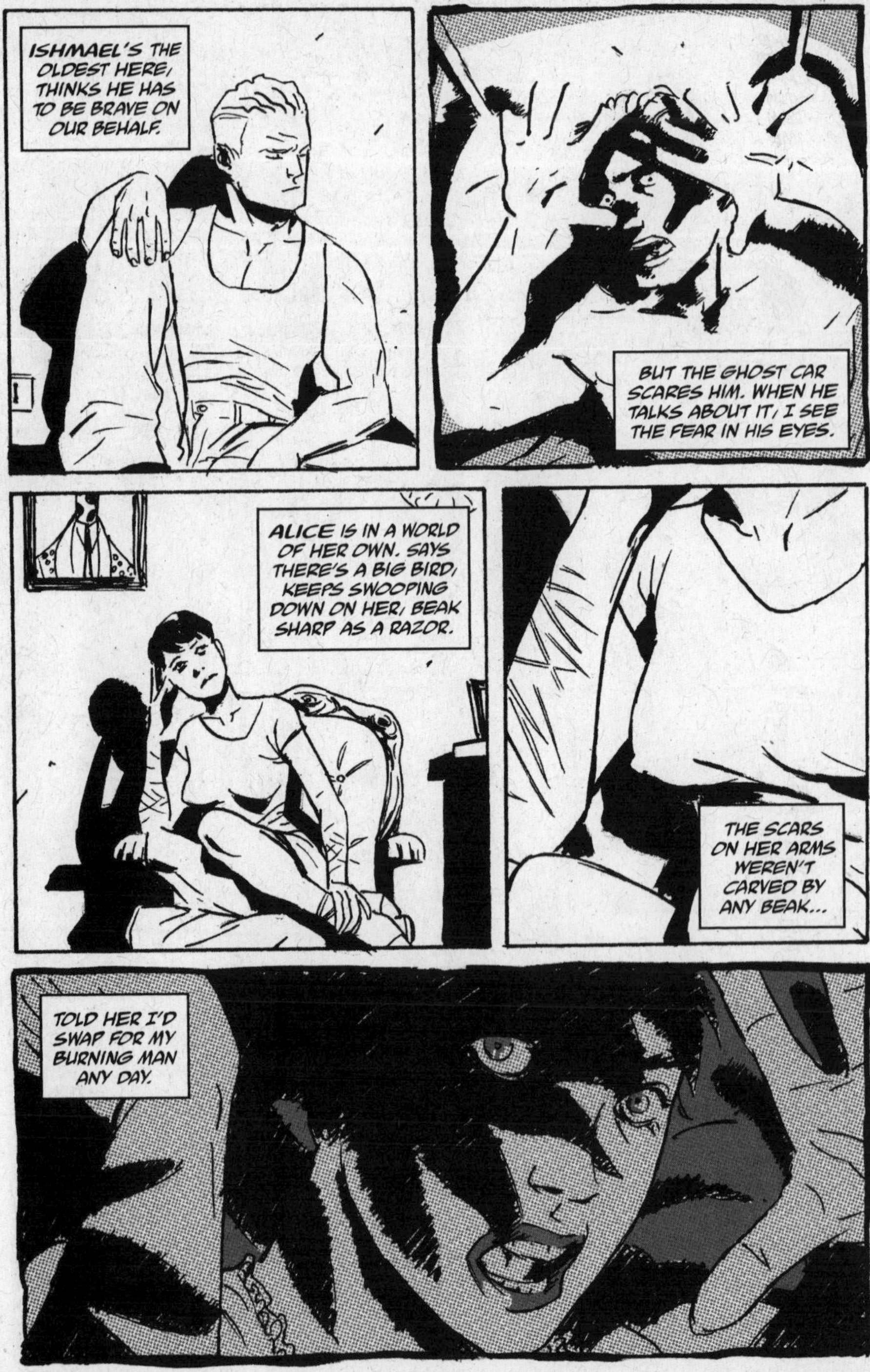
ISHMAEL'S THE OLDEST HERE, THINKS HE HAS TO BE BRAVE ON OUR BEHALF.
BUT THE GHOST CAR SCARES HIM. WHEN HE TALKS ABOUT IT, I SEE THE FEAR IN HIS EYES.
ALICE IS IN A WORLD OF HER OWN. SAYS THERE'S A BIG BIRD, KEEPS SWOOPING DOWN ON HER, BEAK SHARP AS A RAZOR.
THE SCARS ON HER ARMS WEREN'T CARVED BY ANY BEAK...
TOLD HER I'D SWAP FOR MY BURNING MAN ANY DAY.

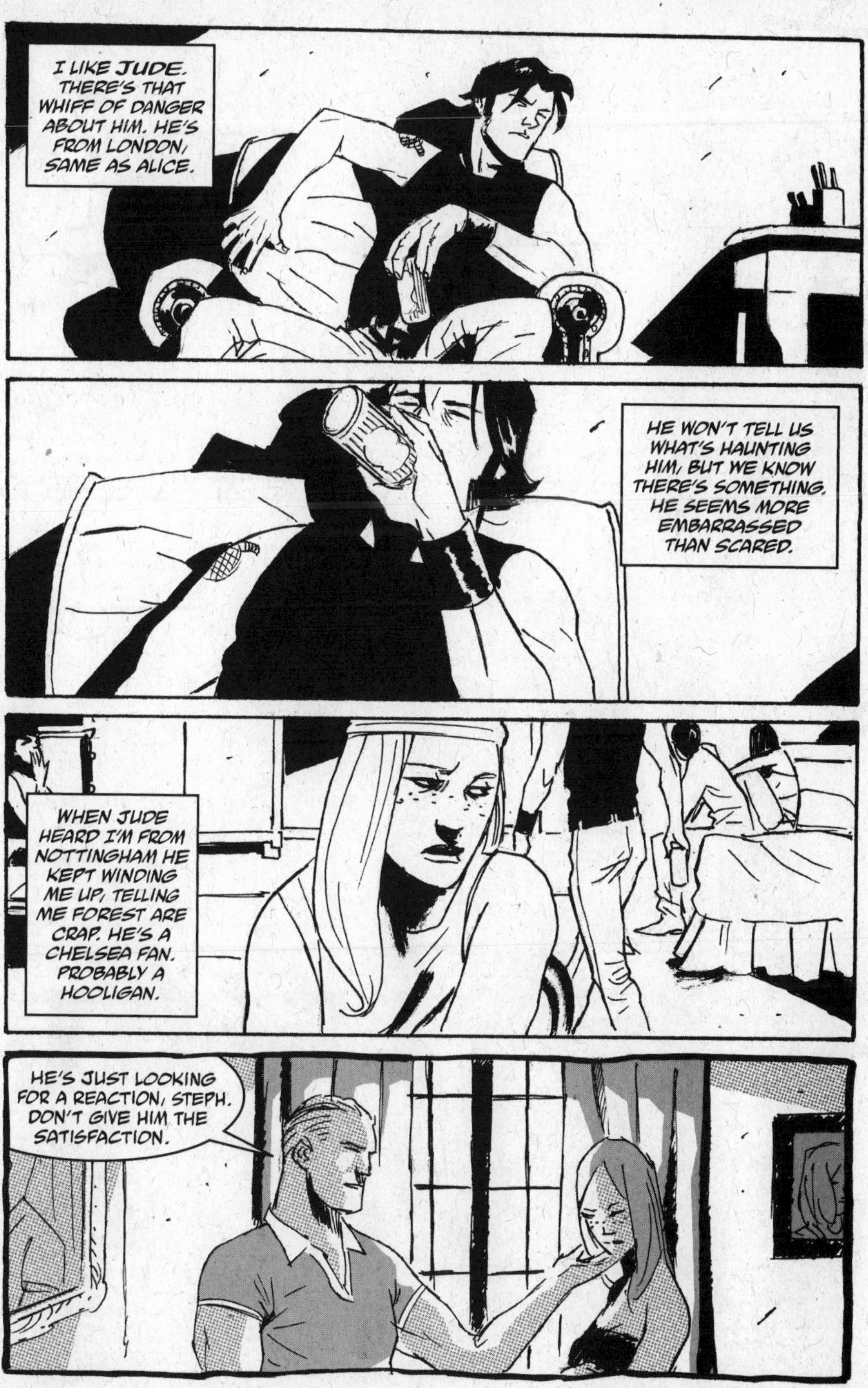
I LIKE JUDE. THERE'S THAT WHIFF OF DANGER ABOUT HIM. HE'S FROM LONDON, SAME AS ALICE.
HE WON'T TELL US WHAT'S HAUNTING HIM, BUT WE KNOW THERE'S SOMETHING. HE SEEMS MORE EMBARRASSED THAN SCARED.
WHEN JUDE HEARD I'M FROM NOTTINGHAM HE KEPT WINDING ME UP, TELLING ME FOREST ARE CRAP. HE'S A CHELSEA FAN. PROBABLY A HOOLIGAN.
HE'S JUST LOOKING FOR A REACTION, STEPH. DON'T GIVE HIM THE SATISFACTION.

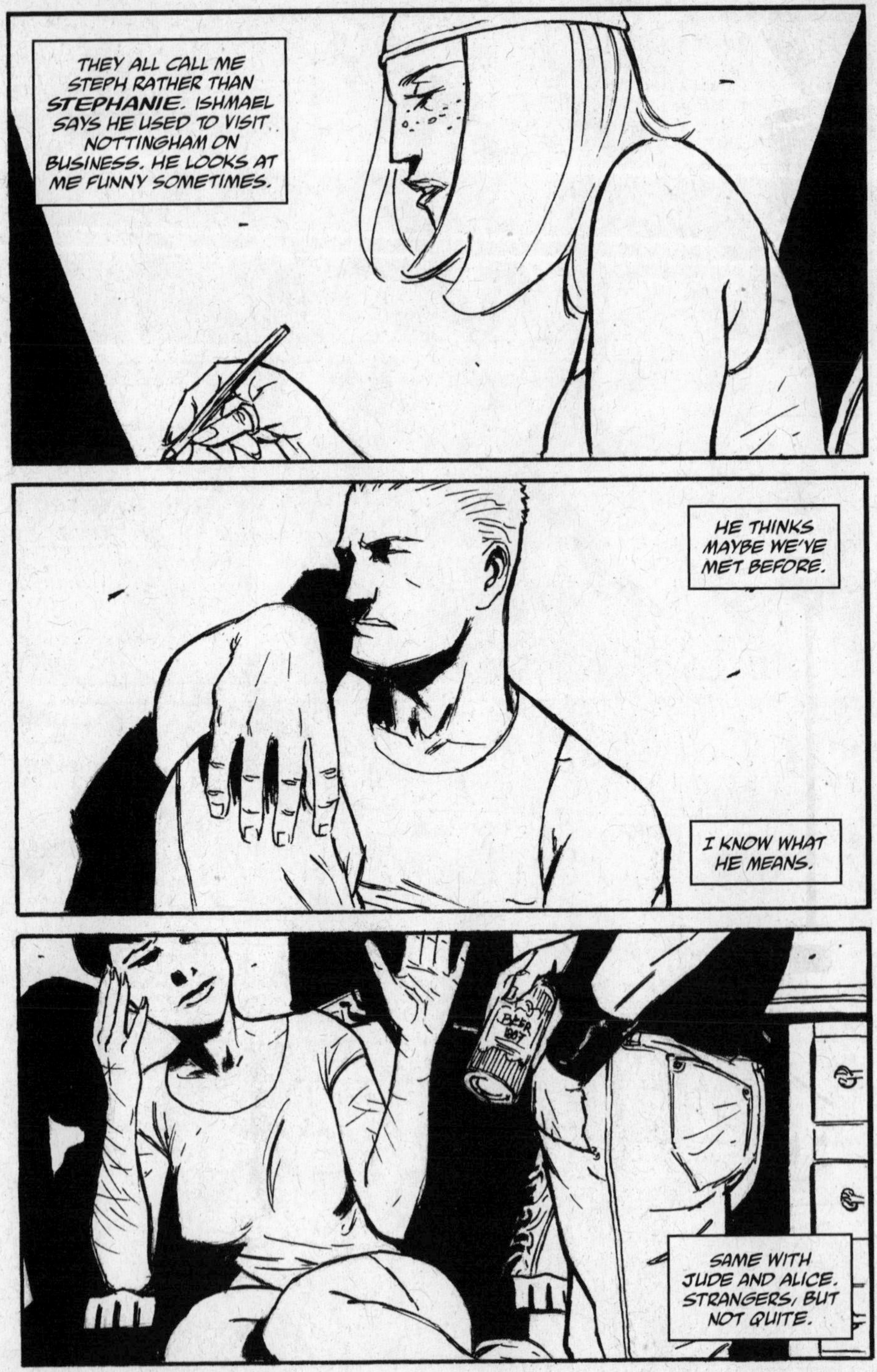
THEY ALL CALL ME STEPH RATHER THAN STEPHANIE. ISHMAEL SAYS HE USED TO VISIT NOTTINGHAM ON BUSINESS. HE LOOKS AT ME FUNNY SOMETIMES.
HE THINKS MAYBE WE'VE MET BEFORE.
I KNOW WHAT HE MEANS.
BEER
SAME WITH JUDE AND ALICE. STRANGERS, BUT NOT QUITE.

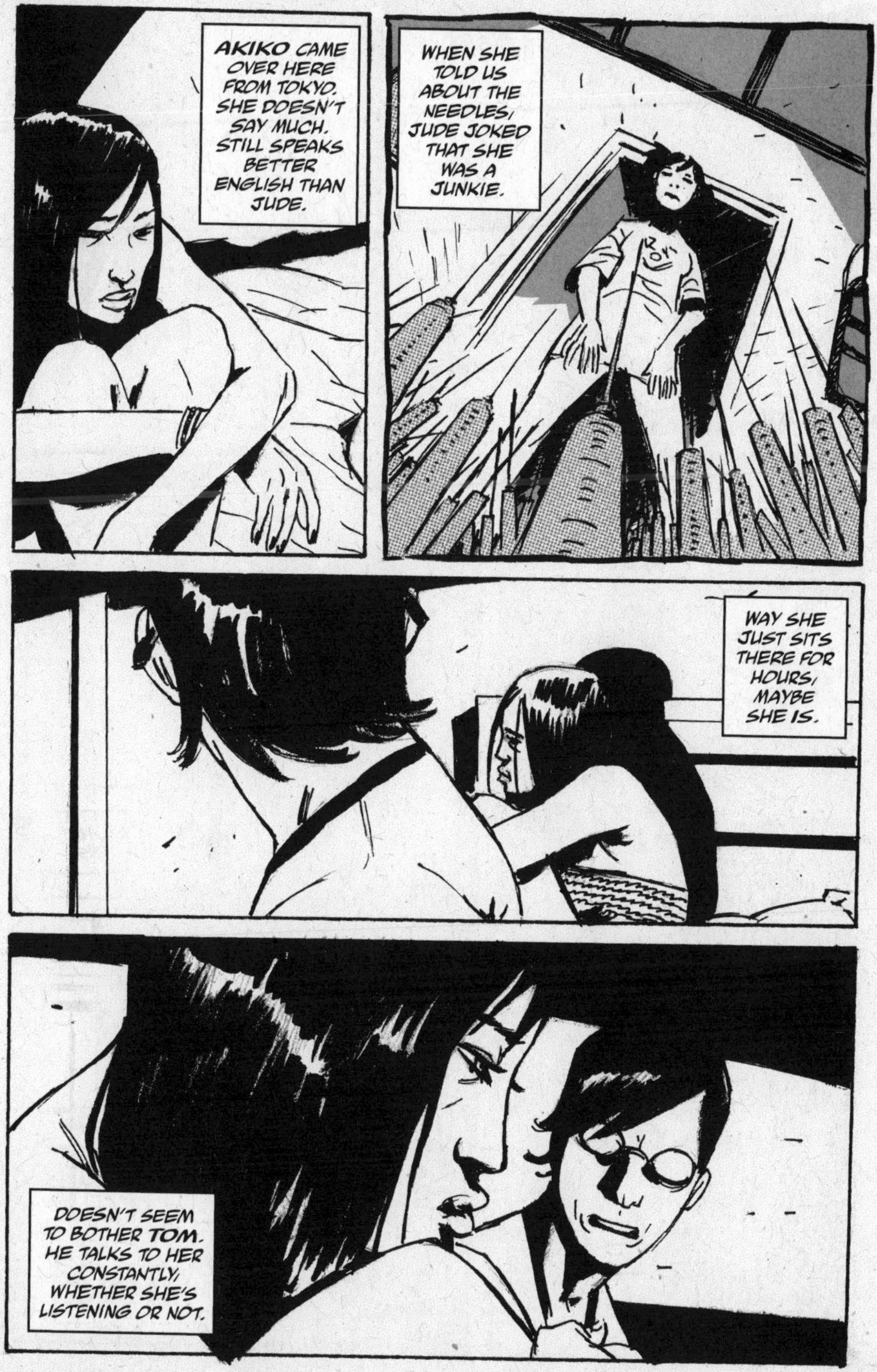
AKIKO CAME OVER HERE FROM TOKYO. SHE DOESN'T SAY MUCH. STILL SPEAKS BETTER ENGLISH THAN JUDE.
WHEN SHE TOLD US ABOUT THE NEEDLES, JUDE JOKED THAT SHE WAS A JUNKIE.
WAY SHE JUST SITS THERE FOR HOURS, MAYBE SHE IS.
DOESN'T SEEM TO BOTHER TOM. HE TALKS TO HER CONSTANTLY, WHETHER SHE'S LISTENING OR NOT.

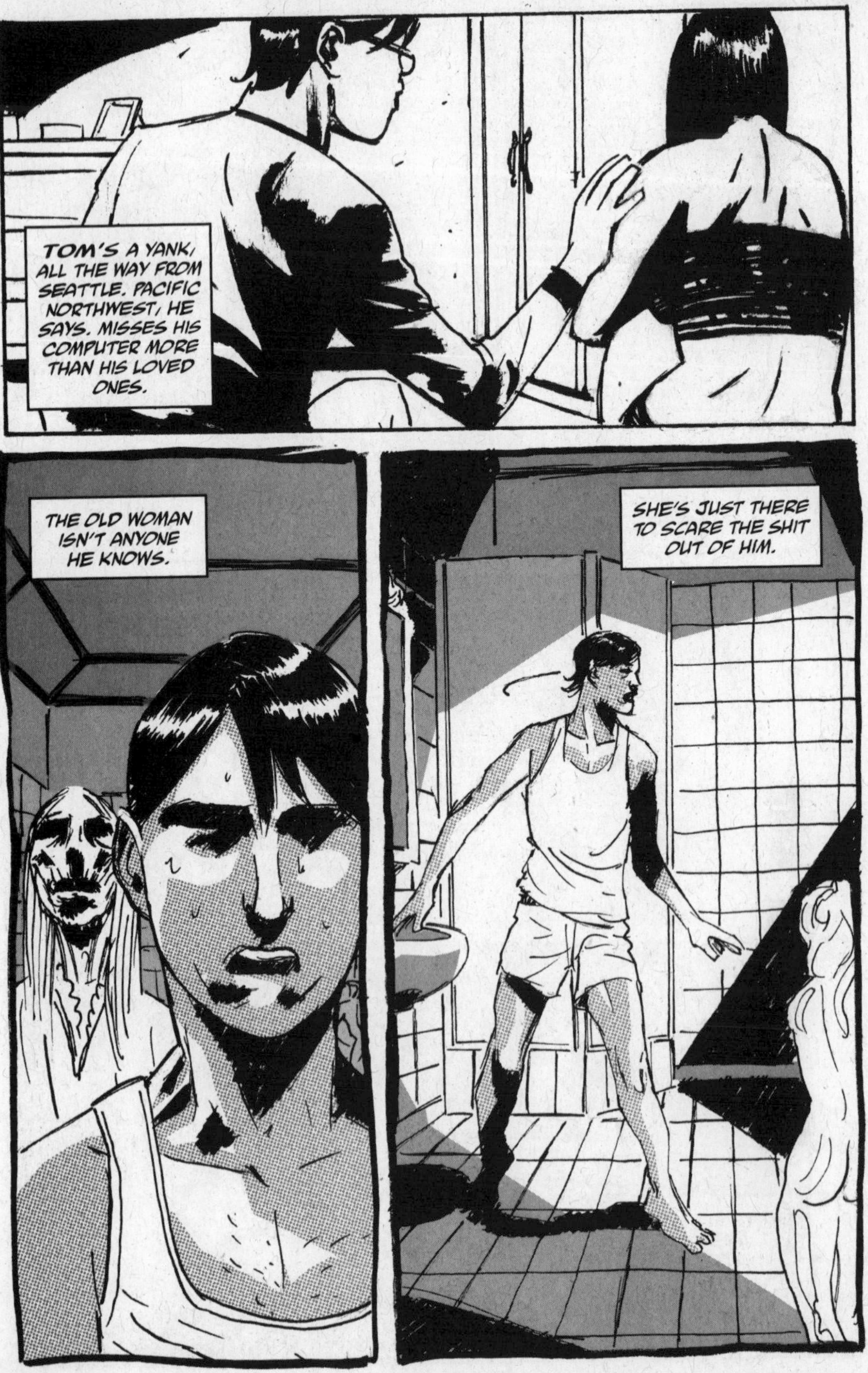
TOM'S A YANK, ALL THE WAY FROM SEATTLE. PACIFIC NORTHWEST, HE SAYS. MISSES HIS COMPUTER MORE THAN HIS LOVED ONES.
THE OLD WOMAN ISN'T ANYONE HE KNOWS.
SHE'S JUST THERE TO SCARE THE SHIT OUT OF HIM.

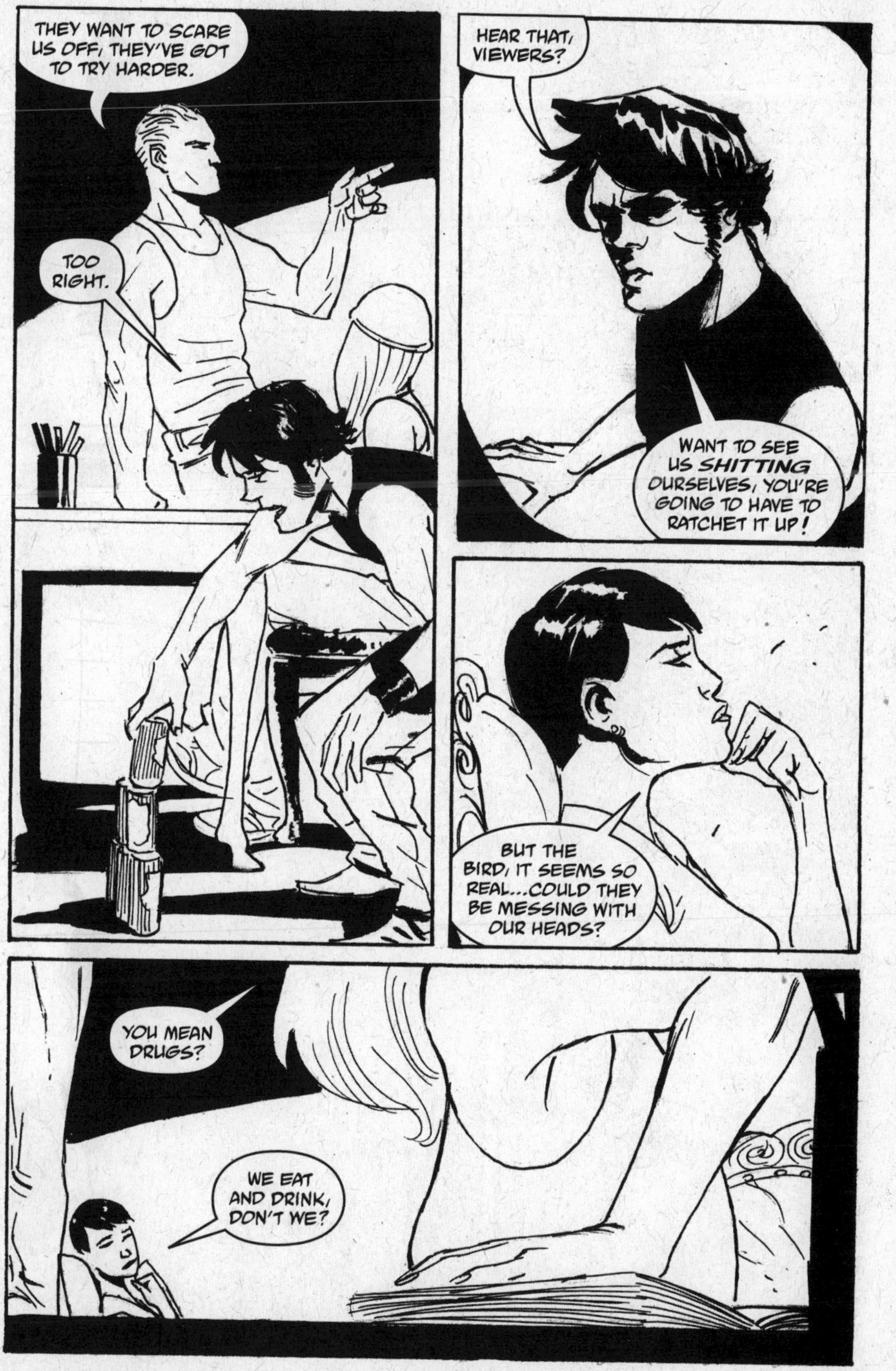

THEY WANT TO SCARE US OFF, THEY'VE GOT TO TRY HARDER.
TOO RIGHT.
HEAR THAT, VIEWERS?
WANT TO SEE US SHITTING OURSELVES, YOU'RE GOING TO HAVE TO RATCHET IT UP!
BUT THE BIRD, IT SEEMS SO REAL...COULD THEY BE MESSING WITH OUR HEADS?
YOU MEAN DRUGS?
WE EAT AND DRINK, DON'T WE?

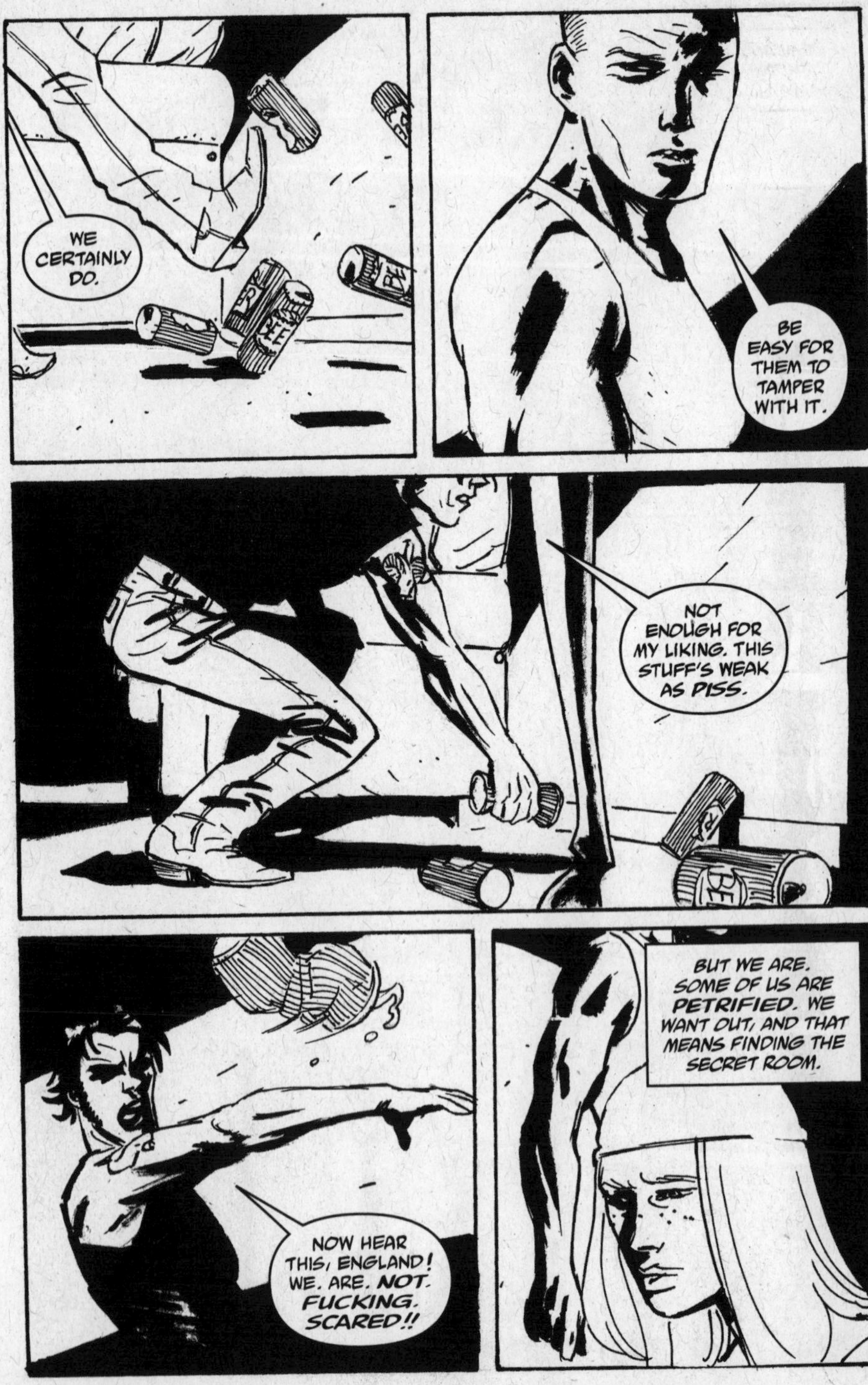
WE CERTAINLY DO.
BE EASY FOR THEM TO TAMPER WITH IT.
NOT ENOUGH FOR MY LIKING. THIS STUFF'S WEAK AS PISS.
NOW HEAR THIS, ENGLAND! WE. ARE. NOT. FUCKING. SCARED!!
BUT WE ARE. SOME OF US ARE PETRIFIED. WE WANT OUT, AND THAT MEANS FINDING THE SECRET ROOM.

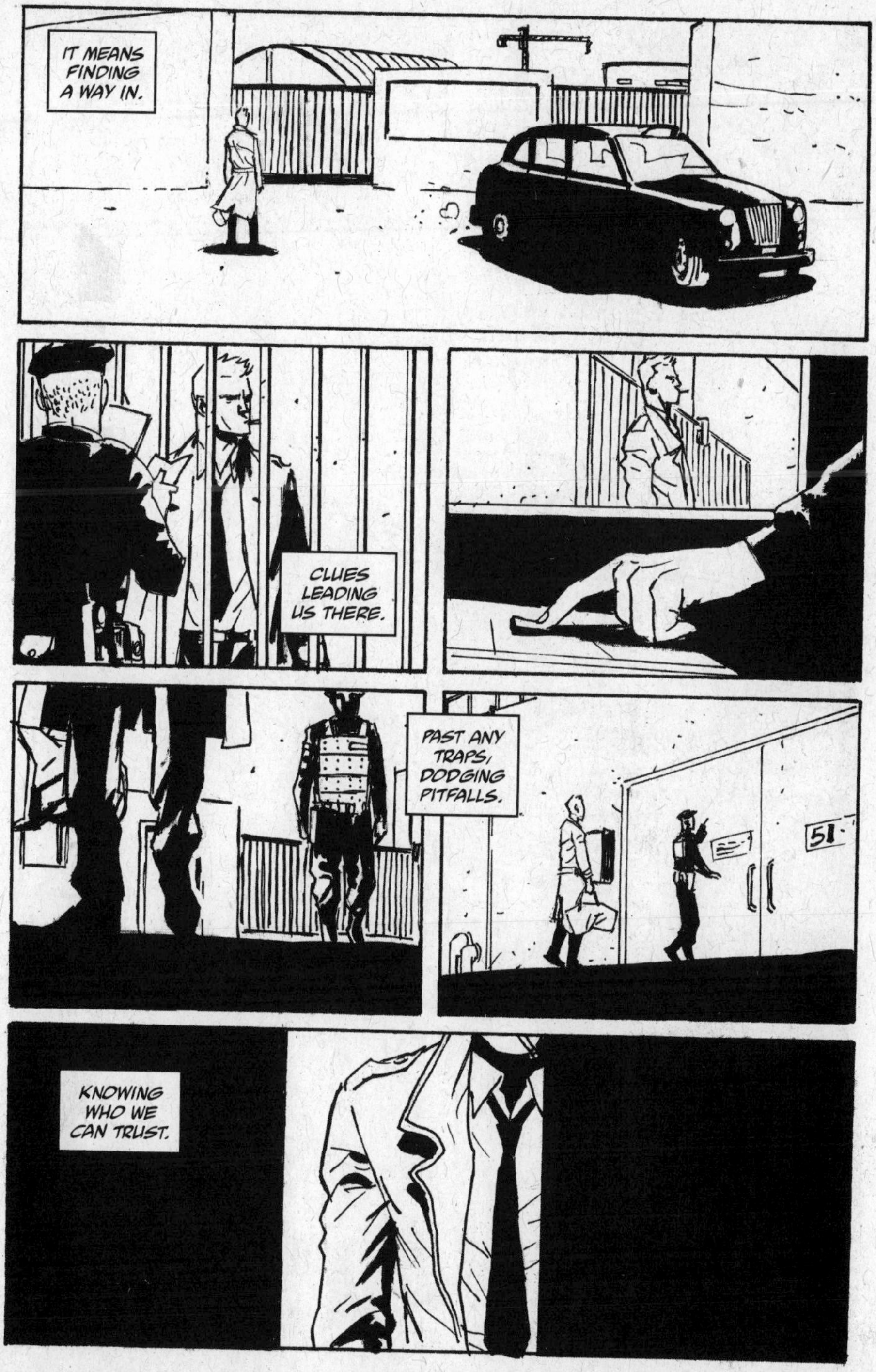
IT MEANS FINDING A WAY IN.
CLUES LEADING US THERE.
PAST ANY TRAPS, DODGING PITFALLS.
51
KNOWING WHO WE CAN TRUST.

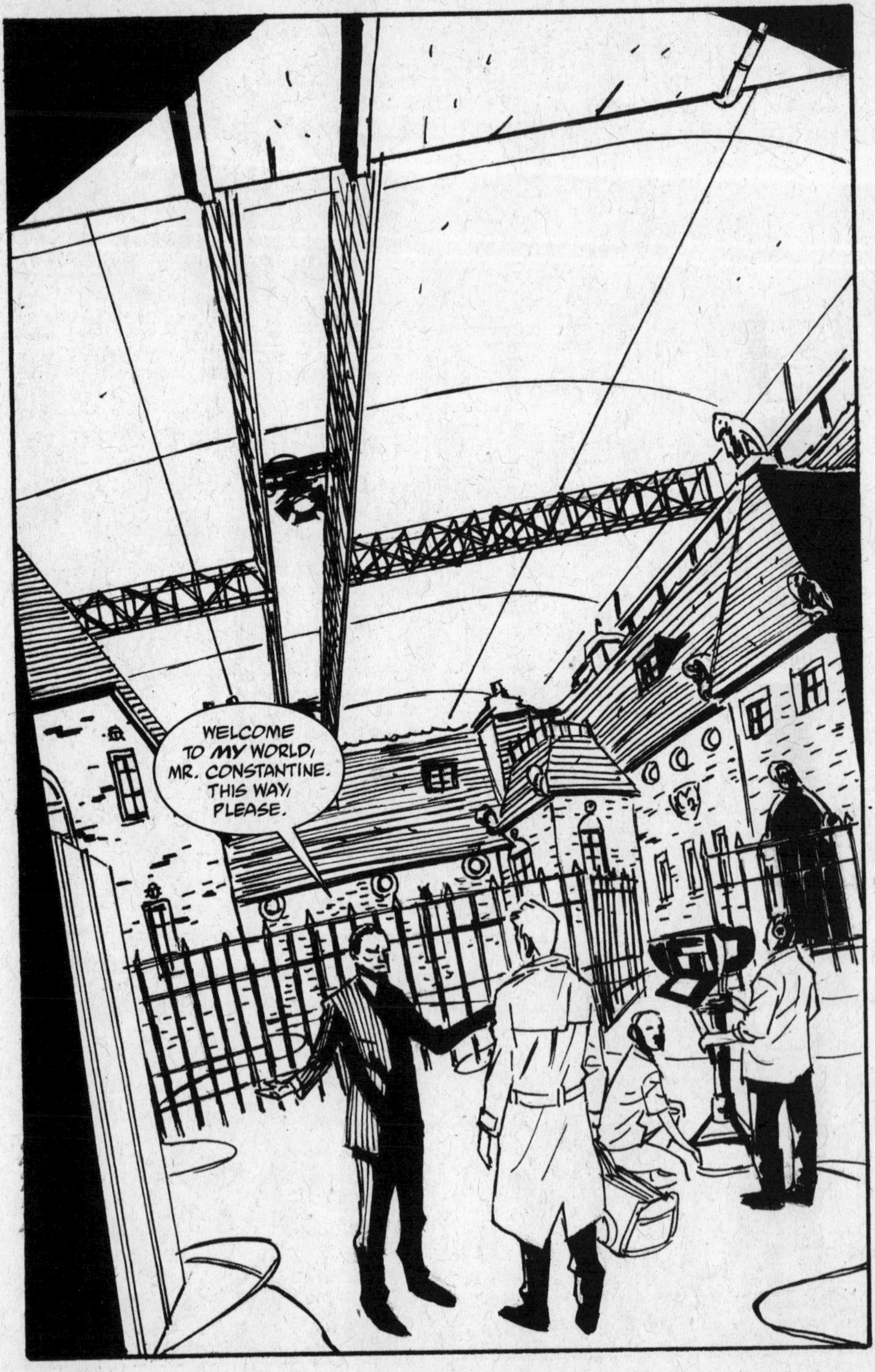
WELCOME TO MY WORLD, MR. CONSTANTINE. THIS WAY, PLEASE.

IT'S QUITE A SETUP, MATTY.

I LIKE TO THINK SO.

AND PUNTERS ACTUALLY *WANT* TO BE STUCK IN THERE?

BECOMING CELEBRITIES IN THE PROCESS. WATCHED BY MILLIONS.

AND THE HANGAR HERE, IT'S NOT BUILT ON THE SITE OF A CEMETERY OR SOMETHING?

AUTHORISED PERSONNEL ONLY

YOU'RE THINKING OF THE FILM "*POLTERGEIST*"?

IF YOU'D SAID "YES," I COULD'VE COLLECTED MY CASH AND HOOFED IT.

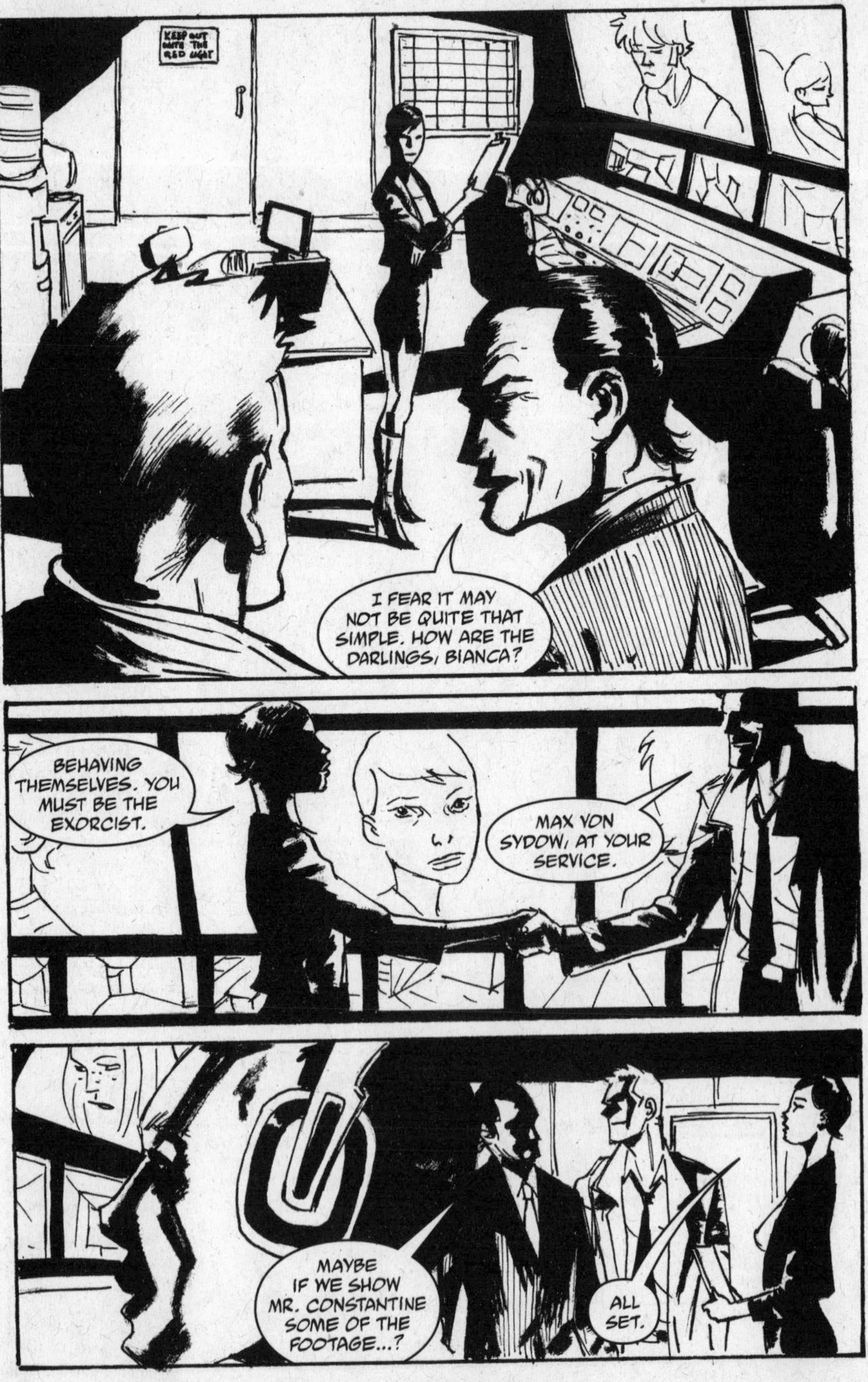
I FEAR IT MAY NOT BE QUITE THAT SIMPLE. HOW ARE THE DARLINGS, BIANCA?
BEHAVING THEMSELVES. YOU MUST BE THE EXORCIST.
MAX VON SYDOW, AT YOUR SERVICE.
MAYBE IF WE SHOW MR. CONSTANTINE SOME OF THE FOOTAGE...?
ALL SET.

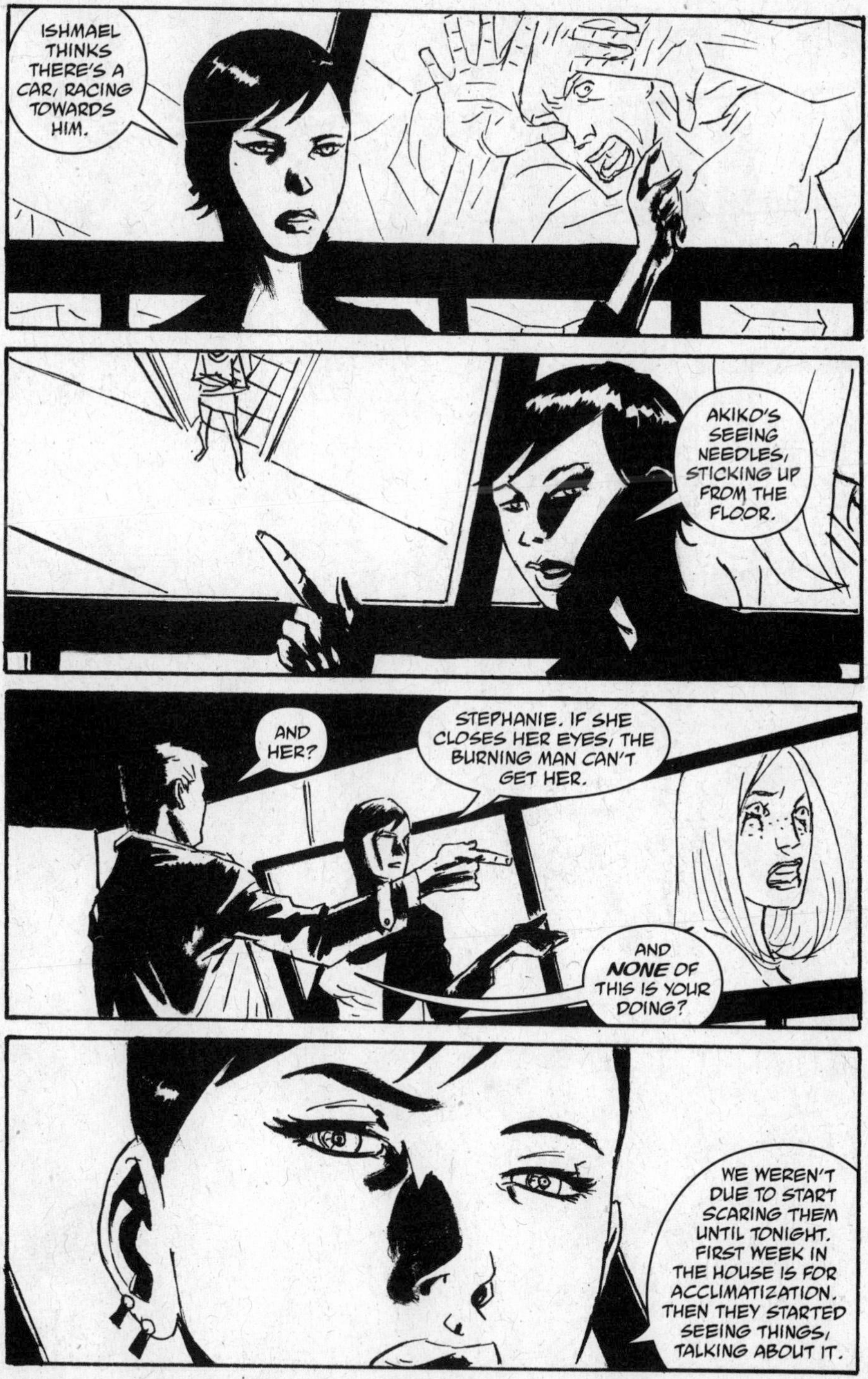
ISHMAEL THINKS THERE'S A CAR, RACING TOWARDS HIM.
AKIKO'S SEEING NEEDLES, STICKING UP FROM THE FLOOR.
AND HER?
STEPHANIE. IF SHE CLOSES HER EYES, THE BURNING MAN CAN'T GET HER.
AND NONE OF THIS IS YOUR DOING?
WE WEREN'T DUE TO START SCARING THEM UNTIL TONIGHT. FIRST WEEK IN THE HOUSE IS FOR ACCLIMATIZATION. THEN THEY STARTED SEEING THINGS, TALKING ABOUT IT.

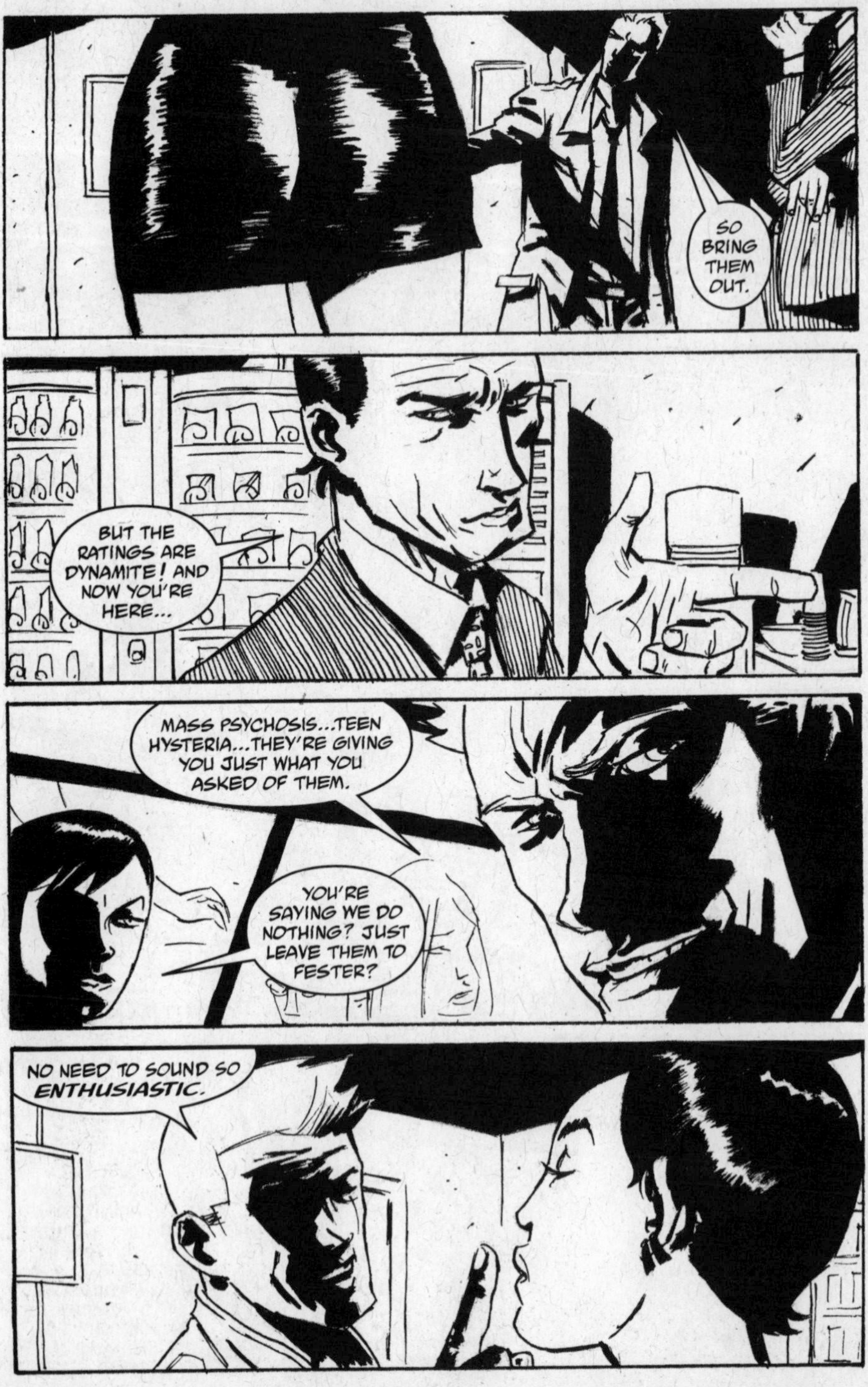
SO BRING THEM OUT.
BUT THE RATINGS ARE DYNAMITE! AND NOW YOU'RE HERE...
MASS PSYCHOSIS...TEEN HYSTERIA...THEY'RE GIVING YOU JUST WHAT YOU ASKED OF THEM.
YOU'RE SAYING WE DO NOTHING? JUST LEAVE THEM TO FESTER?
NO NEED TO SOUND SO *ENTHUSIASTIC.*

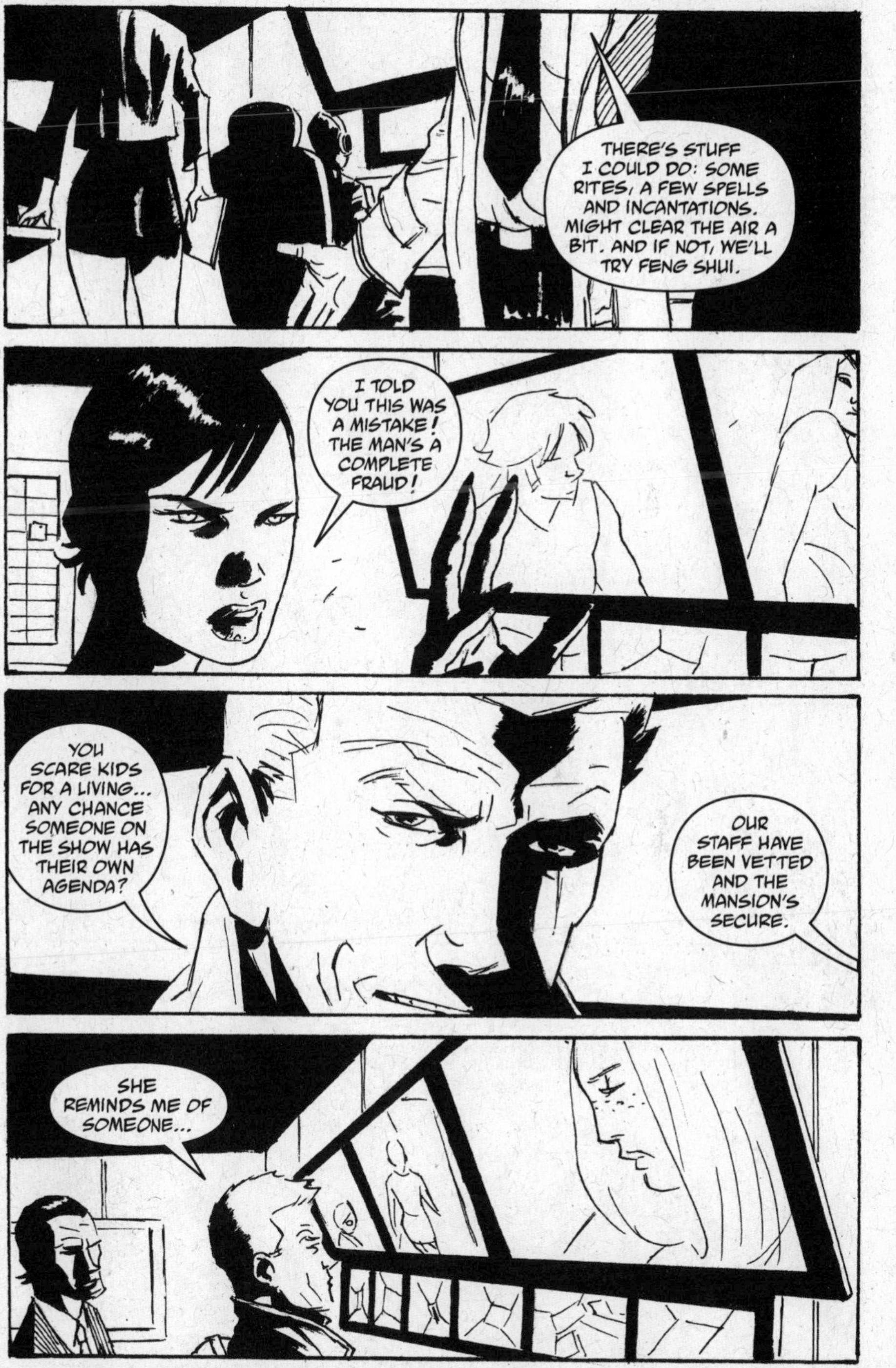
THERE'S STUFF I COULD DO: SOME RITES, A FEW SPELLS AND INCANTATIONS. MIGHT CLEAR THE AIR A BIT. AND IF NOT, WE'LL TRY FENG SHUI.
I TOLD YOU THIS WAS A MISTAKE! THE MAN'S A COMPLETE FRAUD!
YOU SCARE KIDS FOR A LIVING... ANY CHANCE SOMEONE ON THE SHOW HAS THEIR OWN AGENDA?
OUR STAFF HAVE BEEN VETTED AND THE MANSION'S SECURE.
SHE REMINDS ME OF SOMEONE...

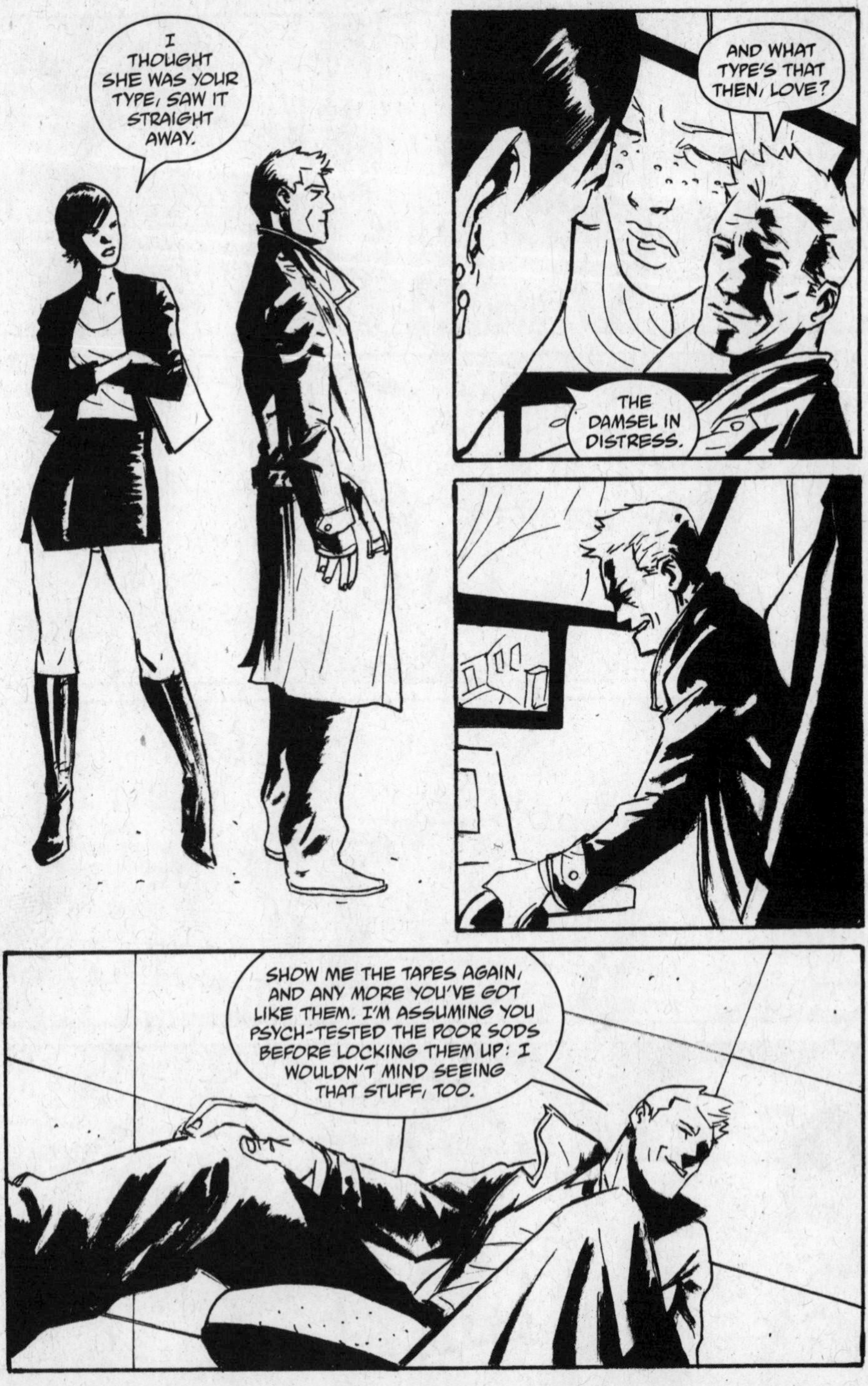
I THOUGHT SHE WAS YOUR TYPE, SAW IT STRAIGHT AWAY.
AND WHAT TYPE'S THAT THEN, LOVE?
THE DAMSEL IN DISTRESS.
SHOW ME THE TAPES AGAIN, AND ANY MORE YOU'VE GOT LIKE THEM. I'M ASSUMING YOU PSYCH-TESTED THE POOR SODS BEFORE LOCKING THEM UP: I WOULDN'T MIND SEEING THAT STUFF, TOO.

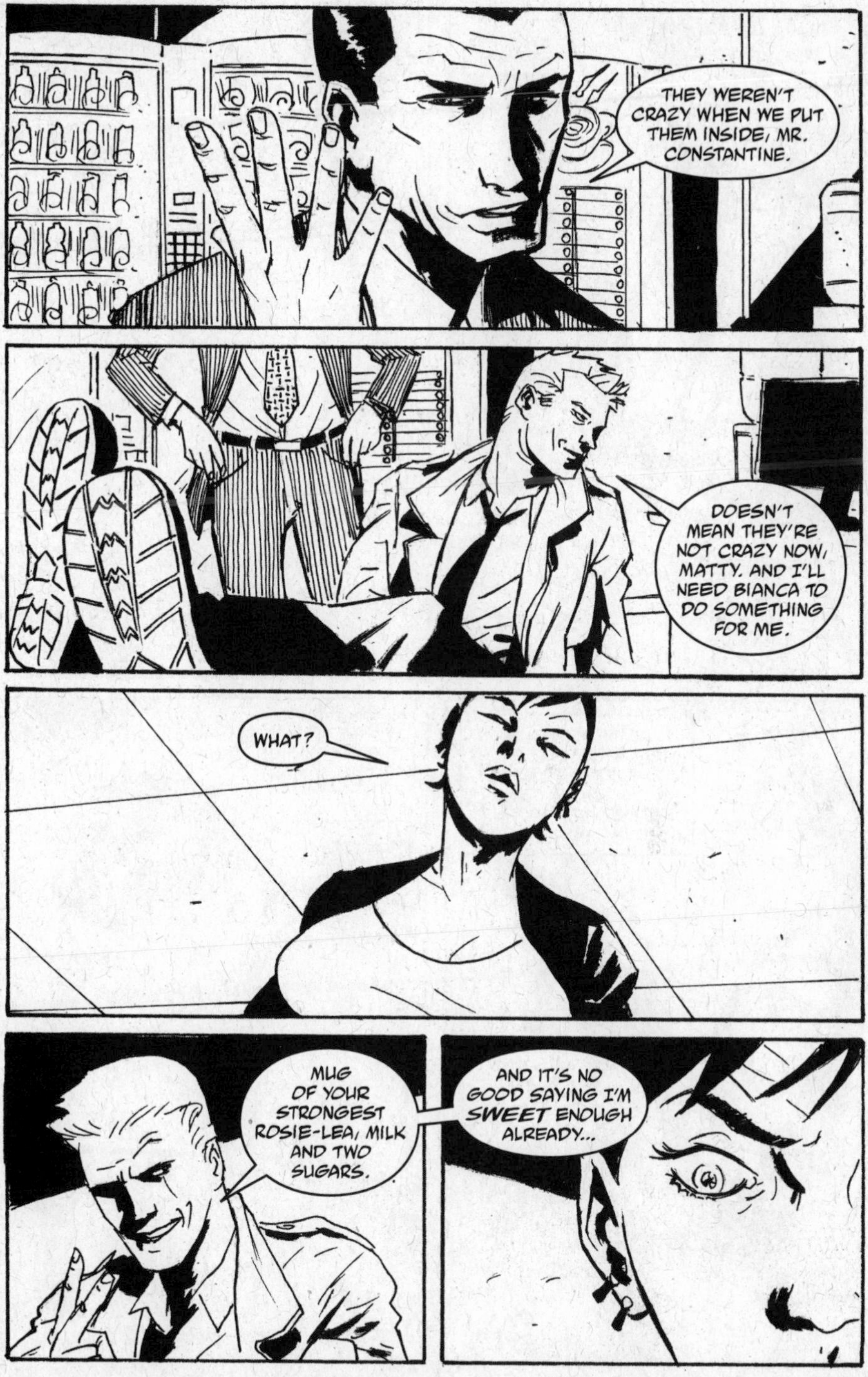
THEY WEREN'T CRAZY WHEN WE PUT THEM INSIDE, MR. CONSTANTINE.
DOESN'T MEAN THEY'RE NOT CRAZY NOW, MATTY. AND I'LL NEED BIANCA TO DO SOMETHING FOR ME.
WHAT?
MUG OF YOUR STRONGEST ROSIE-LEA, MILK AND TWO SUGARS.
AND IT'S NO GOOD SAYING I'M *SWEET* ENOUGH ALREADY...

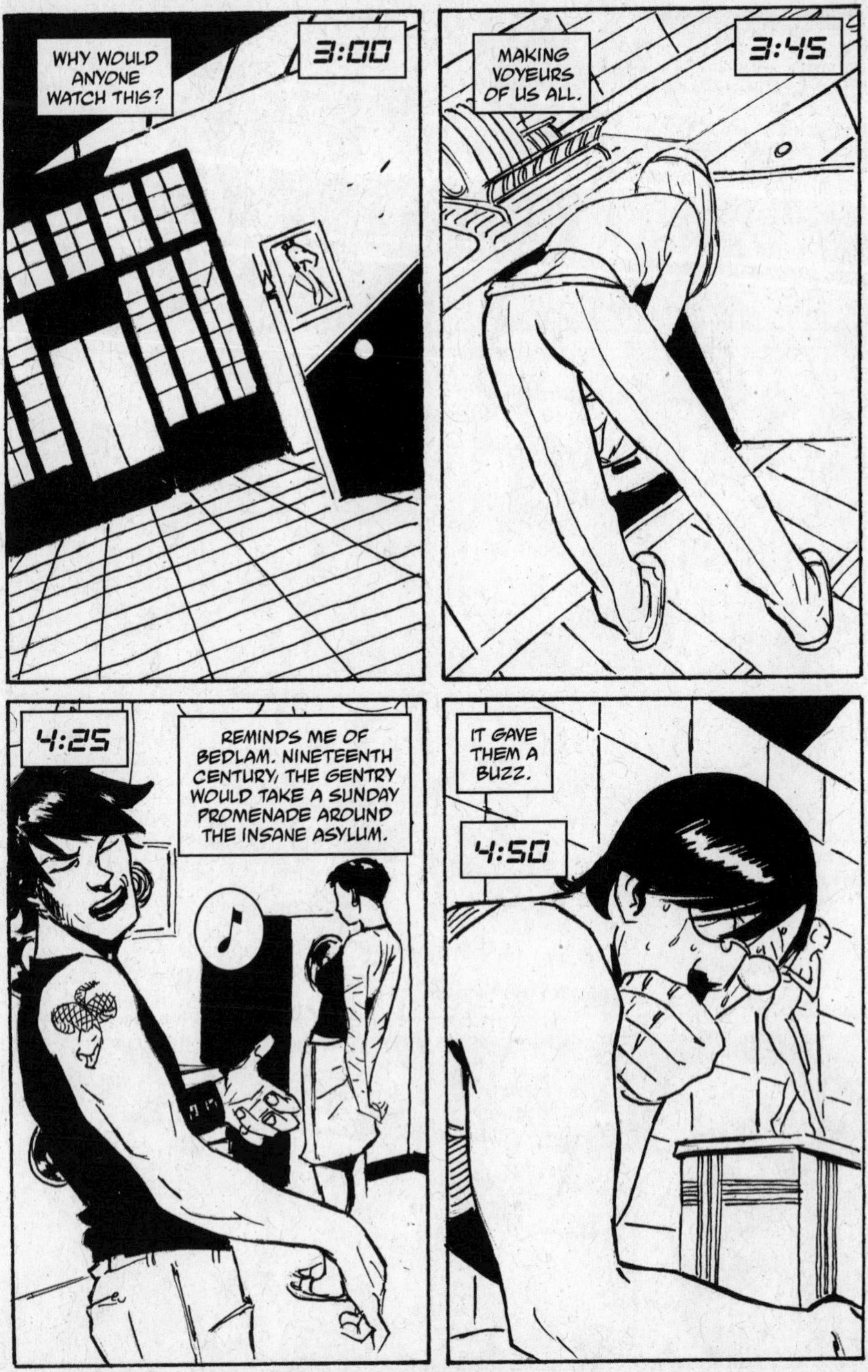
WHY WOULD ANYONE WATCH THIS?
3:00
MAKING VOYEURS OF US ALL.
3:45
4:25
REMINDS ME OF BEDLAM. NINETEENTH CENTURY, THE GENTRY WOULD TAKE A SUNDAY PROMENADE AROUND THE INSANE ASYLUM.
IT GAVE THEM A BUZZ.
4:50

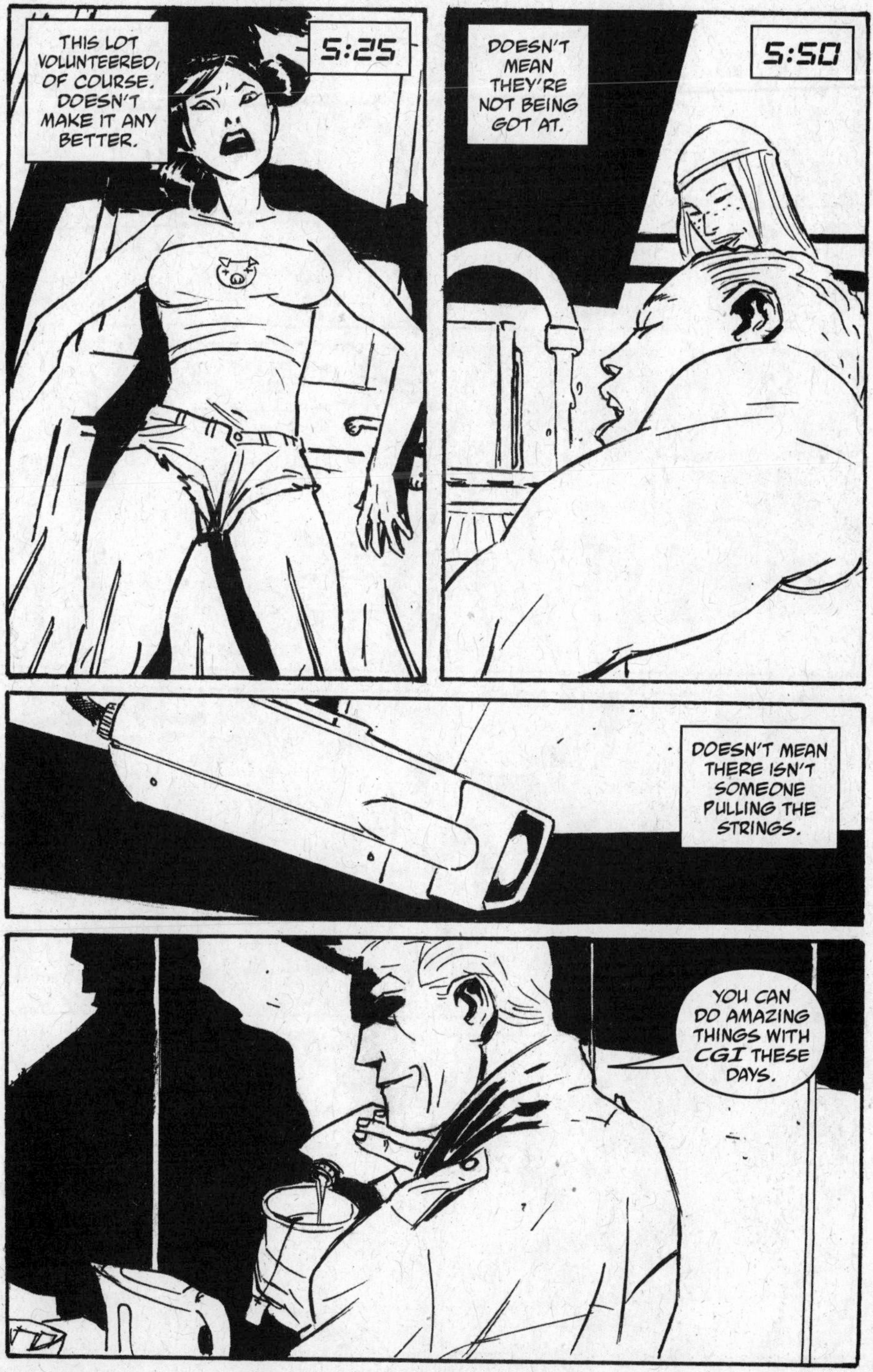
THIS LOT VOLUNTEERED, OF COURSE. DOESN'T MAKE IT ANY BETTER.
5:25
DOESN'T MEAN THEY'RE NOT BEING GOT AT.
5:50
DOESN'T MEAN THERE ISN'T SOMEONE PULLING THE STRINGS.
YOU CAN DO AMAZING THINGS WITH CGI THESE DAYS.

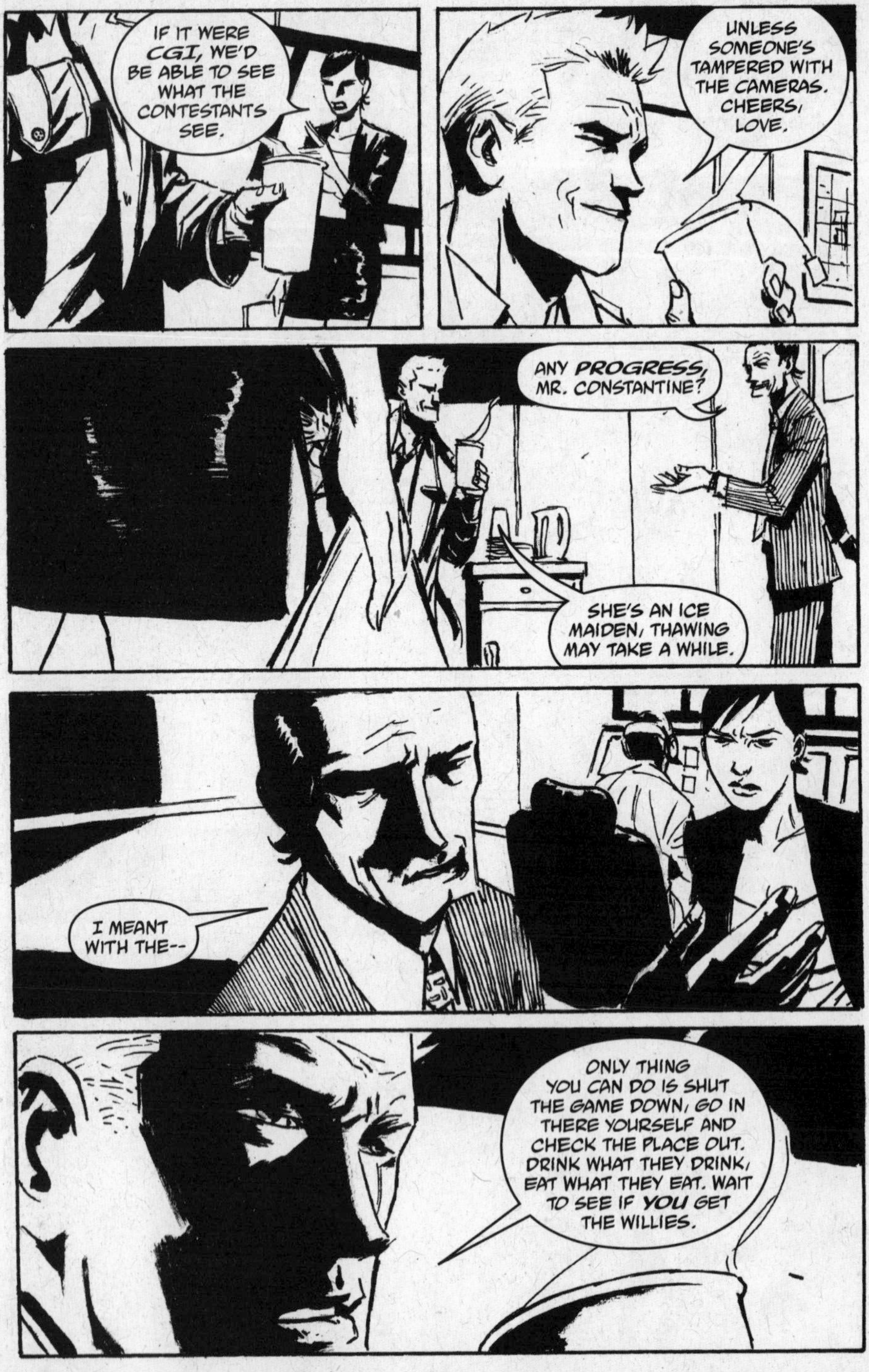

IF IT WERE CGI, WE'D BE ABLE TO SEE WHAT THE CONTESTANTS SEE.
UNLESS SOMEONE'S TAMPERED WITH THE CAMERAS. CHEERS, LOVE.
ANY PROGRESS, MR. CONSTANTINE?
SHE'S AN ICE MAIDEN, THAWING MAY TAKE A WHILE.
I MEANT WITH THE--
ONLY THING YOU CAN DO IS SHUT THE GAME DOWN, GO IN THERE YOURSELF AND CHECK THE PLACE OUT. DRINK WHAT THEY DRINK, EAT WHAT THEY EAT. WAIT TO SEE IF YOU GET THE WILLIES.

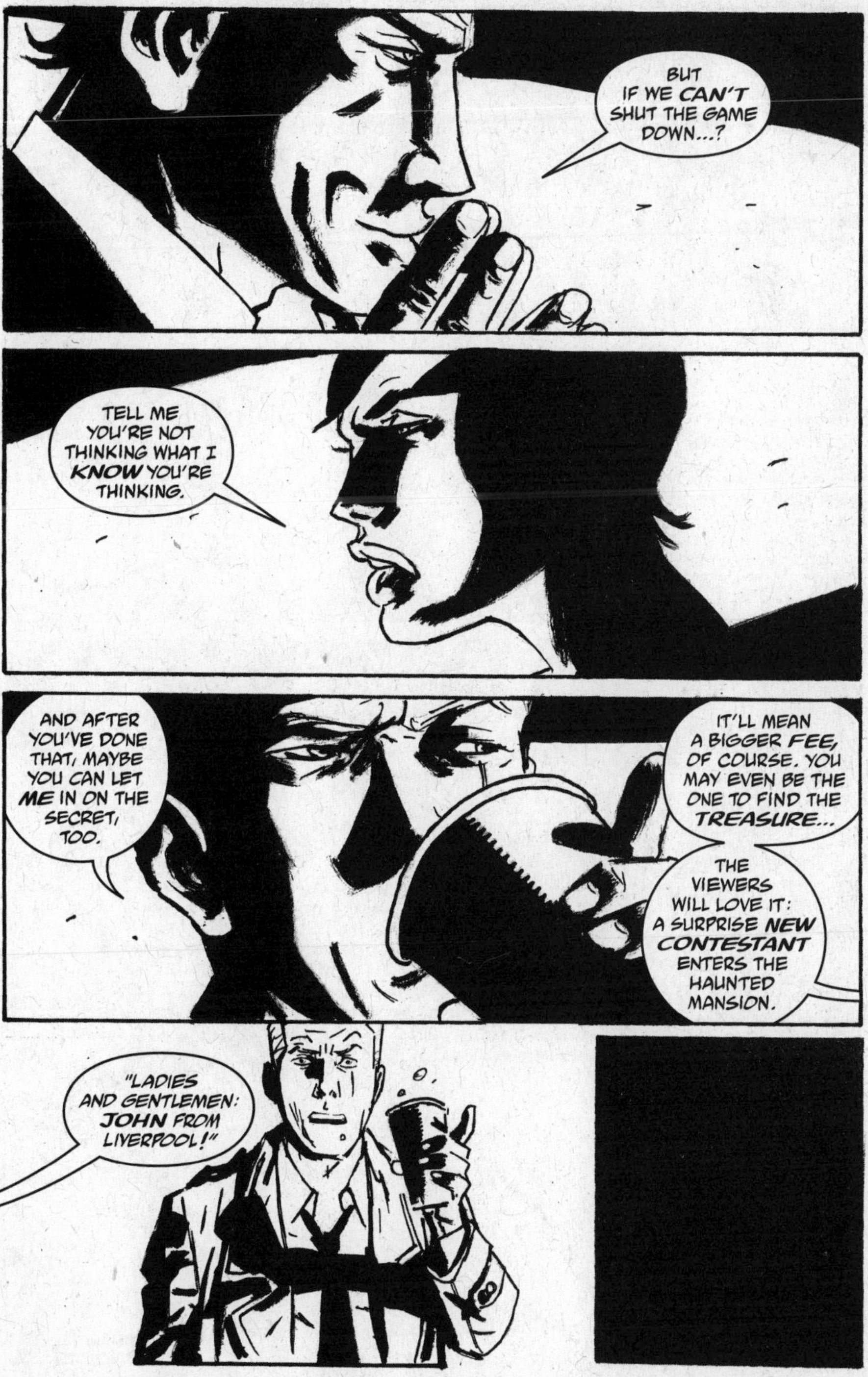
BUT IF WE CAN'T SHUT THE GAME DOWN...?
TELL ME YOU'RE NOT THINKING WHAT I KNOW YOU'RE THINKING.
AND AFTER YOU'VE DONE THAT, MAYBE YOU CAN LET ME IN ON THE SECRET, TOO.
IT'LL MEAN A BIGGER FEE, OF COURSE. YOU MAY EVEN BE THE ONE TO FIND THE TREASURE...
THE VIEWERS WILL LOVE IT: A SURPRISE NEW CONTESTANT ENTERS THE HAUNTED MANSION.
"LADIES AND GENTLEMEN: JOHN FROM LIVERPOOL!"

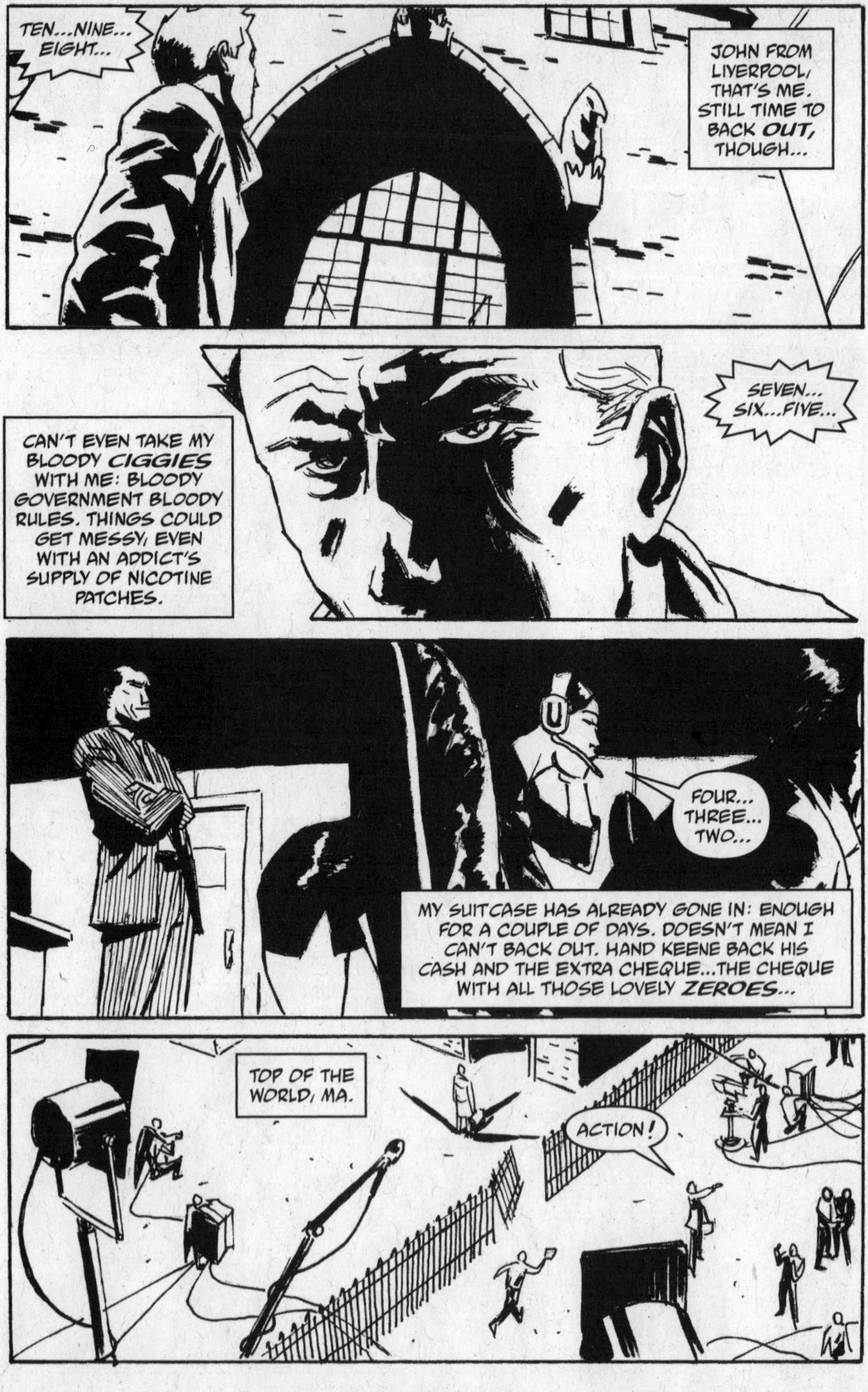

TEN...NINE... EIGHT...
JOHN FROM LIVERPOOL, THAT'S ME. STILL TIME TO BACK OUT, THOUGH...
CAN'T EVEN TAKE MY BLOODY CIGGIES WITH ME: BLOODY GOVERNMENT BLOODY RULES. THINGS COULD GET MESSY, EVEN WITH AN ADDICT'S SUPPLY OF NICOTINE PATCHES.
SEVEN... SIX...FIVE...
FOUR... THREE... TWO...
MY SUITCASE HAS ALREADY GONE IN: ENOUGH FOR A COUPLE OF DAYS. DOESN'T MEAN I CAN'T BACK OUT. HAND KEENE BACK HIS CASH AND THE EXTRA CHEQUE...THE CHEQUE WITH ALL THOSE LOVELY ZEROES...
TOP OF THE WORLD, MA.
ACTION!

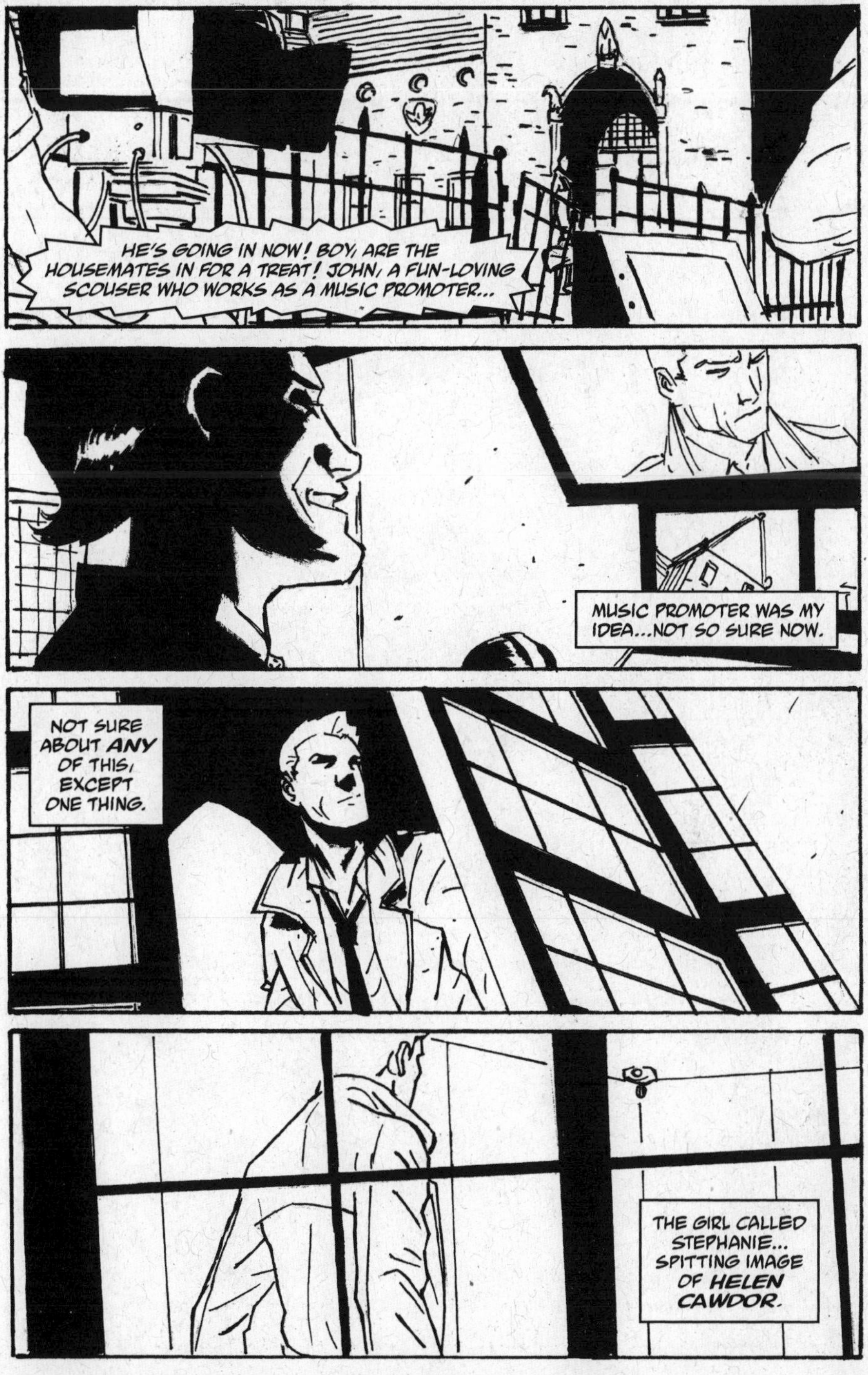
HE'S GOING IN NOW! BOY, ARE THE HOUSEMATES IN FOR A TREAT! JOHN, A FUN-LOVING SCOUSER WHO WORKS AS A MUSIC PROMOTER...
MUSIC PROMOTER WAS MY IDEA...NOT SO SURE NOW.
NOT SURE ABOUT ANY OF THIS, EXCEPT ONE THING.
THE GIRL CALLED STEPHANIE... SPITTING IMAGE OF HELEN CAWDOR.

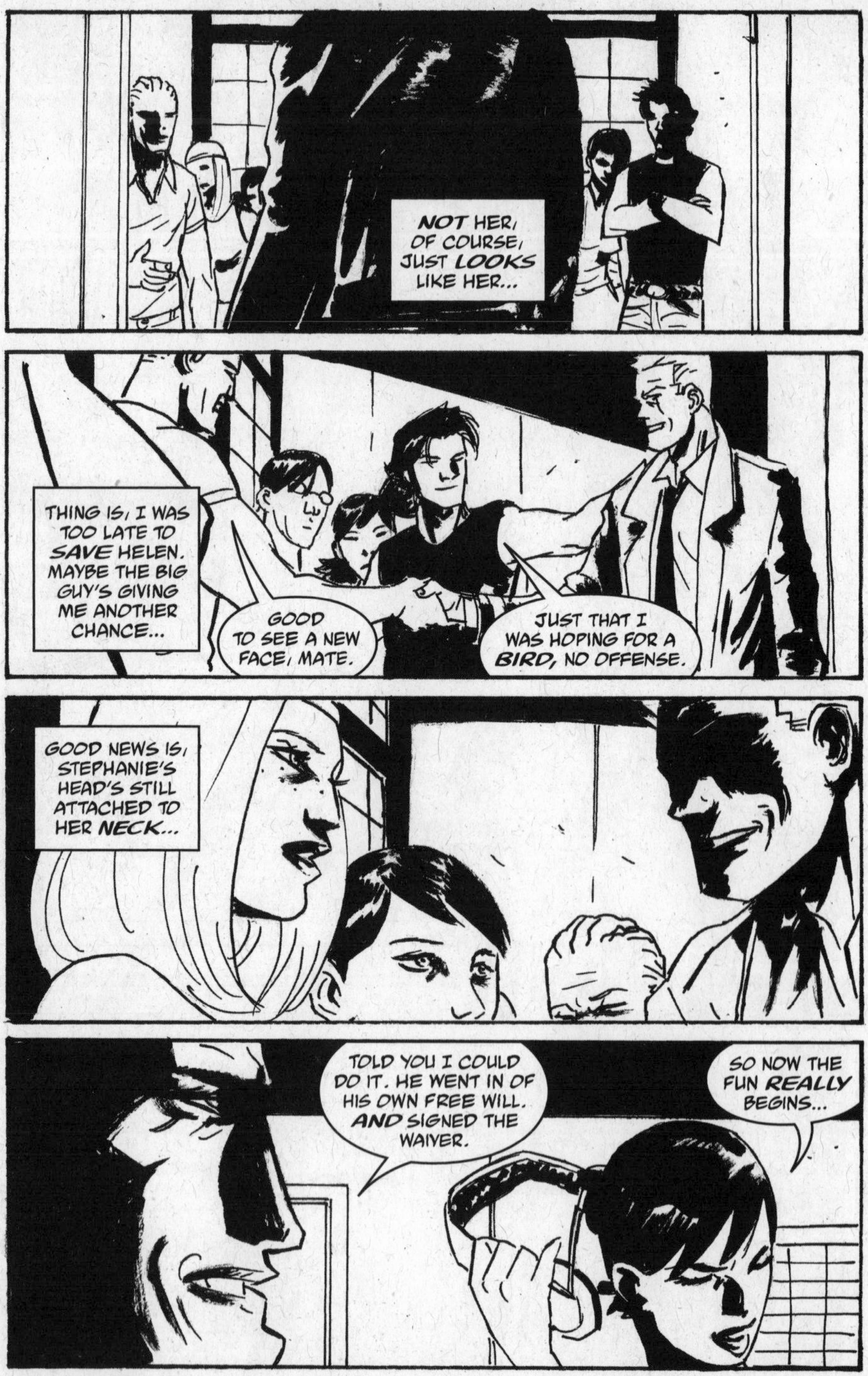
NOT HER, OF COURSE, JUST LOOKS LIKE HER...
THING IS, I WAS TOO LATE TO SAVE HELEN. MAYBE THE BIG GUY'S GIVING ME ANOTHER CHANCE...
GOOD TO SEE A NEW FACE, MATE.
JUST THAT I WAS HOPING FOR A BIRD, NO OFFENSE.
GOOD NEWS IS, STEPHANIE'S HEAD'S STILL ATTACHED TO HER NECK...
TOLD YOU I COULD DO IT. HE WENT IN OF HIS OWN FREE WILL. AND SIGNED THE WAIVER.
SO NOW THE FUN REALLY BEGINS...

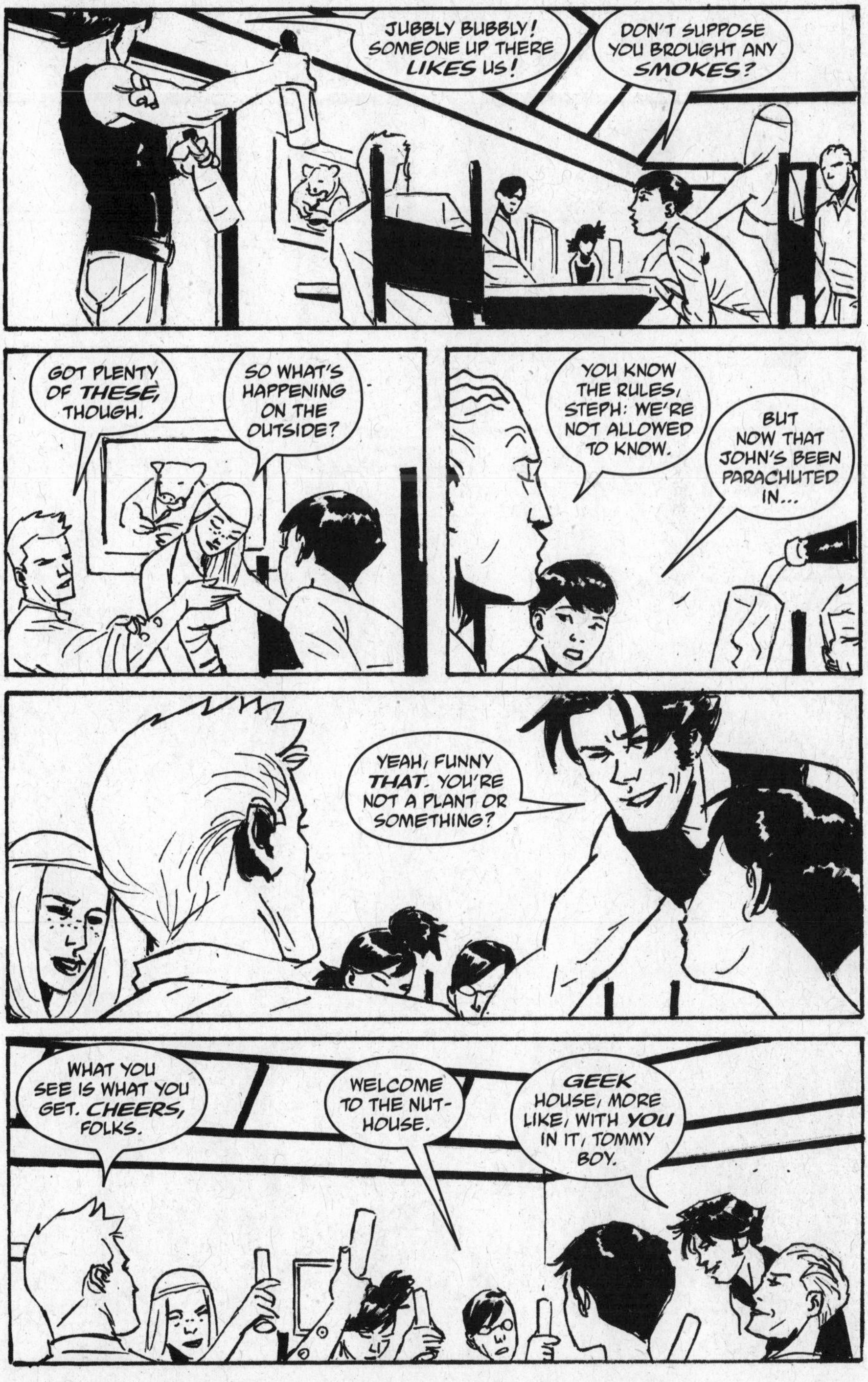
JUBBLY BUBBLY! SOMEONE UP THERE LIKES US!
DON'T SUPPOSE YOU BROUGHT ANY SMOKES?
GOT PLENTY OF THESE, THOUGH.
SO WHAT'S HAPPENING ON THE OUTSIDE?
YOU KNOW THE RULES, STEPH: WE'RE NOT ALLOWED TO KNOW.
BUT NOW THAT JOHN'S BEEN PARACHUTED IN...
YEAH, FUNNY THAT. YOU'RE NOT A PLANT OR SOMETHING?
WHAT YOU SEE IS WHAT YOU GET. CHEERS, FOLKS.
WELCOME TO THE NUT-HOUSE.
GEEK HOUSE, MORE LIKE, WITH YOU IN IT, TOMMY BOY.

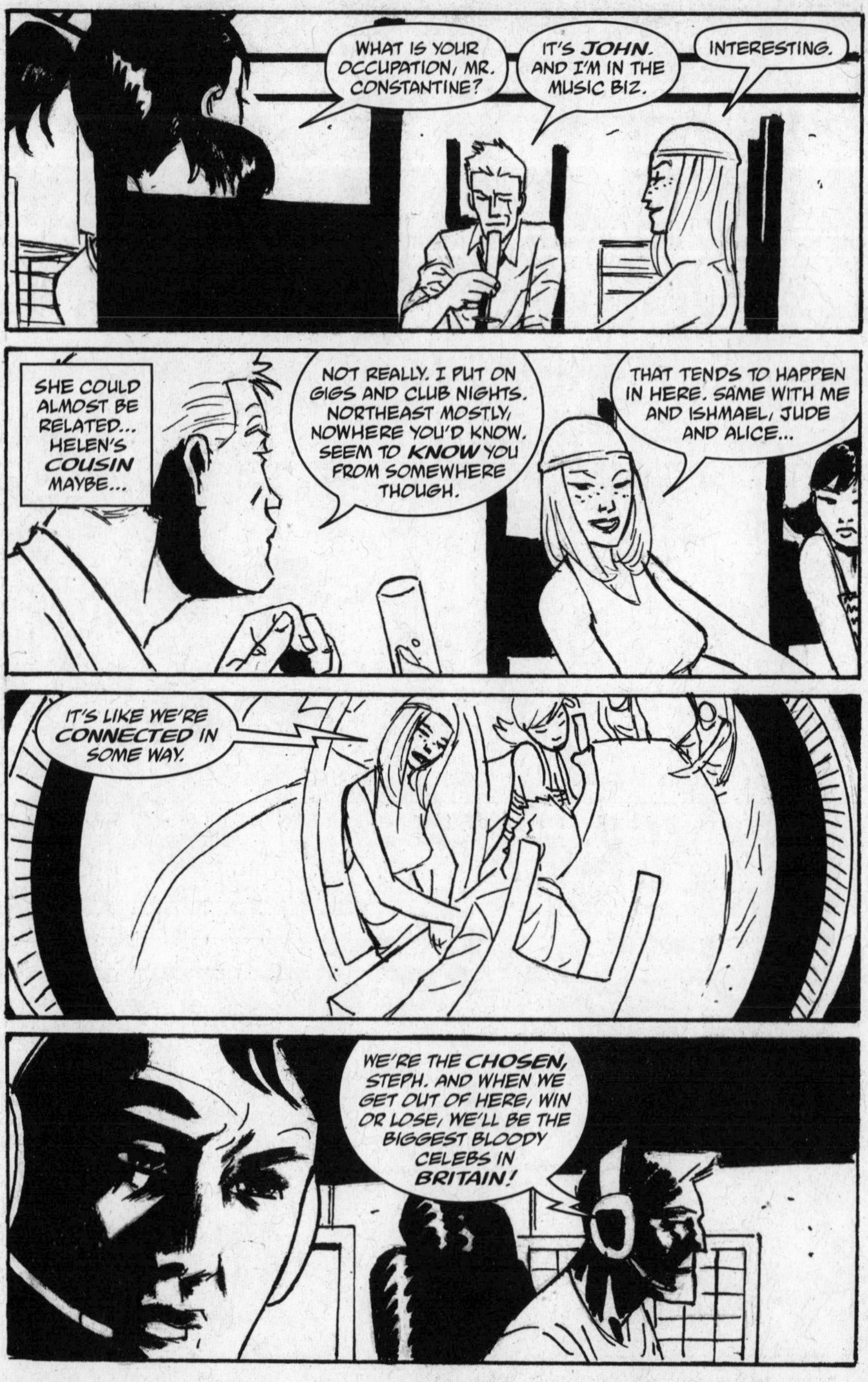
WHAT IS YOUR OCCUPATION, MR. CONSTANTINE?
IT'S JOHN. AND I'M IN THE MUSIC BIZ.
INTERESTING.
SHE COULD ALMOST BE RELATED... HELEN'S COUSIN MAYBE...
NOT REALLY. I PUT ON GIGS AND CLUB NIGHTS. NORTHEAST MOSTLY, NOWHERE YOU'D KNOW. SEEM TO KNOW YOU FROM SOMEWHERE THOUGH.
THAT TENDS TO HAPPEN IN HERE. SAME WITH ME AND ISHMAEL, JUDE AND ALICE...
IT'S LIKE WE'RE CONNECTED IN SOME WAY.
WE'RE THE CHOSEN, STEPH. AND WHEN WE GET OUT OF HERE, WIN OR LOSE, WE'LL BE THE BIGGEST BLOODY CELEBS IN BRITAIN!

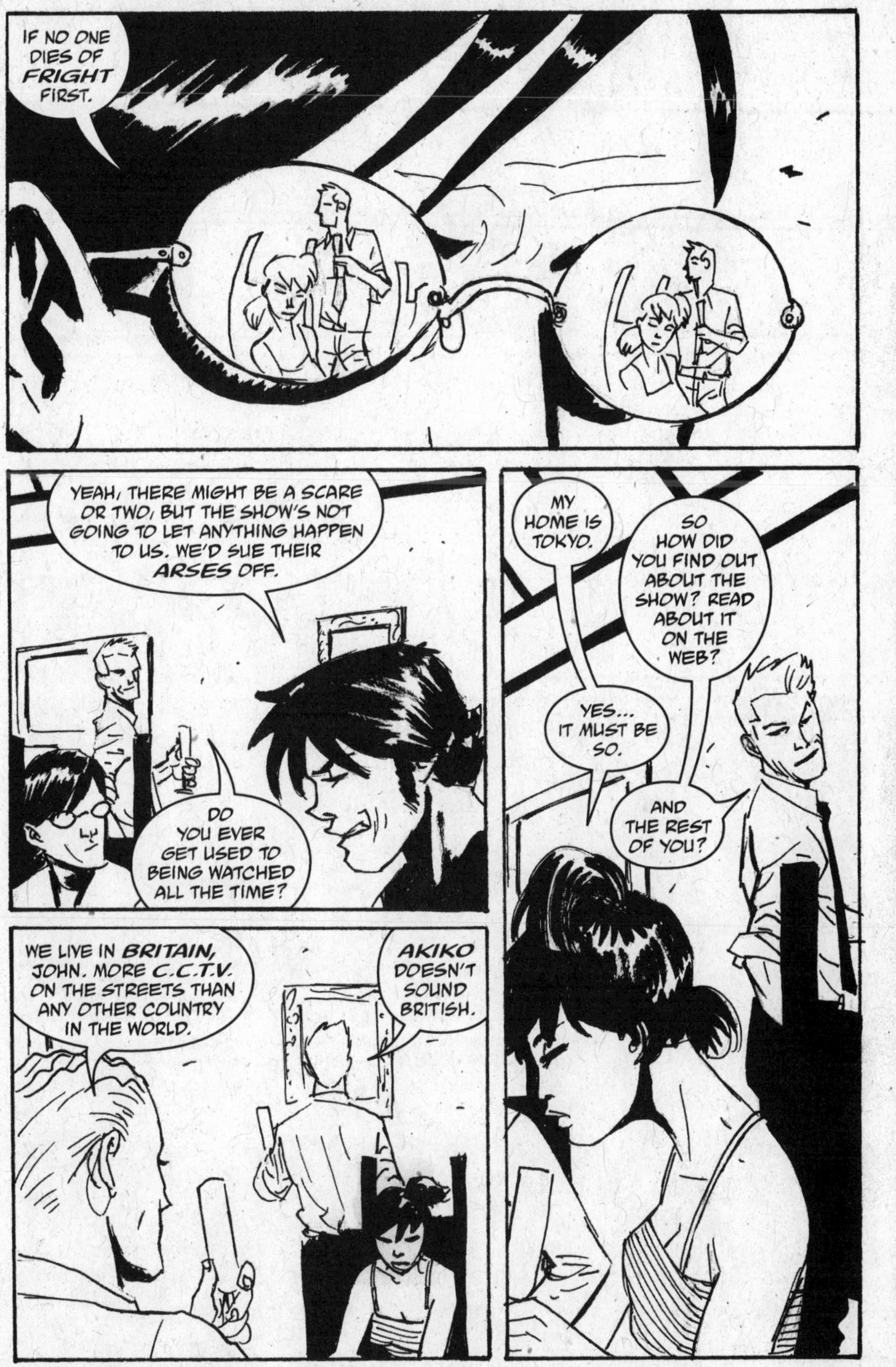
IF NO ONE DIES OF FRIGHT FIRST.
YEAH, THERE MIGHT BE A SCARE OR TWO, BUT THE SHOW'S NOT GOING TO LET ANYTHING HAPPEN TO US. WE'D SUE THEIR ARSES OFF.
DO YOU EVER GET USED TO BEING WATCHED ALL THE TIME?
WE LIVE IN BRITAIN, JOHN. MORE C.C.T.V. ON THE STREETS THAN ANY OTHER COUNTRY IN THE WORLD.
AKIKO DOESN'T SOUND BRITISH.
MY HOME IS TOKYO.
SO HOW DID YOU FIND OUT ABOUT THE SHOW? READ ABOUT IT ON THE WEB?
YES... IT MUST BE SO.
AND THE REST OF YOU?

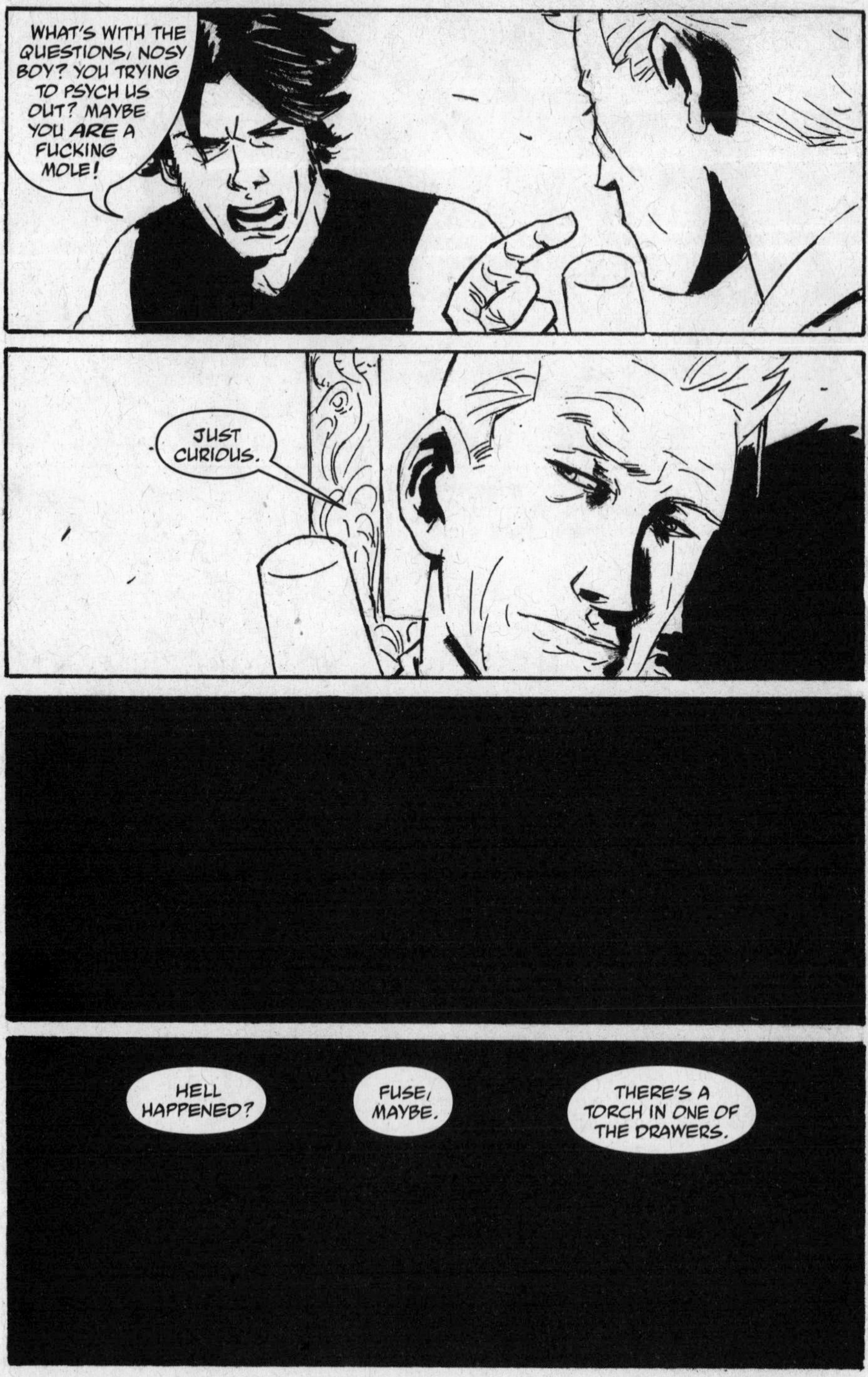
WHAT'S WITH THE QUESTIONS, NOSY BOY? YOU TRYING TO PSYCH US OUT? MAYBE YOU ARE A FUCKING MOLE!
JUST CURIOUS.
HELL HAPPENED?
FUSE, MAYBE.
THERE'S A TORCH IN ONE OF THE DRAWERS.

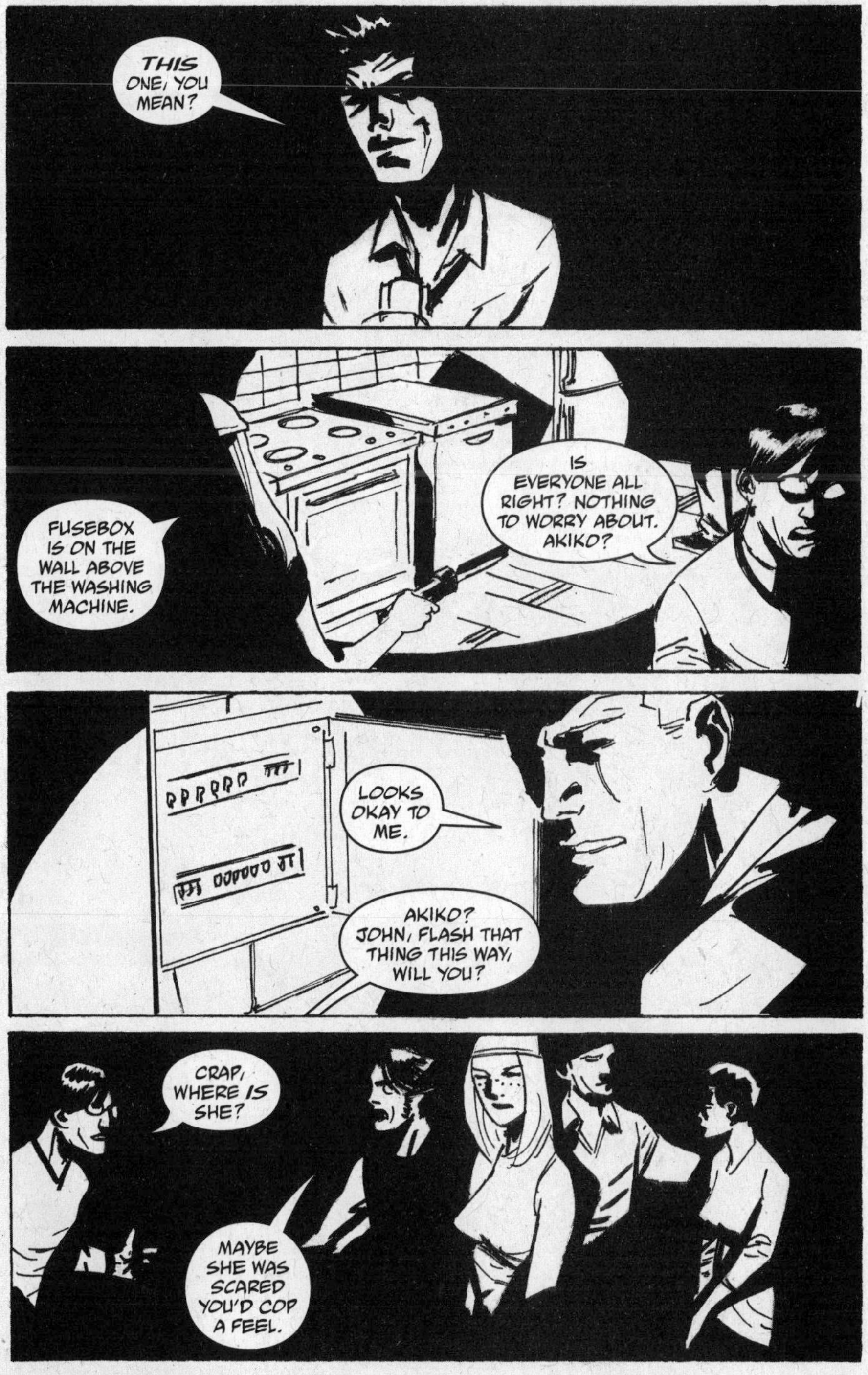
THIS ONE, YOU MEAN?
FUSEBOX IS ON THE WALL ABOVE THE WASHING MACHINE.
IS EVERYONE ALL RIGHT? NOTHING TO WORRY ABOUT. AKIKO?
LOOKS OKAY TO ME.
AKIKO? JOHN, FLASH THAT THING THIS WAY, WILL YOU?
CRAP, WHERE *IS* SHE?
MAYBE SHE WAS SCARED YOU'D COP A FEEL.

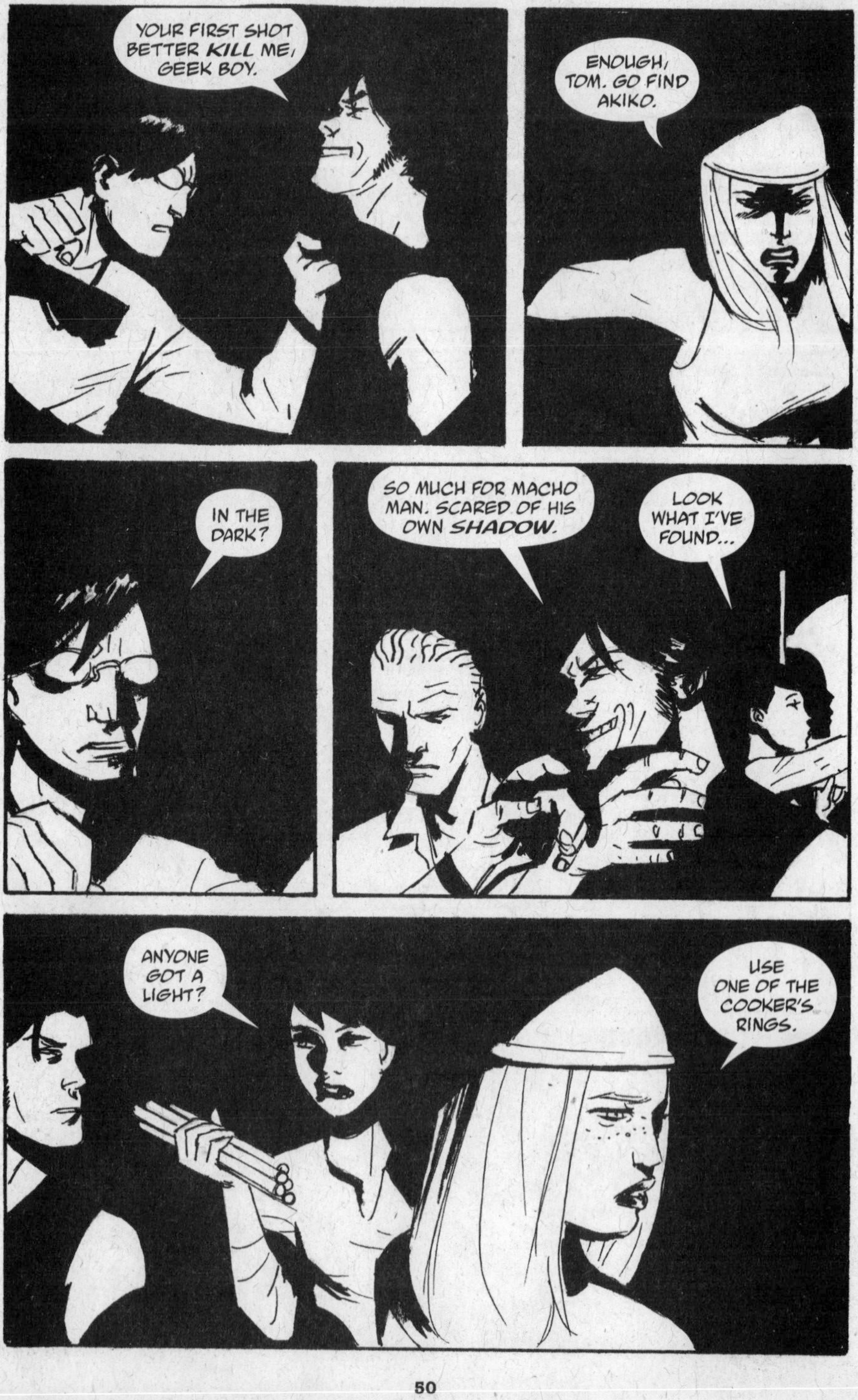
YOUR FIRST SHOT BETTER KILL ME, GEEK BOY.
ENOUGH, TOM. GO FIND AKIKO.
IN THE DARK?
SO MUCH FOR MACHO MAN. SCARED OF HIS OWN SHADOW.
LOOK WHAT I'VE FOUND...
ANYONE GOT A LIGHT?
USE ONE OF THE COOKER'S RINGS.

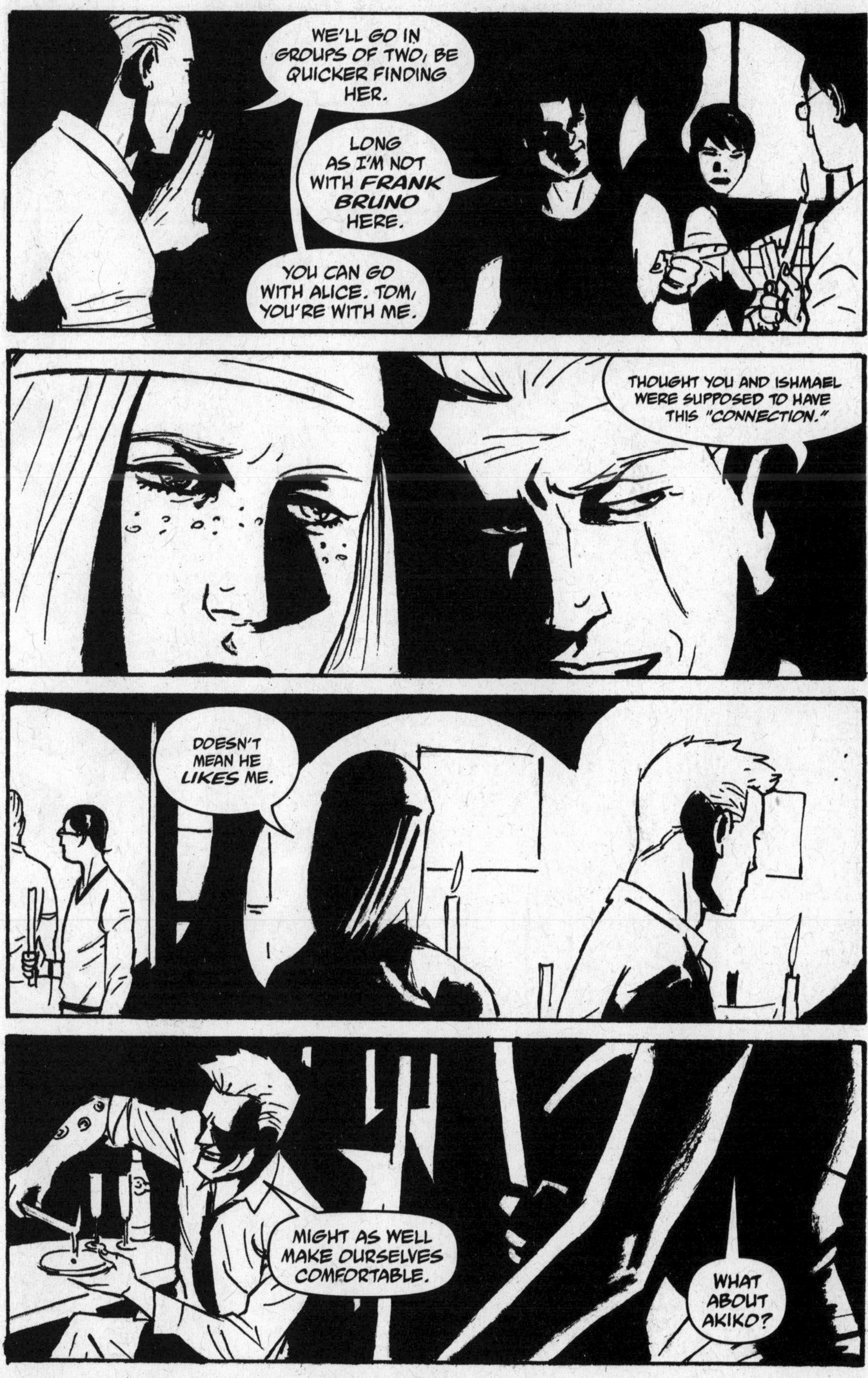
WE'LL GO IN GROUPS OF TWO, BE QUICKER FINDING HER.
LONG AS I'M NOT WITH *FRANK BRUNO* HERE.
YOU CAN GO WITH ALICE. TOM, YOU'RE WITH ME.
THOUGHT YOU AND ISHMAEL WERE SUPPOSED TO HAVE THIS "CONNECTION."
DOESN'T MEAN HE *LIKES* ME.
MIGHT AS WELL MAKE OURSELVES COMFORTABLE.
WHAT ABOUT AKIKO?

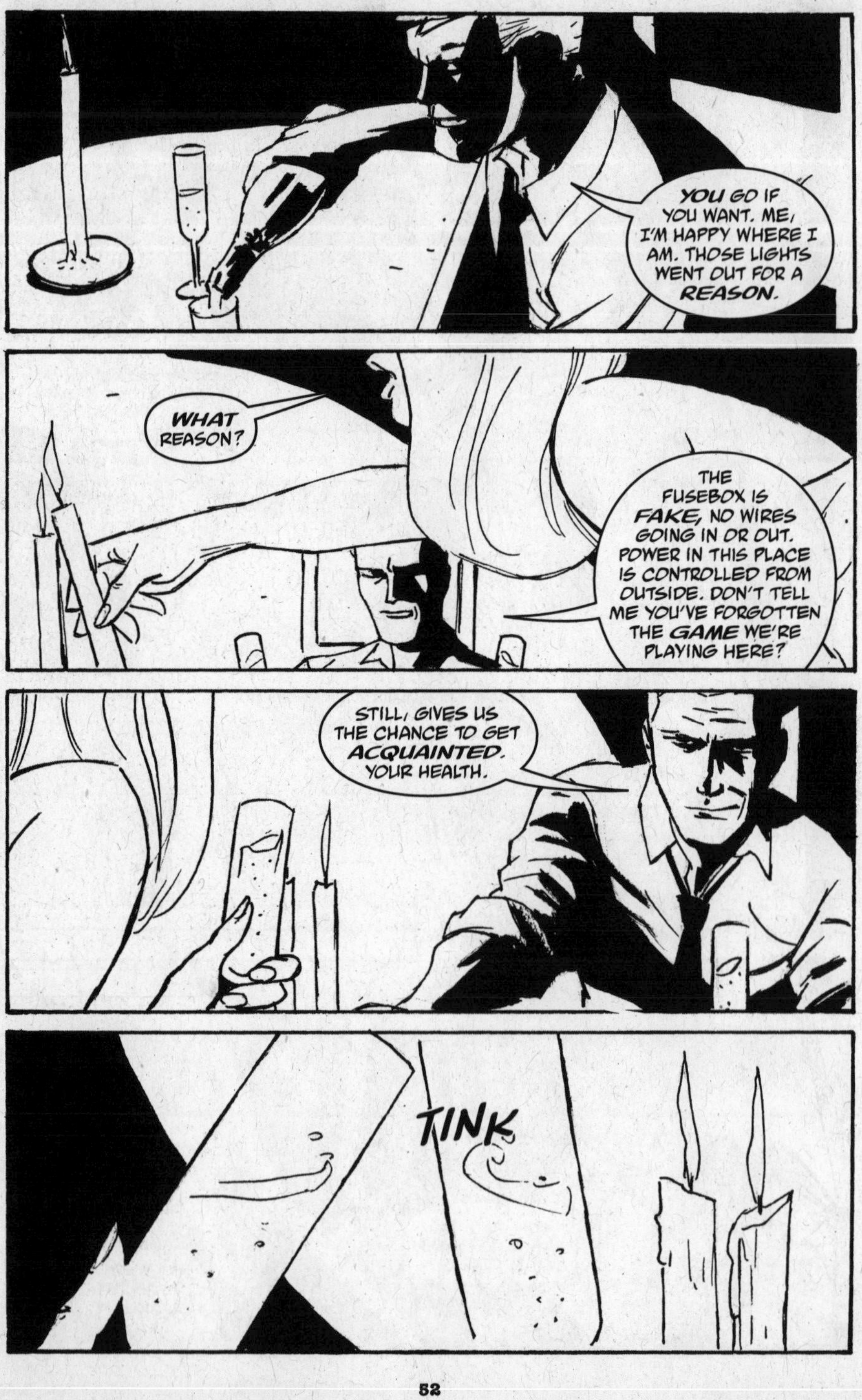
YOU GO IF YOU WANT. ME, I'M HAPPY WHERE I AM. THOSE LIGHTS WENT OUT FOR A REASON.
WHAT REASON?
THE FUSEBOX IS FAKE, NO WIRES GOING IN OR OUT. POWER IN THIS PLACE IS CONTROLLED FROM OUTSIDE. DON'T TELL ME YOU'VE FORGOTTEN THE GAME WE'RE PLAYING HERE?
STILL, GIVES US THE CHANCE TO GET ACQUAINTED. YOUR HEALTH.
TINK

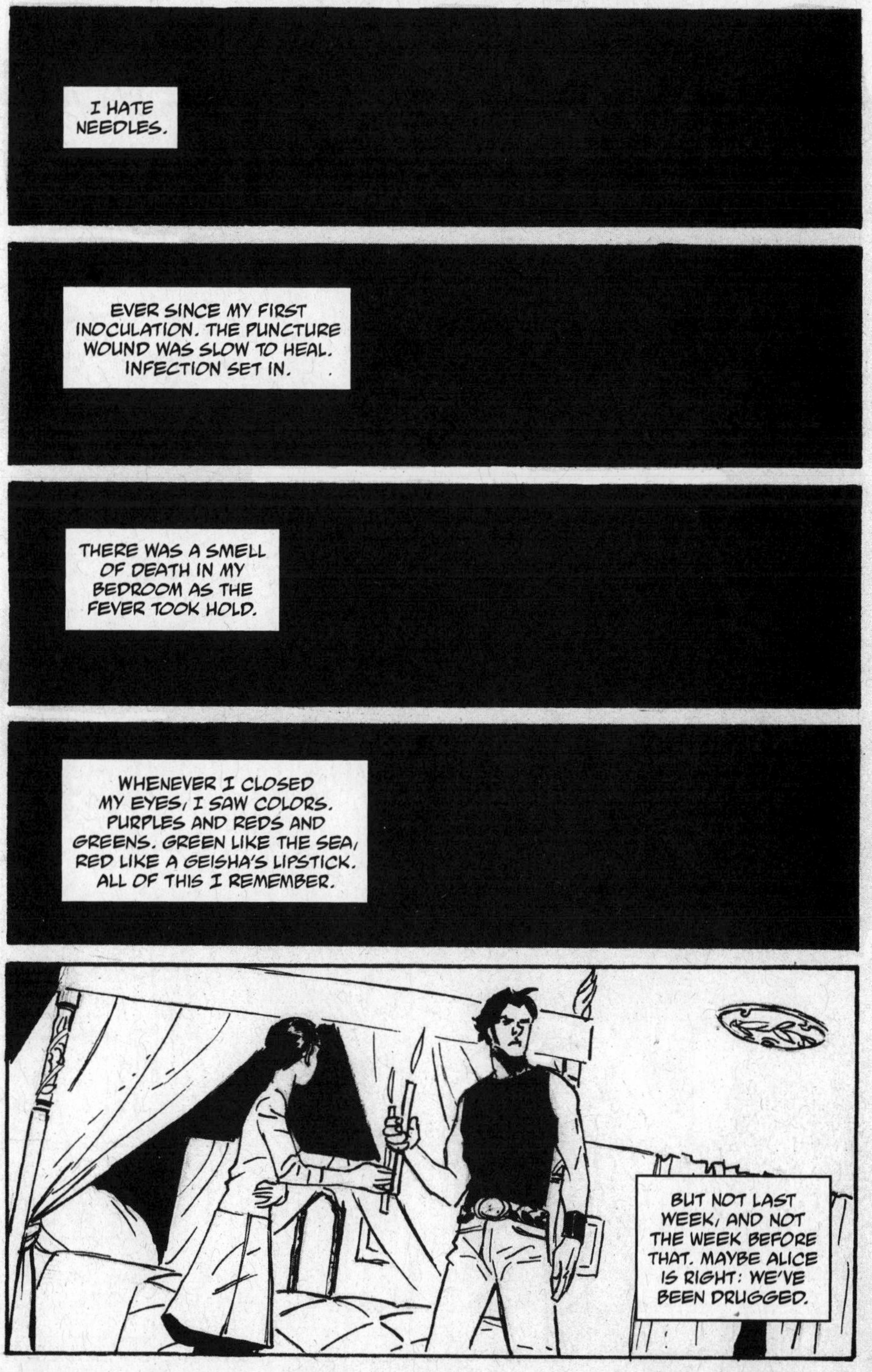
I HATE NEEDLES.
EVER SINCE MY FIRST INOCULATION. THE PUNCTURE WOUND WAS SLOW TO HEAL. INFECTION SET IN.
THERE WAS A SMELL OF DEATH IN MY BEDROOM AS THE FEVER TOOK HOLD.
WHENEVER I CLOSED MY EYES, I SAW COLORS. PURPLES AND REDS AND GREENS. GREEN LIKE THE SEA, RED LIKE A GEISHA'S LIPSTICK. ALL OF THIS I REMEMBER.
BUT NOT LAST WEEK, AND NOT THE WEEK BEFORE THAT. MAYBE ALICE IS RIGHT: WE'VE BEEN DRUGGED.

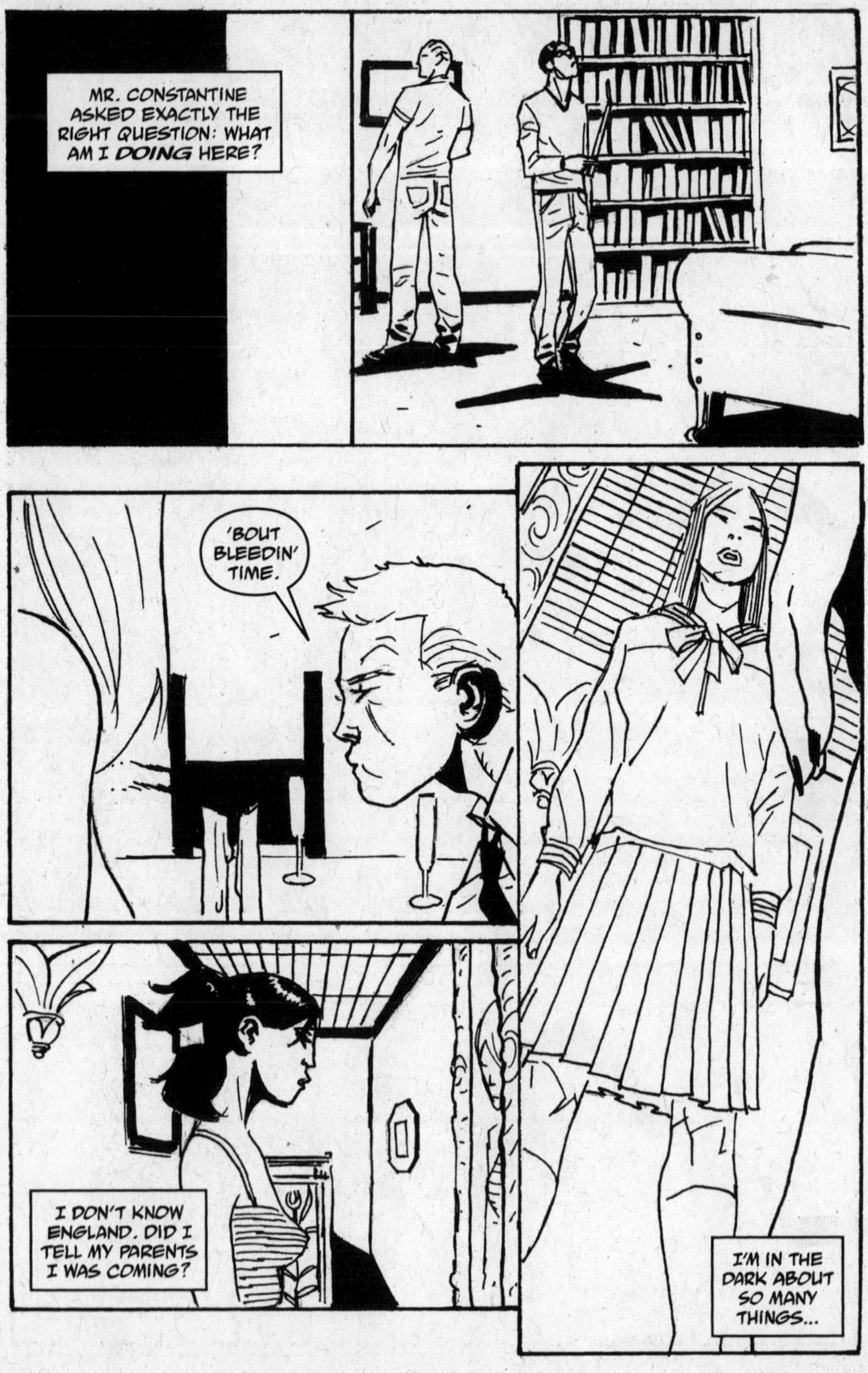
MR. CONSTANTINE ASKED EXACTLY THE RIGHT QUESTION: WHAT AM I DOING HERE?
'BOUT BLEEDIN' TIME.
I DON'T KNOW ENGLAND. DID I TELL MY PARENTS I WAS COMING?
I'M IN THE DARK ABOUT SO MANY THINGS...

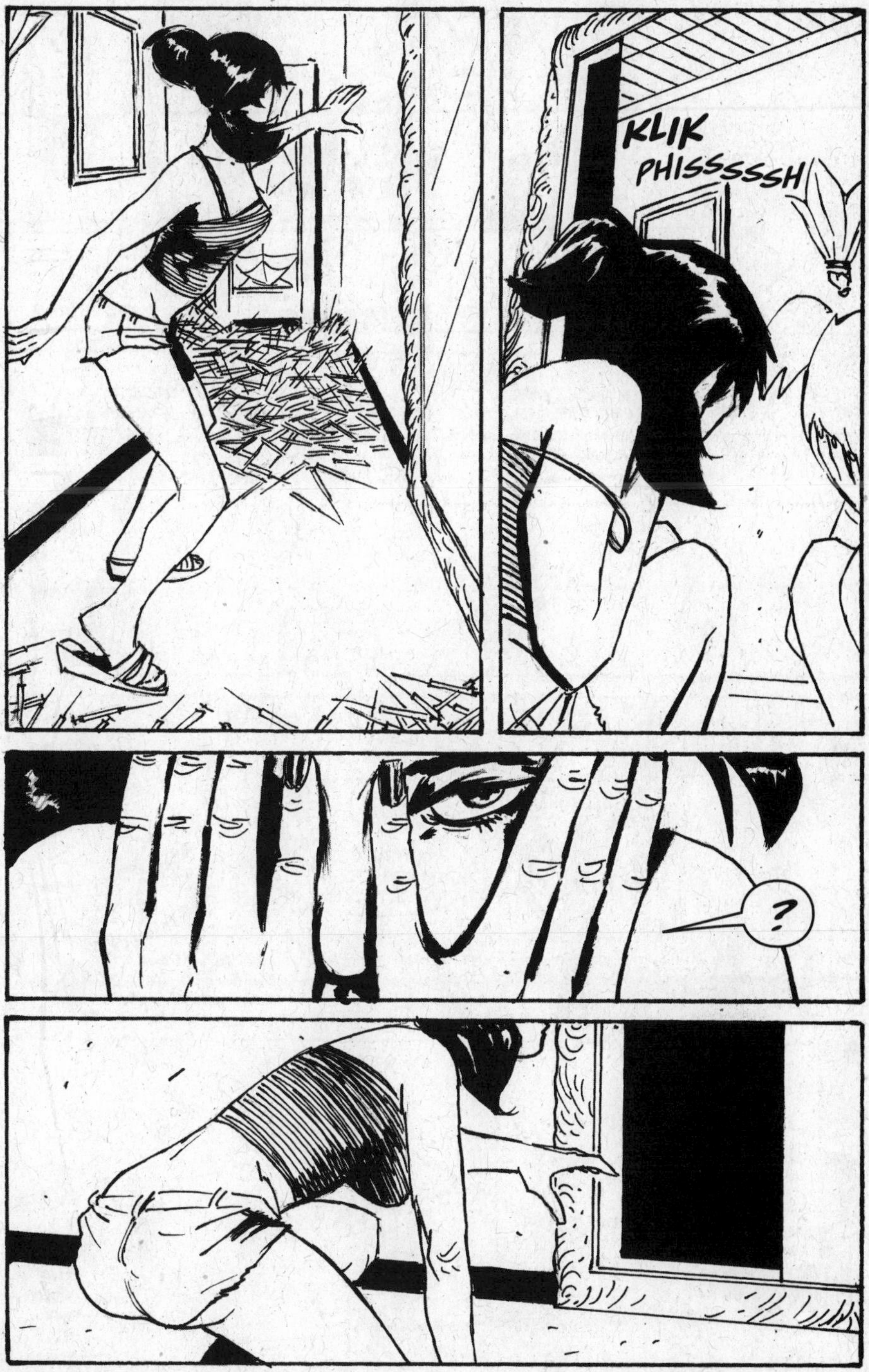
KLIK
PHISSSSSH
?

OPEN SESAME!

YOU TRYING TO GET ME SOZZLED?

DUNNO... WOULD IT HELP MY CHANCES?

IN FRONT OF AN AUDIENCE OF *EIGHT MILLION?* GET REAL.

BUT WITH ME UNCONSCIOUS, YOU CAN GO EXPLORING, MAYBE FIND THE SECRET ROOM.

GOOD POINT. SOUNDS SOLID ENOUGH.

SO WHAT BRINGS *YOU* HERE, JOHN? THE FAME? THE TREASURE?

MAYBE THE *COMPANY.* HOW ABOUT YOU?

SOUNDS STUPID, BUT I'M NOT REALLY *SURE* NOW.

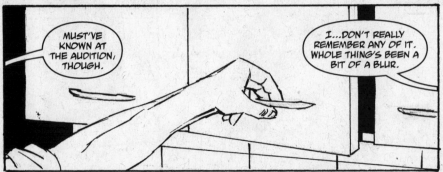

MUST'VE KNOWN AT THE AUDITION, THOUGH.

I...DON'T REALLY REMEMBER ANY OF IT. WHOLE THING'S BEEN A BIT OF A BLUR.

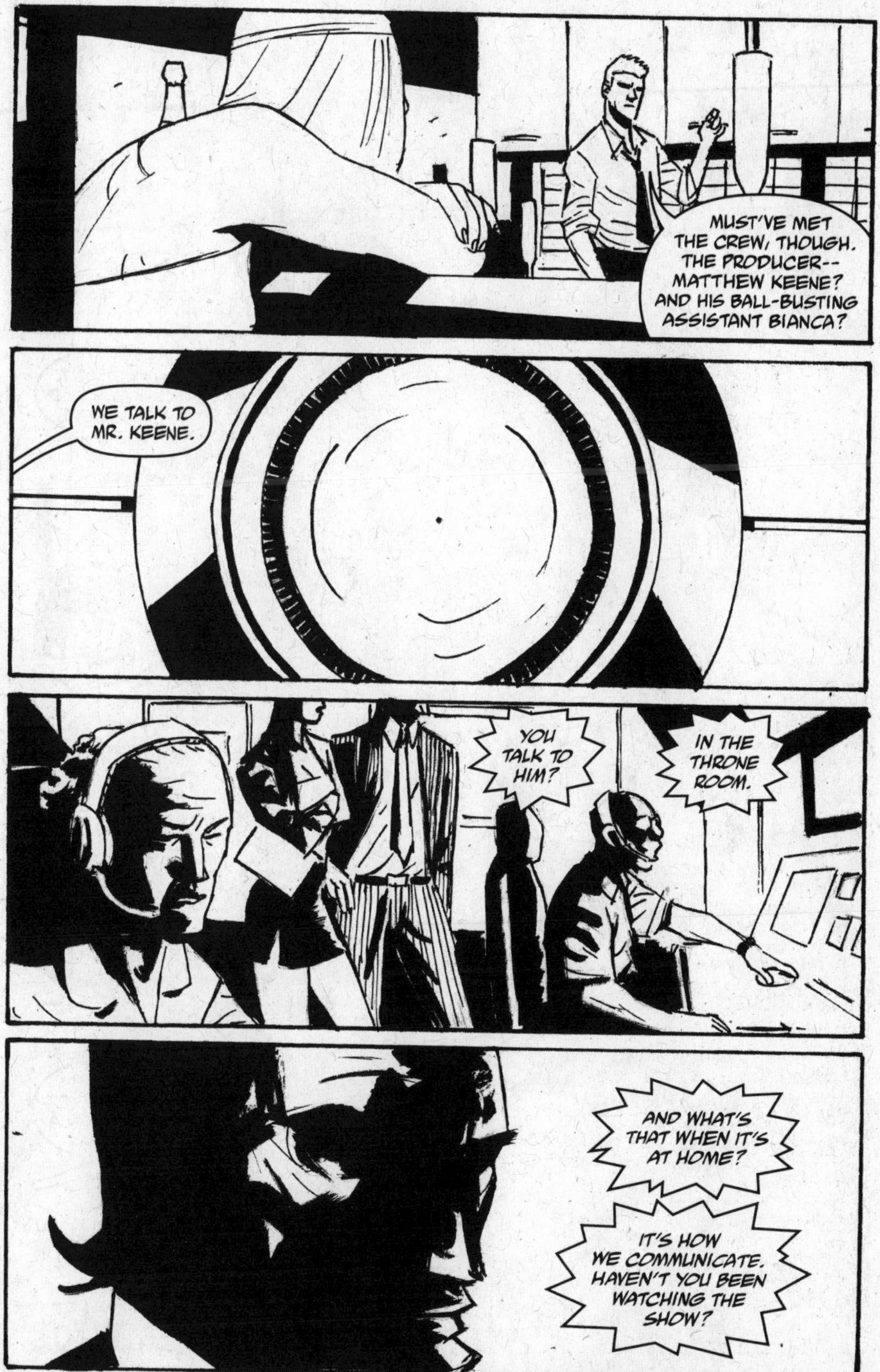
MUST'VE MET THE CREW, THOUGH. THE PRODUCER-- MATTHEW KEENE? AND HIS BALL-BUSTING ASSISTANT BIANCA?
WE TALK TO MR. KEENE.
YOU TALK TO HIM?
IN THE THRONE ROOM.
AND WHAT'S THAT WHEN IT'S AT HOME?
IT'S HOW WE COMMUNICATE. HAVEN'T YOU BEEN WATCHING THE SHOW?

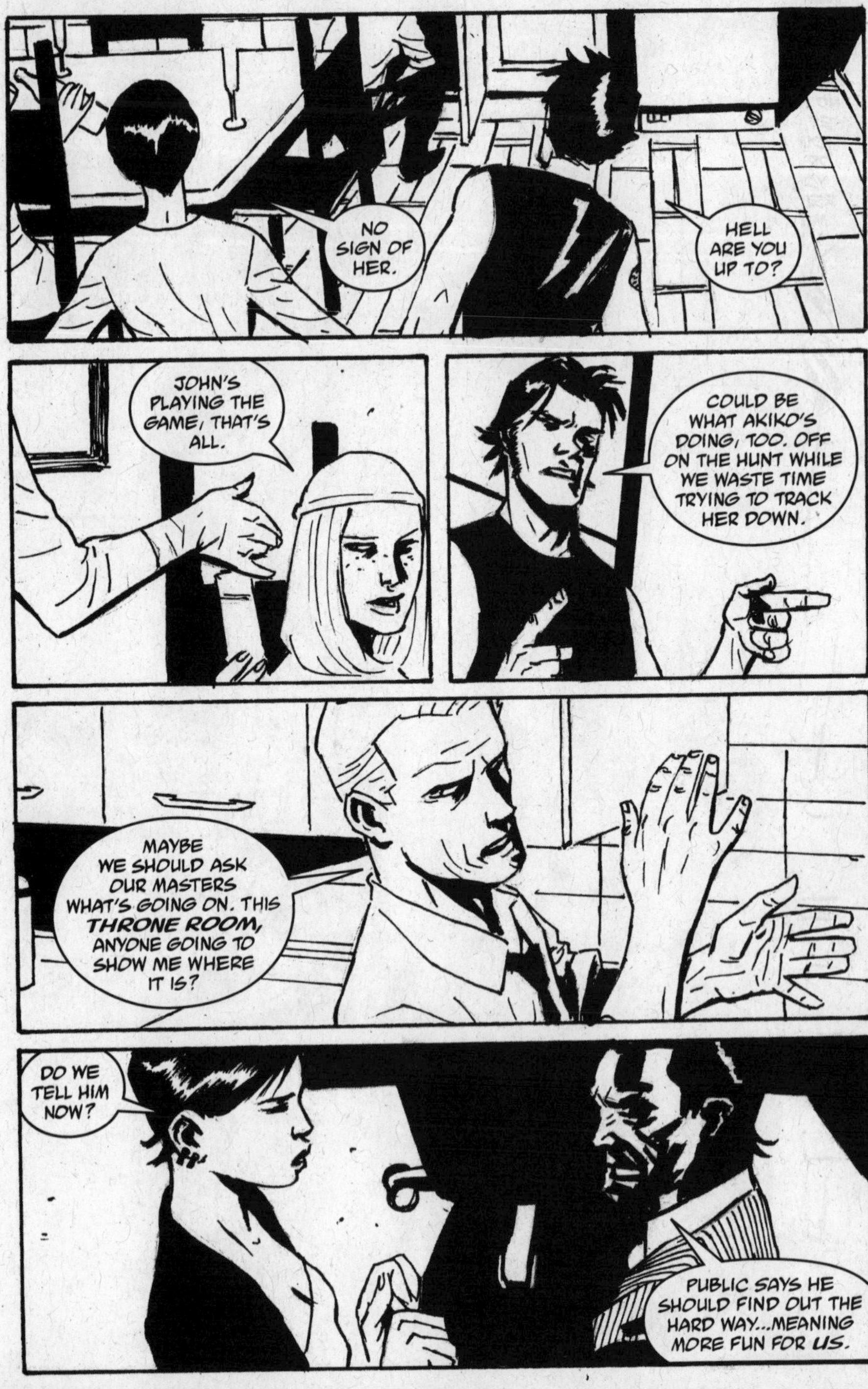
NO SIGN OF HER.
HELL ARE YOU UP TO?
JOHN'S PLAYING THE GAME, THAT'S ALL.
COULD BE WHAT AKIKO'S DOING, TOO. OFF ON THE HUNT WHILE WE WASTE TIME TRYING TO TRACK HER DOWN.
MAYBE WE SHOULD ASK OUR MASTERS WHAT'S GOING ON. THIS *THRONE ROOM*, ANYONE GOING TO SHOW ME WHERE IT IS?
DO WE TELL HIM NOW?
PUBLIC SAYS HE SHOULD FIND OUT THE HARD WAY...MEANING MORE FUN FOR *US*.

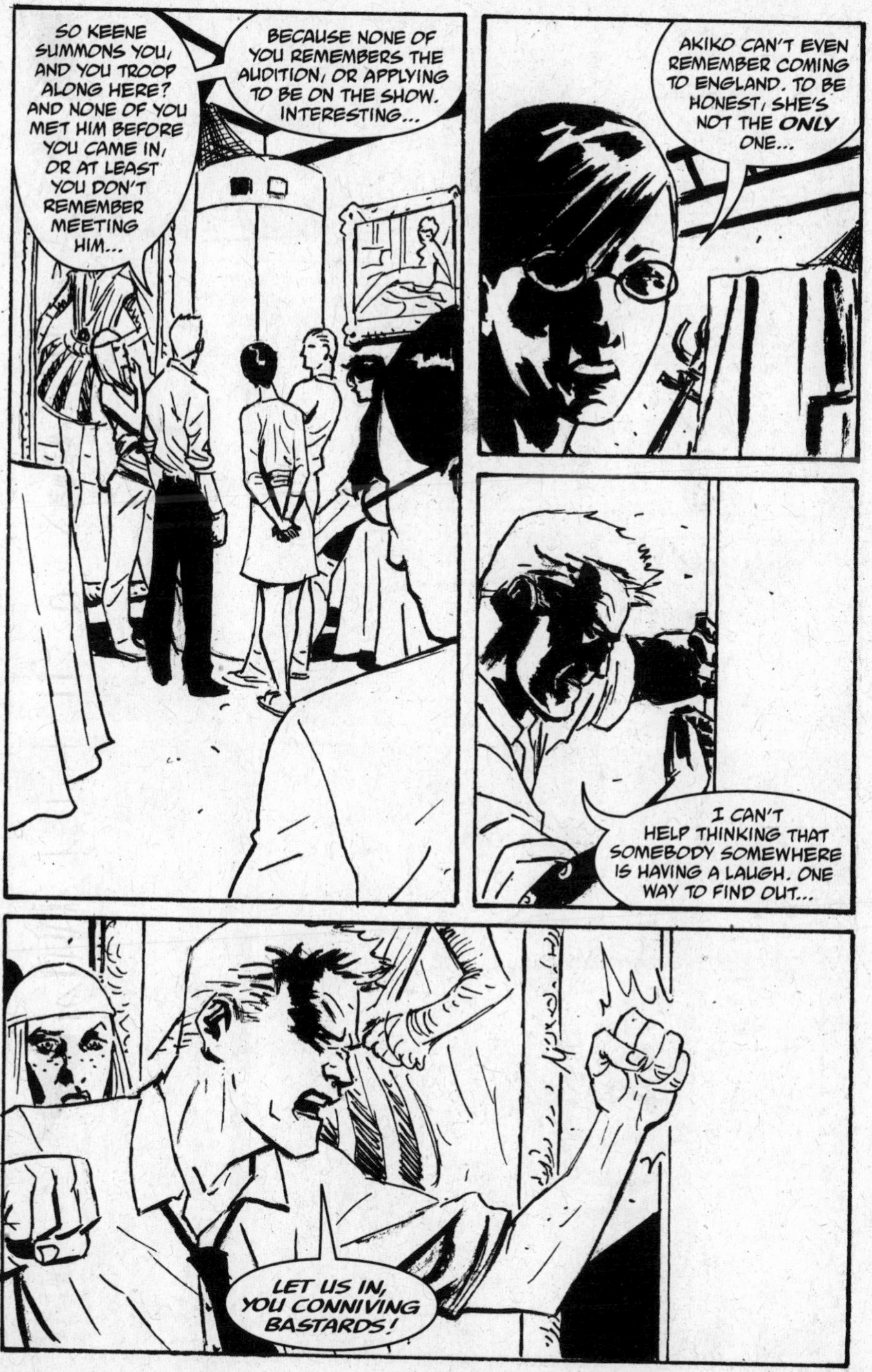
SO KEENE SUMMONS YOU, AND YOU TROOP ALONG HERE? AND NONE OF YOU MET HIM BEFORE YOU CAME IN, OR AT LEAST YOU DON'T REMEMBER MEETING HIM...
BECAUSE NONE OF YOU REMEMBERS THE AUDITION, OR APPLYING TO BE ON THE SHOW. INTERESTING...
AKIKO CAN'T EVEN REMEMBER COMING TO ENGLAND. TO BE HONEST, SHE'S NOT THE ONLY ONE...
I CAN'T HELP THINKING THAT SOMEBODY SOMEWHERE IS HAVING A LAUGH. ONE WAY TO FIND OUT...
LET US IN, YOU CONNIVING BASTARDS!

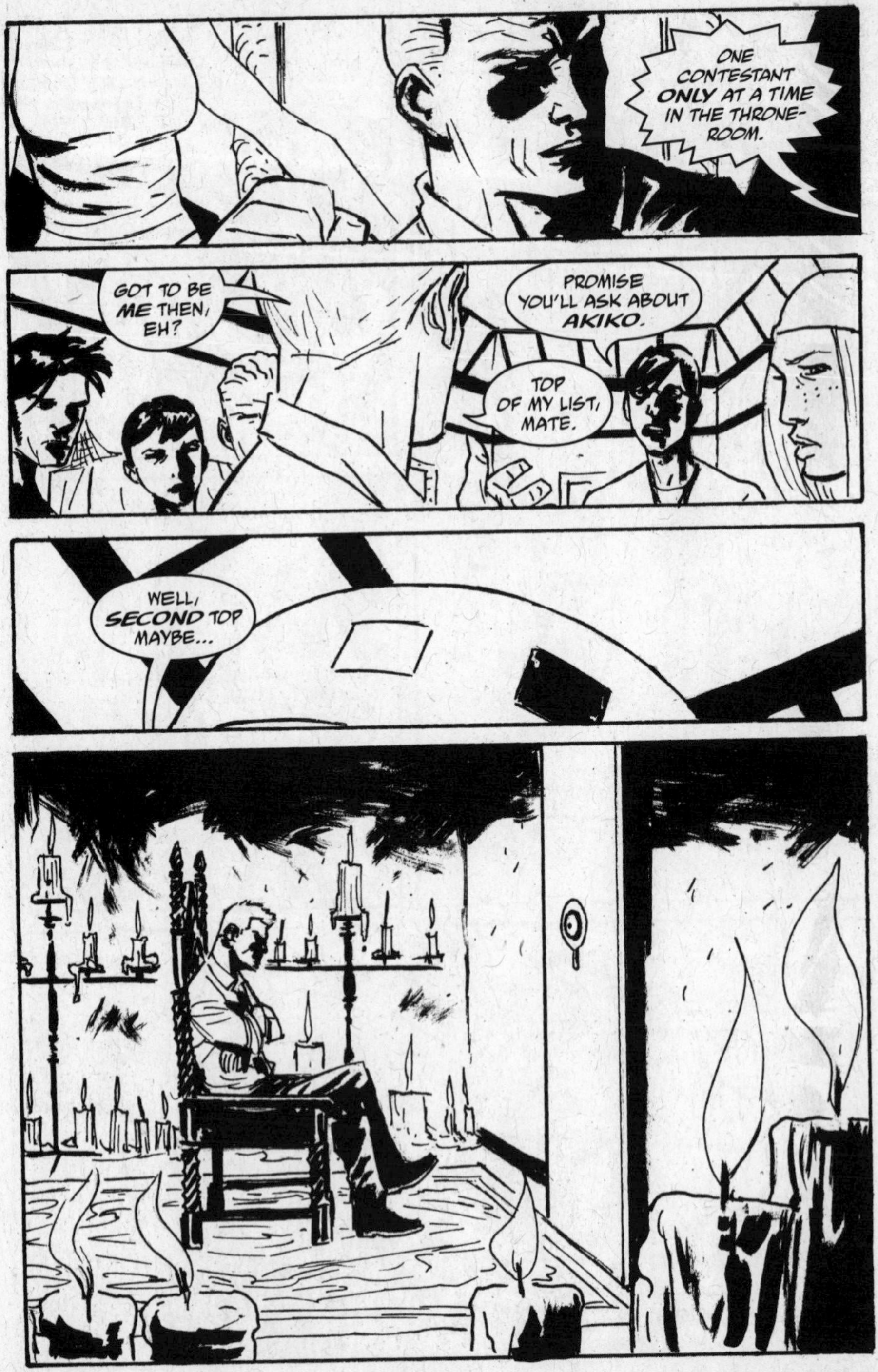
ONE CONTESTANT ONLY AT A TIME IN THE THRONE-ROOM.
GOT TO BE ME THEN, EH?
PROMISE YOU'LL ASK ABOUT AKIKO.
TOP OF MY LIST, MATE.
WELL, SECOND TOP MAYBE...

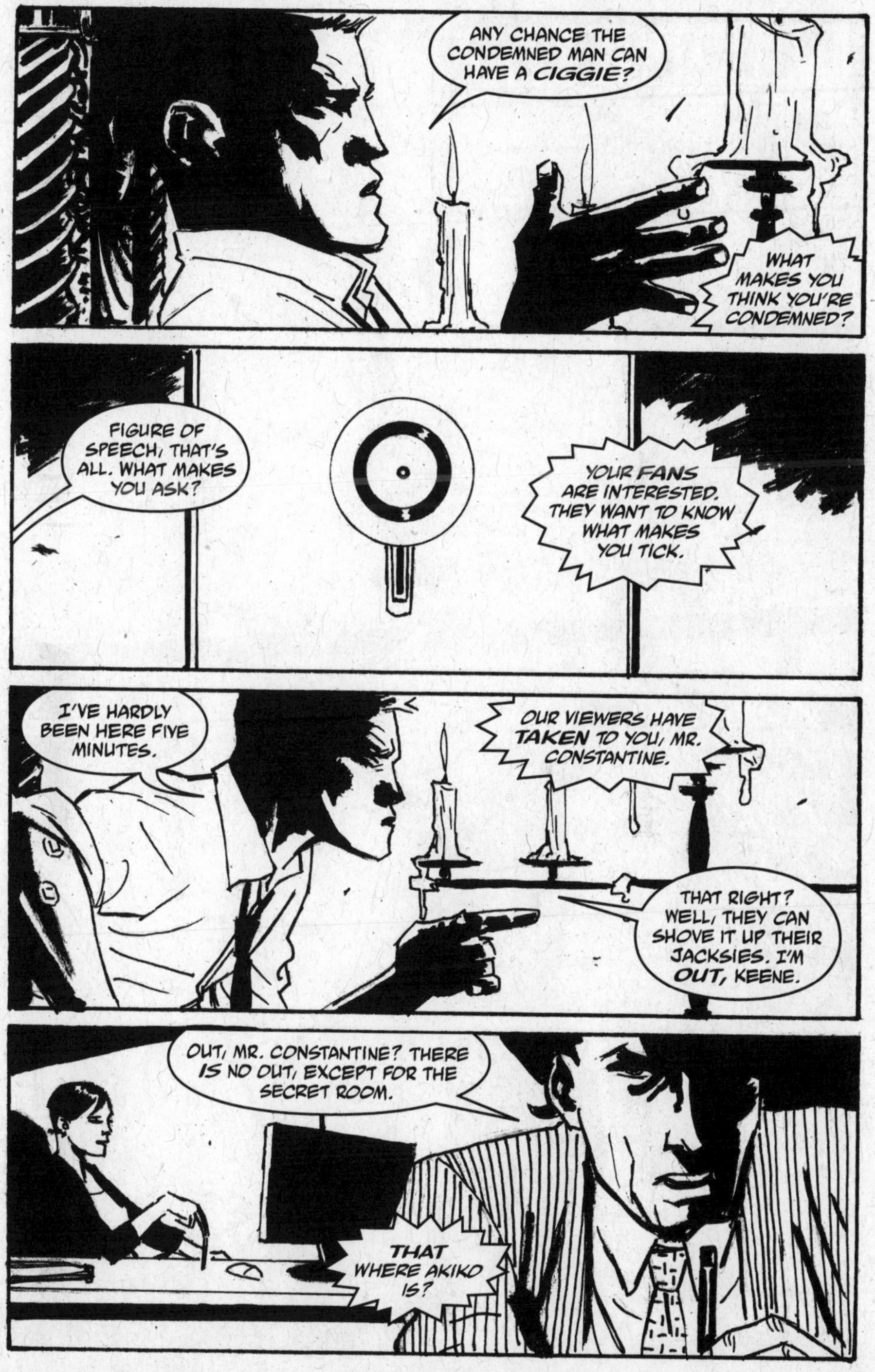
ANY CHANCE THE CONDEMNED MAN CAN HAVE A *CIGGIE*?
WHAT MAKES YOU THINK YOU'RE CONDEMNED?
FIGURE OF SPEECH, THAT'S ALL. WHAT MAKES YOU ASK?
YOUR **FANS** ARE INTERESTED. THEY WANT TO KNOW WHAT MAKES YOU TICK.
I'VE HARDLY BEEN HERE FIVE MINUTES.
OUR VIEWERS HAVE **TAKEN** TO YOU, MR. CONSTANTINE.
THAT RIGHT? WELL, THEY CAN SHOVE IT UP THEIR JACKSIES. I'M **OUT**, KEENE.
OUT, MR. CONSTANTINE? THERE **IS** NO OUT, EXCEPT FOR THE SECRET ROOM.
THAT WHERE AKIKO IS?

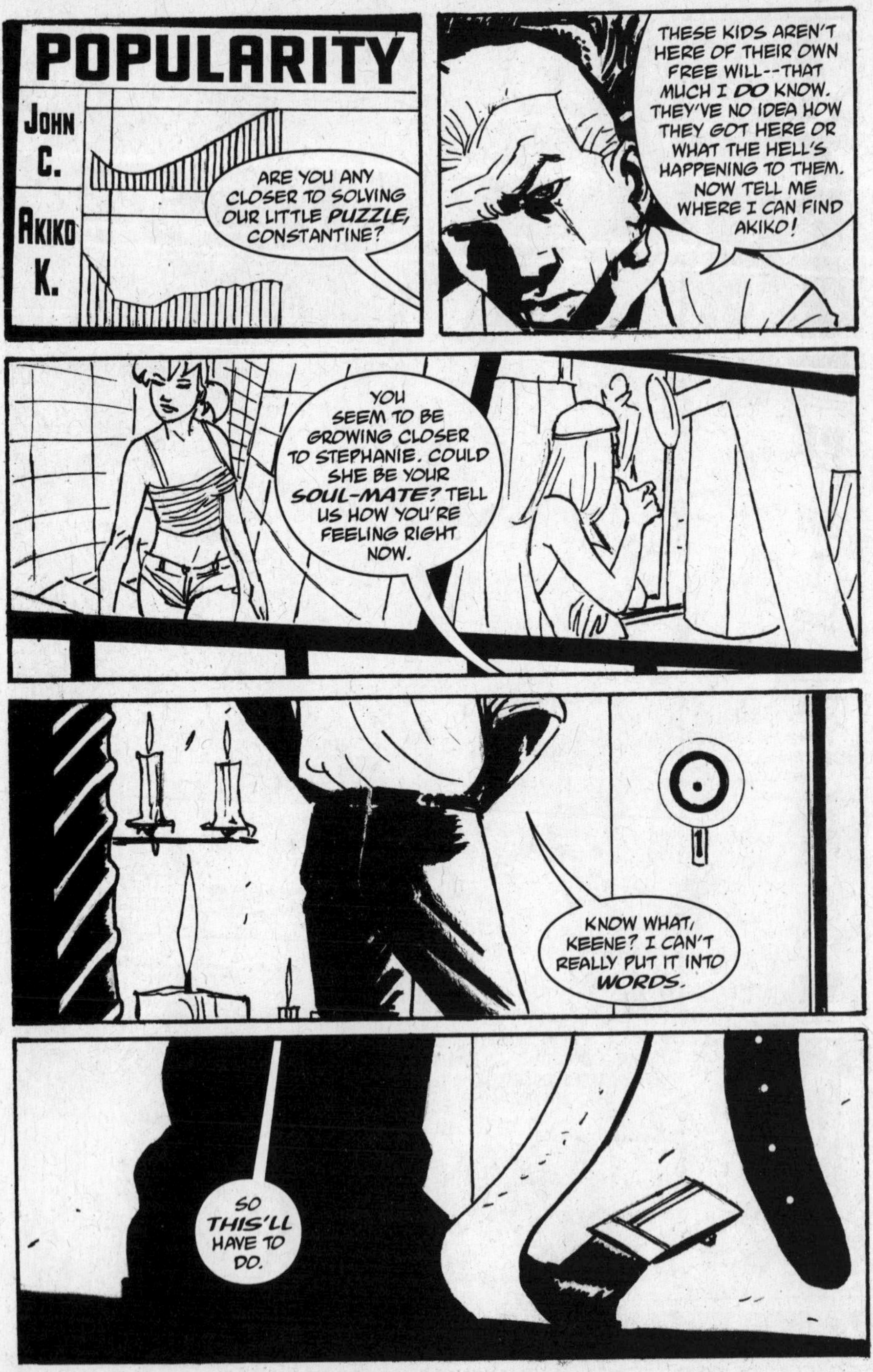
POPULARITY
JOHN C.
AKIKO K.
ARE YOU ANY CLOSER TO SOLVING OUR LITTLE PUZZLE, CONSTANTINE?
THESE KIDS AREN'T HERE OF THEIR OWN FREE WILL--THAT MUCH I DO KNOW. THEY'VE NO IDEA HOW THEY GOT HERE OR WHAT THE HELL'S HAPPENING TO THEM. NOW TELL ME WHERE I CAN FIND AKIKO!
YOU SEEM TO BE GROWING CLOSER TO STEPHANIE. COULD SHE BE YOUR SOUL-MATE? TELL US HOW YOU'RE FEELING RIGHT NOW.
KNOW WHAT, KEENE? I CAN'T REALLY PUT IT INTO WORDS.
SO THIS'LL HAVE TO DO.

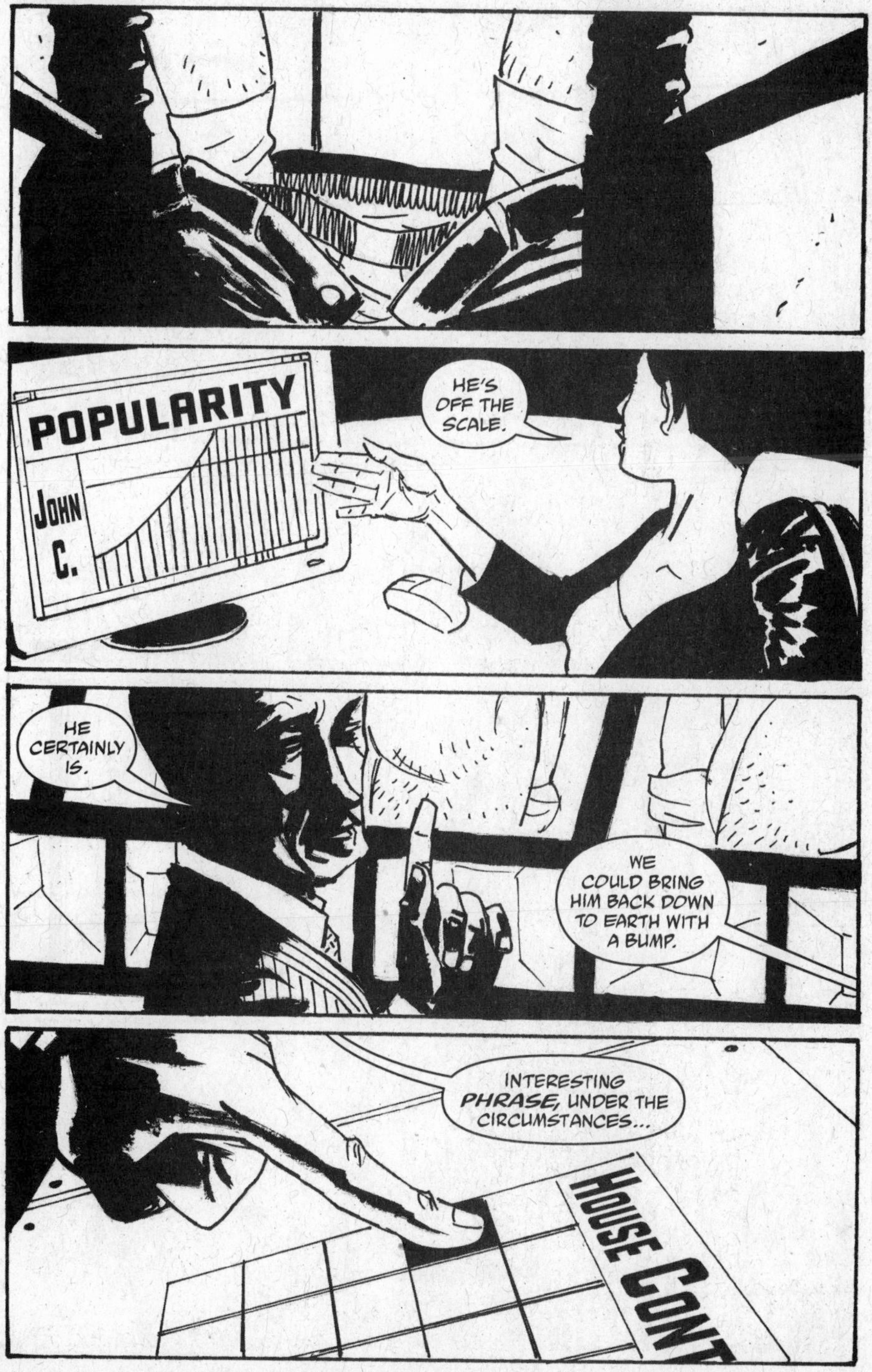
POPULARITY
JOHN C.
HE'S OFF THE SCALE.
HE CERTAINLY IS.
WE COULD BRING HIM BACK DOWN TO EARTH WITH A BUMP.
INTERESTING *PHRASE*, UNDER THE CIRCUMSTANCES...
HOUSE CONT

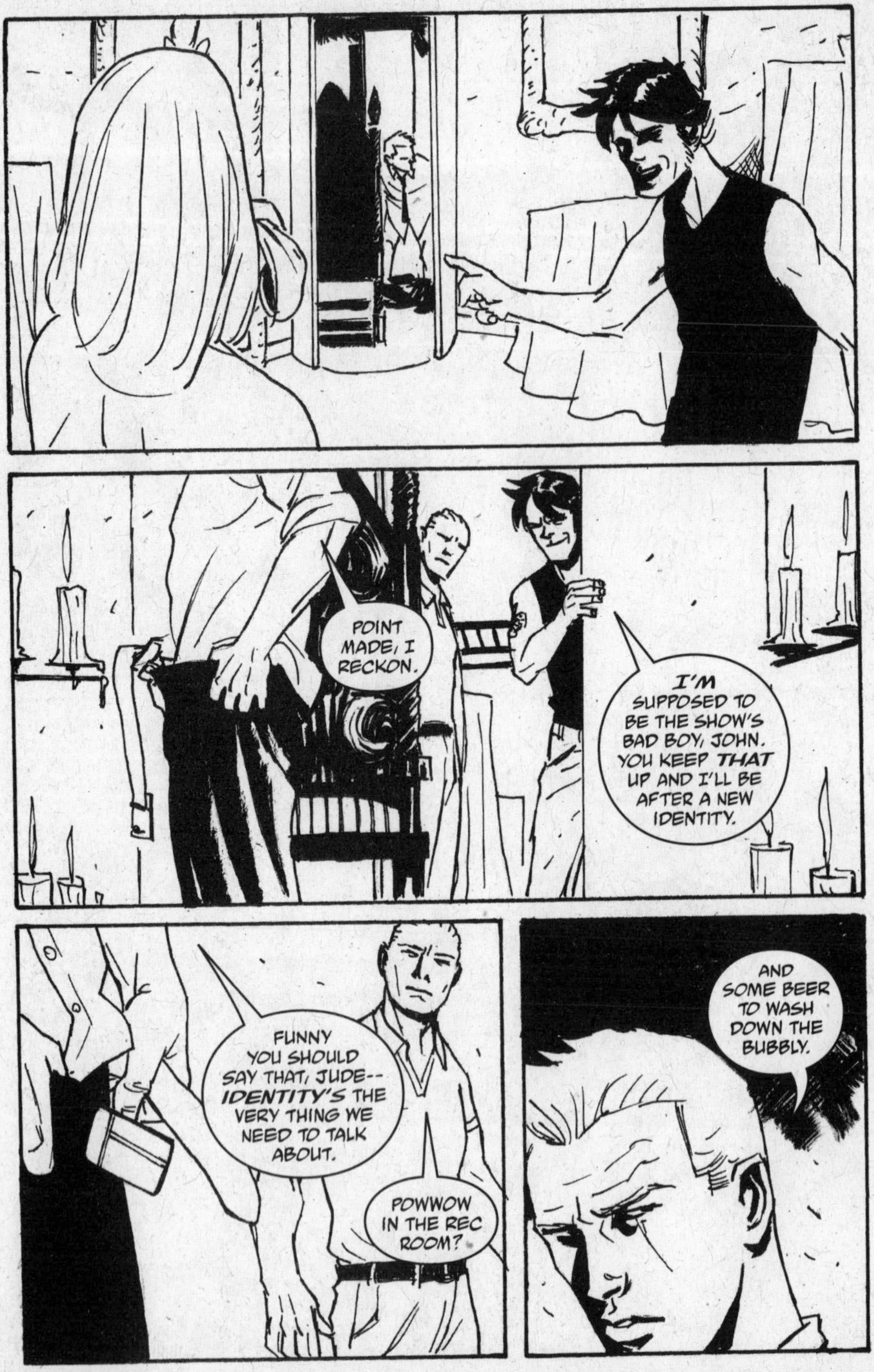
POINT MADE, I RECKON.
I'M SUPPOSED TO BE THE SHOW'S BAD BOY, JOHN. YOU KEEP THAT UP AND I'LL BE AFTER A NEW IDENTITY.
FUNNY YOU SHOULD SAY THAT, JUDE-- IDENTITY'S THE VERY THING WE NEED TO TALK ABOUT.
POWWOW IN THE REC ROOM?
AND SOME BEER TO WASH DOWN THE BUBBLY.

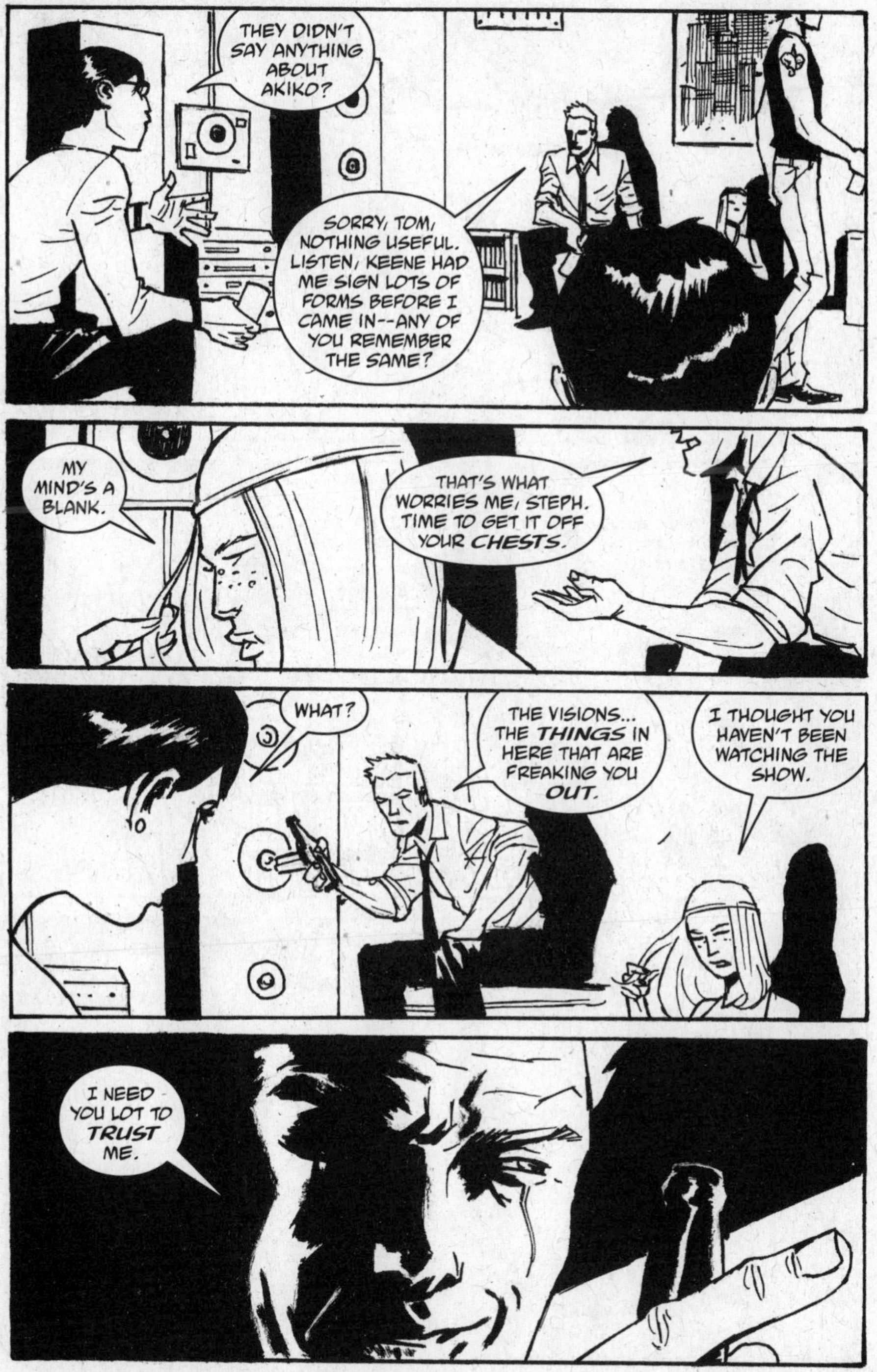
THEY DIDN'T SAY ANYTHING ABOUT AKIKO?
SORRY, TOM, NOTHING USEFUL. LISTEN, KEENE HAD ME SIGN LOTS OF FORMS BEFORE I CAME IN--ANY OF YOU REMEMBER THE SAME?
MY MIND'S A BLANK.
THAT'S WHAT WORRIES ME, STEPH. TIME TO GET IT OFF YOUR CHESTS.
WHAT?
THE VISIONS... THE THINGS IN HERE THAT ARE FREAKING YOU OUT.
I THOUGHT YOU HAVEN'T BEEN WATCHING THE SHOW.
I NEED YOU LOT TO TRUST ME.

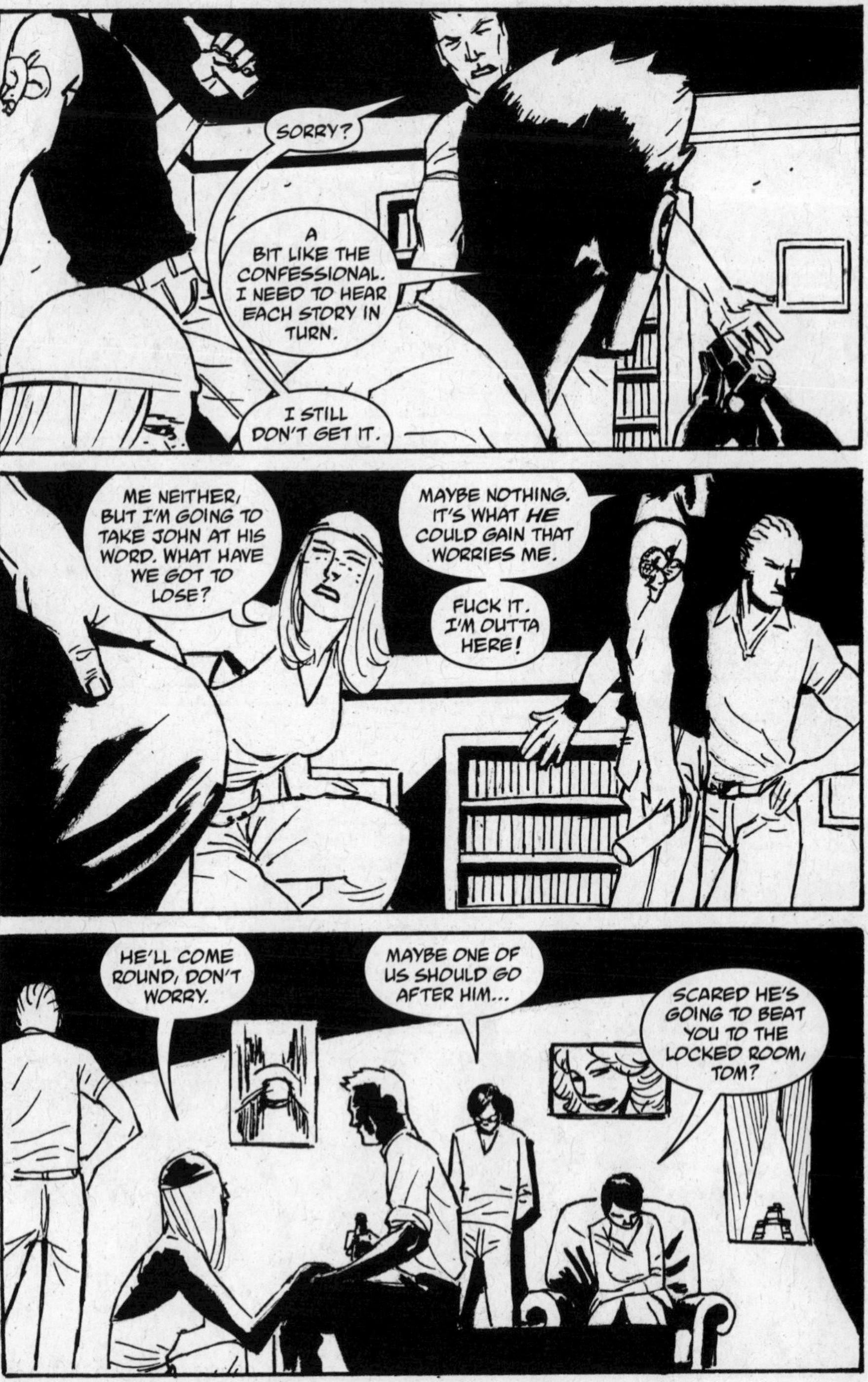
SORRY?
A BIT LIKE THE CONFESSIONAL. I NEED TO HEAR EACH STORY IN TURN.
I STILL DON'T GET IT.
ME NEITHER, BUT I'M GOING TO TAKE JOHN AT HIS WORD. WHAT HAVE WE GOT TO LOSE?
MAYBE NOTHING. IT'S WHAT *HE* COULD GAIN THAT WORRIES ME.
FUCK IT. I'M OUTTA HERE!
HE'LL COME ROUND, DON'T WORRY.
MAYBE ONE OF US SHOULD GO AFTER HIM...
SCARED HE'S GOING TO BEAT YOU TO THE LOCKED ROOM, TOM?

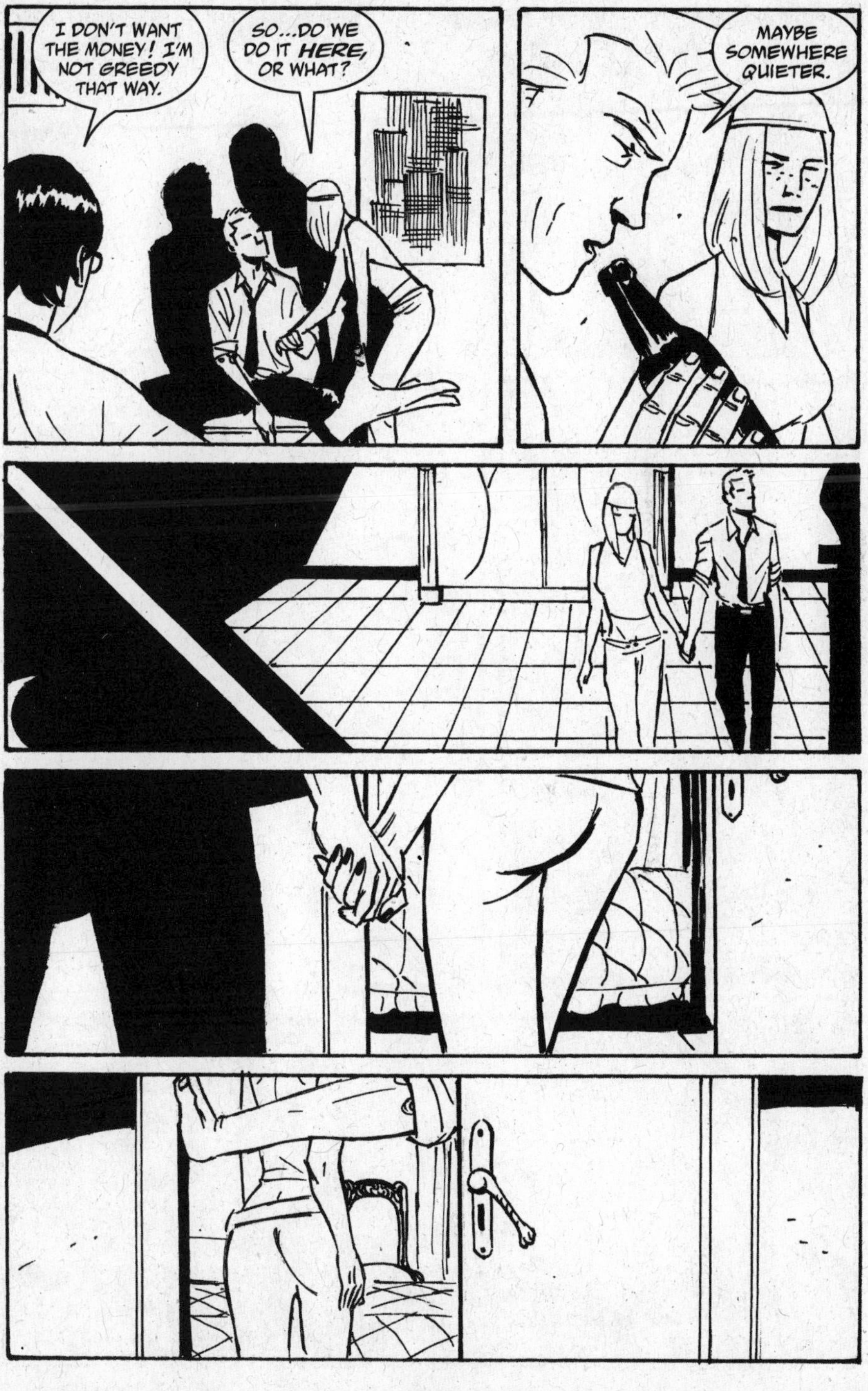
I DON'T WANT THE MONEY! I'M NOT GREEDY THAT WAY.
SO...DO WE DO IT HERE, OR WHAT?
MAYBE SOMEWHERE QUIETER.

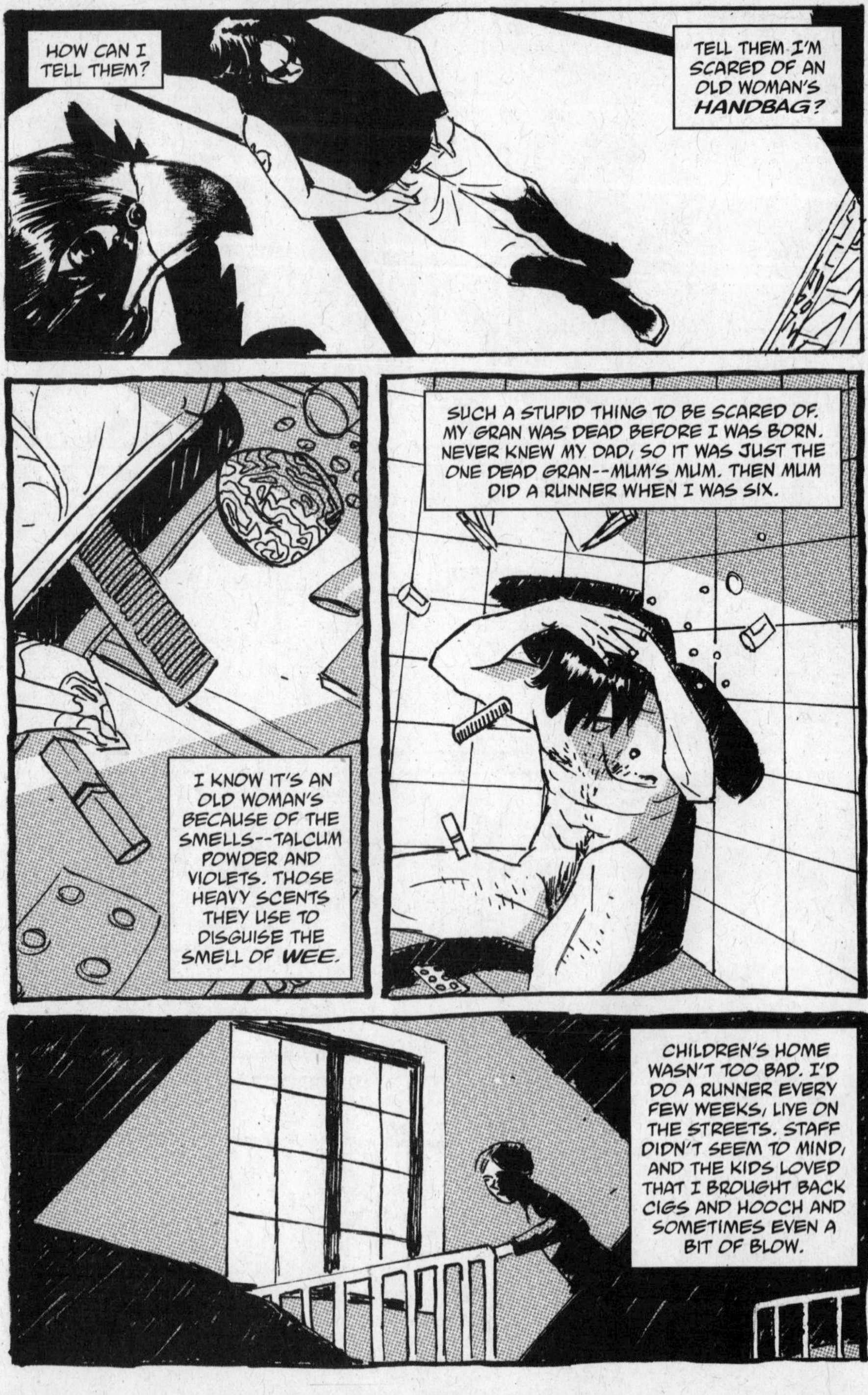
HOW CAN I TELL THEM?
TELL THEM I'M SCARED OF AN OLD WOMAN'S HANDBAG?
I KNOW IT'S AN OLD WOMAN'S BECAUSE OF THE SMELLS--TALCUM POWDER AND VIOLETS. THOSE HEAVY SCENTS THEY USE TO DISGUISE THE SMELL OF WEE.
SUCH A STUPID THING TO BE SCARED OF. MY GRAN WAS DEAD BEFORE I WAS BORN. NEVER KNEW MY DAD, SO IT WAS JUST THE ONE DEAD GRAN--MUM'S MUM. THEN MUM DID A RUNNER WHEN I WAS SIX.
CHILDREN'S HOME WASN'T TOO BAD. I'D DO A RUNNER EVERY FEW WEEKS, LIVE ON THE STREETS. STAFF DIDN'T SEEM TO MIND, AND THE KIDS LOVED THAT I BROUGHT BACK CIGS AND HOOCH AND SOMETIMES EVEN A BIT OF BLOW.

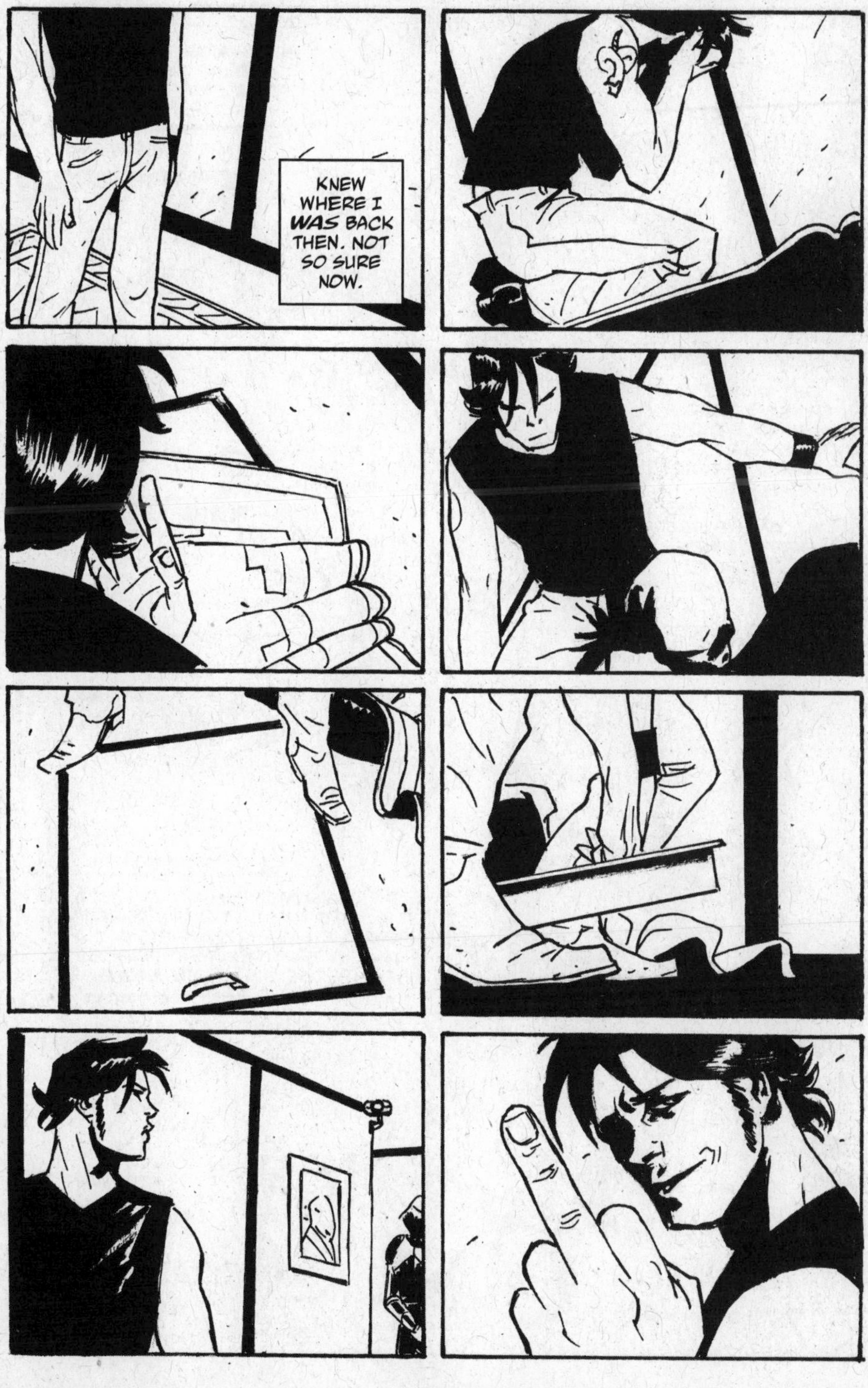
KNEW WHERE I *WAS* BACK THEN. NOT SO SURE NOW.

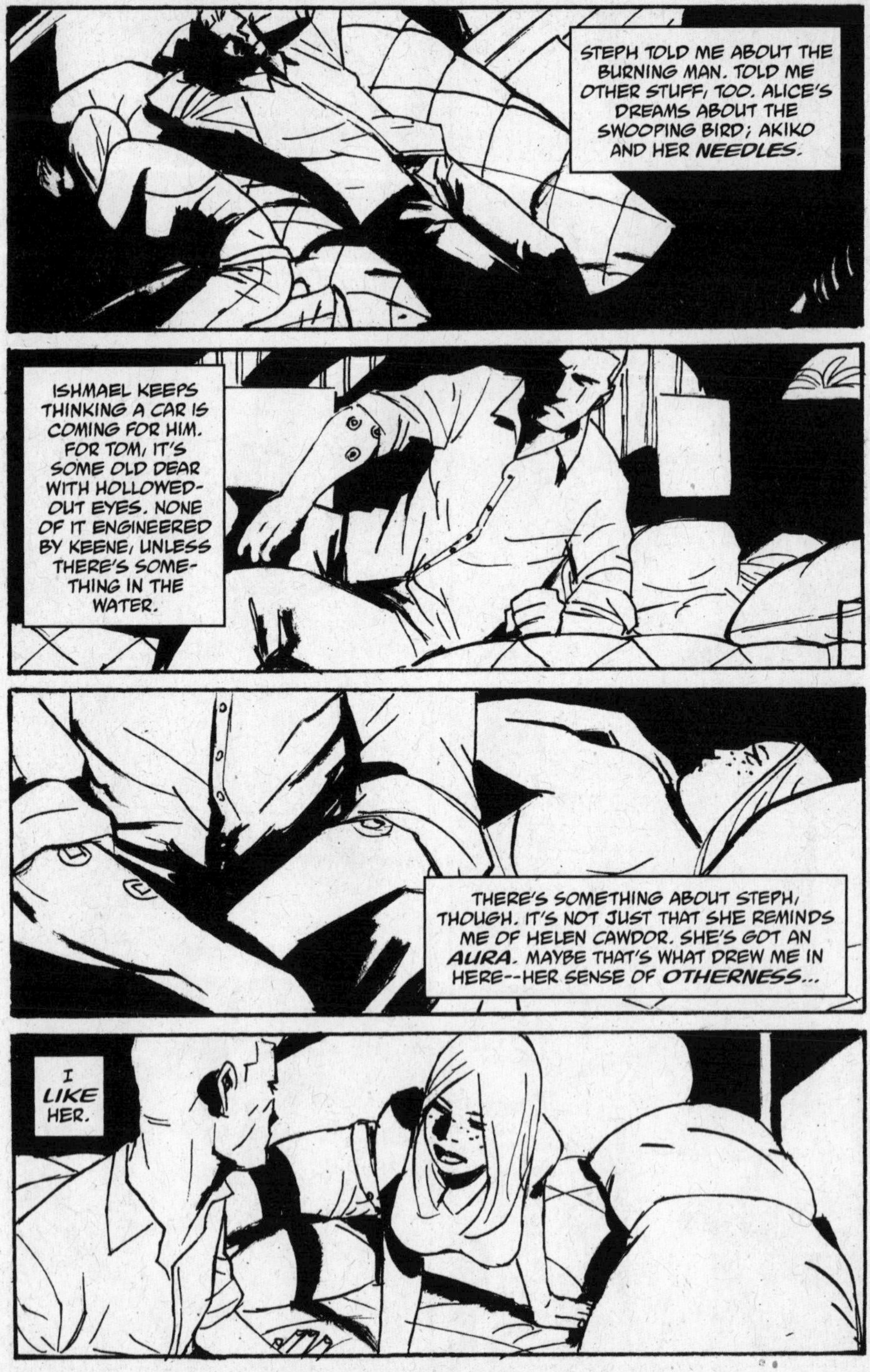

STEPH TOLD ME ABOUT THE BURNING MAN. TOLD ME OTHER STUFF, TOO. ALICE'S DREAMS ABOUT THE SWOOPING BIRD; AKIKO AND HER NEEDLES.
ISHMAEL KEEPS THINKING A CAR IS COMING FOR HIM. FOR TOM, IT'S SOME OLD DEAR WITH HOLLOWED-OUT EYES. NONE OF IT ENGINEERED BY KEENE, UNLESS THERE'S SOMETHING IN THE WATER.
THERE'S SOMETHING ABOUT STEPH, THOUGH. IT'S NOT JUST THAT SHE REMINDS ME OF HELEN CAWDOR. SHE'S GOT AN AURA. MAYBE THAT'S WHAT DREW ME IN HERE--HER SENSE OF OTHERNESS...
I LIKE HER.

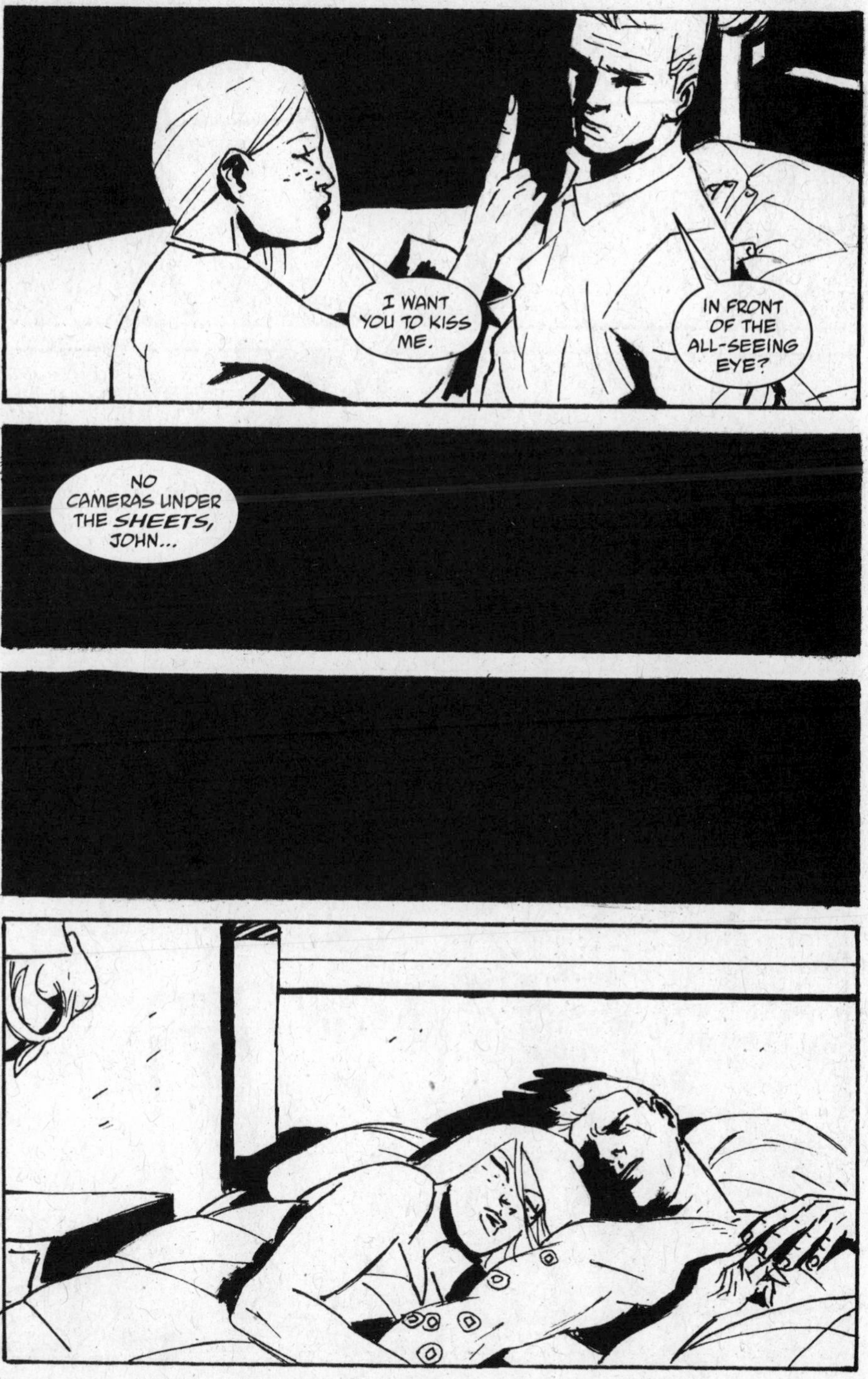
I WANT YOU TO KISS ME.
IN FRONT OF THE ALL-SEEING EYE?
NO CAMERAS UNDER THE *SHEETS,* JOHN...

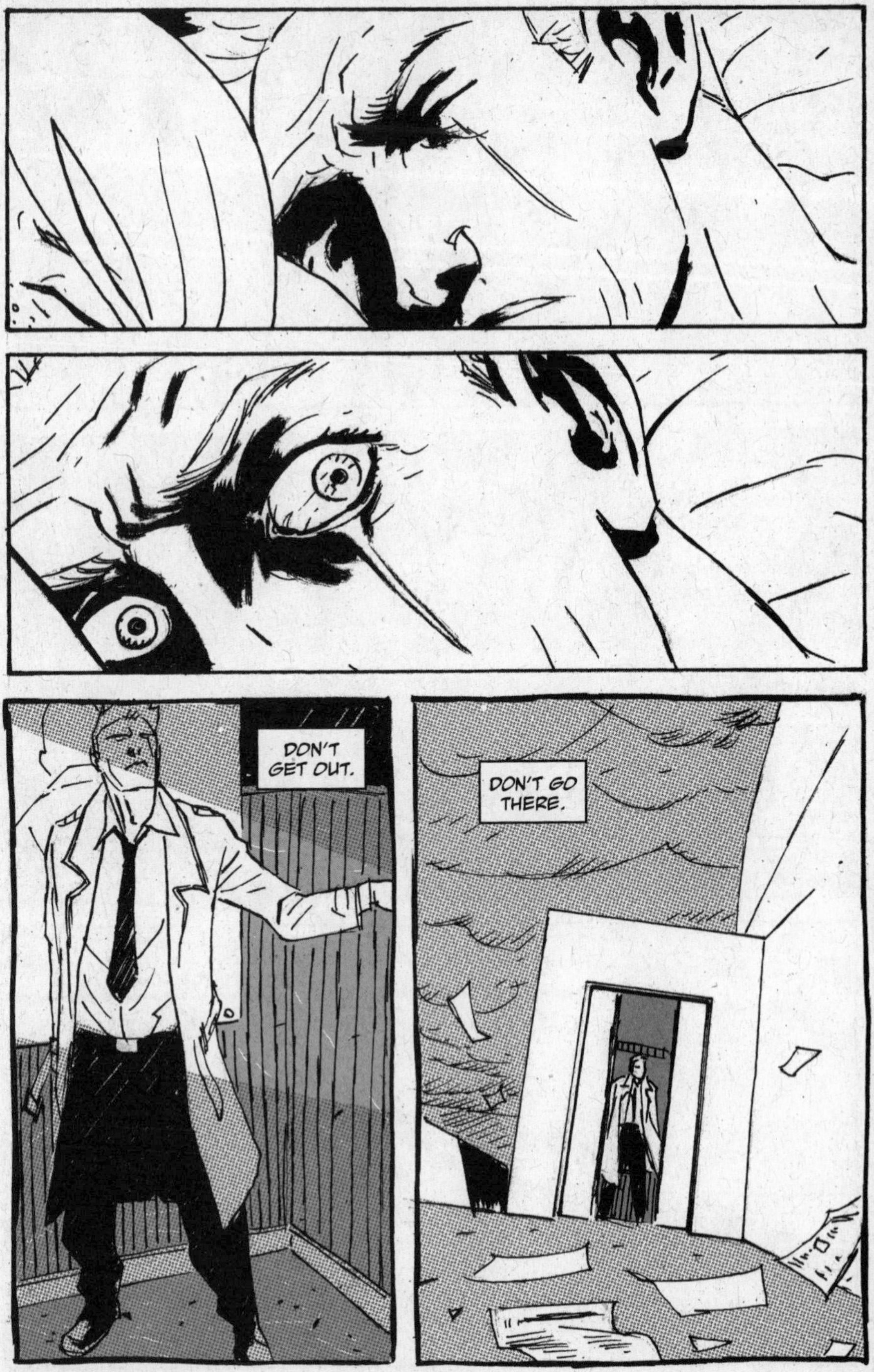
DON'T GET OUT.
DON'T GO THERE.

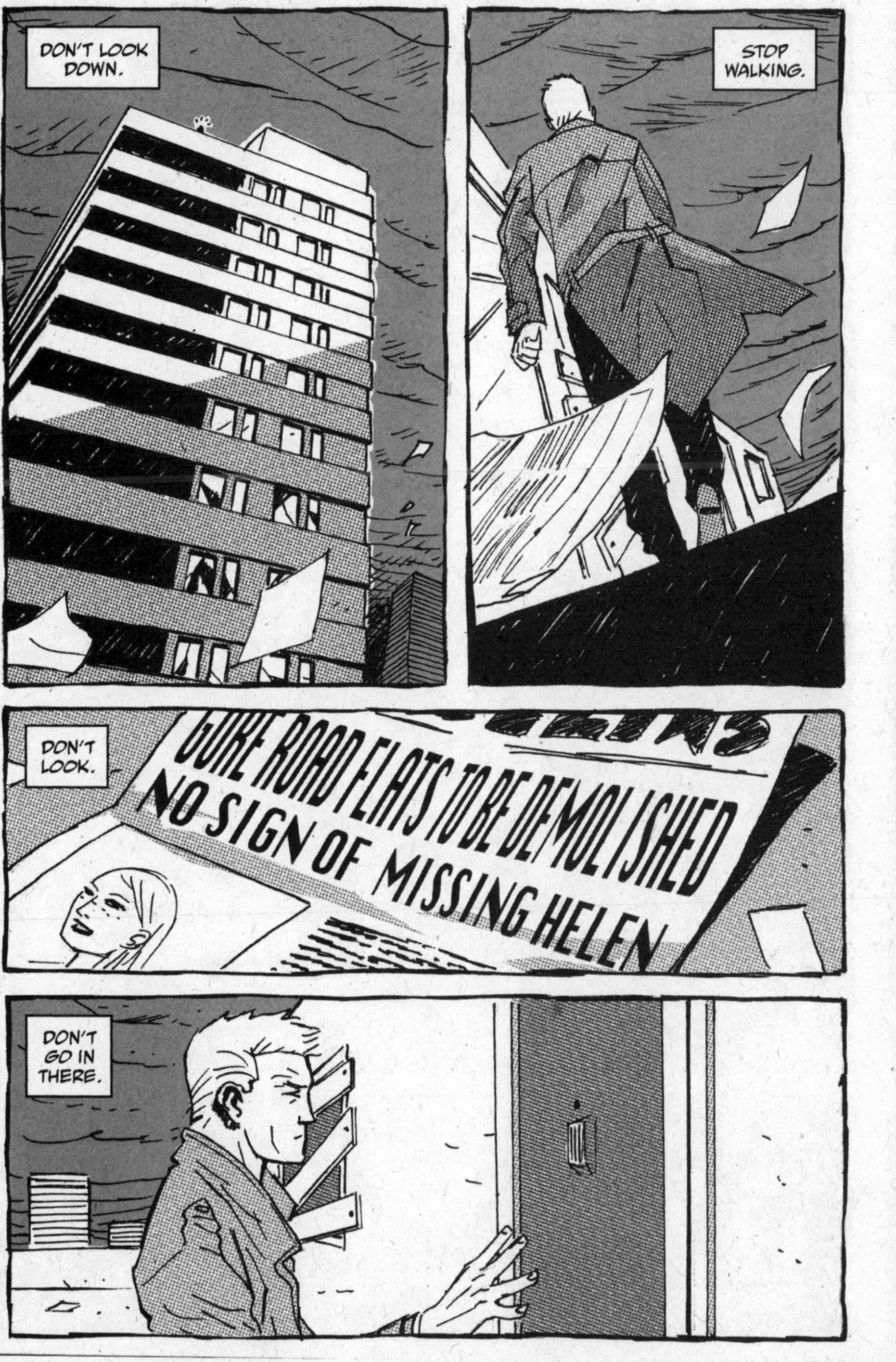
DON'T LOOK DOWN.
STOP WALKING.
DON'T LOOK.
GORE ROAD FLATS TO BE DEMOLISHED
NO SIGN OF MISSING HELEN
DON'T GO IN THERE.

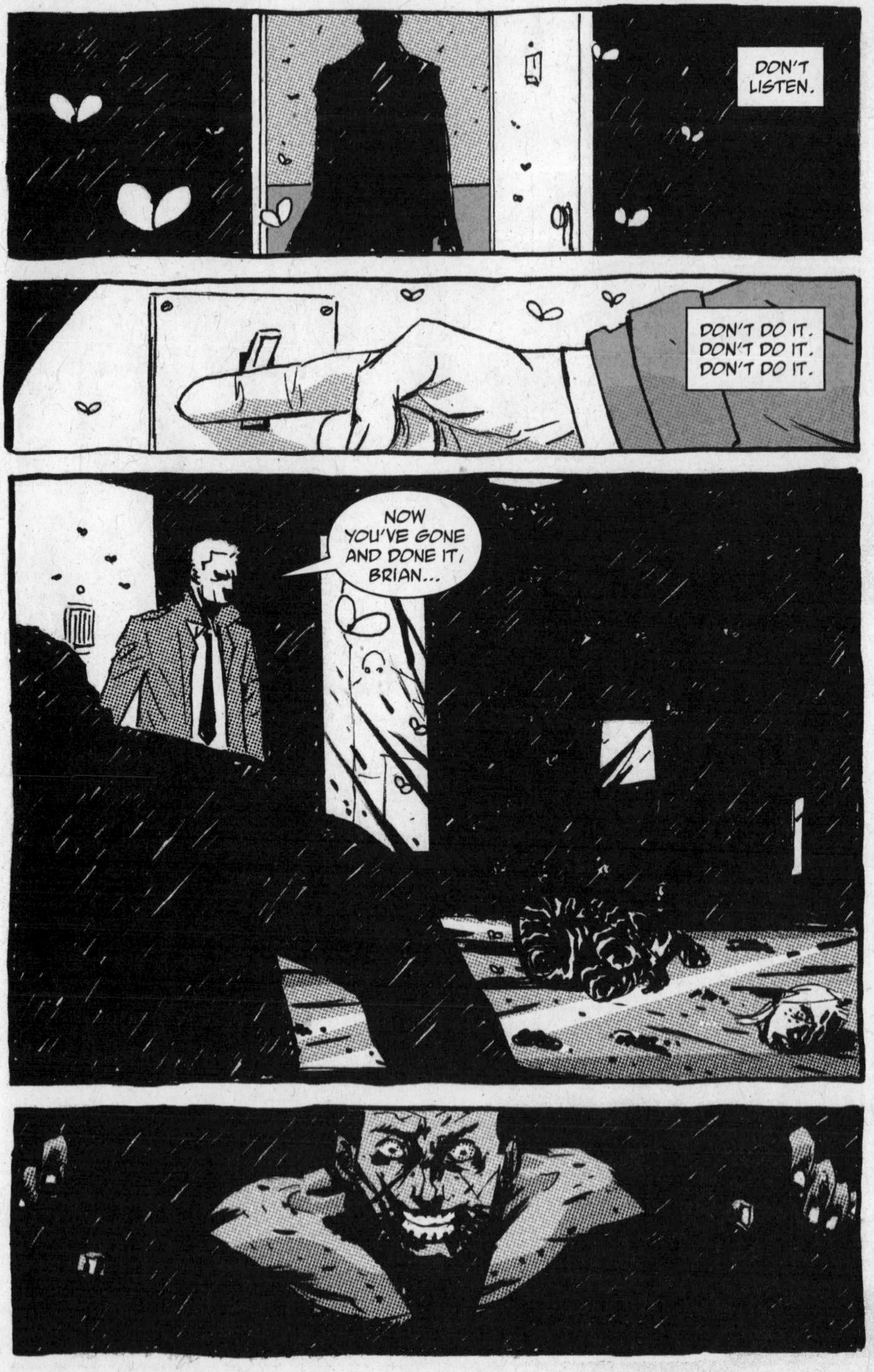
DON'T LISTEN.
DON'T DO IT. DON'T DO IT. DON'T DO IT.
NOW YOU'VE GONE AND DONE IT, BRIAN...

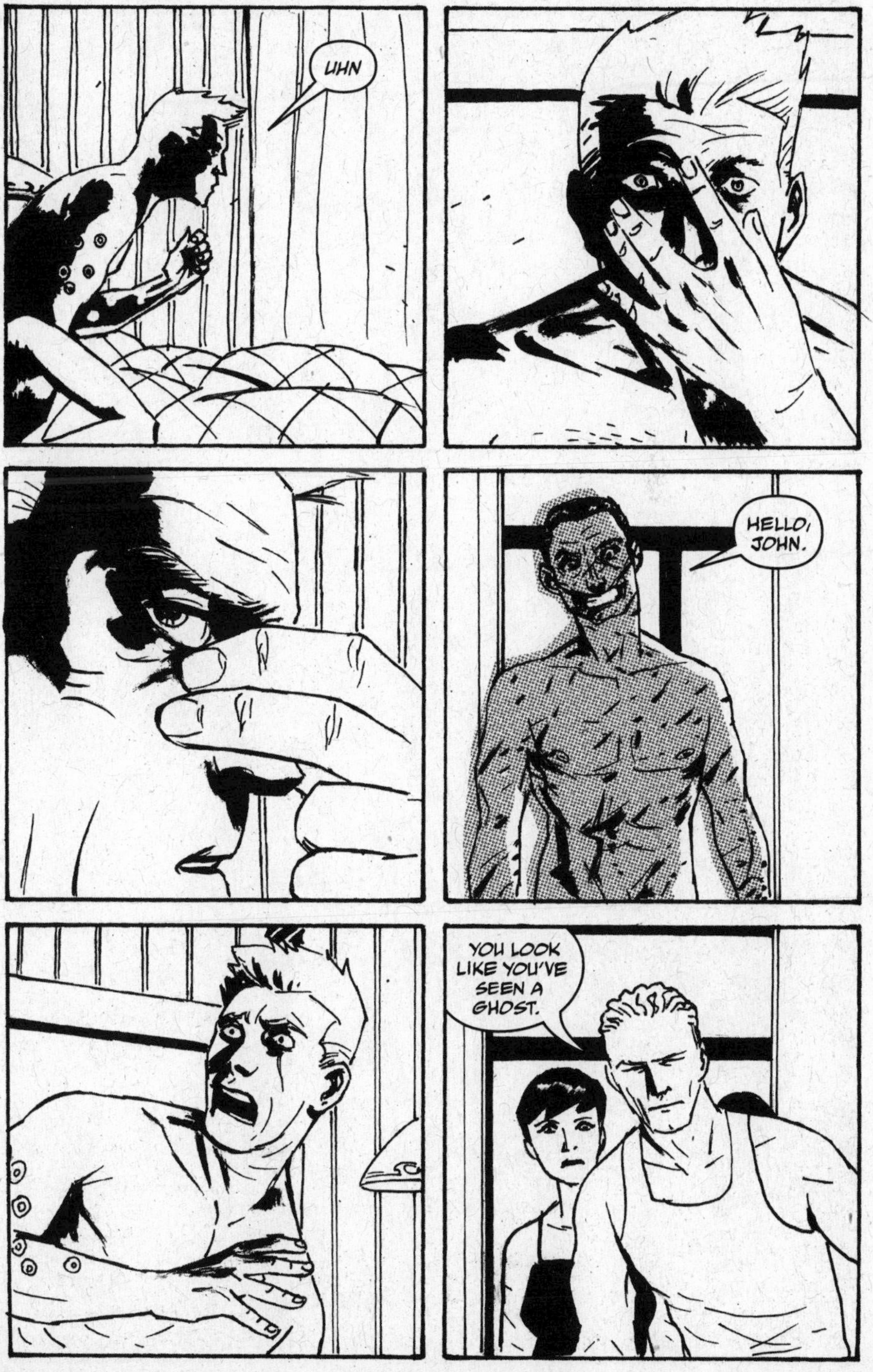
UHN
HELLO, JOHN.
YOU LOOK LIKE YOU'VE SEEN A GHOST.

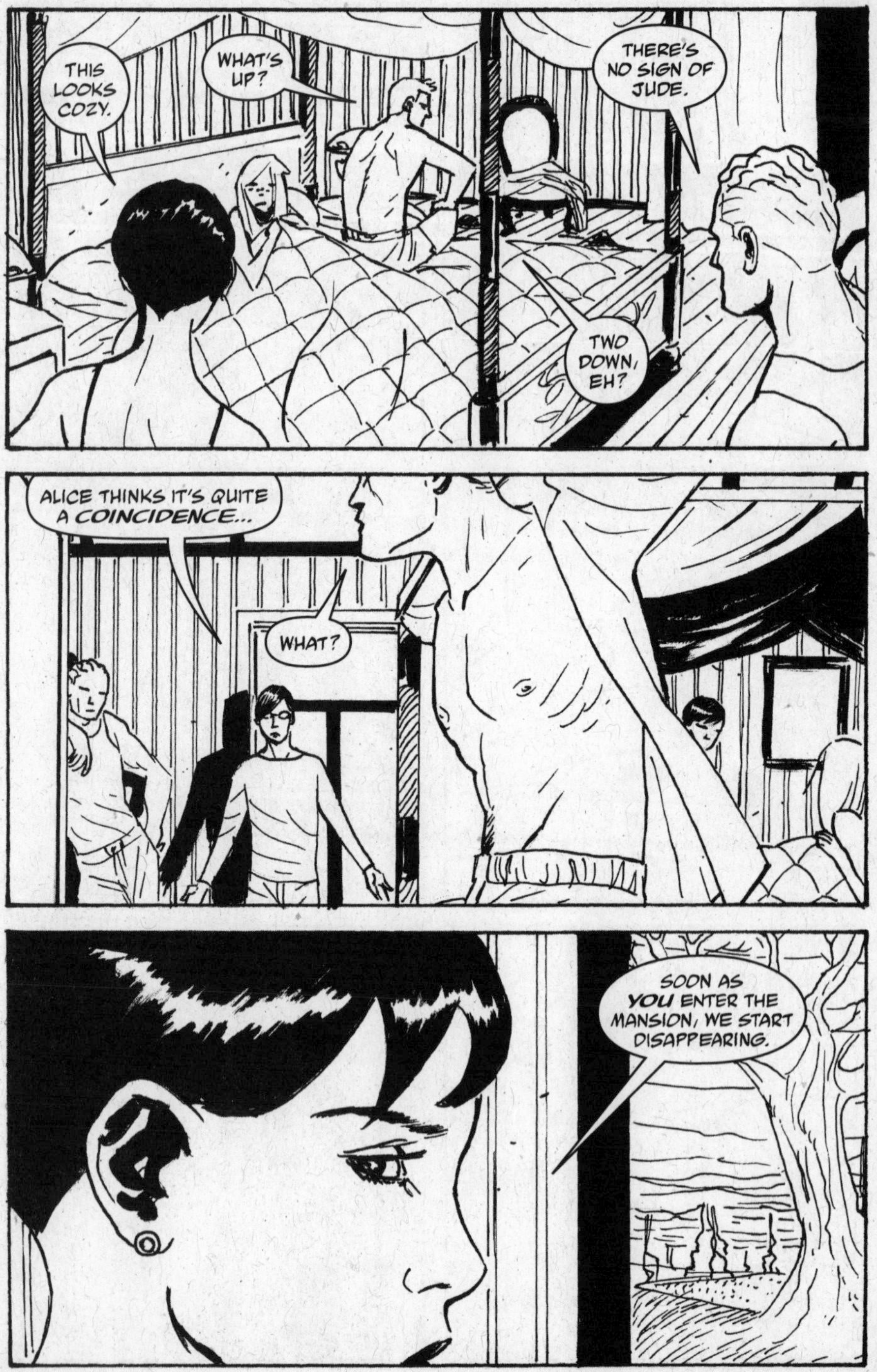
THIS LOOKS COZY.
WHAT'S UP?
THERE'S NO SIGN OF JUDE.
TWO DOWN, EH?
ALICE THINKS IT'S QUITE A *COINCIDENCE*...
WHAT?
SOON AS *YOU* ENTER THE MANSION, WE START DISAPPEARING.

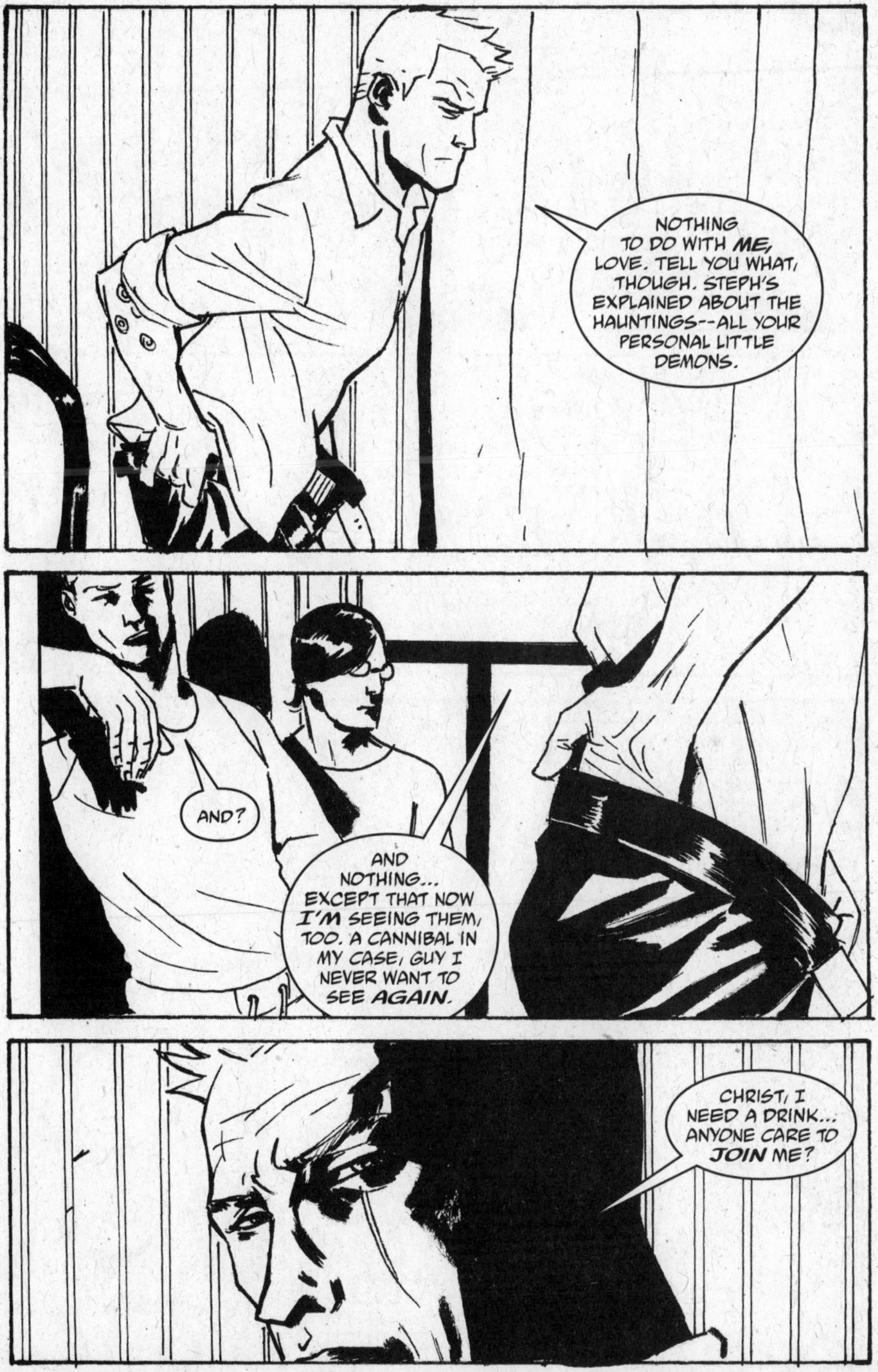
NOTHING TO DO WITH ME, LOVE. TELL YOU WHAT, THOUGH. STEPH'S EXPLAINED ABOUT THE HAUNTINGS--ALL YOUR PERSONAL LITTLE DEMONS.
AND?
AND NOTHING... EXCEPT THAT NOW I'M SEEING THEM, TOO. A CANNIBAL IN MY CASE, GUY I NEVER WANT TO SEE AGAIN.
CHRIST, I NEED A DRINK... ANYONE CARE TO JOIN ME?

SO TELL US THE STORY, JOHN.

NOT MUCH TO TELL. IT WAS SIX YEARS BACK, GUY I KNEW CALLED *BRIAN McARTHUR.*

ACTUALLY, IT WASN'T BRIAN I KNEW AS MUCH AS HIS *GIRLFRIEND...*

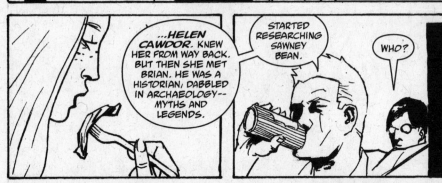

...*HELEN CAWDOR.* KNEW HER FROM WAY BACK. BUT THEN SHE MET BRIAN. HE WAS A HISTORIAN, DABBLED IN ARCHAEOLOGY-- MYTHS AND LEGENDS.

STARTED RESEARCHING SAWNEY BEAN.

WHO?

"HE LIVED IN THE SCOTTISH COUNTRYSIDE. COULDN'T MAKE MUCH OF A GO OF IT, WHICH MIGHT EXPLAIN WHY HE DID WHAT HE DID."

CANNIBALISM?

SO THE STORY GOES. FAR AS BRIAN WAS CONCERNED, THAT'S ALL IT *WAS,* THOUGH--A *STORY.*

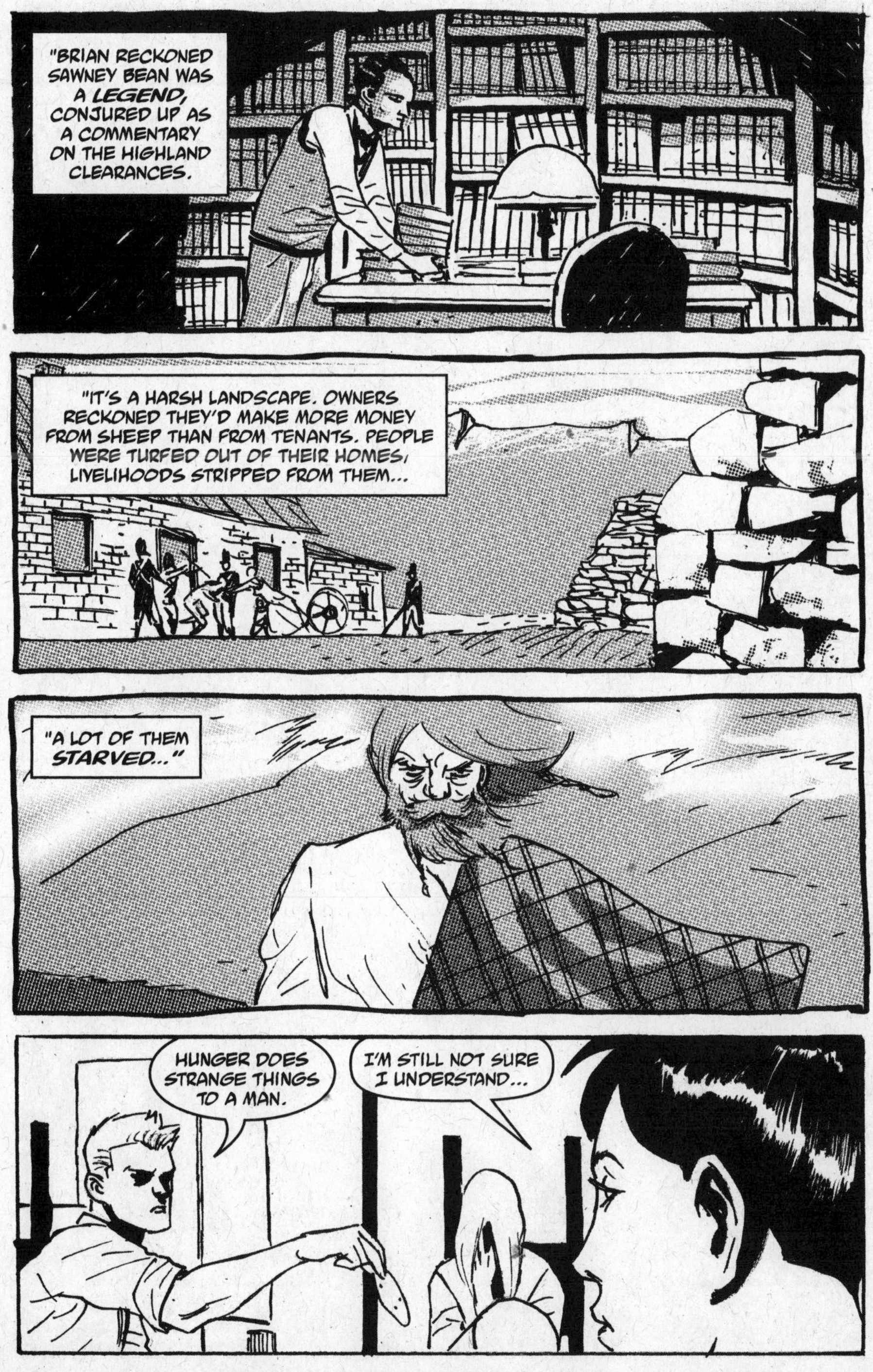
"BRIAN RECKONED SAWNEY BEAN WAS A *LEGEND*, CONJURED UP AS A COMMENTARY ON THE HIGHLAND CLEARANCES.
"IT'S A HARSH LANDSCAPE. OWNERS RECKONED THEY'D MAKE MORE MONEY FROM SHEEP THAN FROM TENANTS. PEOPLE WERE TURFED OUT OF THEIR HOMES, LIVELIHOODS STRIPPED FROM THEM...
"A LOT OF THEM *STARVED*..."
HUNGER DOES STRANGE THINGS TO A MAN.
I'M STILL NOT SURE I UNDERSTAND...

BRIAN GREW OBSESSED. HELEN CALLED ME; SAID SHE WAS WORRIED ABOUT HIM. TOLD ME HE WAS *CHANGING*.

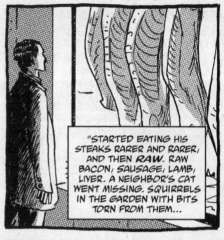

"STARTED EATING HIS STEAKS RARER AND RARER, AND THEN *RAW*. RAW BACON, SAUSAGE, LAMB, LIVER. A NEIGHBOR'S CAT WENT MISSING. SQUIRRELS IN THE GARDEN WITH BITS TORN FROM THEM..."

"PSYCHIATRIST COULDN'T FIND ANYTHING WRONG WITH HIM. HELEN RECKONED IT WENT *BEYOND* THAT, ANYWAY. HER THEORY WAS, SAWNEY HIMSELF HAD TAKEN POSSESSION. BRIAN WASN'T *BRIAN* ANY MORE..."

THE PAIR OF THEM WENT *AWOL*. I TRACKED BRIAN DOWN. HE'D *KILLED* HELEN...

"END OF STORY."

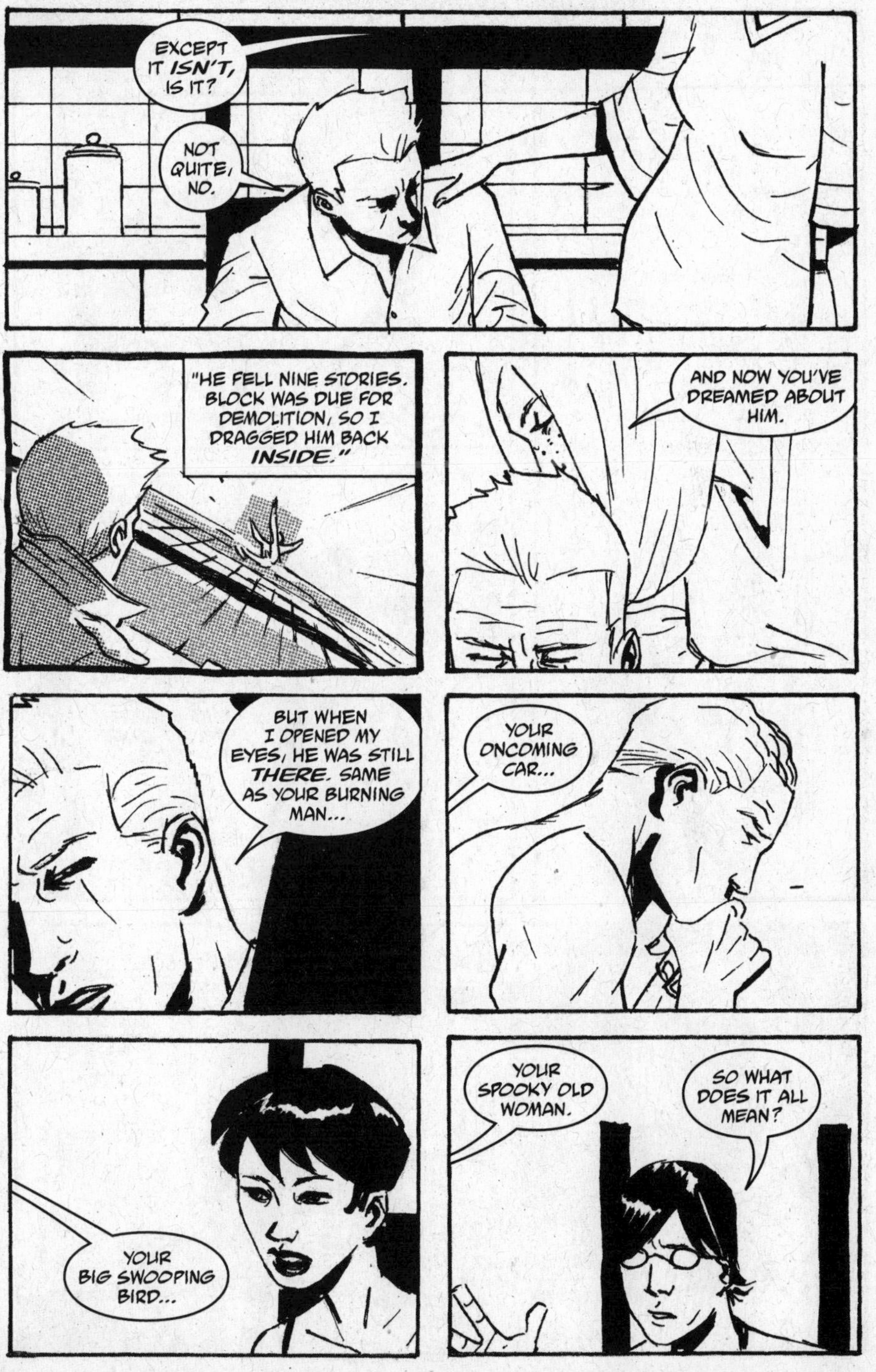
EXCEPT IT ISN'T, IS IT?
NOT QUITE, NO.
"HE FELL NINE STORIES. BLOCK WAS DUE FOR DEMOLITION, SO I DRAGGED HIM BACK INSIDE."
AND NOW YOU'VE DREAMED ABOUT HIM.
BUT WHEN I OPENED MY EYES, HE WAS STILL THERE. SAME AS YOUR BURNING MAN...
YOUR ONCOMING CAR...
YOUR BIG SWOOPING BIRD...
YOUR SPOOKY OLD WOMAN.
SO WHAT DOES IT ALL MEAN?

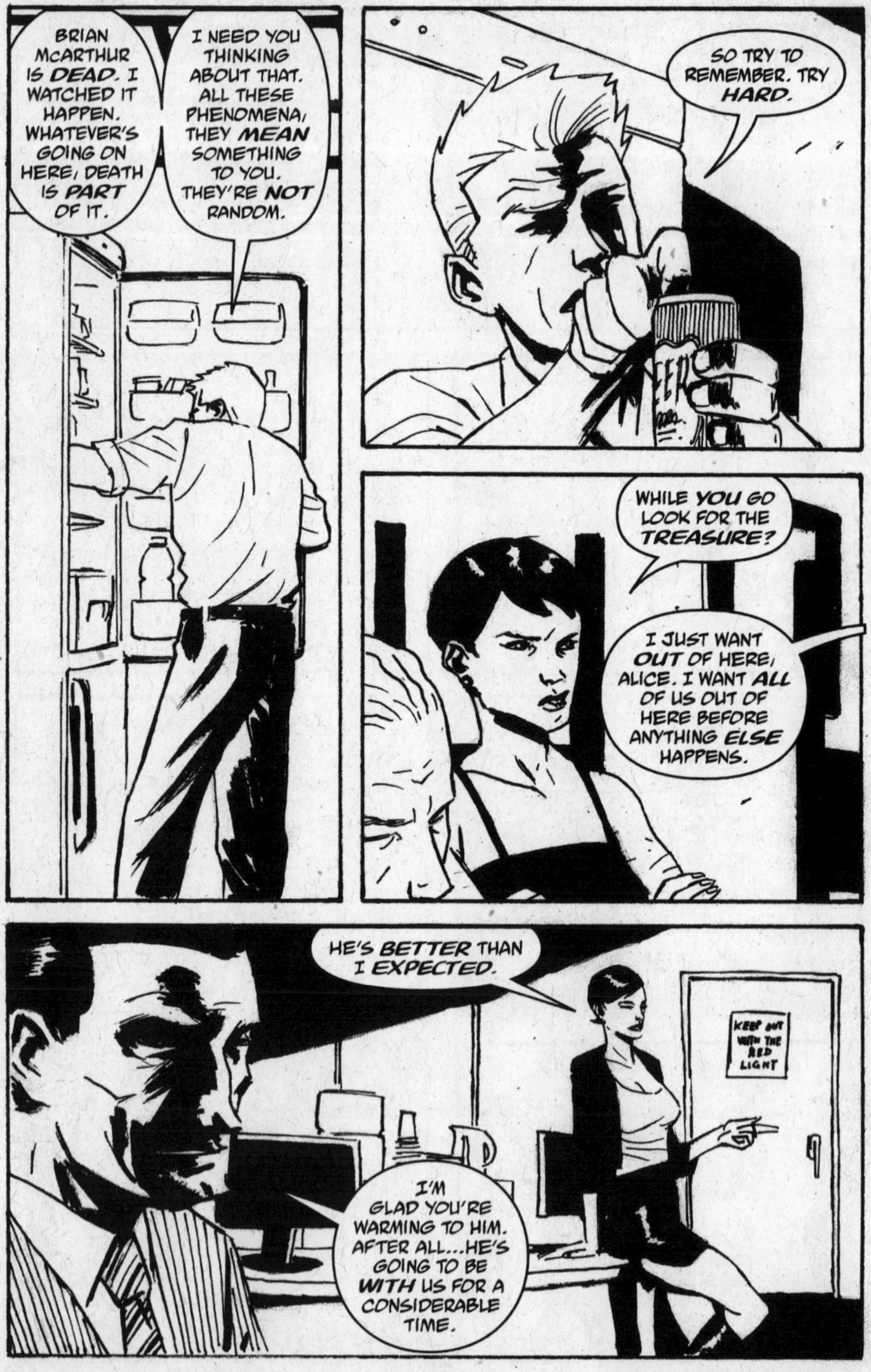
BRIAN McARTHUR IS DEAD. I WATCHED IT HAPPEN. WHATEVER'S GOING ON HERE, DEATH IS PART OF IT.
I NEED YOU THINKING ABOUT THAT. ALL THESE PHENOMENA, THEY MEAN SOMETHING TO YOU. THEY'RE NOT RANDOM.
SO TRY TO REMEMBER. TRY HARD.
WHILE YOU GO LOOK FOR THE TREASURE?
I JUST WANT OUT OF HERE, ALICE. I WANT ALL OF US OUT OF HERE BEFORE ANYTHING ELSE HAPPENS.
HE'S BETTER THAN I EXPECTED.
KEEP OUT WITH THE RED LIGHT
I'M GLAD YOU'RE WARMING TO HIM. AFTER ALL...HE'S GOING TO BE WITH US FOR A CONSIDERABLE TIME.

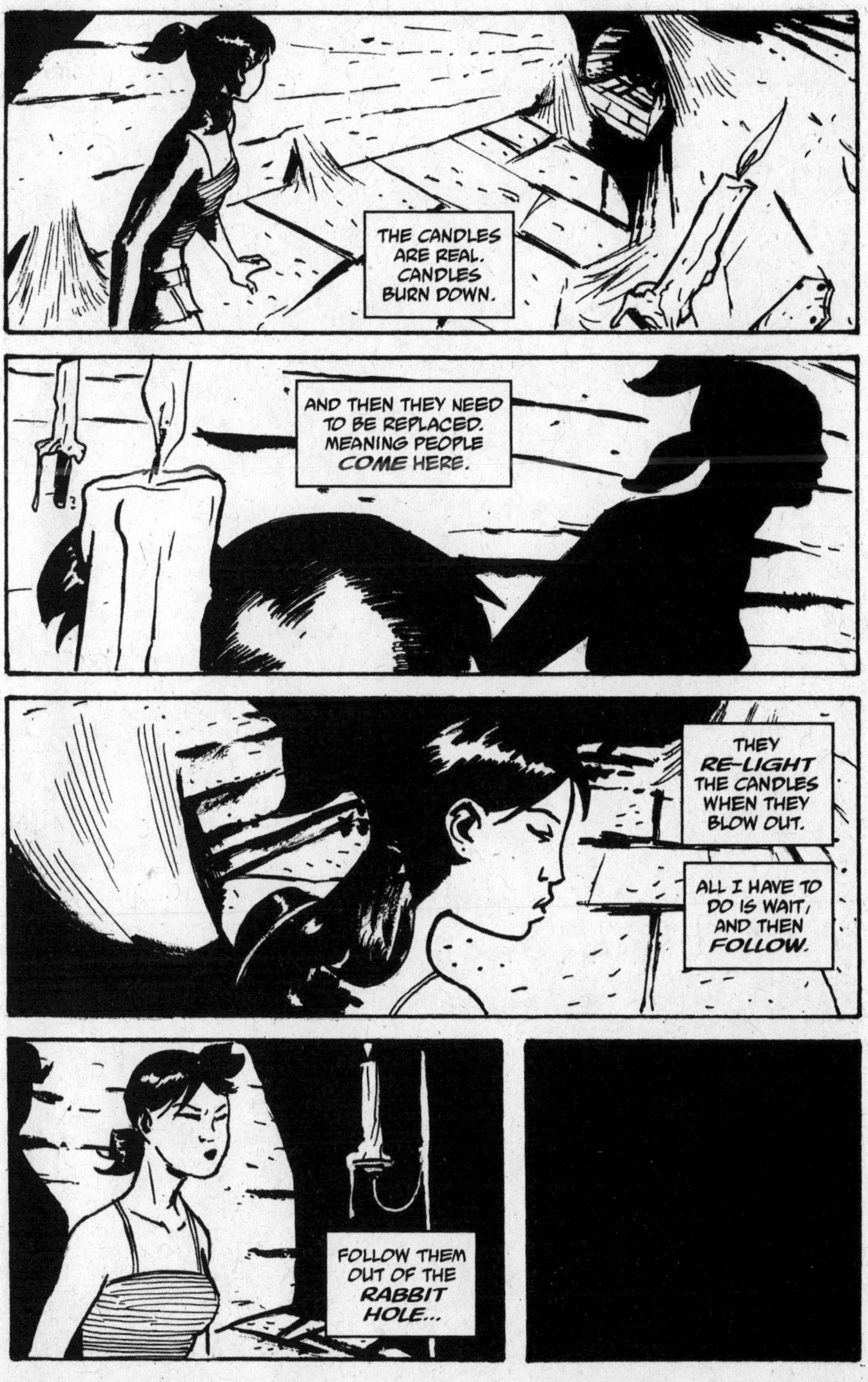
THE CANDLES ARE REAL. CANDLES BURN DOWN.
AND THEN THEY NEED TO BE REPLACED. MEANING PEOPLE COME HERE.
THEY RE-LIGHT THE CANDLES WHEN THEY BLOW OUT.
ALL I HAVE TO DO IS WAIT, AND THEN FOLLOW.
FOLLOW THEM OUT OF THE RABBIT HOLE...

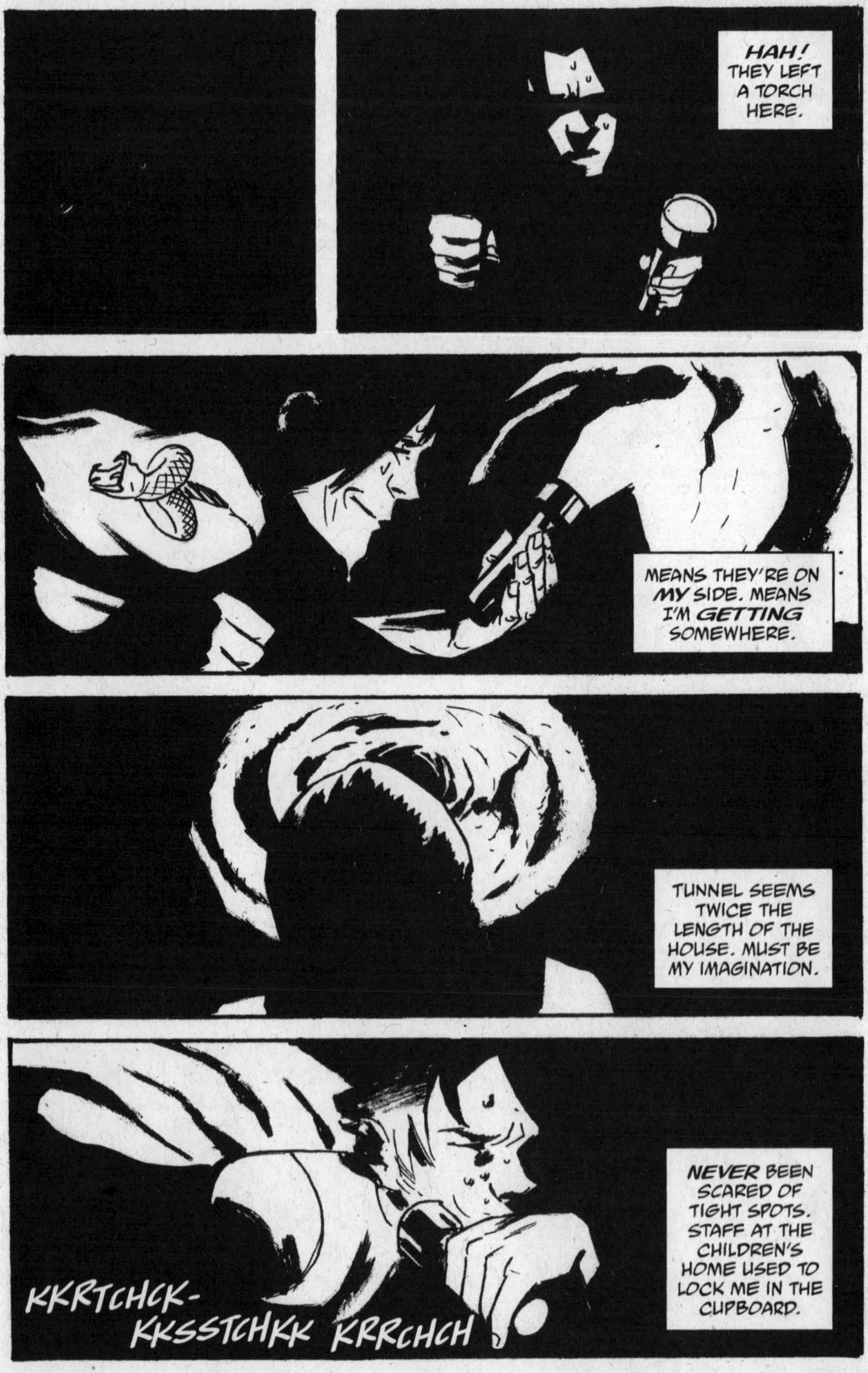
HAH! THEY LEFT A TORCH HERE.
MEANS THEY'RE ON MY SIDE. MEANS I'M GETTING SOMEWHERE.
TUNNEL SEEMS TWICE THE LENGTH OF THE HOUSE. MUST BE MY IMAGINATION.
NEVER BEEN SCARED OF TIGHT SPOTS. STAFF AT THE CHILDREN'S HOME USED TO LOCK ME IN THE CUPBOARD.
KKRTCHCK-
KKSSTCHKK KRRCHCH

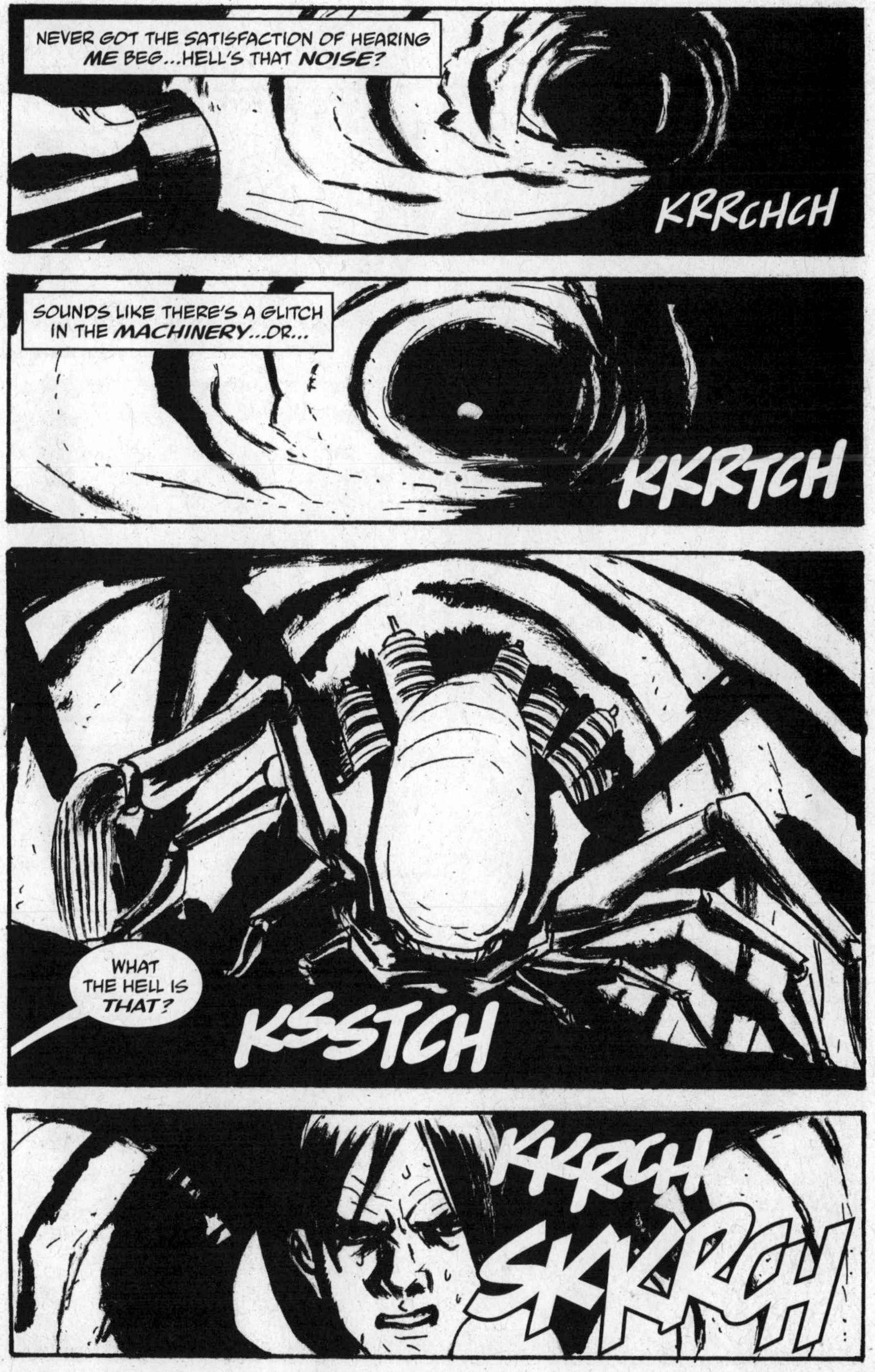
NEVER GOT THE SATISFACTION OF HEARING *ME* BEG...HELL'S THAT *NOISE?*
KRRCHCH
SOUNDS LIKE THERE'S A GLITCH IN THE *MACHINERY*...OR...
KKRTCH
WHAT THE HELL IS *THAT?*
KSSTCH
KKRCH
SKKRCH

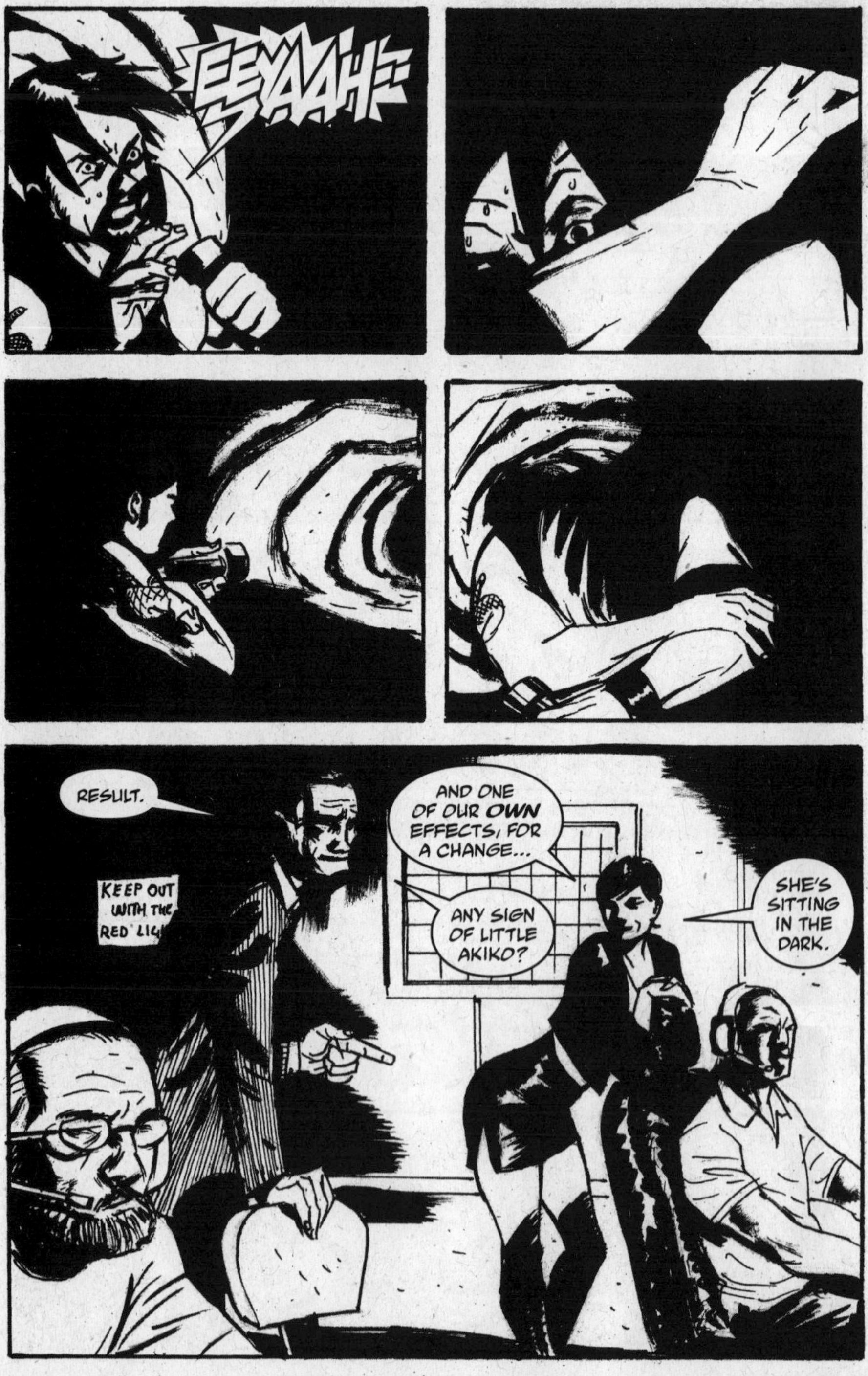
EEYAAH!
RESULT.
AND ONE OF OUR OWN EFFECTS, FOR A CHANGE...
KEEP OUT WITH THE RED LIG
ANY SIGN OF LITTLE AKIKO?
SHE'S SITTING IN THE DARK.

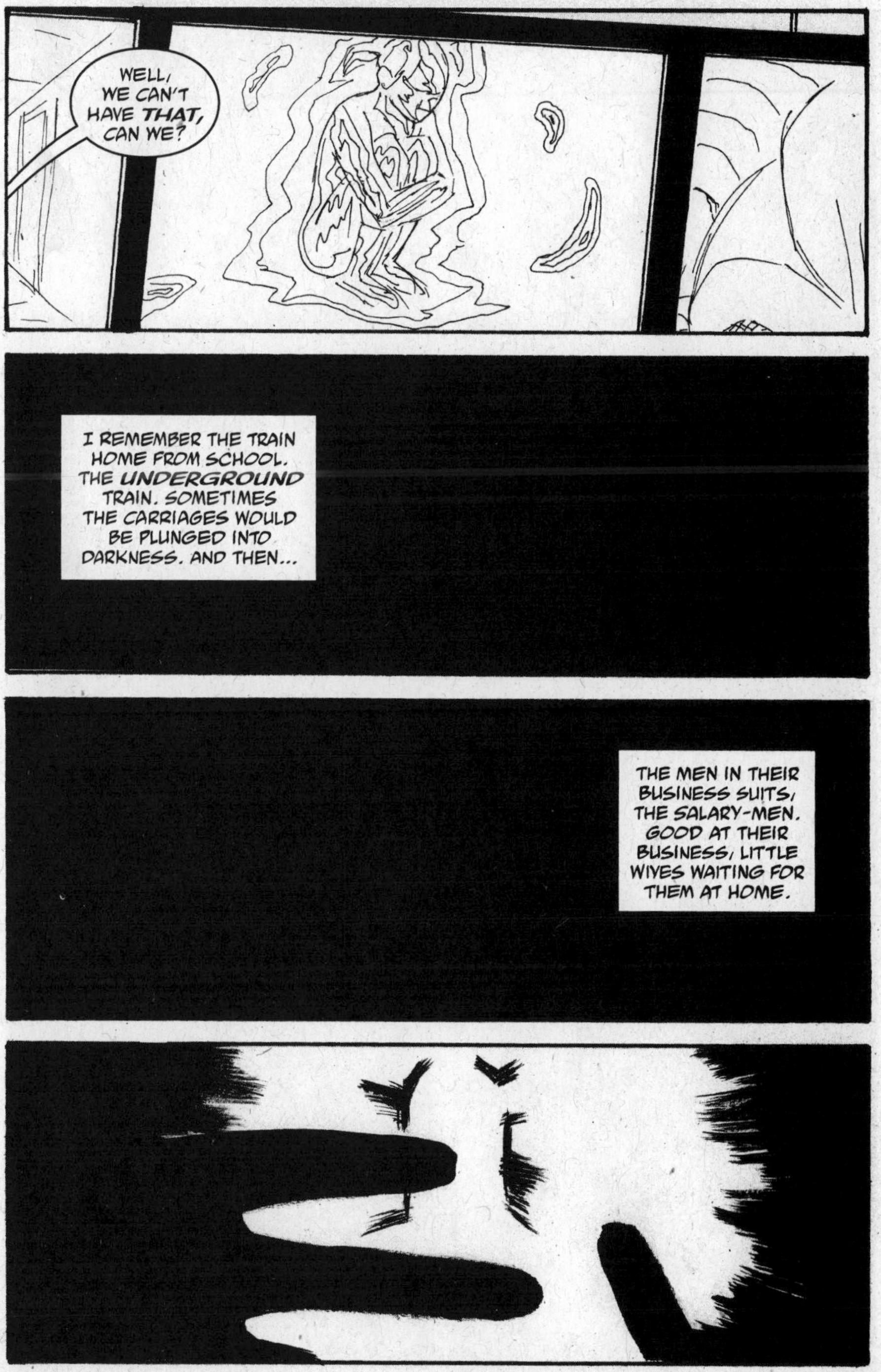
WELL, WE CAN'T HAVE *THAT,* CAN WE?
I REMEMBER THE TRAIN HOME FROM SCHOOL. THE *UNDERGROUND* TRAIN. SOMETIMES THE CARRIAGES WOULD BE PLUNGED INTO DARKNESS. AND THEN...
THE MEN IN THEIR BUSINESS SUITS, THE SALARY-MEN. GOOD AT THEIR BUSINESS, LITTLE WIVES WAITING FOR THEM AT HOME.

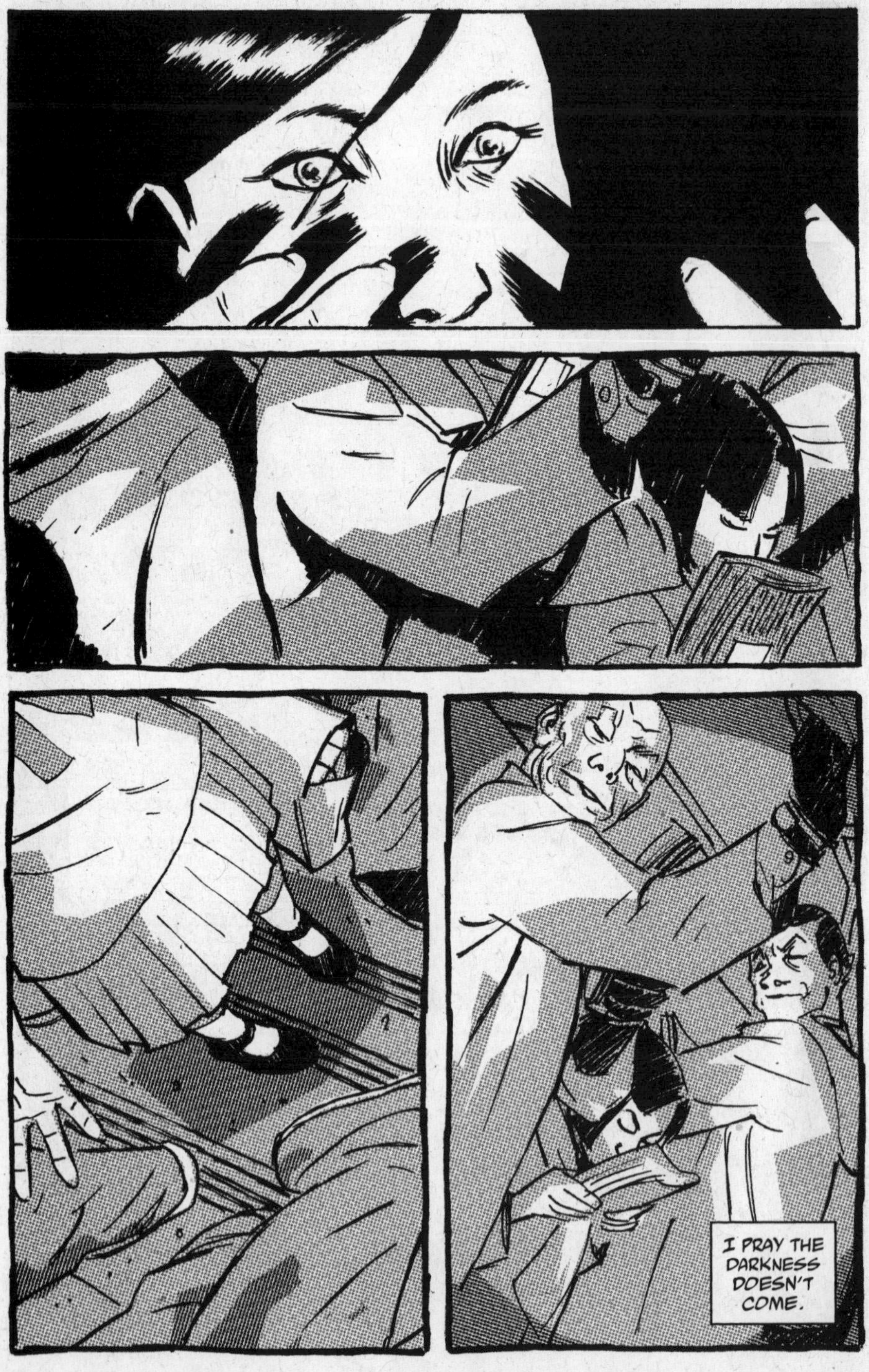
I PRAY THE DARKNESS DOESN'T COME.

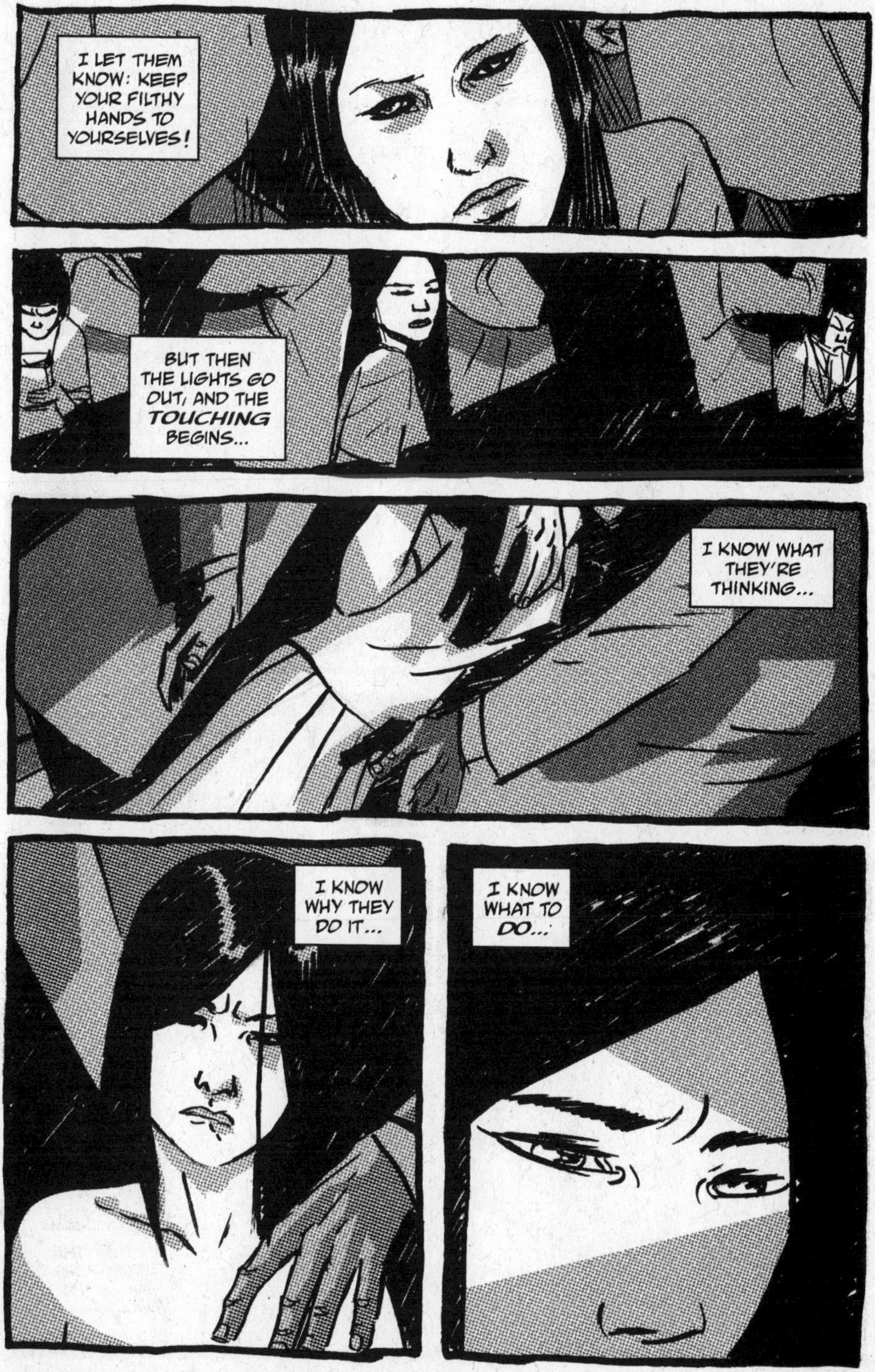
I LET THEM KNOW: KEEP YOUR FILTHY HANDS TO YOURSELVES!
BUT THEN THE LIGHTS GO OUT, AND THE *TOUCHING* BEGINS...
I KNOW WHAT THEY'RE THINKING...
I KNOW WHY THEY DO IT...
I KNOW WHAT TO *DO*...

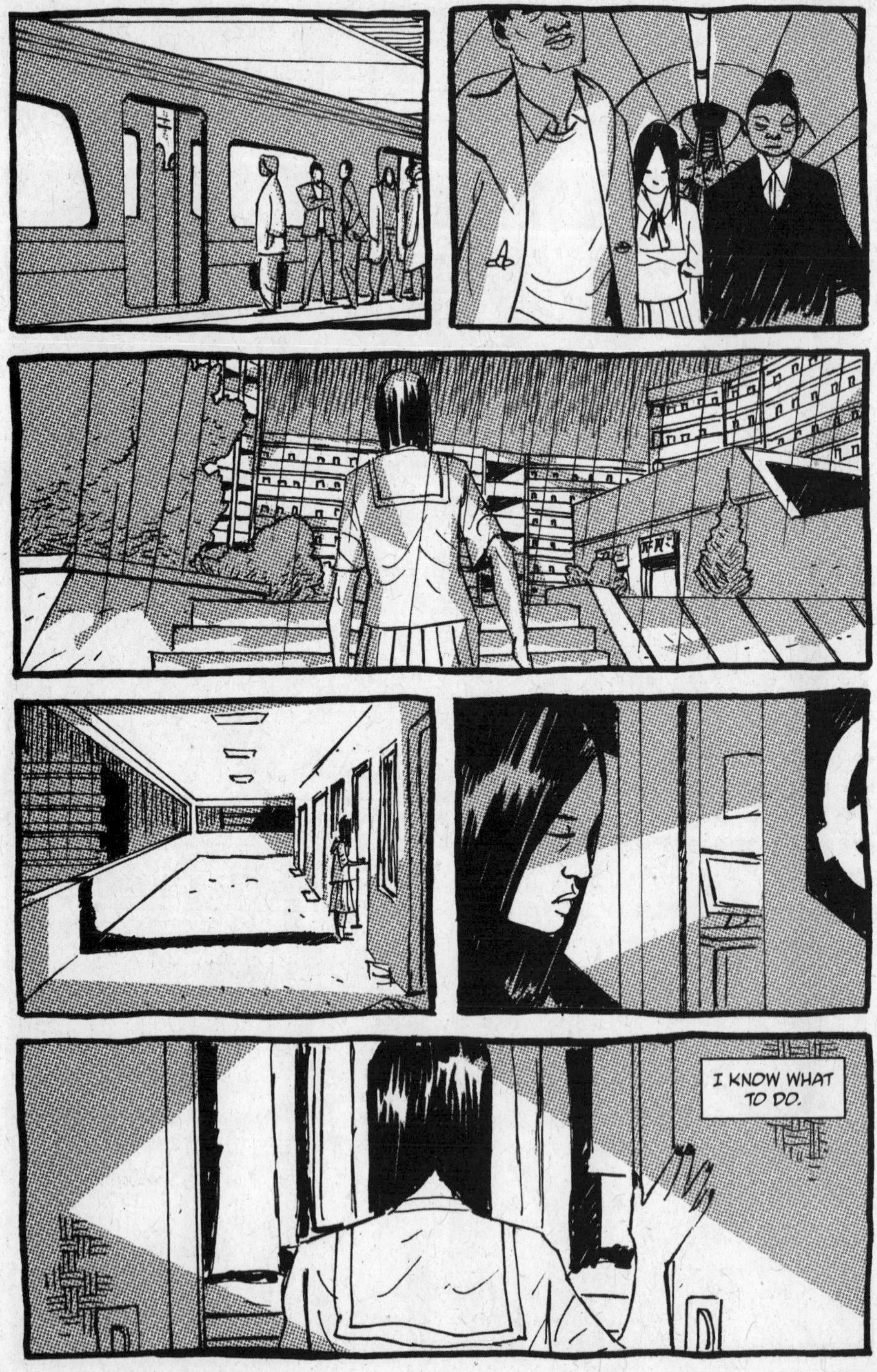
I KNOW WHAT TO DO.

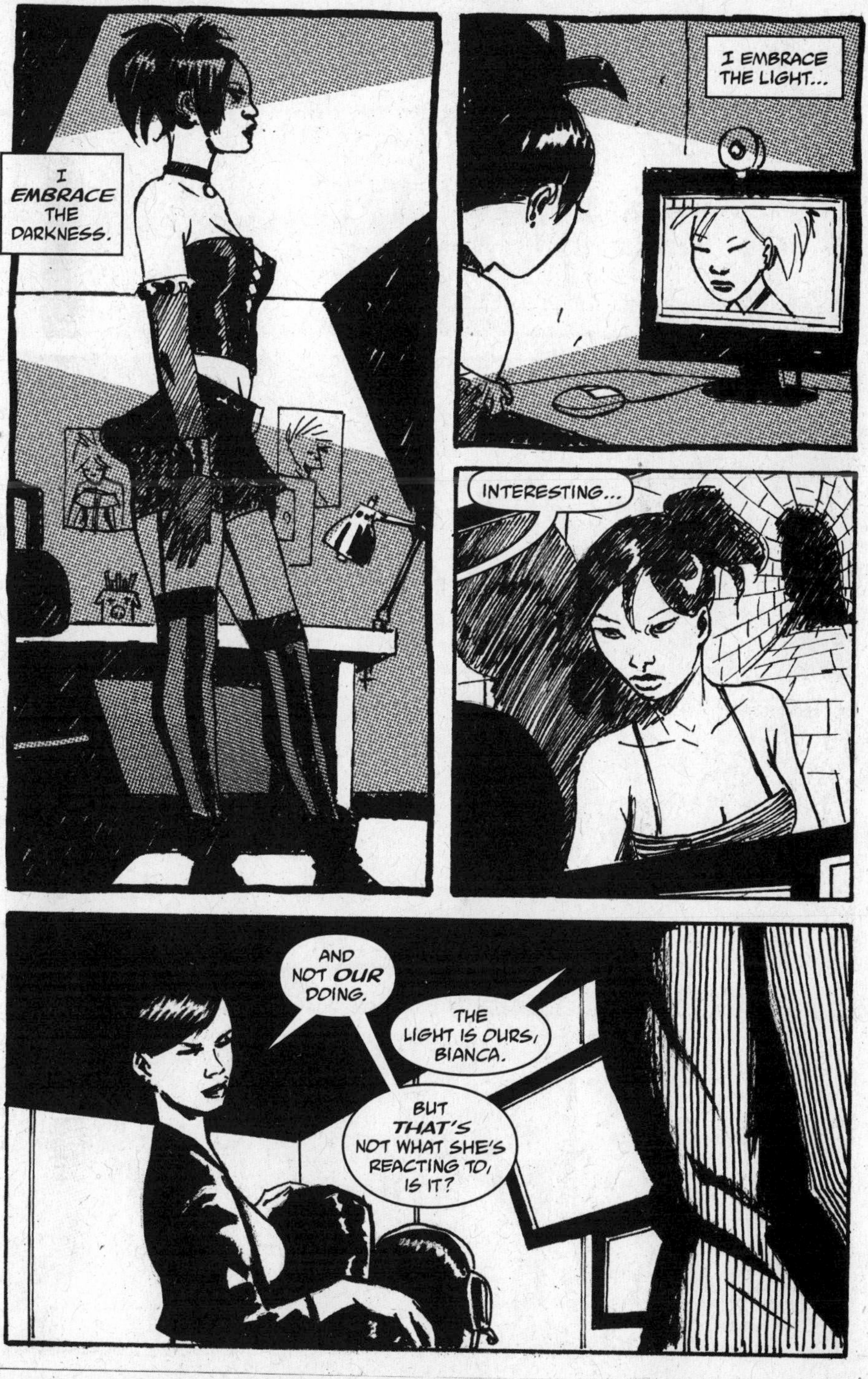
I EMBRACE THE DARKNESS.
I EMBRACE THE LIGHT...
INTERESTING...
AND NOT OUR DOING.
THE LIGHT IS OURS, BIANCA.
BUT THAT'S NOT WHAT SHE'S REACTING TO, IS IT?

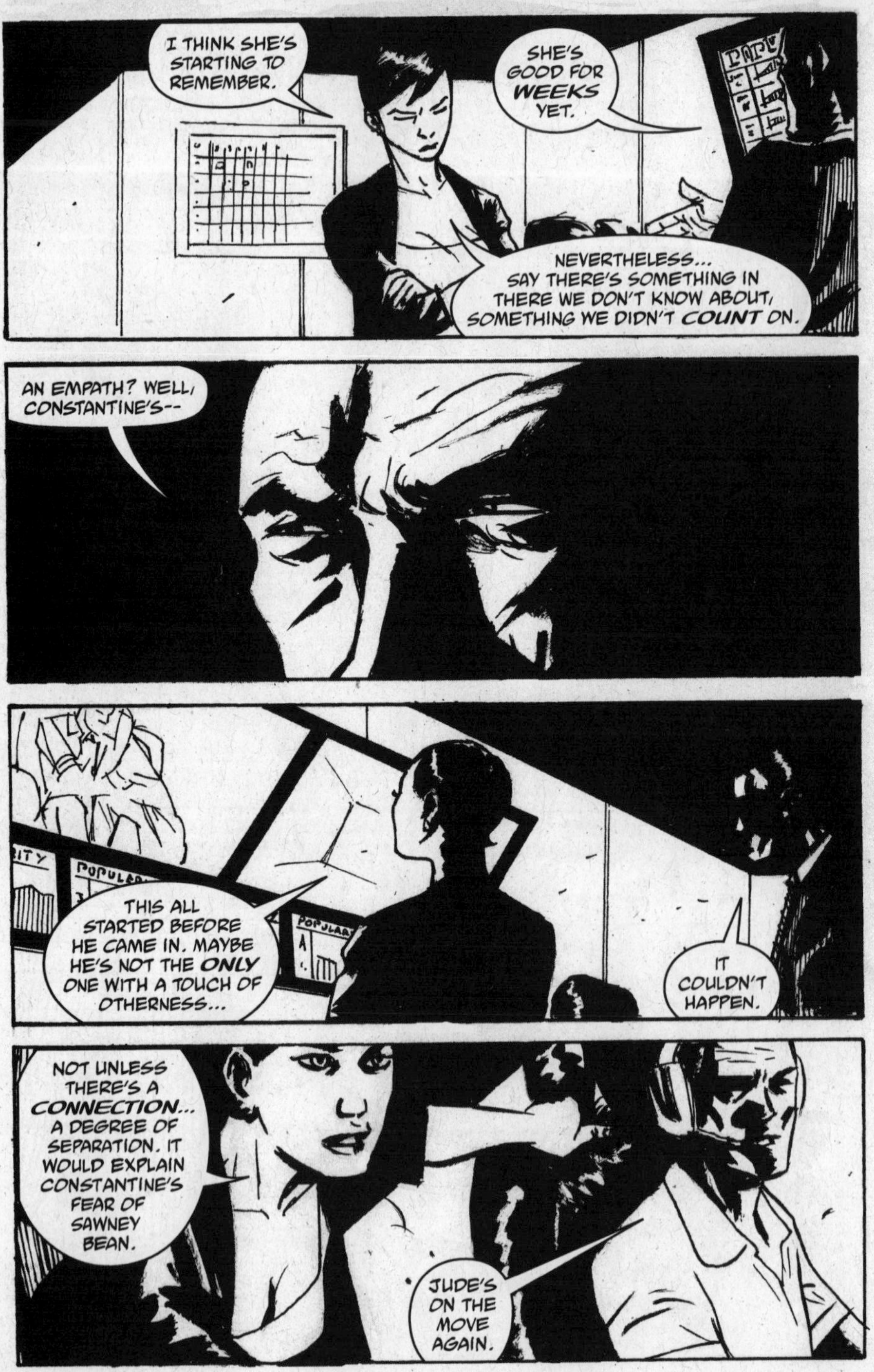
I THINK SHE'S STARTING TO REMEMBER.
SHE'S GOOD FOR WEEKS YET.
NEVERTHELESS... SAY THERE'S SOMETHING IN THERE WE DON'T KNOW ABOUT, SOMETHING WE DIDN'T COUNT ON.
AN EMPATH? WELL, CONSTANTINE'S--
THIS ALL STARTED BEFORE HE CAME IN. MAYBE HE'S NOT THE ONLY ONE WITH A TOUCH OF OTHERNESS...
IT COULDN'T HAPPEN.
NOT UNLESS THERE'S A CONNECTION... A DEGREE OF SEPARATION. IT WOULD EXPLAIN CONSTANTINE'S FEAR OF SAWNEY BEAN.
JUDE'S ON THE MOVE AGAIN.

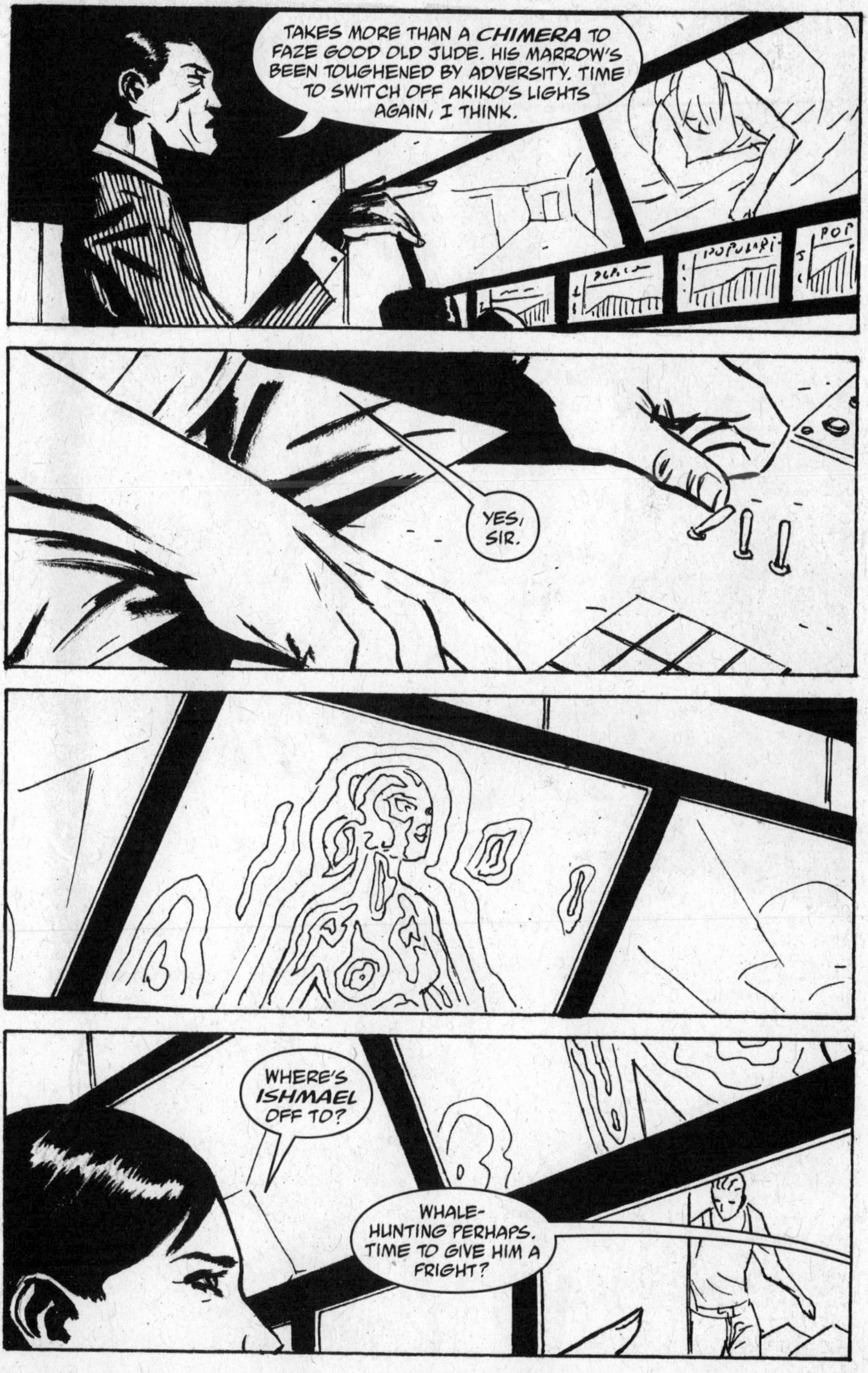
TAKES MORE THAN A CHIMERA TO FAZE GOOD OLD JUDE. HIS MARROW'S BEEN TOUGHENED BY ADVERSITY. TIME TO SWITCH OFF AKIKO'S LIGHTS AGAIN, I THINK.
YES, SIR.
WHERE'S ISHMAEL OFF TO?
WHALE-HUNTING PERHAPS. TIME TO GIVE HIM A FRIGHT?

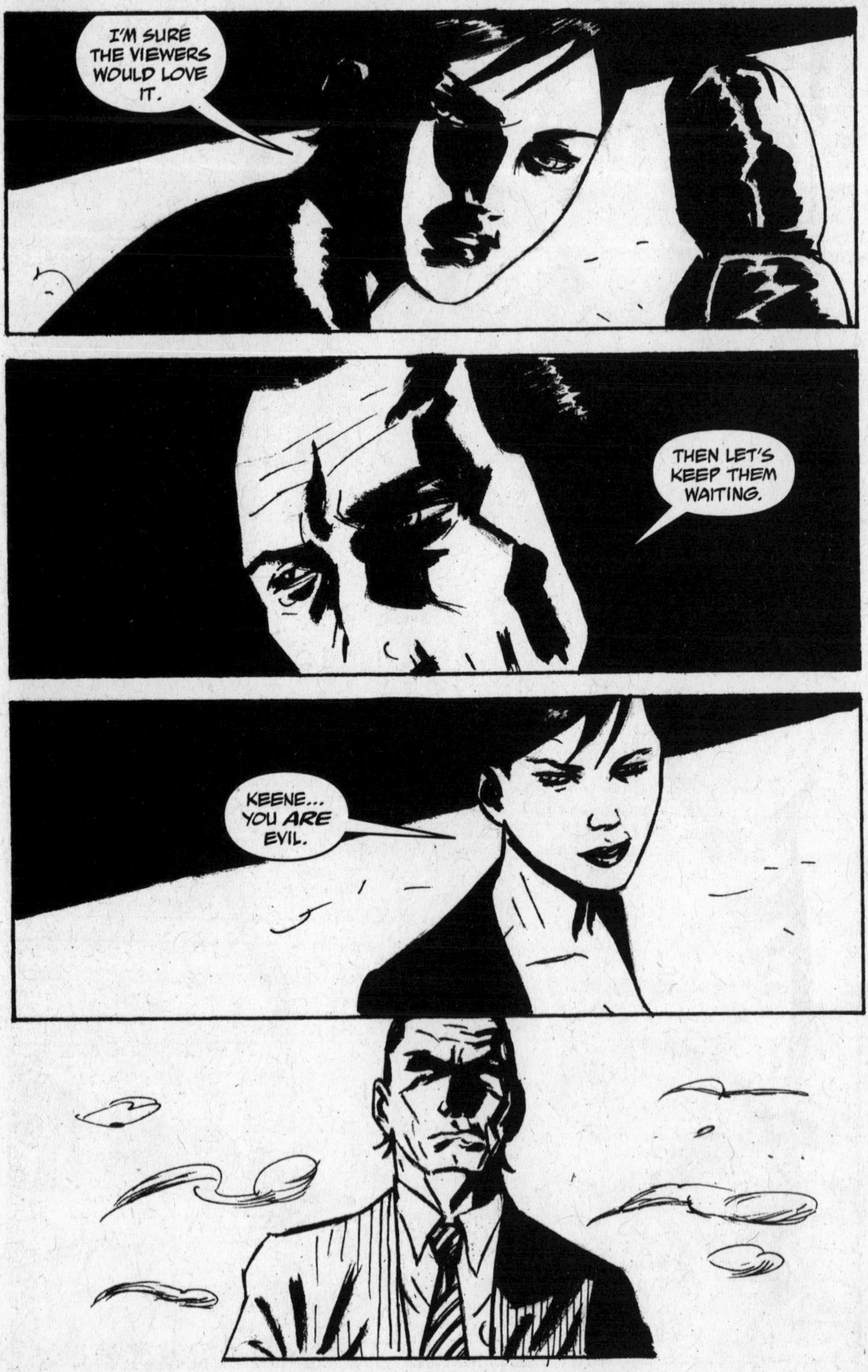
I'M SURE THE VIEWERS WOULD LOVE IT.
THEN LET'S KEEP THEM WAITING.
KEENE... YOU ARE EVIL.

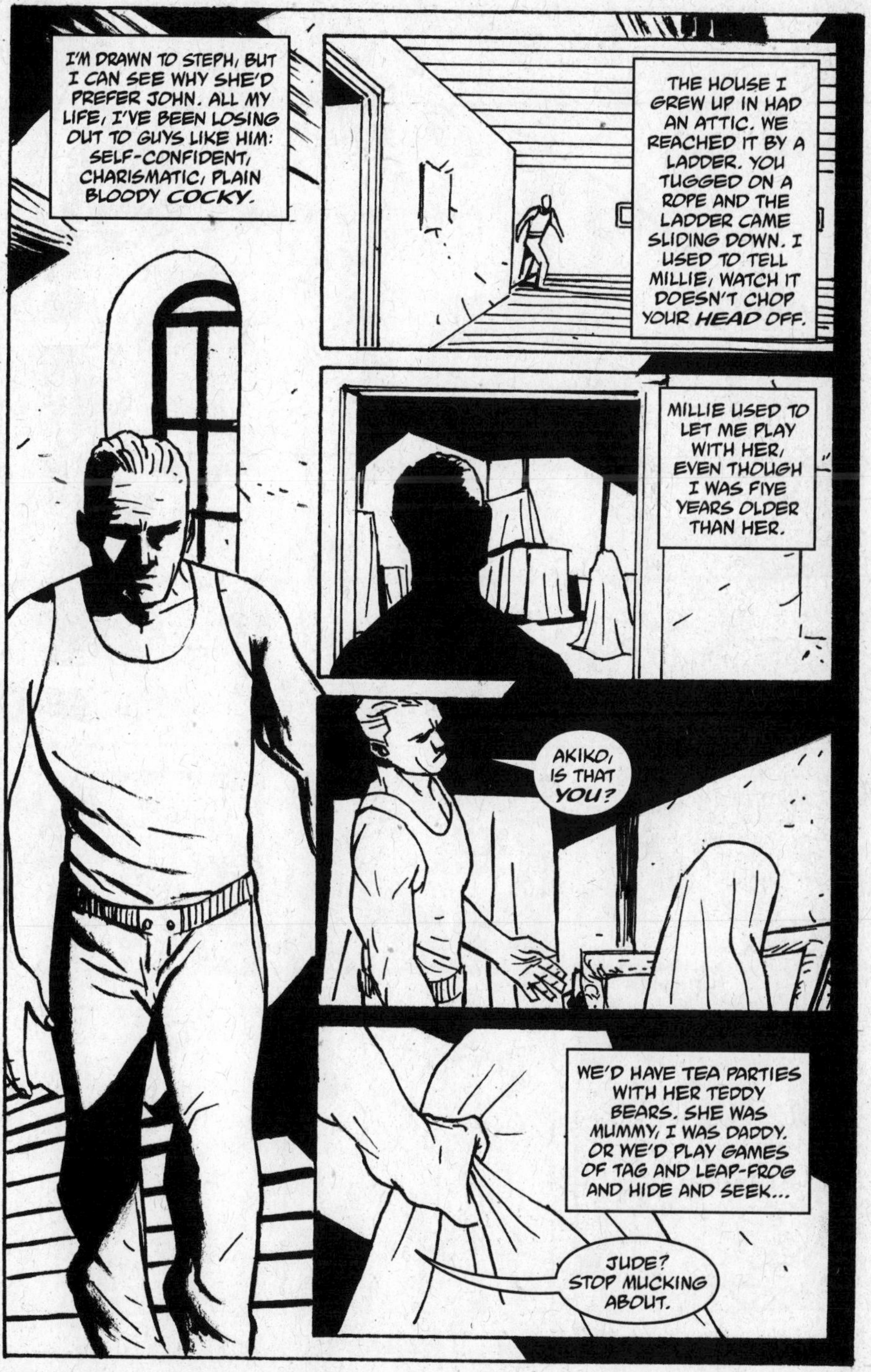
I'M DRAWN TO STEPH, BUT I CAN SEE WHY SHE'D PREFER JOHN. ALL MY LIFE, I'VE BEEN LOSING OUT TO GUYS LIKE HIM: SELF-CONFIDENT, CHARISMATIC, PLAIN BLOODY *COCKY*.
THE HOUSE I GREW UP IN HAD AN ATTIC. WE REACHED IT BY A LADDER. YOU TUGGED ON A ROPE AND THE LADDER CAME SLIDING DOWN. I USED TO TELL MILLIE, WATCH IT DOESN'T CHOP YOUR *HEAD* OFF.
MILLIE USED TO LET ME PLAY WITH HER, EVEN THOUGH I WAS FIVE YEARS OLDER THAN HER.
AKIKO, IS THAT *YOU*?
WE'D HAVE TEA PARTIES WITH HER TEDDY BEARS. SHE WAS MUMMY, I WAS DADDY. OR WE'D PLAY GAMES OF TAG AND LEAP-FROG AND HIDE AND SEEK...
JUDE? STOP MUCKING ABOUT.

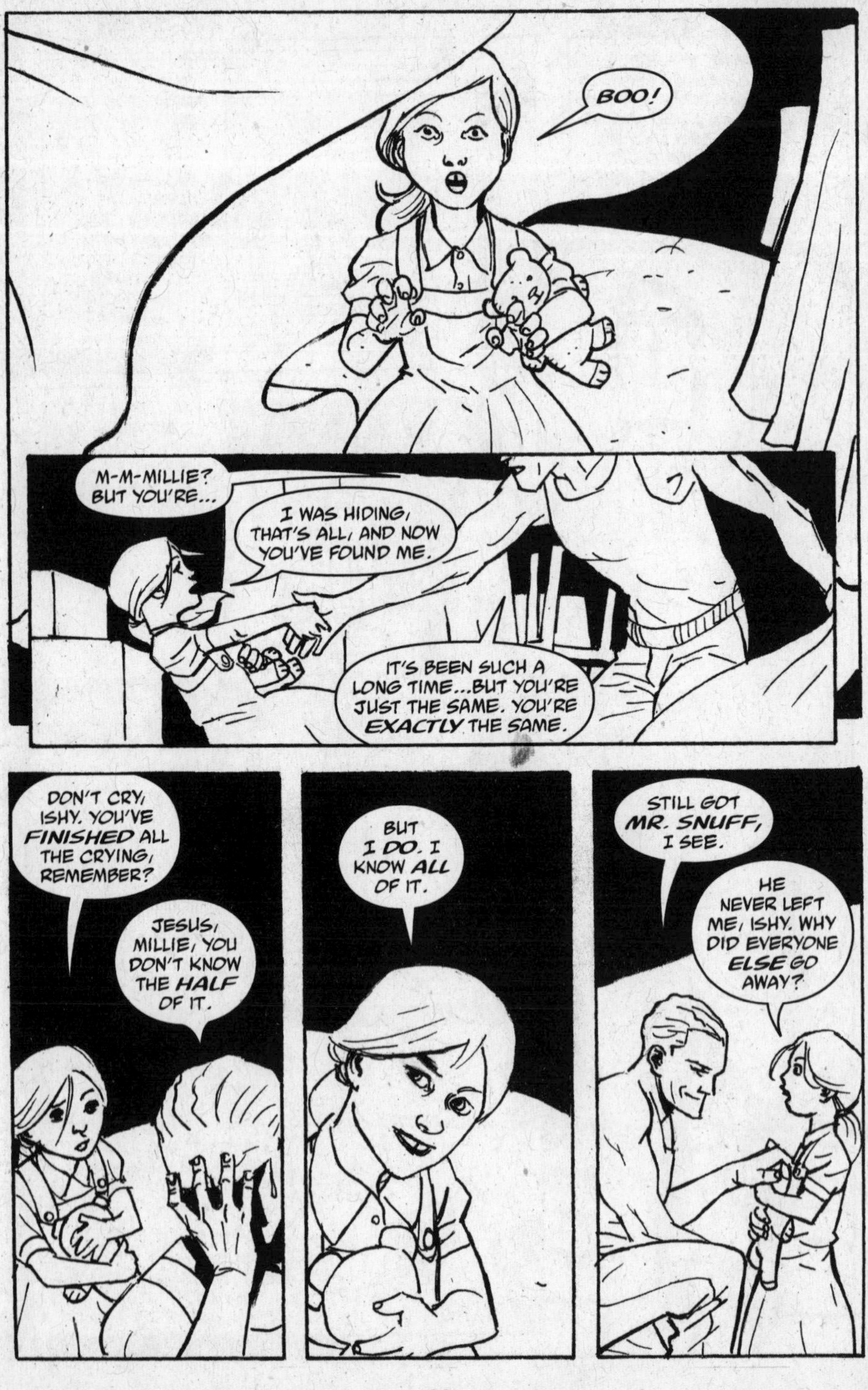
BOO!
M-M-MILLIE? BUT YOU'RE...
I WAS HIDING, THAT'S ALL, AND NOW YOU'VE FOUND ME.
IT'S BEEN SUCH A LONG TIME...BUT YOU'RE JUST THE SAME. YOU'RE EXACTLY THE SAME.
DON'T CRY, ISHY. YOU'VE FINISHED ALL THE CRYING, REMEMBER?
JESUS, MILLIE, YOU DON'T KNOW THE HALF OF IT.
BUT I DO. I KNOW ALL OF IT.
STILL GOT MR. SNUFF, I SEE.
HE NEVER LEFT ME, ISHY. WHY DID EVERYONE ELSE GO AWAY?

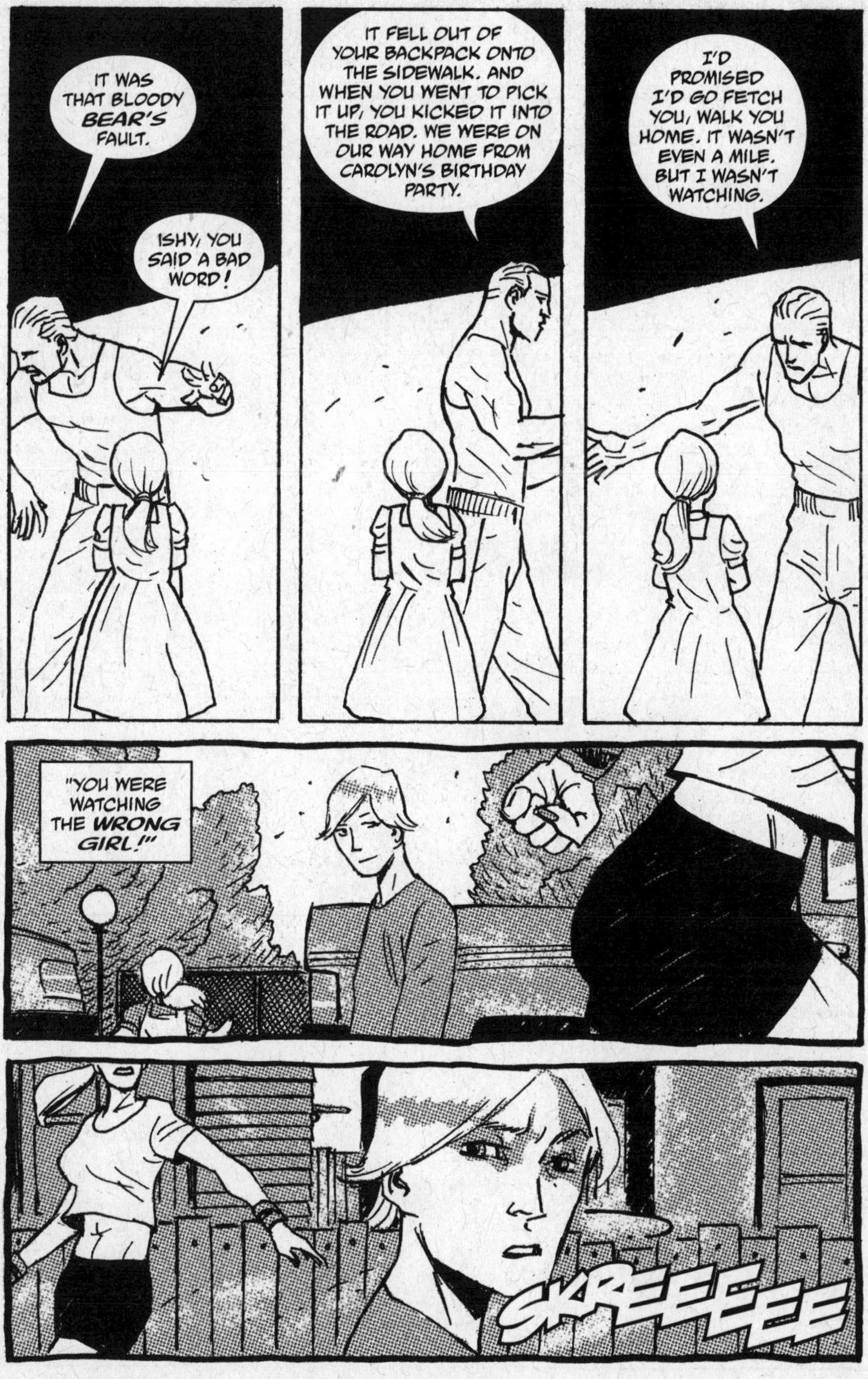
IT WAS THAT BLOODY BEAR'S FAULT.
ISHY, YOU SAID A BAD WORD!
IT FELL OUT OF YOUR BACKPACK ONTO THE SIDEWALK. AND WHEN YOU WENT TO PICK IT UP, YOU KICKED IT INTO THE ROAD. WE WERE ON OUR WAY HOME FROM CAROLYN'S BIRTHDAY PARTY.
I'D PROMISED I'D GO FETCH YOU, WALK YOU HOME. IT WASN'T EVEN A MILE. BUT I WASN'T WATCHING.
"YOU WERE WATCHING THE WRONG GIRL!"
SKREEEEEE

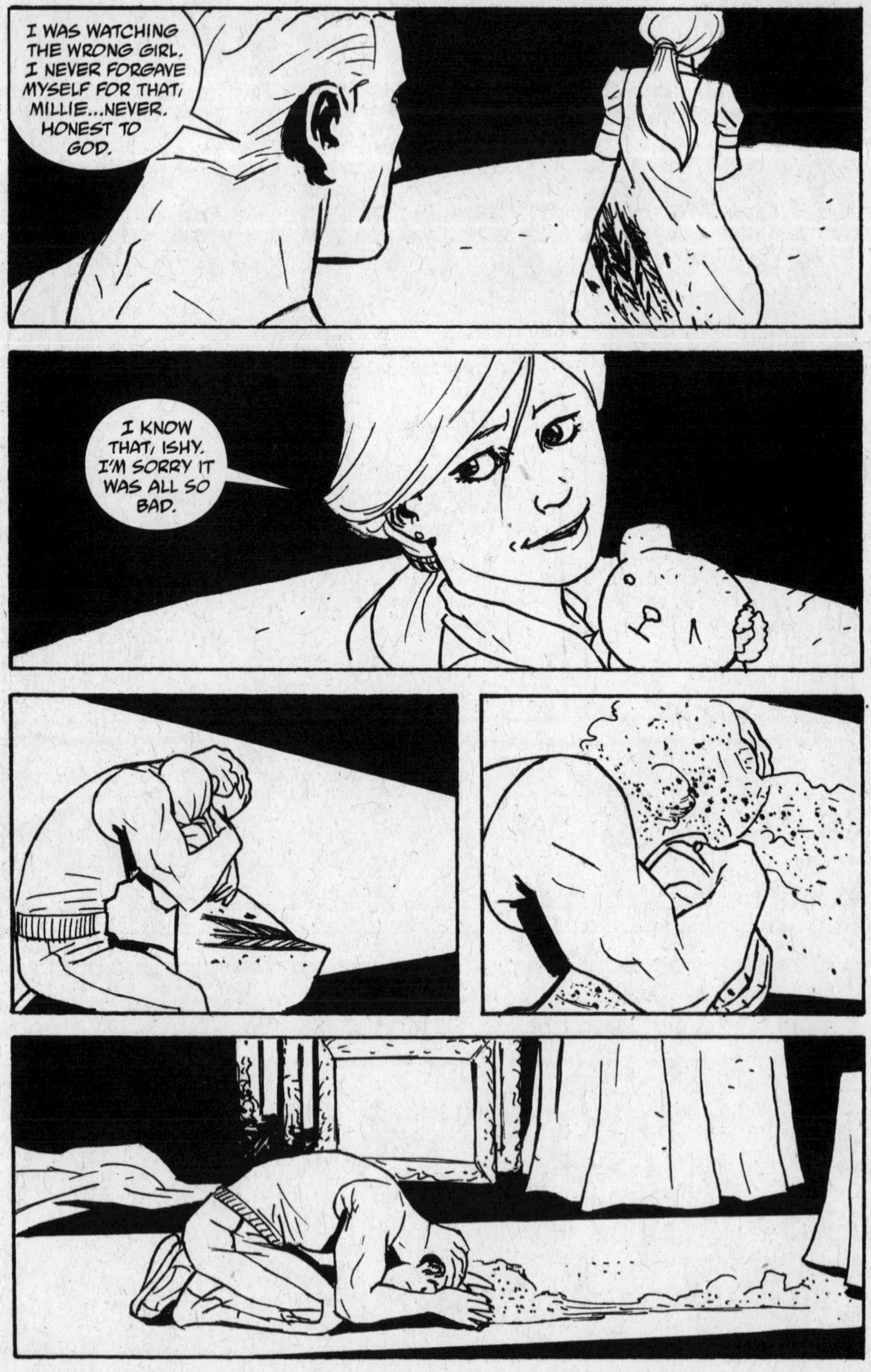
I WAS WATCHING THE WRONG GIRL. I NEVER FORGAVE MYSELF FOR THAT, MILLIE...NEVER. HONEST TO GOD.
I KNOW THAT, ISHY. I'M SORRY IT WAS ALL SO BAD.

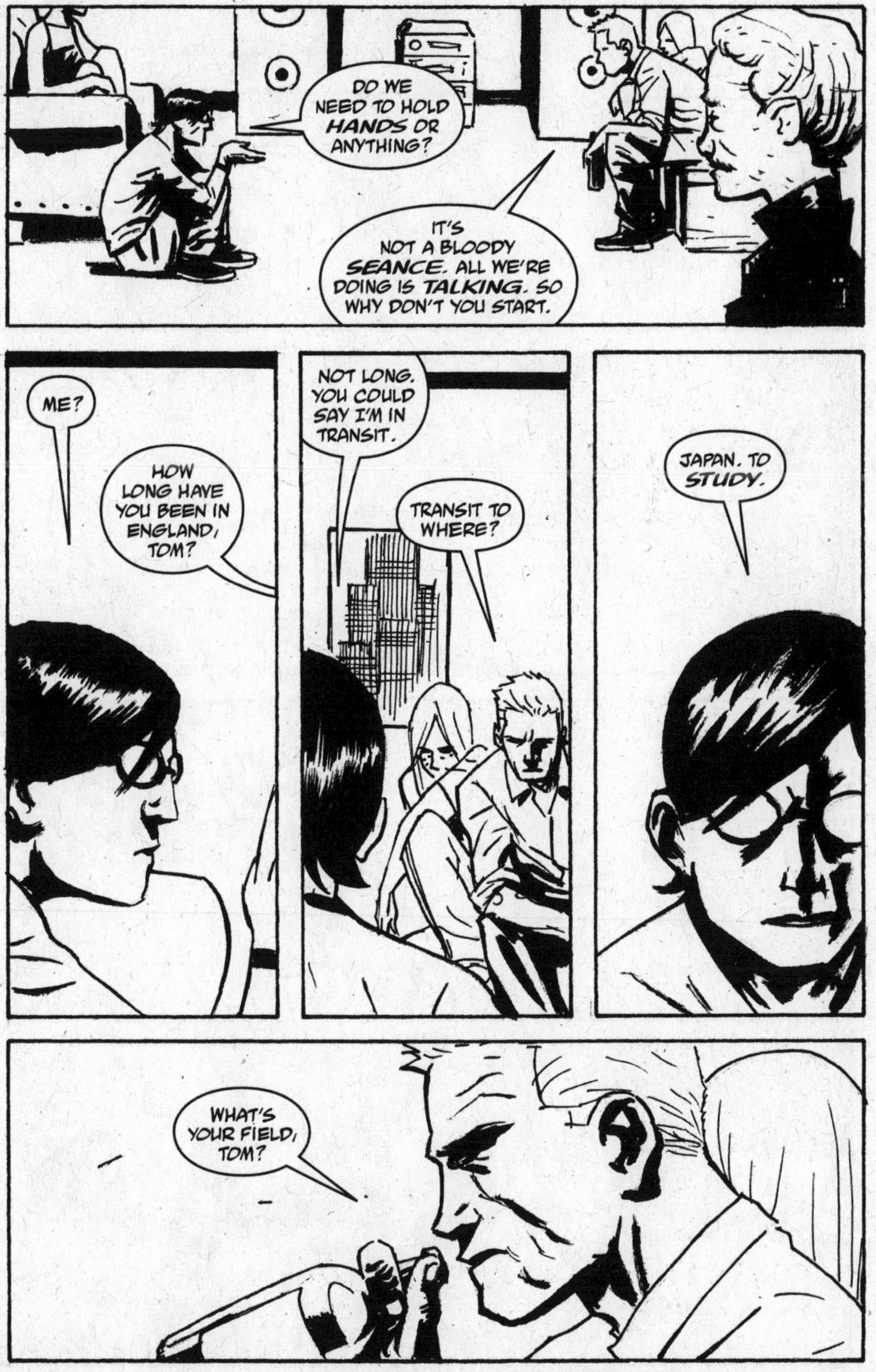
DO WE NEED TO HOLD HANDS OR ANYTHING?
IT'S NOT A BLOODY SEANCE. ALL WE'RE DOING IS TALKING. SO WHY DON'T YOU START.
ME?
HOW LONG HAVE YOU BEEN IN ENGLAND, TOM?
NOT LONG. YOU COULD SAY I'M IN TRANSIT.
TRANSIT TO WHERE?
JAPAN. TO STUDY.
WHAT'S YOUR FIELD, TOM?

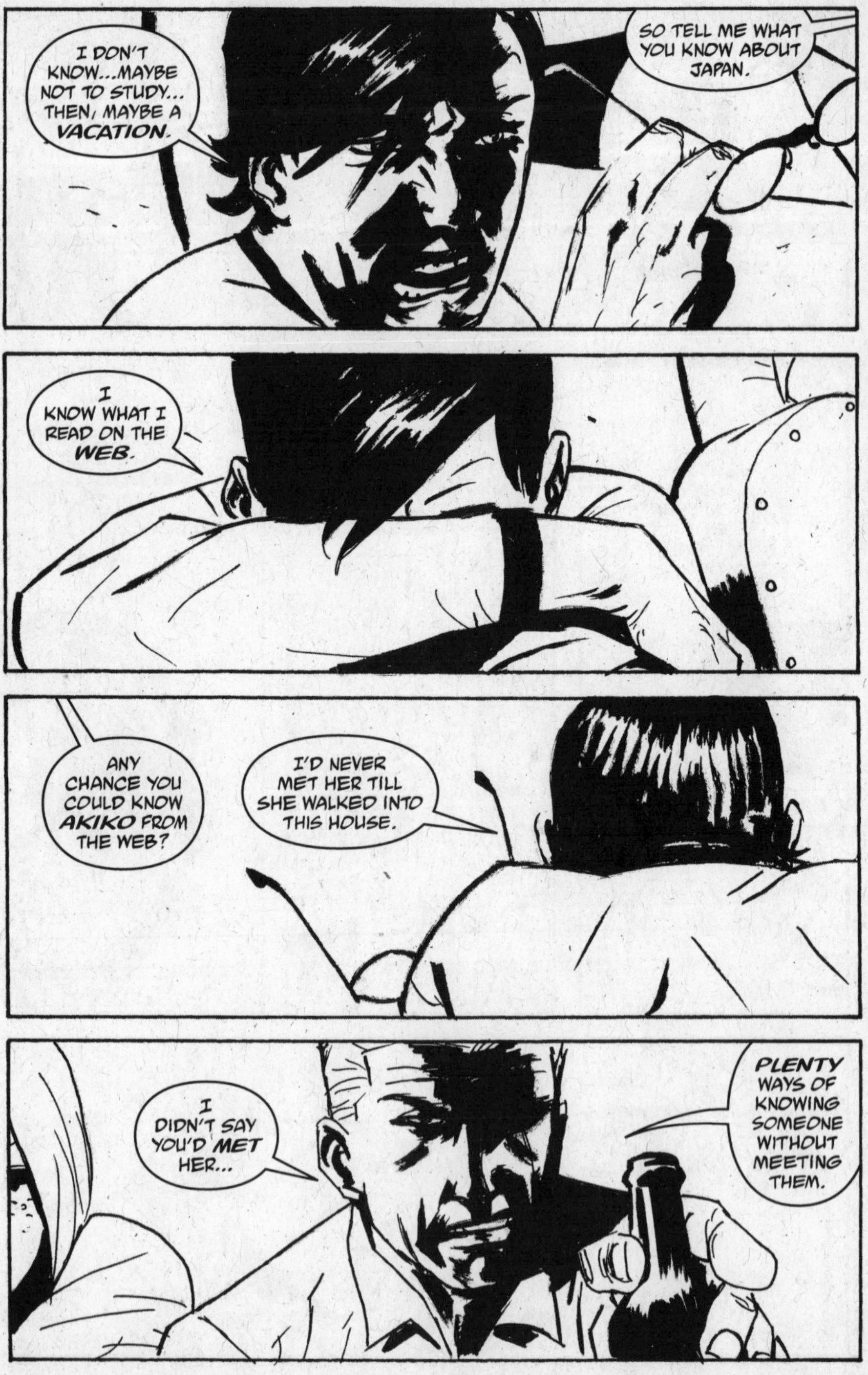

I DON'T KNOW...MAYBE NOT TO STUDY... THEN, MAYBE A VACATION.
SO TELL ME WHAT YOU KNOW ABOUT JAPAN.
I KNOW WHAT I READ ON THE WEB.
ANY CHANCE YOU COULD KNOW AKIKO FROM THE WEB?
I'D NEVER MET HER TILL SHE WALKED INTO THIS HOUSE.
I DIDN'T SAY YOU'D MET HER...
PLENTY WAYS OF KNOWING SOMEONE WITHOUT MEETING THEM.

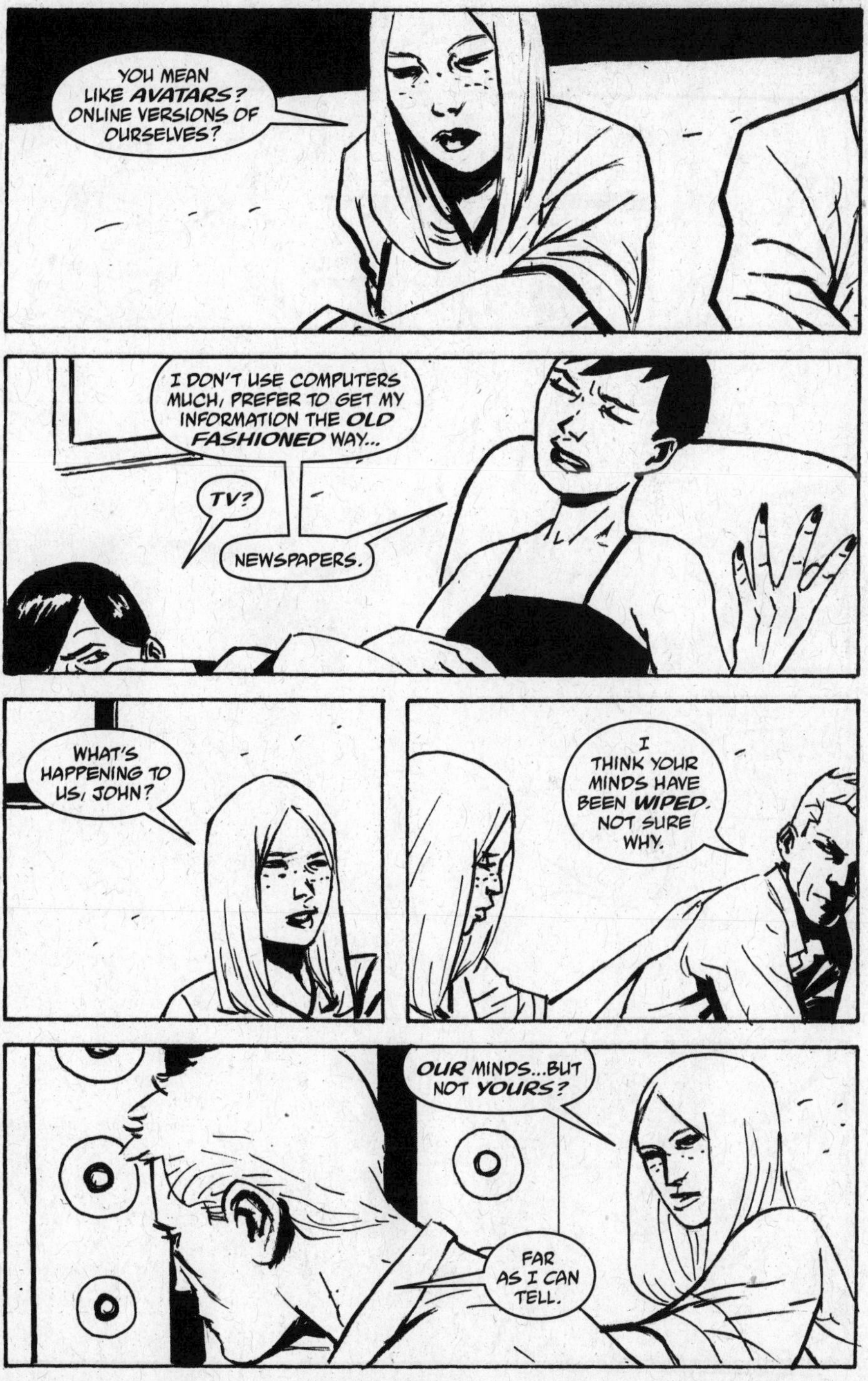
YOU MEAN LIKE AVATARS? ONLINE VERSIONS OF OURSELVES?
I DON'T USE COMPUTERS MUCH, PREFER TO GET MY INFORMATION THE OLD FASHIONED WAY...
TV?
NEWSPAPERS.
WHAT'S HAPPENING TO US, JOHN?
I THINK YOUR MINDS HAVE BEEN WIPED. NOT SURE WHY.
OUR MINDS...BUT NOT YOURS?
FAR AS I CAN TELL.

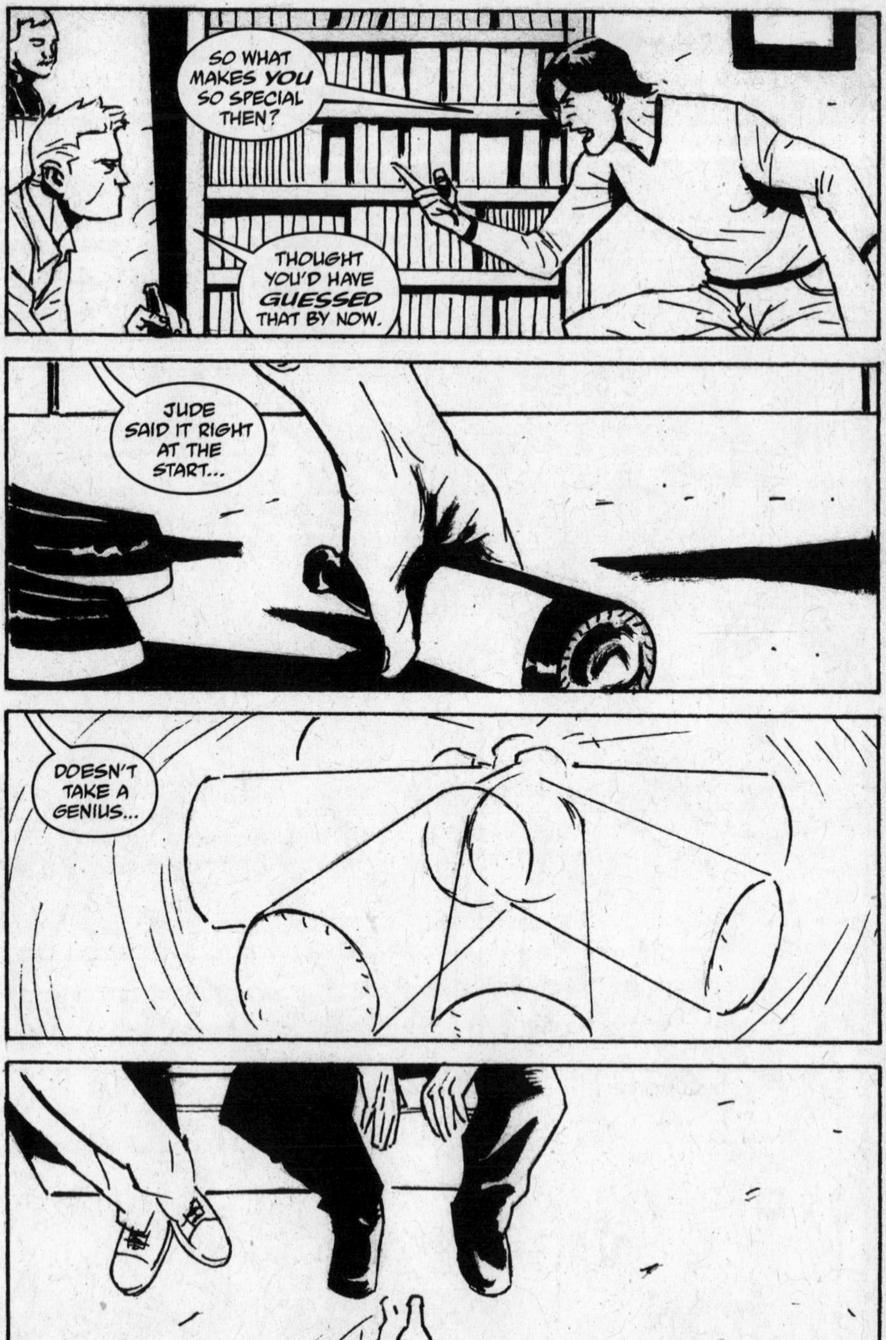
SO WHAT MAKES YOU SO SPECIAL THEN?
THOUGHT YOU'D HAVE GUESSED THAT BY NOW.
JUDE SAID IT RIGHT AT THE START...
DOESN'T TAKE A GENIUS...

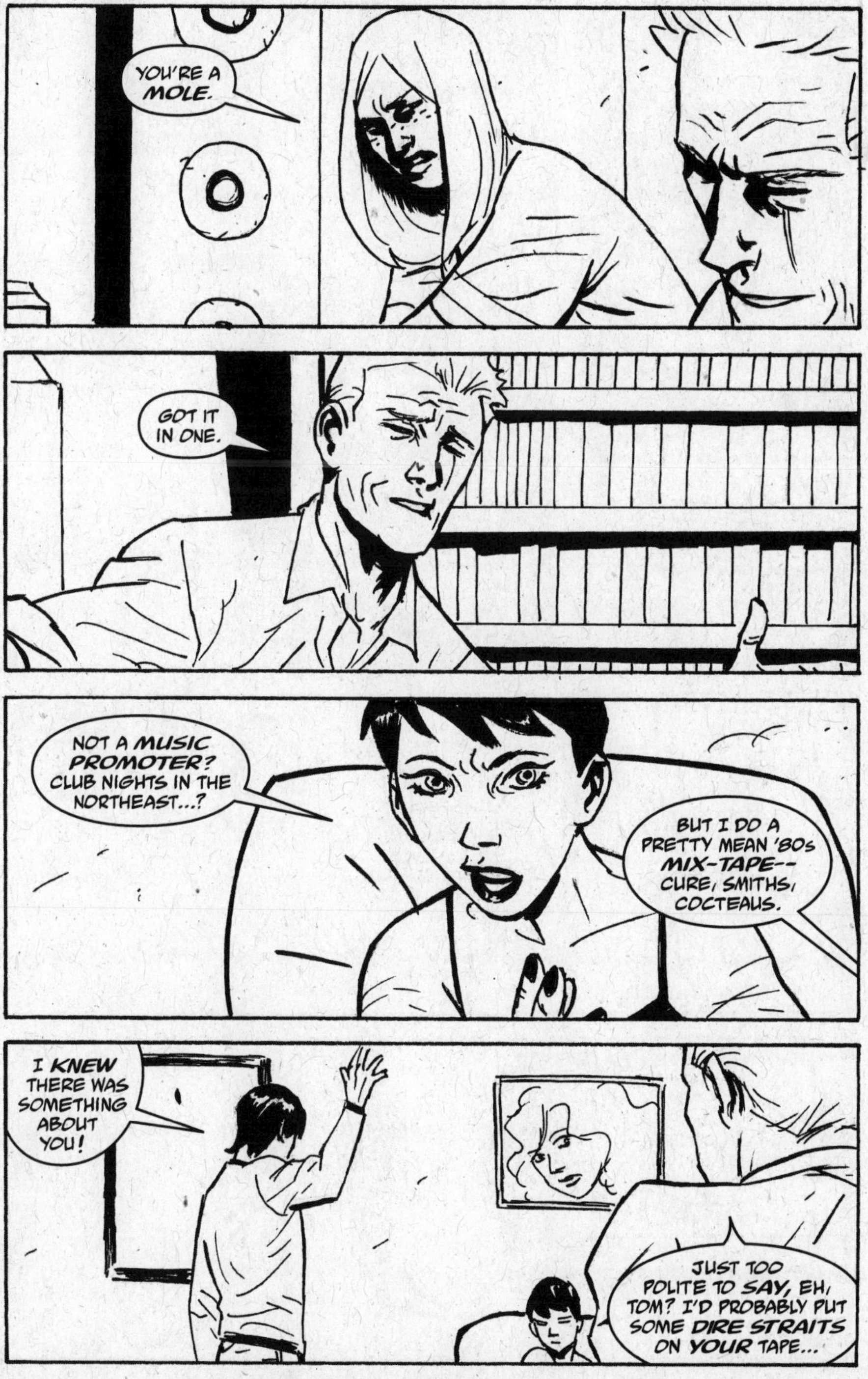
YOU'RE A MOLE.
GOT IT IN ONE.
NOT A MUSIC PROMOTER? CLUB NIGHTS IN THE NORTHEAST...?
BUT I DO A PRETTY MEAN '80s MIX-TAPE-- CURE, SMITHS, COCTEAUS.
I KNEW THERE WAS SOMETHING ABOUT YOU!
JUST TOO POLITE TO SAY, EH, TOM? I'D PROBABLY PUT SOME DIRE STRAITS ON YOUR TAPE...

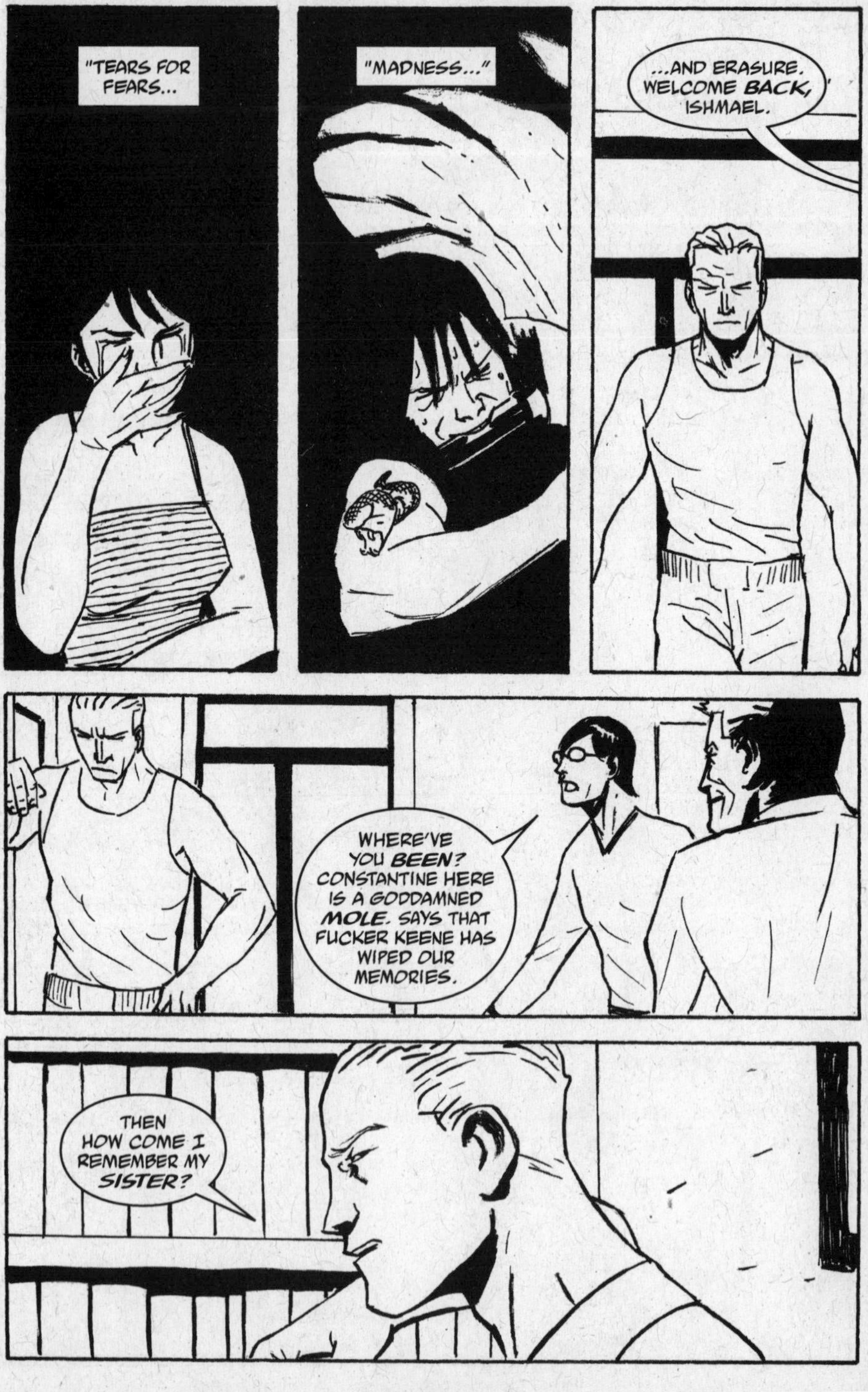
"TEARS FOR FEARS...
"MADNESS..."
...AND ERASURE. WELCOME BACK, ISHMAEL.
WHERE'VE YOU BEEN? CONSTANTINE HERE IS A GODDAMNED MOLE. SAYS THAT FUCKER KEENE HAS WIPED OUR MEMORIES.
THEN HOW COME I REMEMBER MY SISTER?

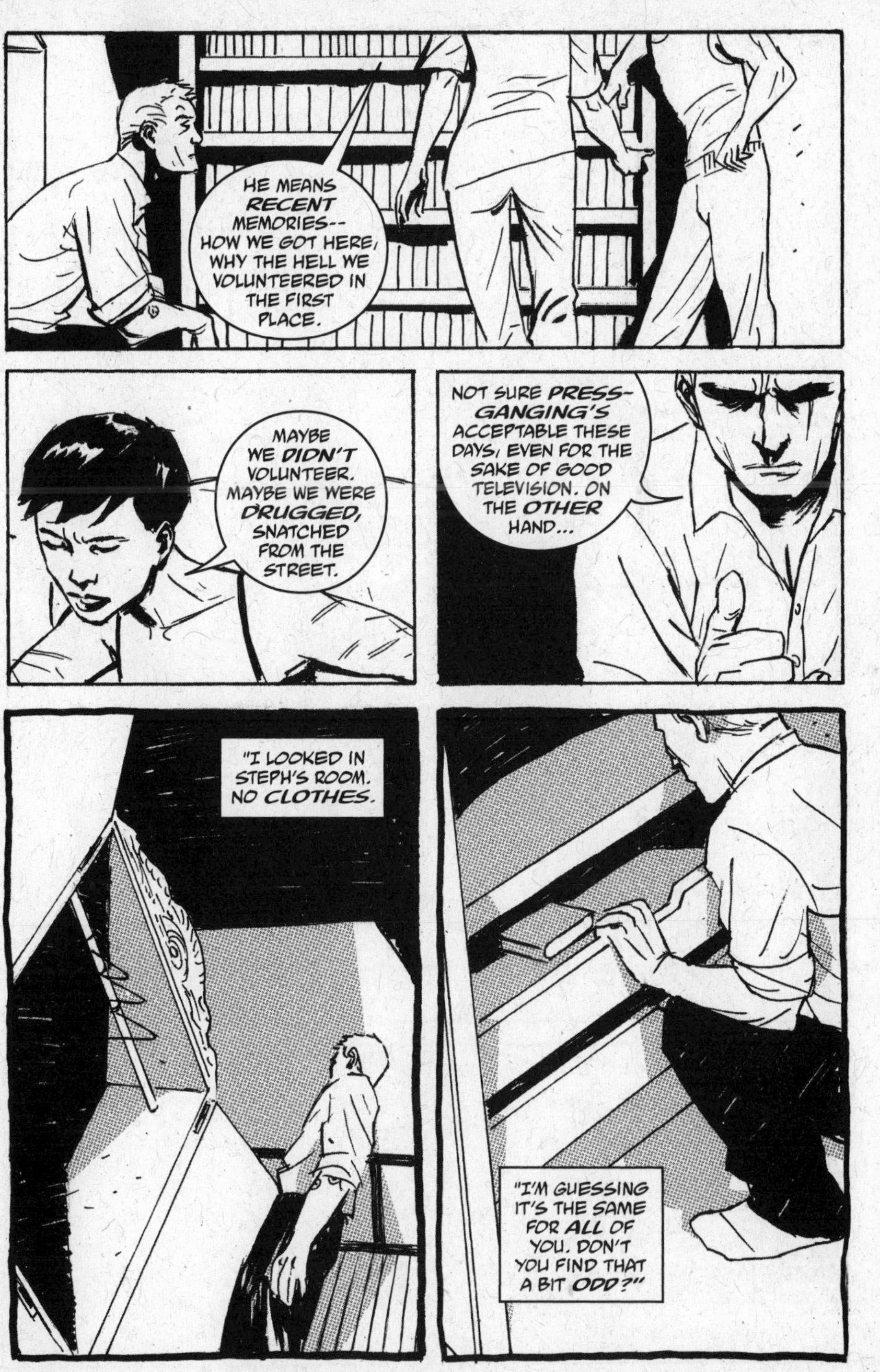
HE MEANS RECENT MEMORIES-- HOW WE GOT HERE, WHY THE HELL WE VOLUNTEERED IN THE FIRST PLACE.
MAYBE WE DIDN'T VOLUNTEER. MAYBE WE WERE DRUGGED, SNATCHED FROM THE STREET.
NOT SURE PRESS-GANGING'S ACCEPTABLE THESE DAYS, EVEN FOR THE SAKE OF GOOD TELEVISION. ON THE OTHER HAND...
"I LOOKED IN STEPH'S ROOM. NO CLOTHES.
"I'M GUESSING IT'S THE SAME FOR ALL OF YOU. DON'T YOU FIND THAT A BIT ODD?"

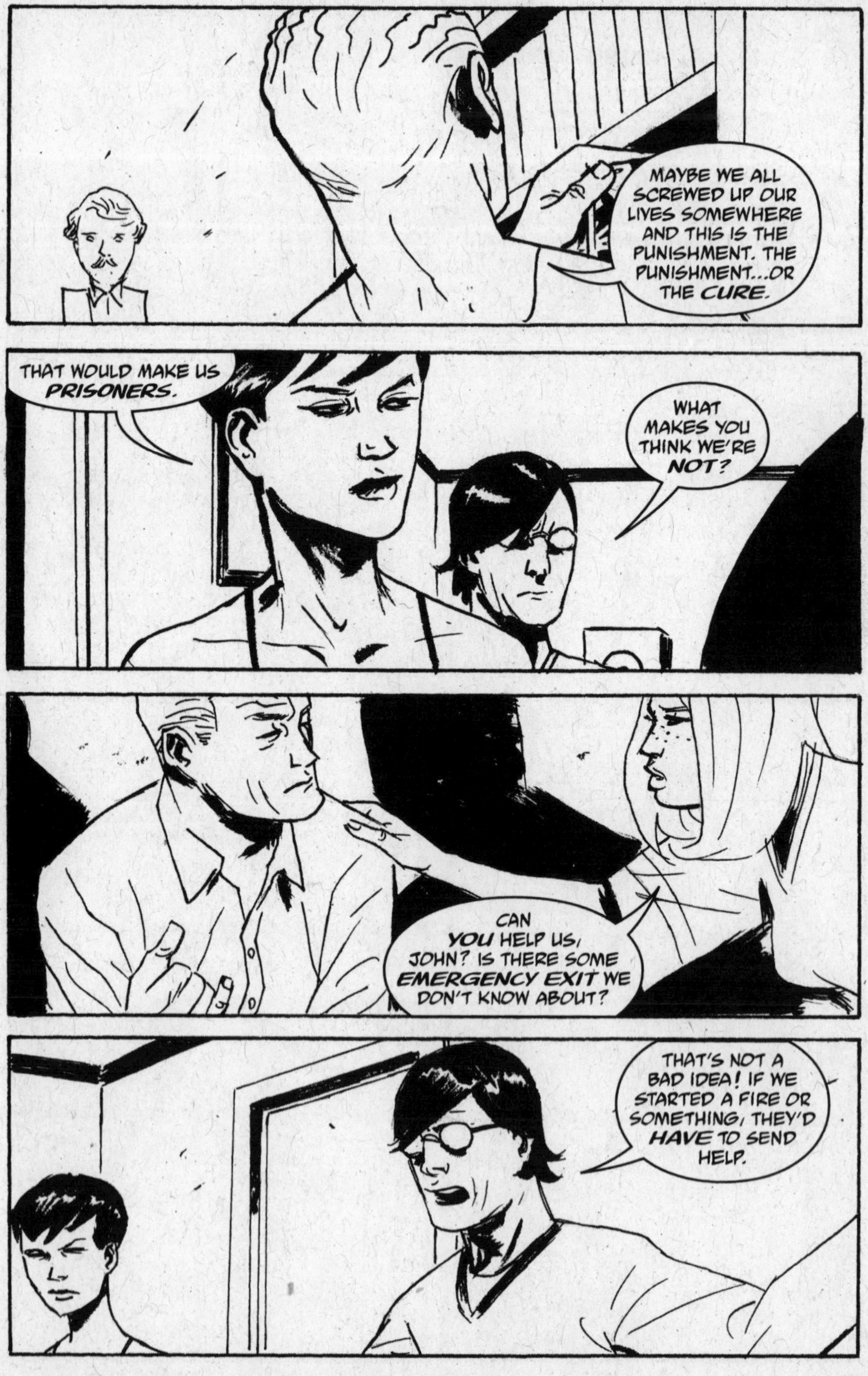
MAYBE WE ALL SCREWED UP OUR LIVES SOMEWHERE AND THIS IS THE PUNISHMENT. THE PUNISHMENT...OR THE CURE.
THAT WOULD MAKE US PRISONERS.
WHAT MAKES YOU THINK WE'RE NOT?
CAN YOU HELP US, JOHN? IS THERE SOME EMERGENCY EXIT WE DON'T KNOW ABOUT?
THAT'S NOT A BAD IDEA! IF WE STARTED A FIRE OR SOMETHING, THEY'D HAVE TO SEND HELP.

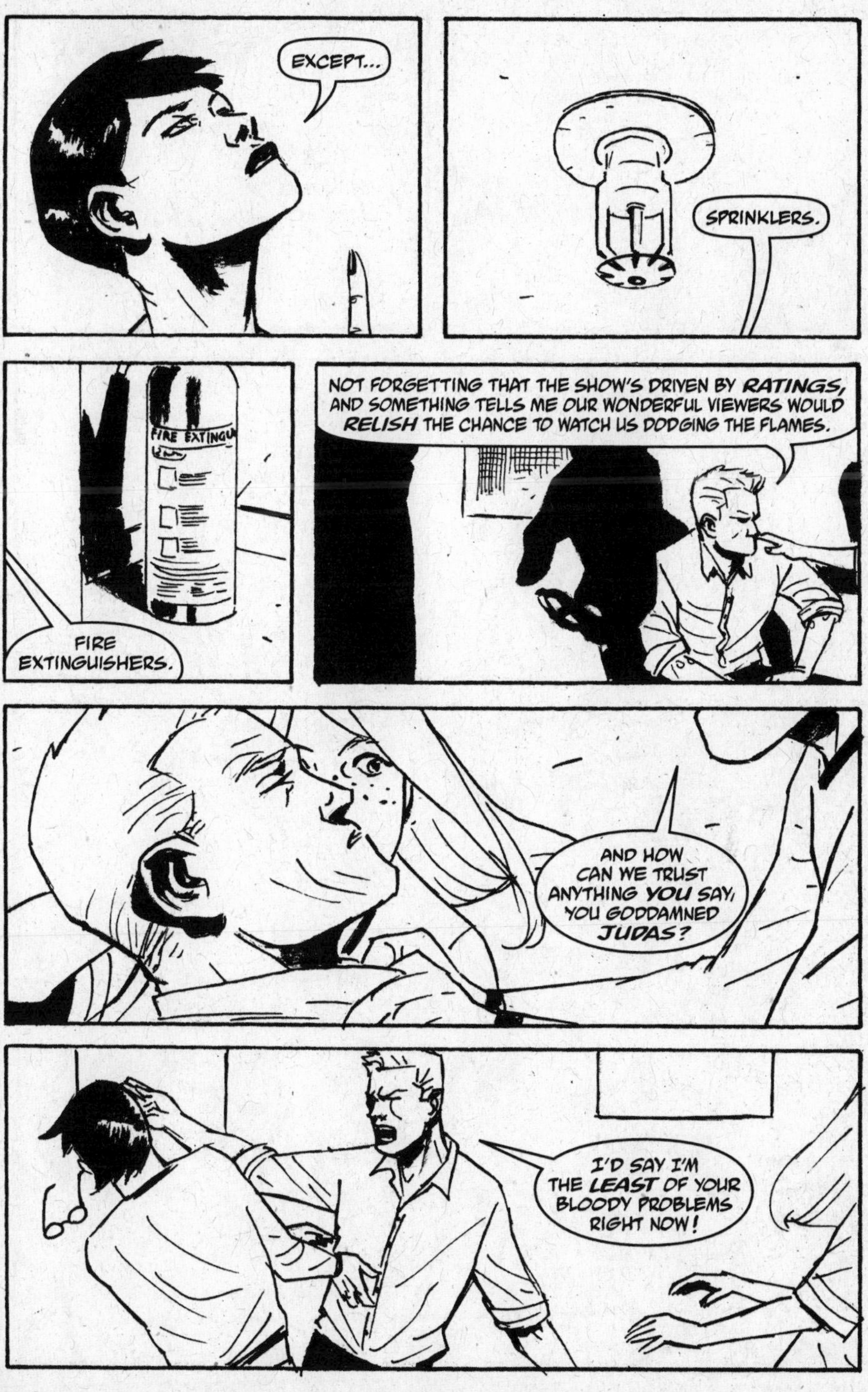
EXCEPT...
SPRINKLERS.
FIRE EXTINGU
FIRE EXTINGUISHERS.
NOT FORGETTING THAT THE SHOW'S DRIVEN BY RATINGS, AND SOMETHING TELLS ME OUR WONDERFUL VIEWERS WOULD RELISH THE CHANCE TO WATCH US DODGING THE FLAMES.
AND HOW CAN WE TRUST ANYTHING YOU SAY, YOU GODDAMNED JUDAS?
I'D SAY I'M THE LEAST OF YOUR BLOODY PROBLEMS RIGHT NOW!

JOHN'S RIGHT. THE WAY OUT OF HERE IS TO FIND WHAT CONNECTS US. FIGHTING AMONG OURSELVES IS JUST WHAT THEY *WANT*. THIS WHOLE GAME'S ABOUT SETTING US IN OPPOSITION TO EACH OTHER.

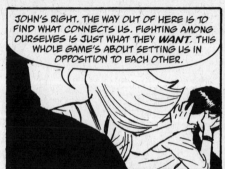

I WAS UPSTAIRS. THEY SHOWED ME MY *SISTER*. SHE SEEMED SO REAL, BUT I WAS JUST A KID WHEN SHE DIED.

WAS IT A *CAR ACCIDENT?*

HOW DID *YOU* KNOW?

YOU DREAM ABOUT HEADLIGHTS, A CAR COMING TOWARDS YOU. THESE NIGHTMARES, THEY'RE THINGS WE'RE AFRAID OF...THINGS FROM OUR *PAST.*

SO *TELL* ME, ALICE, JUST WHEN DID A HUGE *BIRD* SWOOP DOWN AND CARRY YOU OFF TO ITS *EYRIE?*

IT MIGHT *NOT* BE AN ACTUAL BIRD.

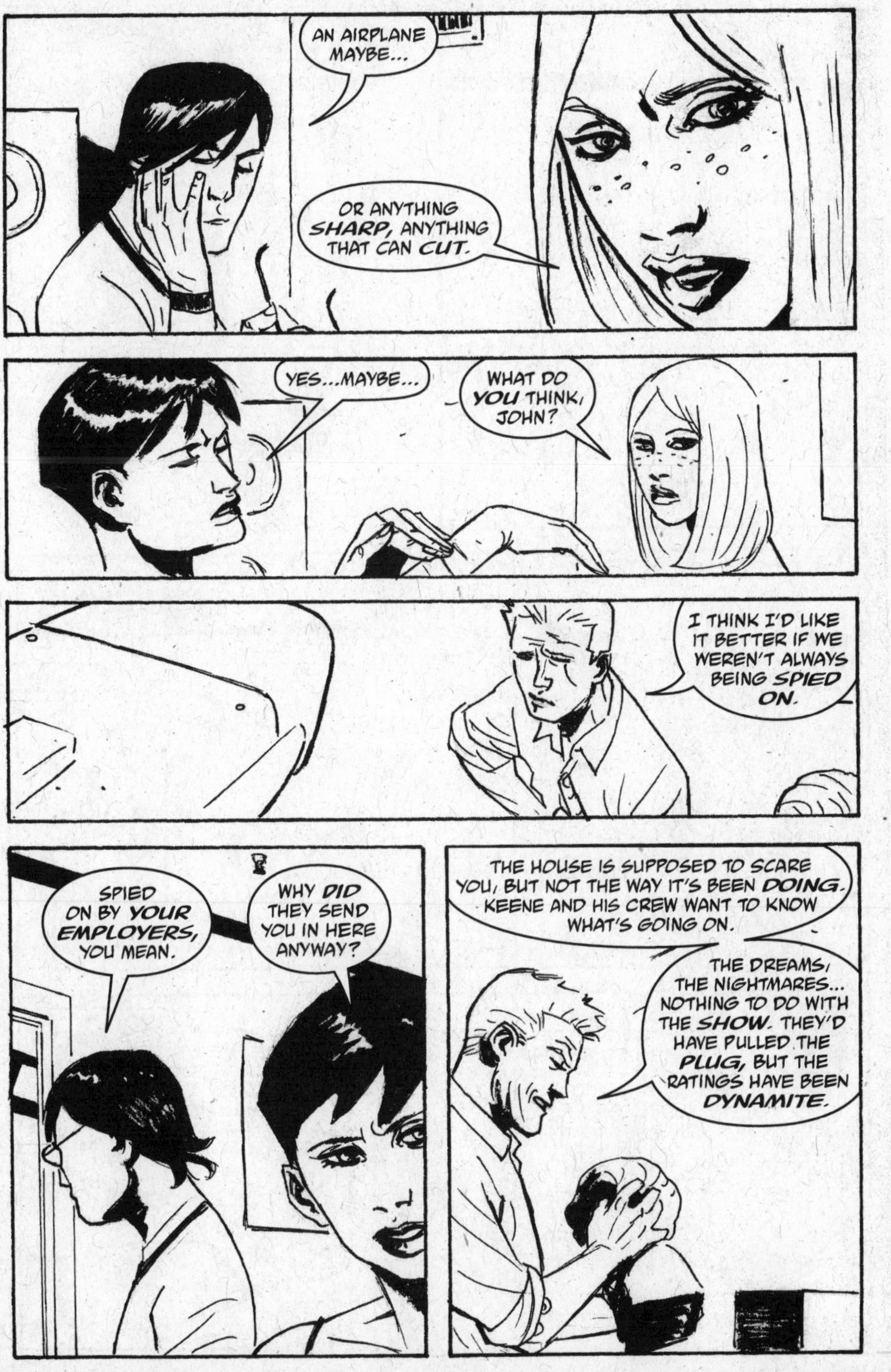
AN AIRPLANE MAYBE...
OR ANYTHING SHARP, ANYTHING THAT CAN CUT.
YES...MAYBE...
WHAT DO YOU THINK, JOHN?
I THINK I'D LIKE IT BETTER IF WE WEREN'T ALWAYS BEING SPIED ON.
SPIED ON BY YOUR EMPLOYERS, YOU MEAN.
WHY DID THEY SEND YOU IN HERE ANYWAY?
THE HOUSE IS SUPPOSED TO SCARE YOU, BUT NOT THE WAY IT'S BEEN DOING. KEENE AND HIS CREW WANT TO KNOW WHAT'S GOING ON.
THE DREAMS, THE NIGHTMARES... NOTHING TO DO WITH THE SHOW. THEY'D HAVE PULLED THE PLUG, BUT THE RATINGS HAVE BEEN DYNAMITE.

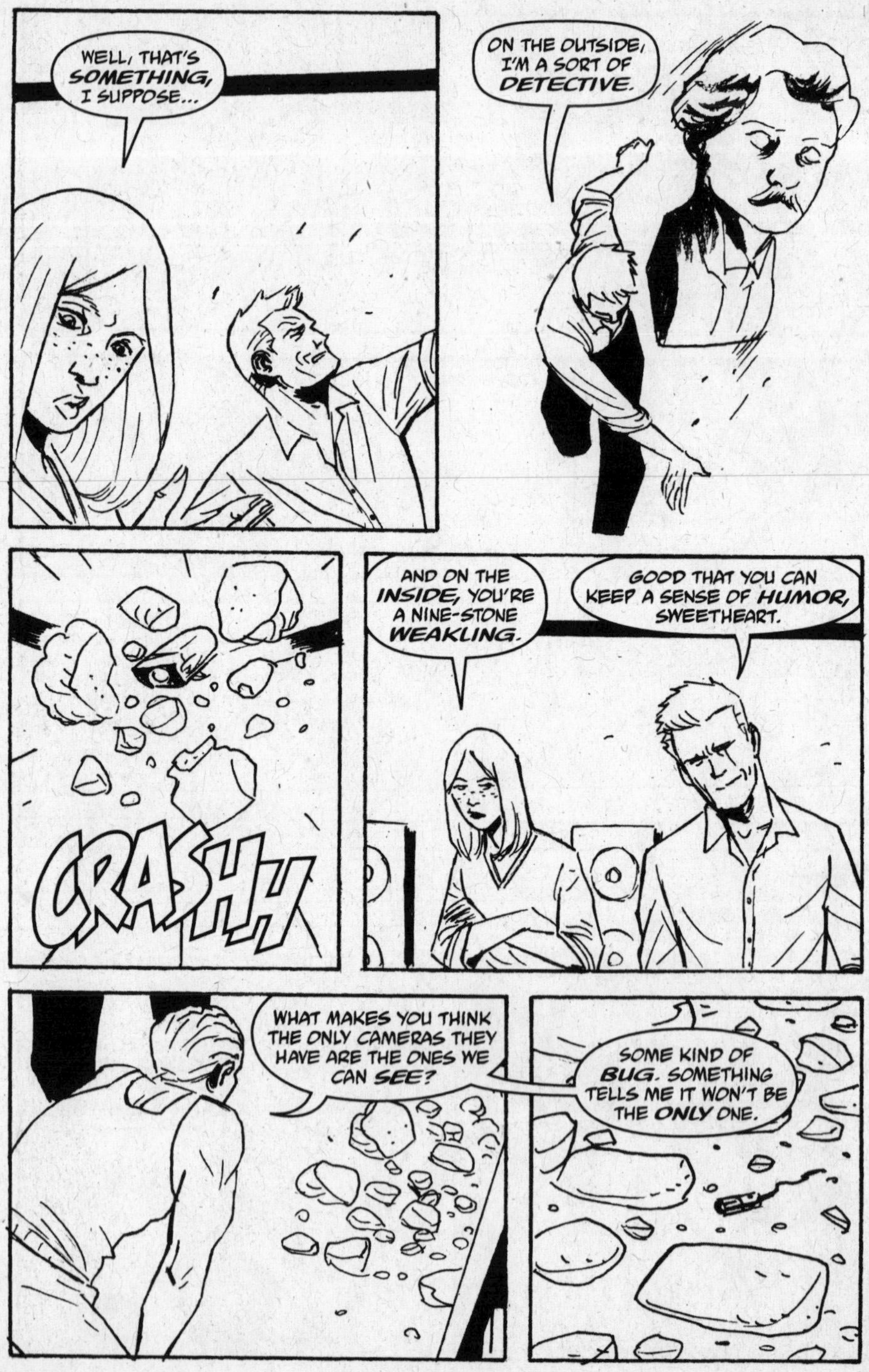
WELL, THAT'S SOMETHING, I SUPPOSE...
ON THE OUTSIDE, I'M A SORT OF DETECTIVE.
CRASHH
AND ON THE INSIDE, YOU'RE A NINE-STONE WEAKLING.
GOOD THAT YOU CAN KEEP A SENSE OF HUMOR, SWEETHEART.
WHAT MAKES YOU THINK THE ONLY CAMERAS THEY HAVE ARE THE ONES WE CAN SEE?
SOME KIND OF BUG. SOMETHING TELLS ME IT WON'T BE THE ONLY ONE.

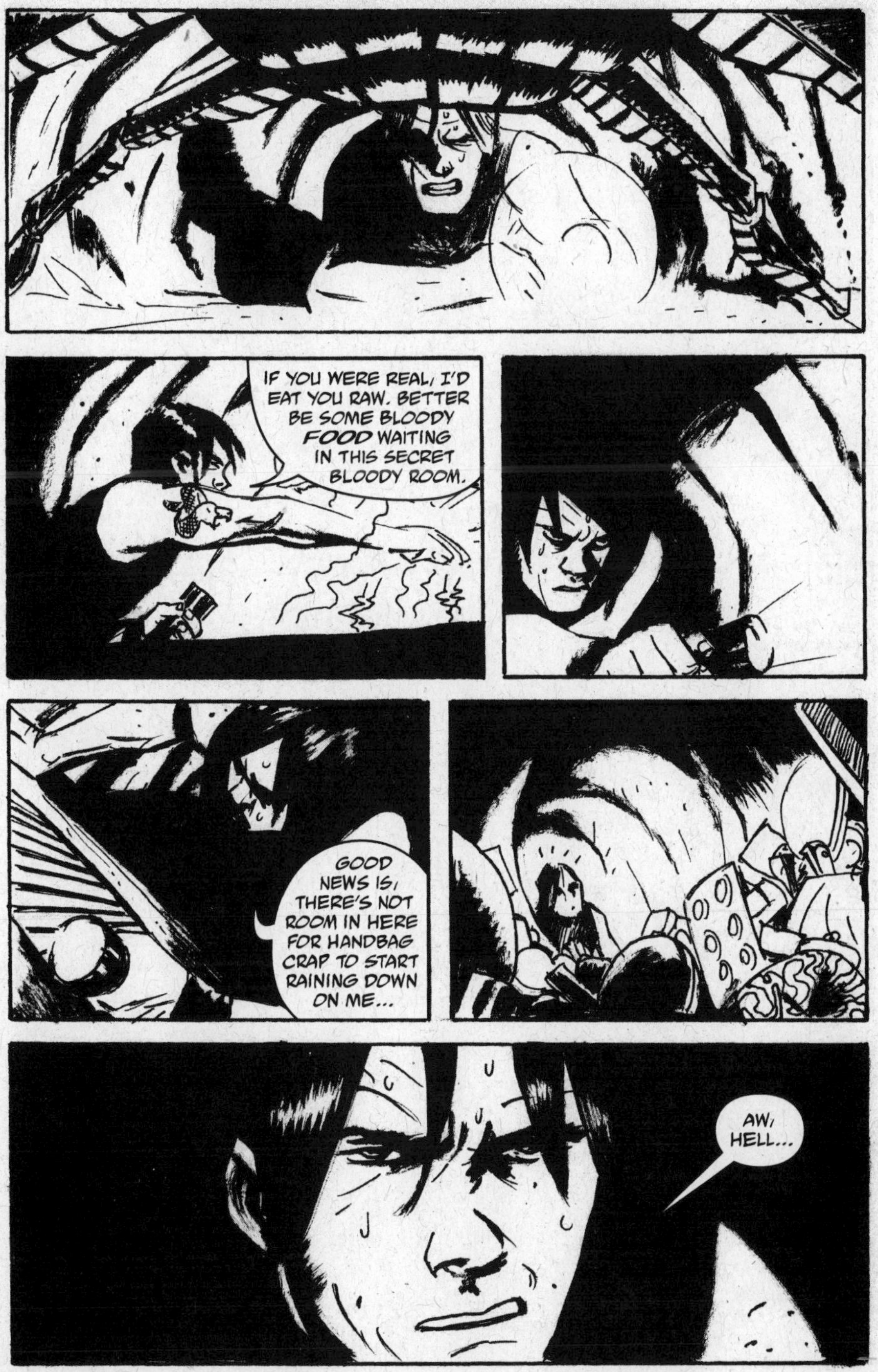
IF YOU WERE REAL, I'D EAT YOU RAW. BETTER BE SOME BLOODY FOOD WAITING IN THIS SECRET BLOODY ROOM.
GOOD NEWS IS, THERE'S NOT ROOM IN HERE FOR HANDBAG CRAP TO START RAINING DOWN ON ME...
AW, HELL...

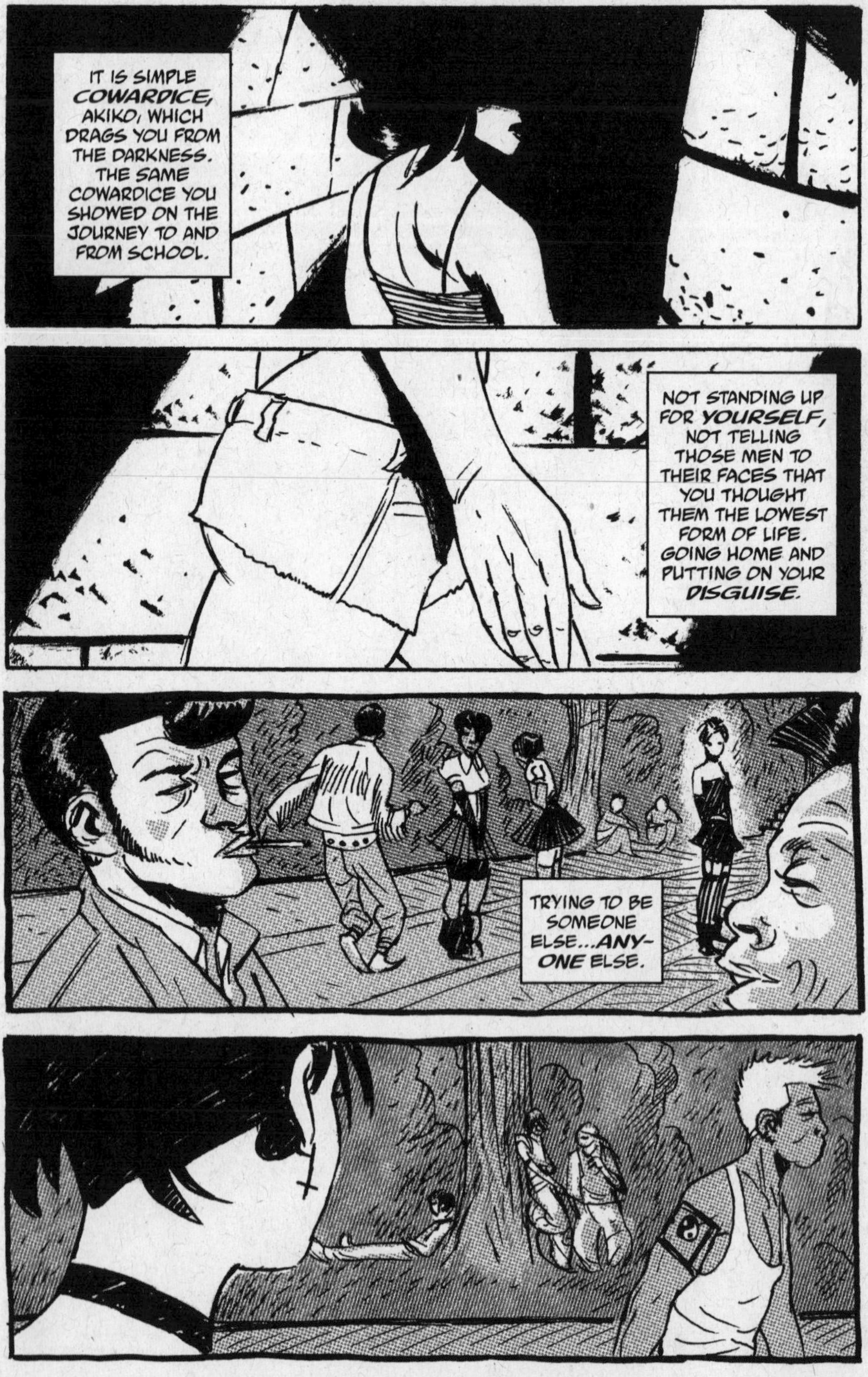
IT IS SIMPLE COWARDICE, AKIKO, WHICH DRAGS YOU FROM THE DARKNESS. THE SAME COWARDICE YOU SHOWED ON THE JOURNEY TO AND FROM SCHOOL.
NOT STANDING UP FOR YOURSELF, NOT TELLING THOSE MEN TO THEIR FACES THAT YOU THOUGHT THEM THE LOWEST FORM OF LIFE. GOING HOME AND PUTTING ON YOUR DISGUISE.
TRYING TO BE SOMEONE ELSE...ANY-ONE ELSE.

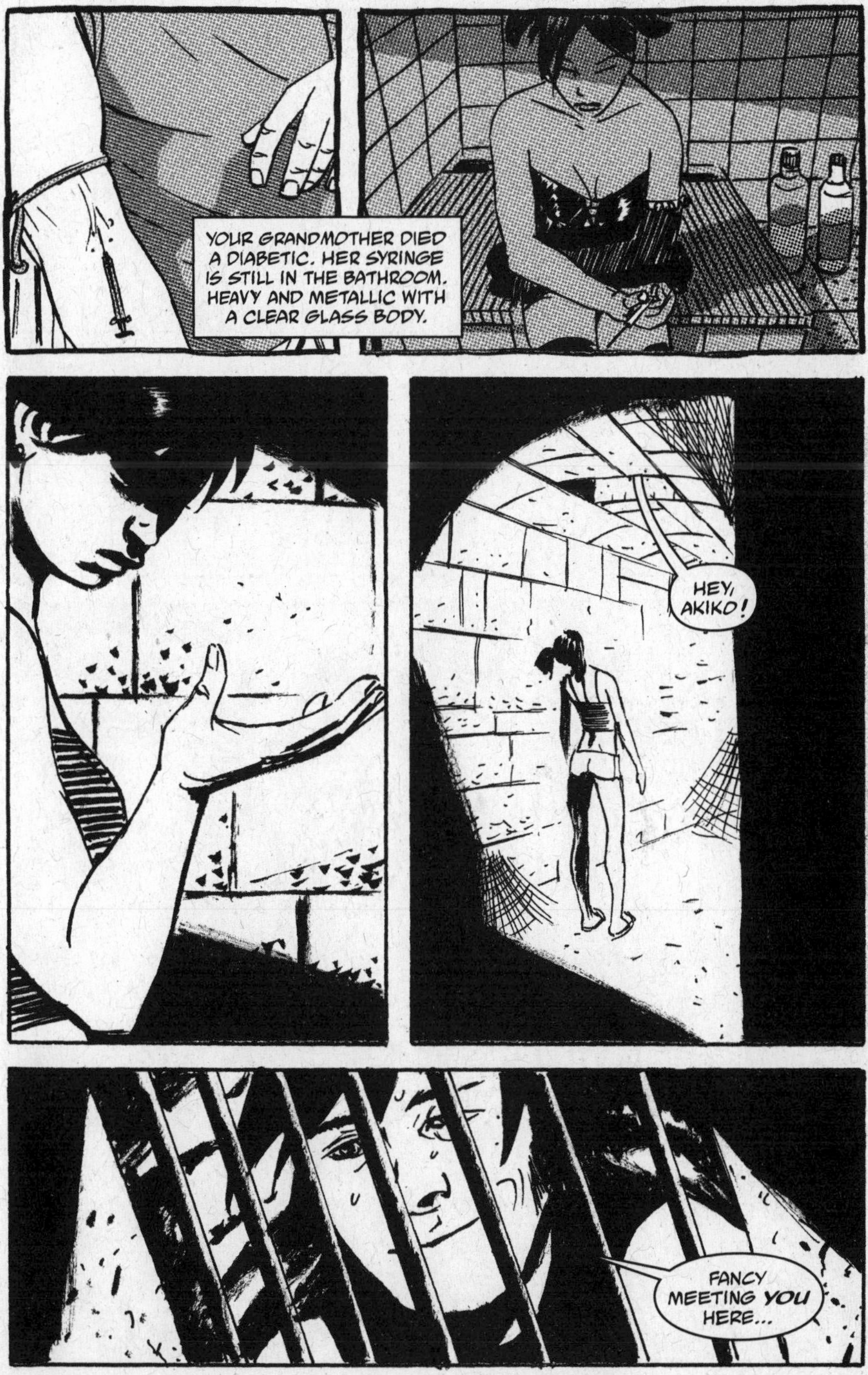
YOUR GRANDMOTHER DIED A DIABETIC. HER SYRINGE IS STILL IN THE BATHROOM. HEAVY AND METALLIC WITH A CLEAR GLASS BODY.
HEY, AKIKO!
FANCY MEETING YOU HERE...

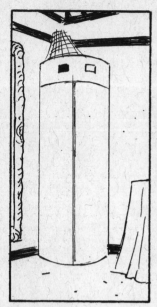

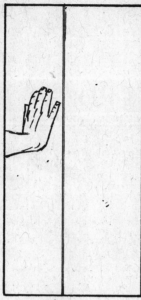

PHissH

WHAT CAN I DO FOR YOU, CONSTANTINE?

THOUGHT YOU'D WANT A *PROGRESS REPORT*, KEENE.

SO YOU *HAVE* MADE SOME *PROGRESS*?

I'VE DONE THE *SHERLOCK HOLMES* THING, COME TO A FEW *DEDUCTIONS*.

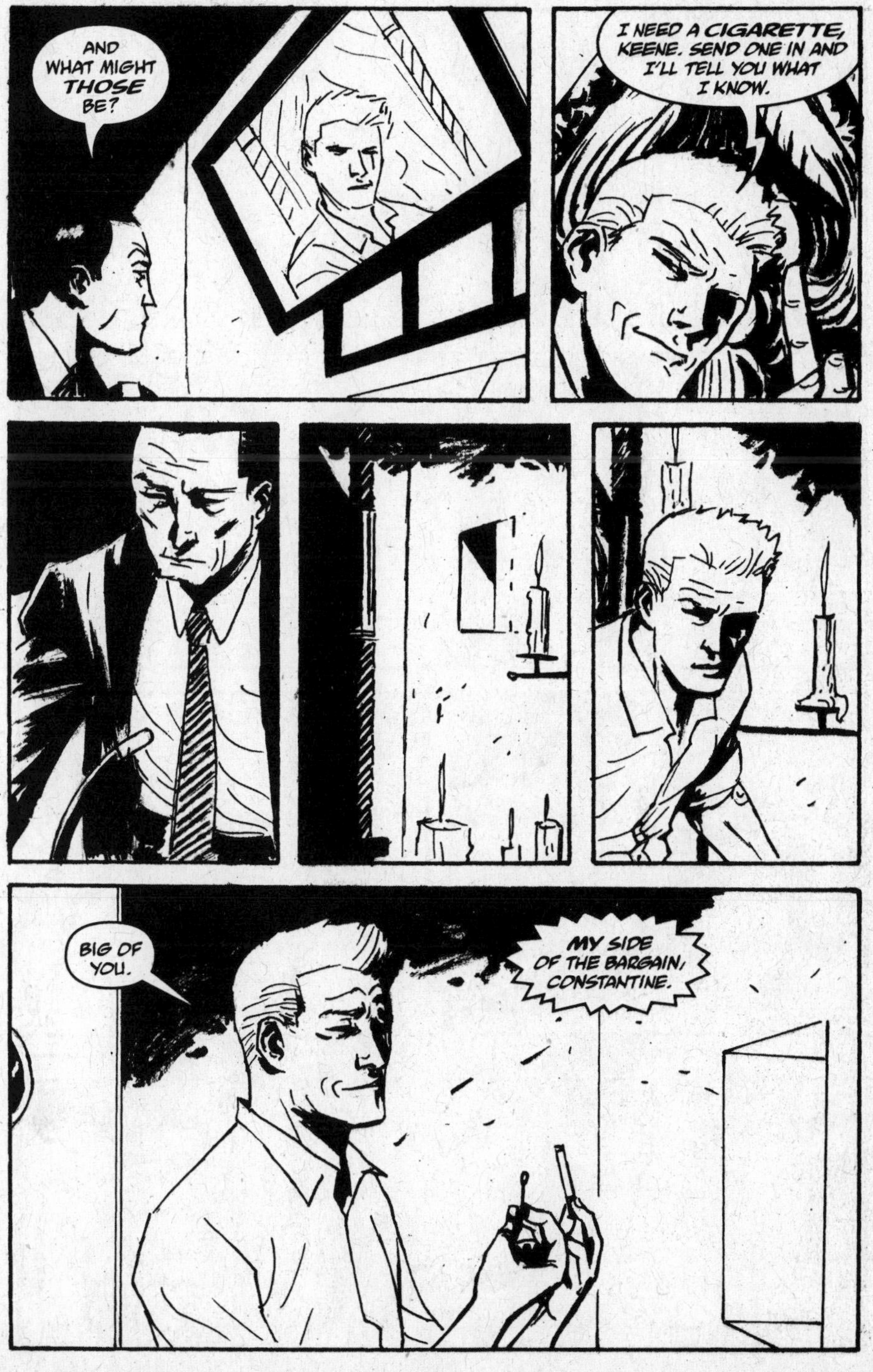
AND WHAT MIGHT THOSE BE?
I NEED A CIGARETTE, KEENE. SEND ONE IN AND I'LL TELL YOU WHAT I KNOW.
MY SIDE OF THE BARGAIN, CONSTANTINE.
BIG OF YOU.

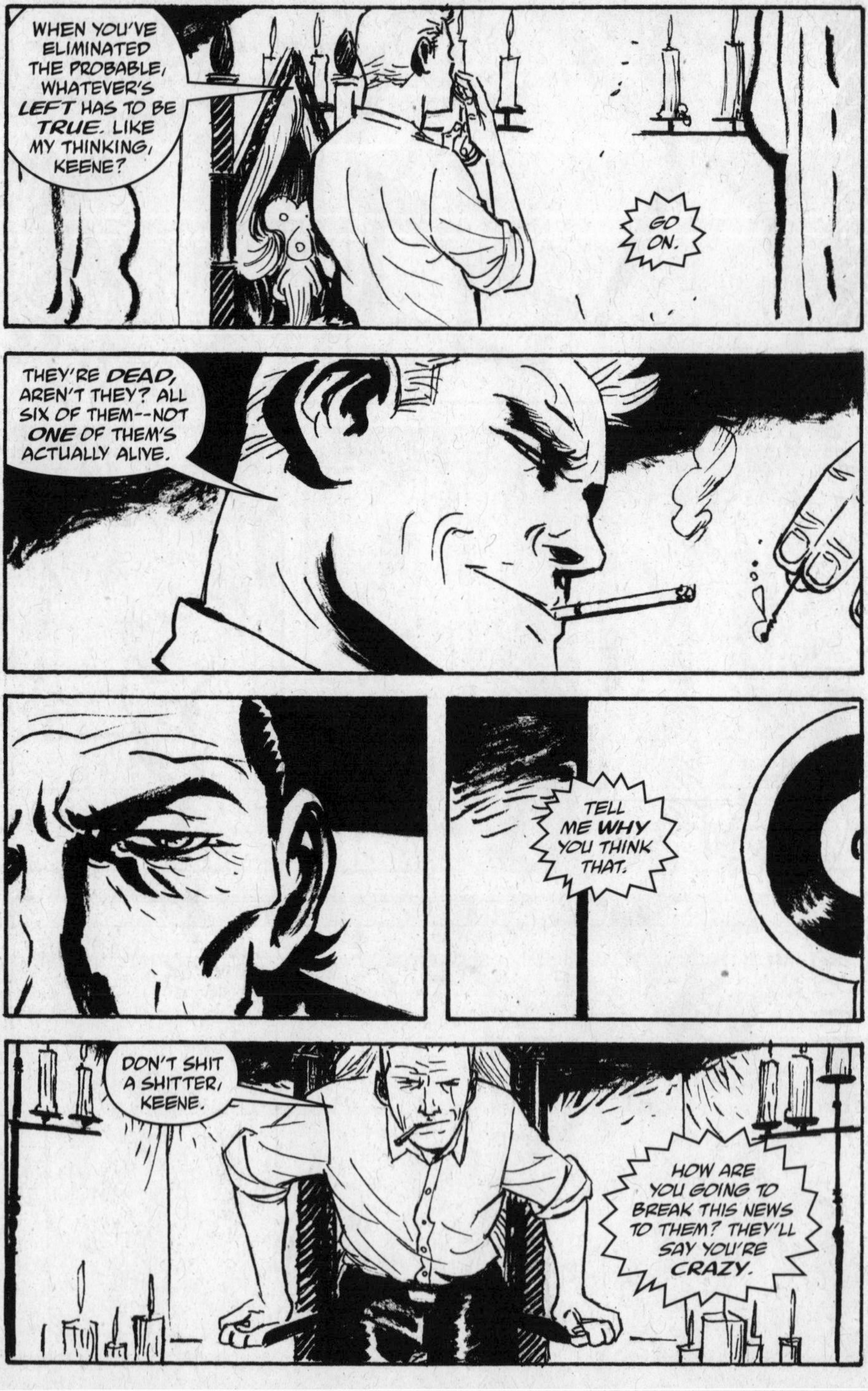
WHEN YOU'VE ELIMINATED THE PROBABLE, WHATEVER'S *LEFT* HAS TO BE *TRUE*. LIKE MY THINKING, KEENE?
GO ON.
THEY'RE *DEAD*, AREN'T THEY? ALL SIX OF THEM--NOT *ONE* OF THEM'S ACTUALLY ALIVE.
TELL ME *WHY* YOU THINK THAT.
DON'T SHIT A SHITTER, KEENE.
HOW ARE YOU GOING TO BREAK THIS NEWS TO THEM? THEY'LL SAY YOU'RE *CRAZY*.

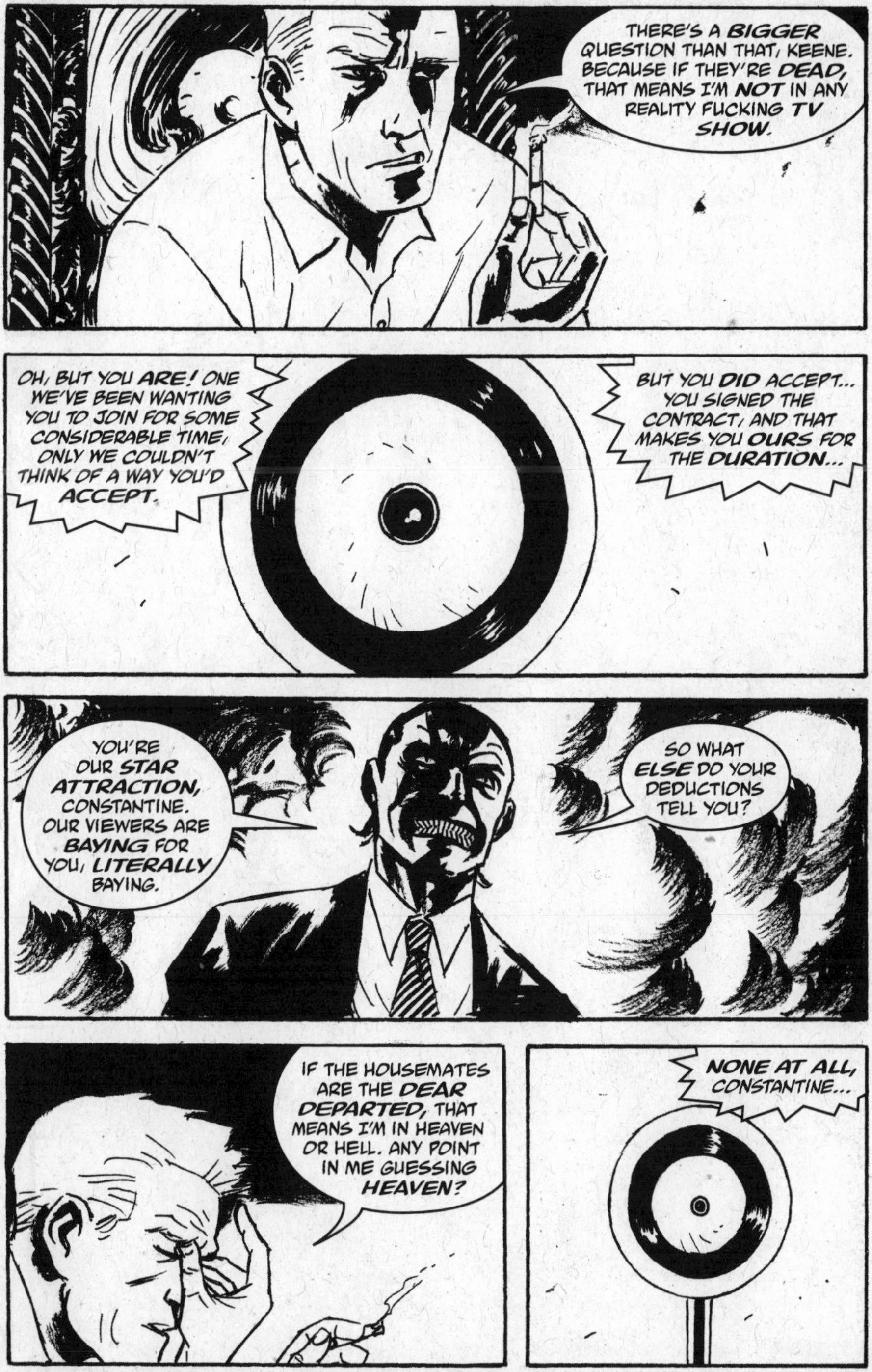
THERE'S A BIGGER QUESTION THAN THAT, KEENE. BECAUSE IF THEY'RE DEAD, THAT MEANS I'M NOT IN ANY REALITY FUCKING TV SHOW.
OH, BUT YOU ARE! ONE WE'VE BEEN WANTING YOU TO JOIN FOR SOME CONSIDERABLE TIME, ONLY WE COULDN'T THINK OF A WAY YOU'D ACCEPT.
BUT YOU DID ACCEPT... YOU SIGNED THE CONTRACT, AND THAT MAKES YOU OURS FOR THE DURATION...
YOU'RE OUR STAR ATTRACTION, CONSTANTINE. OUR VIEWERS ARE BAYING FOR YOU, LITERALLY BAYING.
SO WHAT ELSE DO YOUR DEDUCTIONS TELL YOU?
IF THE HOUSEMATES ARE THE DEAR DEPARTED, THAT MEANS I'M IN HEAVEN OR HELL. ANY POINT IN ME GUESSING HEAVEN?
NONE AT ALL, CONSTANTINE...

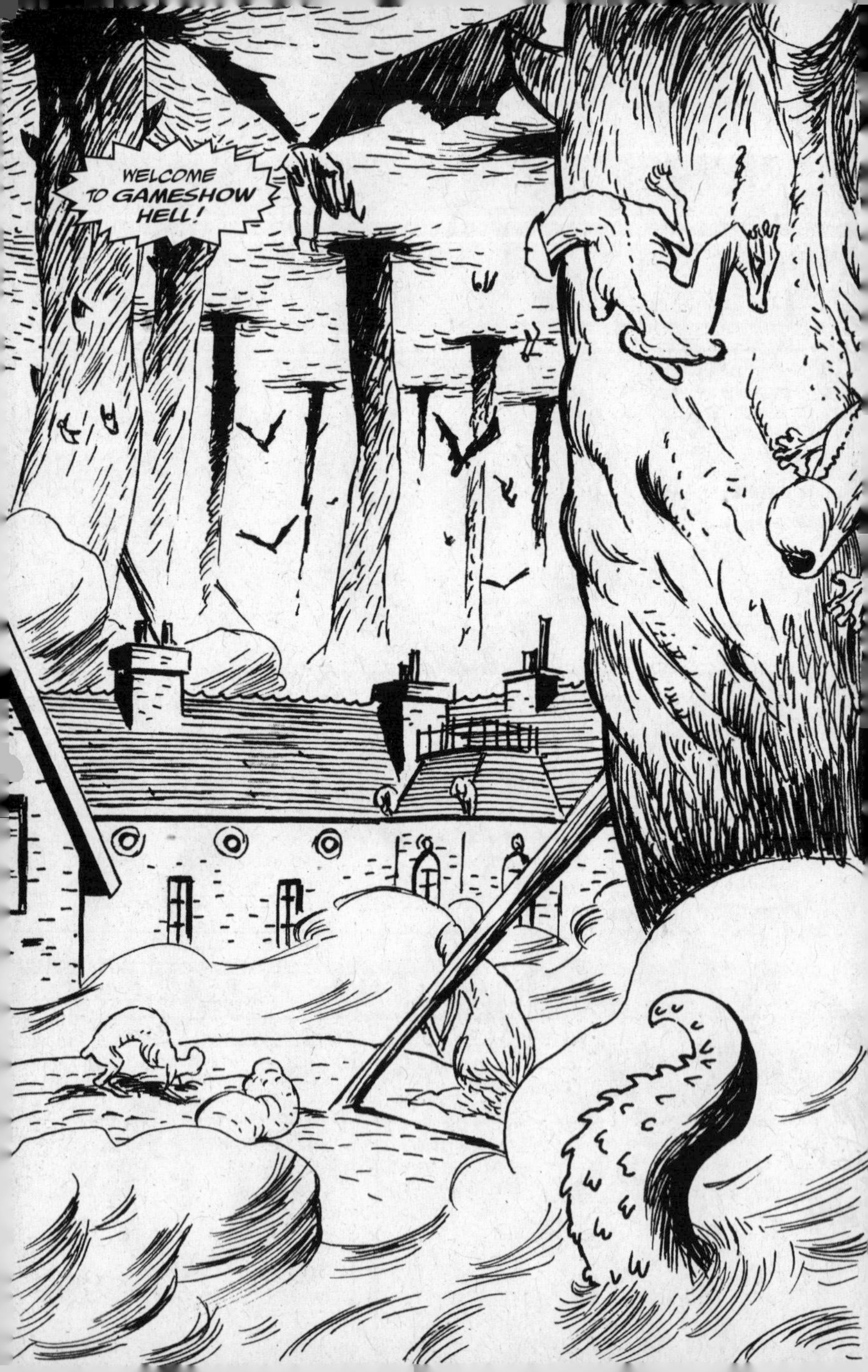
WELCOME TO GAMESHOW HELL!

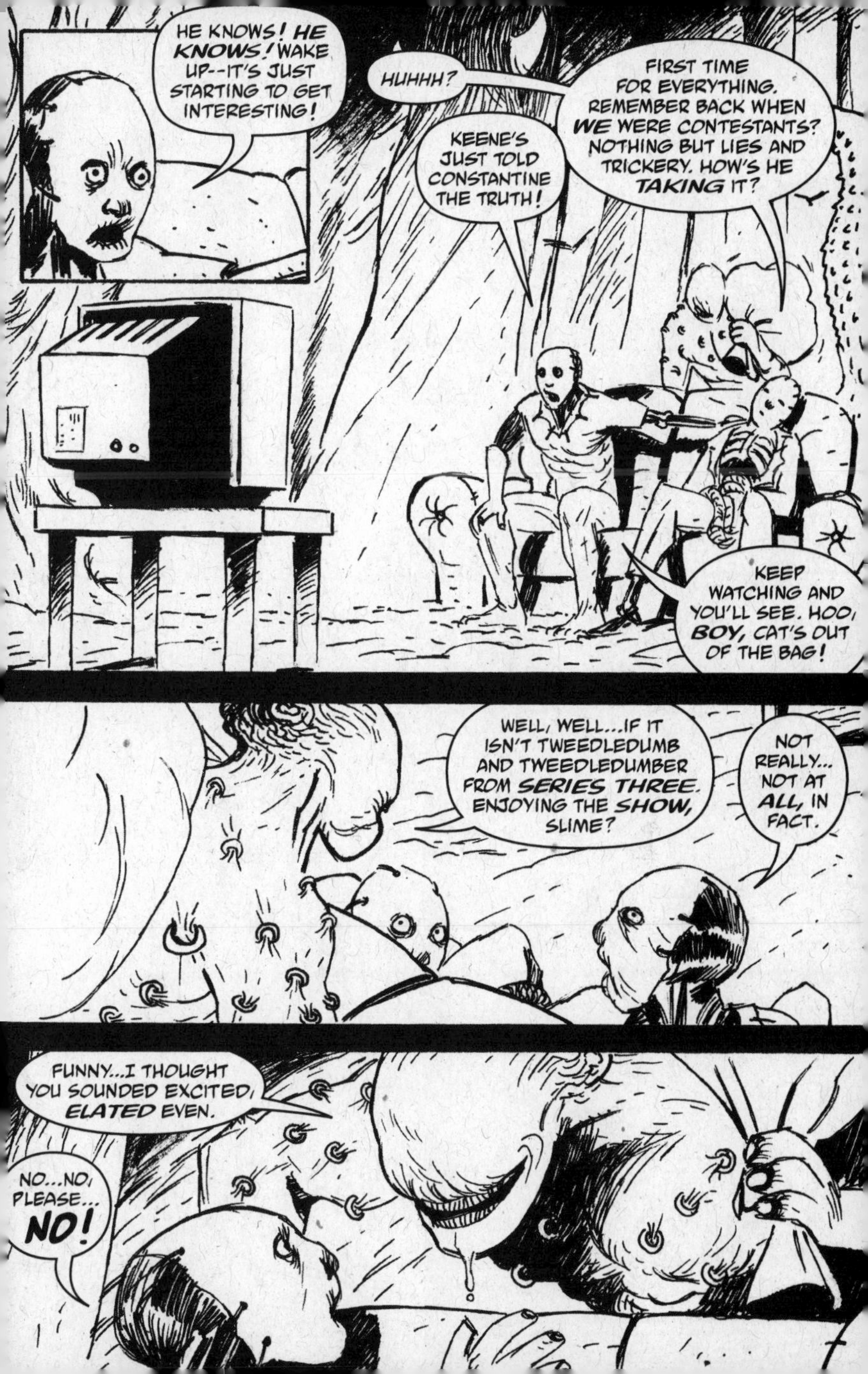
HE KNOWS! HE KNOWS! WAKE UP--IT'S JUST STARTING TO GET INTERESTING!
HUHHH?
KEENE'S JUST TOLD CONSTANTINE THE TRUTH!
FIRST TIME FOR EVERYTHING. REMEMBER BACK WHEN WE WERE CONTESTANTS? NOTHING BUT LIES AND TRICKERY. HOW'S HE TAKING IT?
KEEP WATCHING AND YOU'LL SEE. HOO, BOY, CAT'S OUT OF THE BAG!
WELL, WELL...IF IT ISN'T TWEEDLEDUMB AND TWEEDLEDUMBER FROM SERIES THREE. ENJOYING THE SHOW, SLIME?
NOT REALLY... NOT AT ALL, IN FACT.
FUNNY...I THOUGHT YOU SOUNDED EXCITED, ELATED EVEN.
NO...NO, PLEASE... NO!

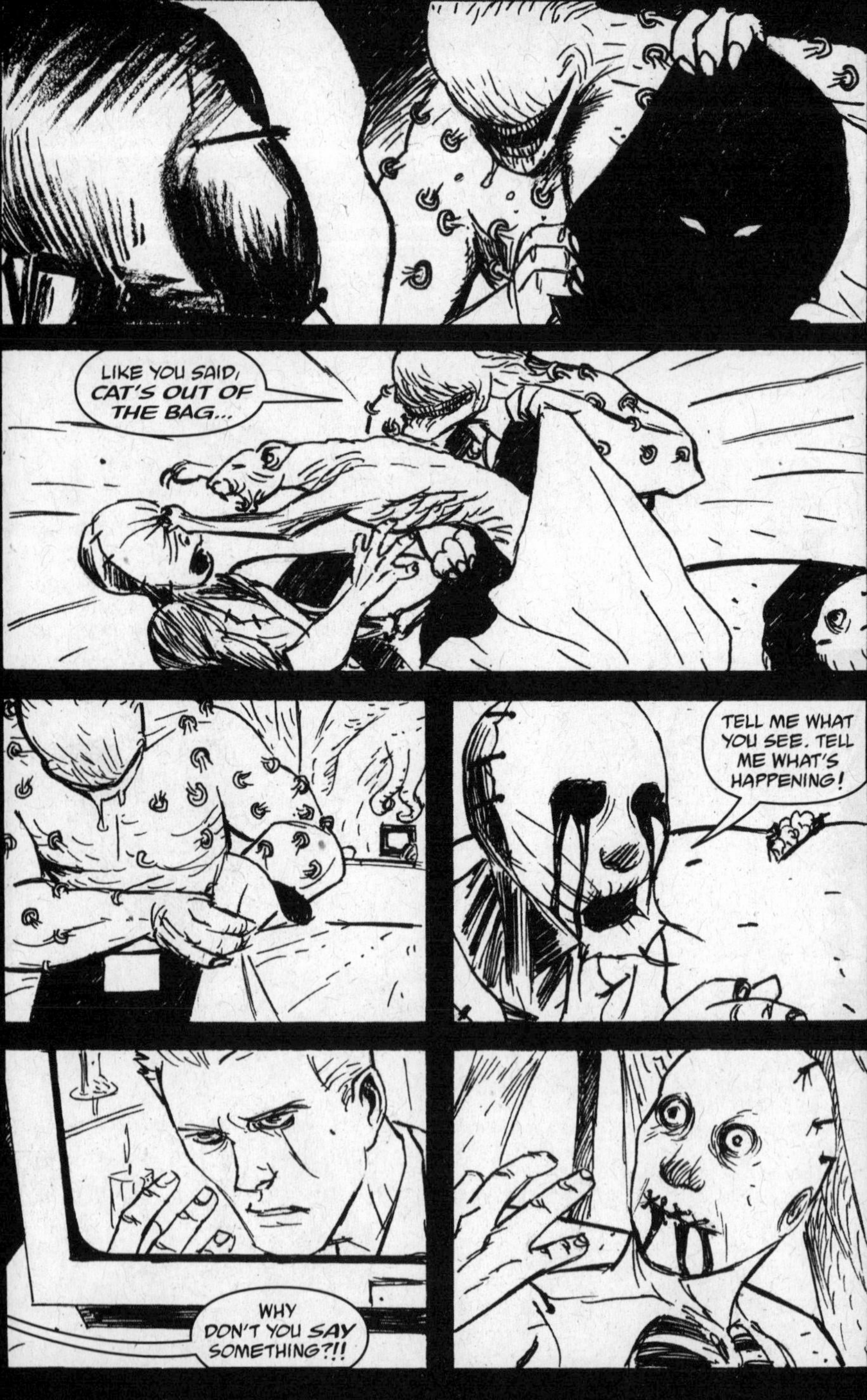
LIKE YOU SAID, CAT'S OUT OF THE BAG...
TELL ME WHAT YOU SEE. TELL ME WHAT'S HAPPENING!
WHY DON'T YOU SAY SOMETHING?!!

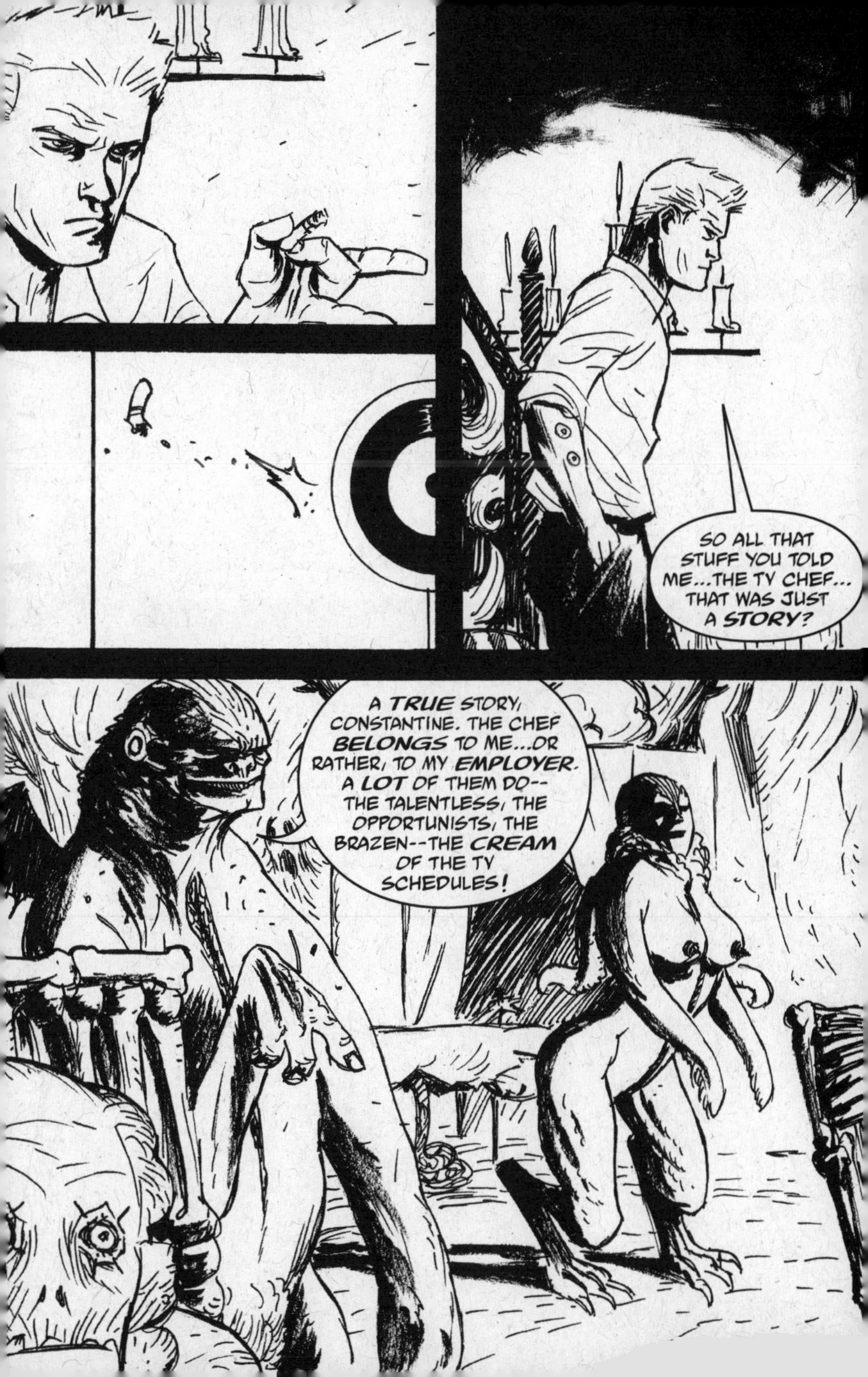

SO ALL THAT STUFF YOU TOLD ME...THE TV CHEF... THAT WAS JUST A *STORY?*
A ***TRUE*** STORY, CONSTANTINE. THE CHEF ***BELONGS*** TO ME...OR RATHER, TO MY ***EMPLOYER***. A ***LOT*** OF THEM DO-- THE TALENTLESS, THE OPPORTUNISTS, THE BRAZEN--THE ***CREAM*** OF THE TV SCHEDULES!

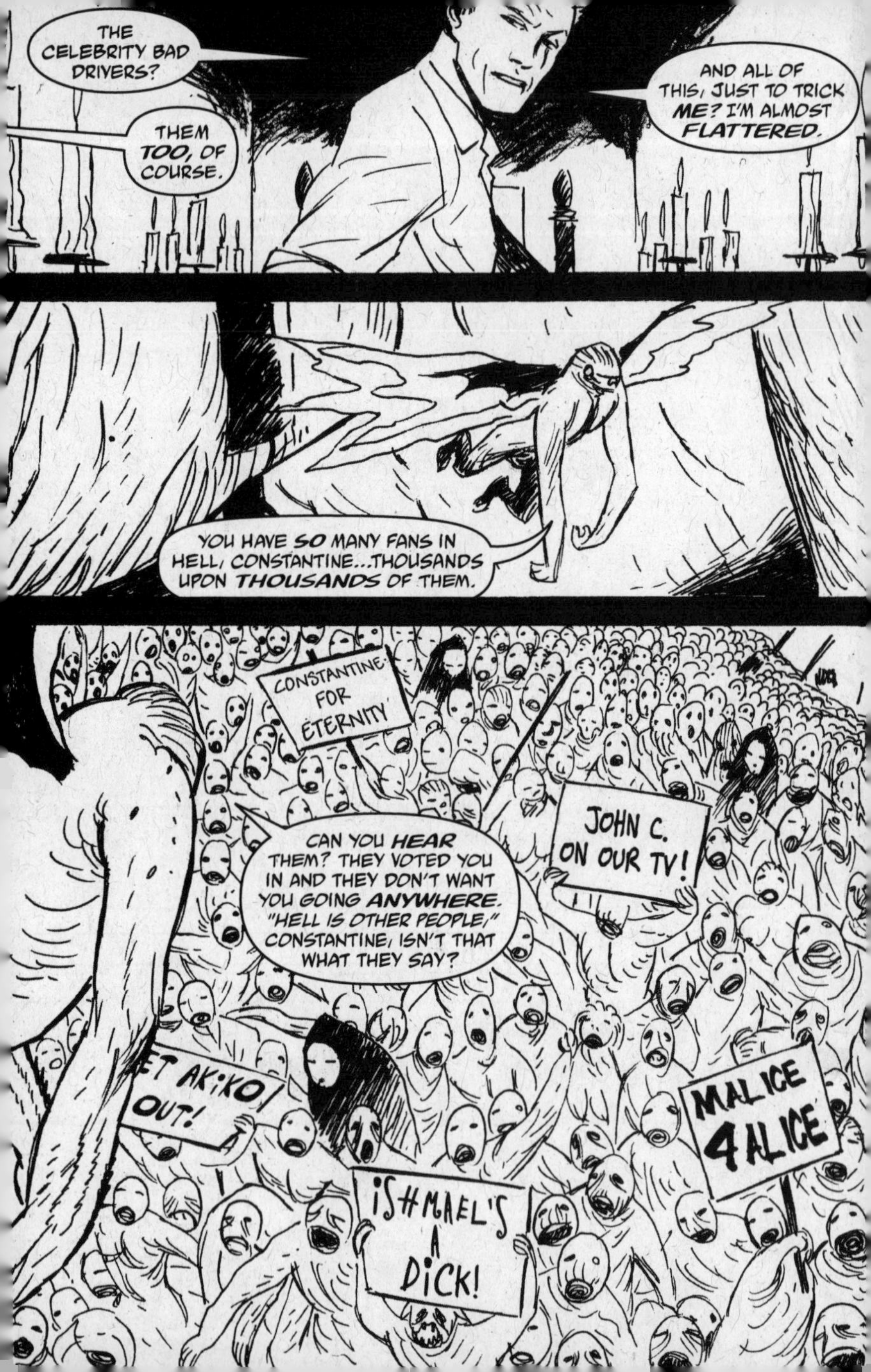
THE CELEBRITY BAD DRIVERS?
THEM TOO, OF COURSE.
AND ALL OF THIS, JUST TO TRICK ME? I'M ALMOST FLATTERED.
YOU HAVE SO MANY FANS IN HELL, CONSTANTINE...THOUSANDS UPON THOUSANDS OF THEM.
CONSTANTINE FOR ETERNITY
JOHN C. ON OUR TV!
CAN YOU HEAR THEM? THEY VOTED YOU IN AND THEY DON'T WANT YOU GOING ANYWHERE. "HELL IS OTHER PEOPLE," CONSTANTINE, ISN'T THAT WHAT THEY SAY?
AKiKO OUT!
MALICE 4 ALICE
iSHMAEL'S A DiCK!

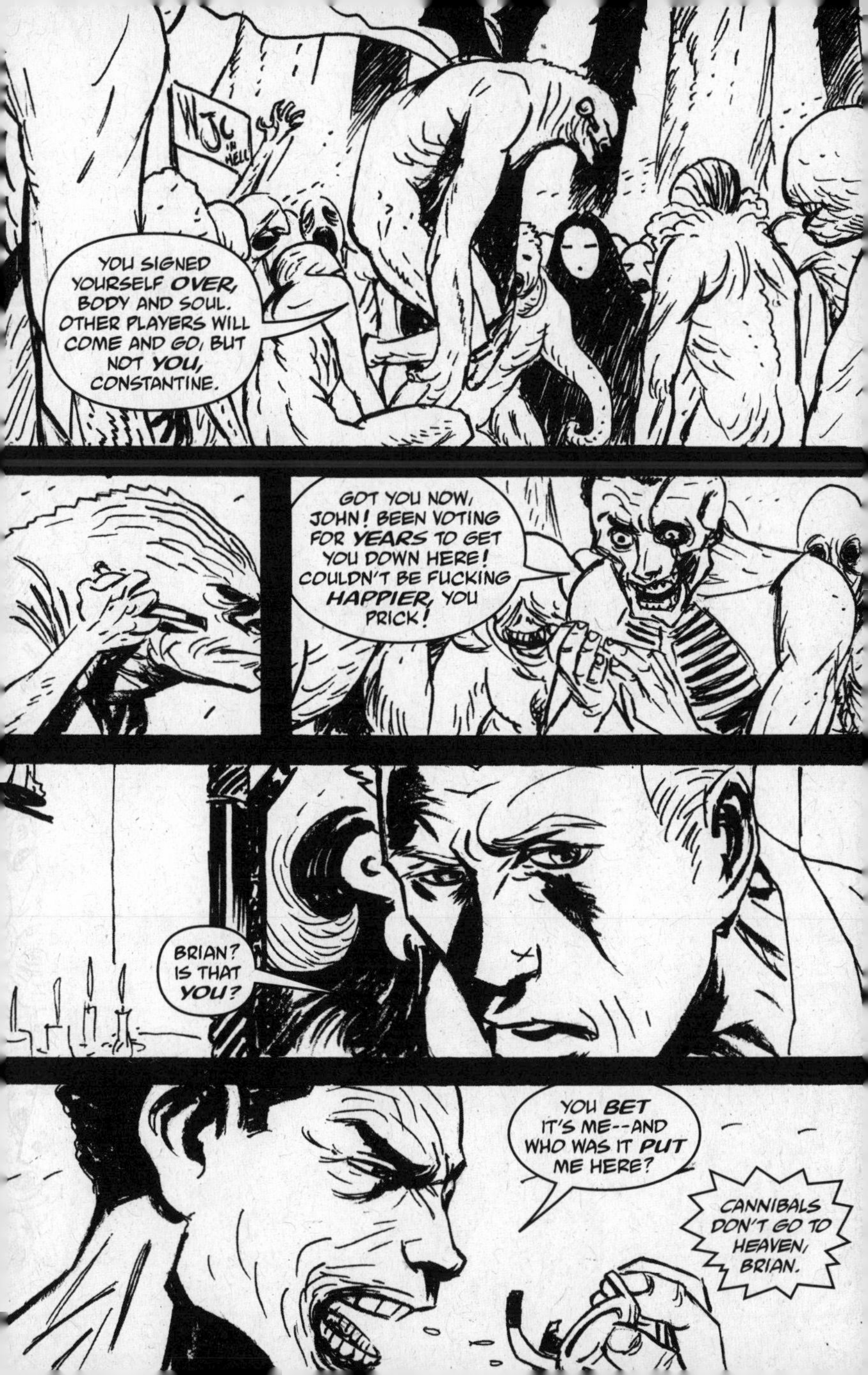
WJC IN HELL
YOU SIGNED YOURSELF OVER, BODY AND SOUL. OTHER PLAYERS WILL COME AND GO, BUT NOT YOU, CONSTANTINE.
GOT YOU NOW, JOHN! BEEN VOTING FOR YEARS TO GET YOU DOWN HERE! COULDN'T BE FUCKING HAPPIER, YOU PRICK!
BRIAN? IS THAT YOU?
YOU BET IT'S ME--AND WHO WAS IT PUT ME HERE?
CANNIBALS DON'T GO TO HEAVEN, BRIAN.

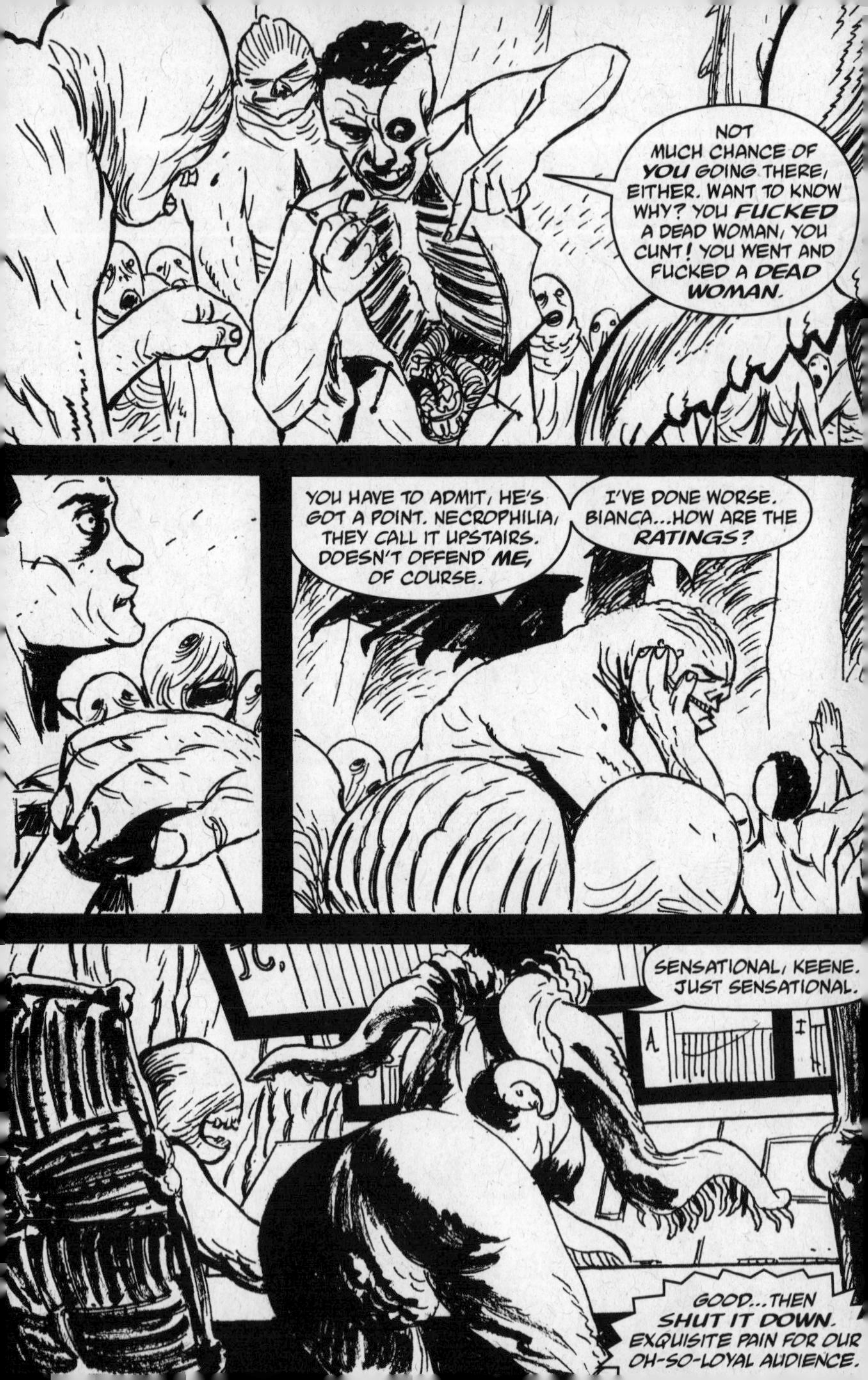
NOT MUCH CHANCE OF YOU GOING THERE, EITHER. WANT TO KNOW WHY? YOU FUCKED A DEAD WOMAN, YOU CUNT! YOU WENT AND FUCKED A DEAD WOMAN.
YOU HAVE TO ADMIT, HE'S GOT A POINT. NECROPHILIA, THEY CALL IT UPSTAIRS. DOESN'T OFFEND ME, OF COURSE.
I'VE DONE WORSE. BIANCA...HOW ARE THE RATINGS?
SENSATIONAL, KEENE. JUST SENSATIONAL.
GOOD...THEN SHUT IT DOWN. EXQUISITE PAIN FOR OUR OH-SO-LOYAL AUDIENCE.

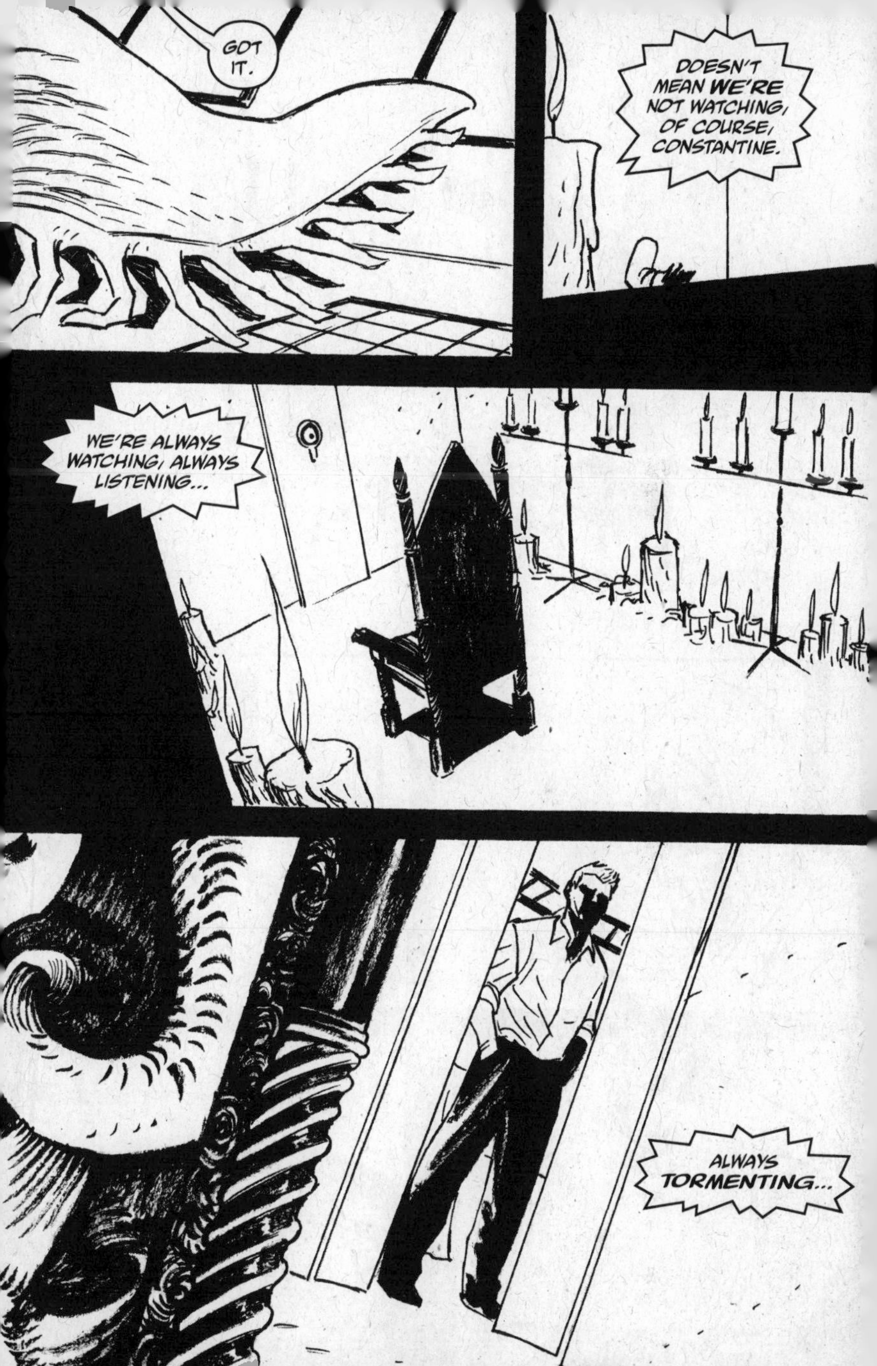
GOT IT.
DOESN'T MEAN WE'RE NOT WATCHING, OF COURSE, CONSTANTINE.
WE'RE ALWAYS WATCHING, ALWAYS LISTENING...
ALWAYS TORMENTING...

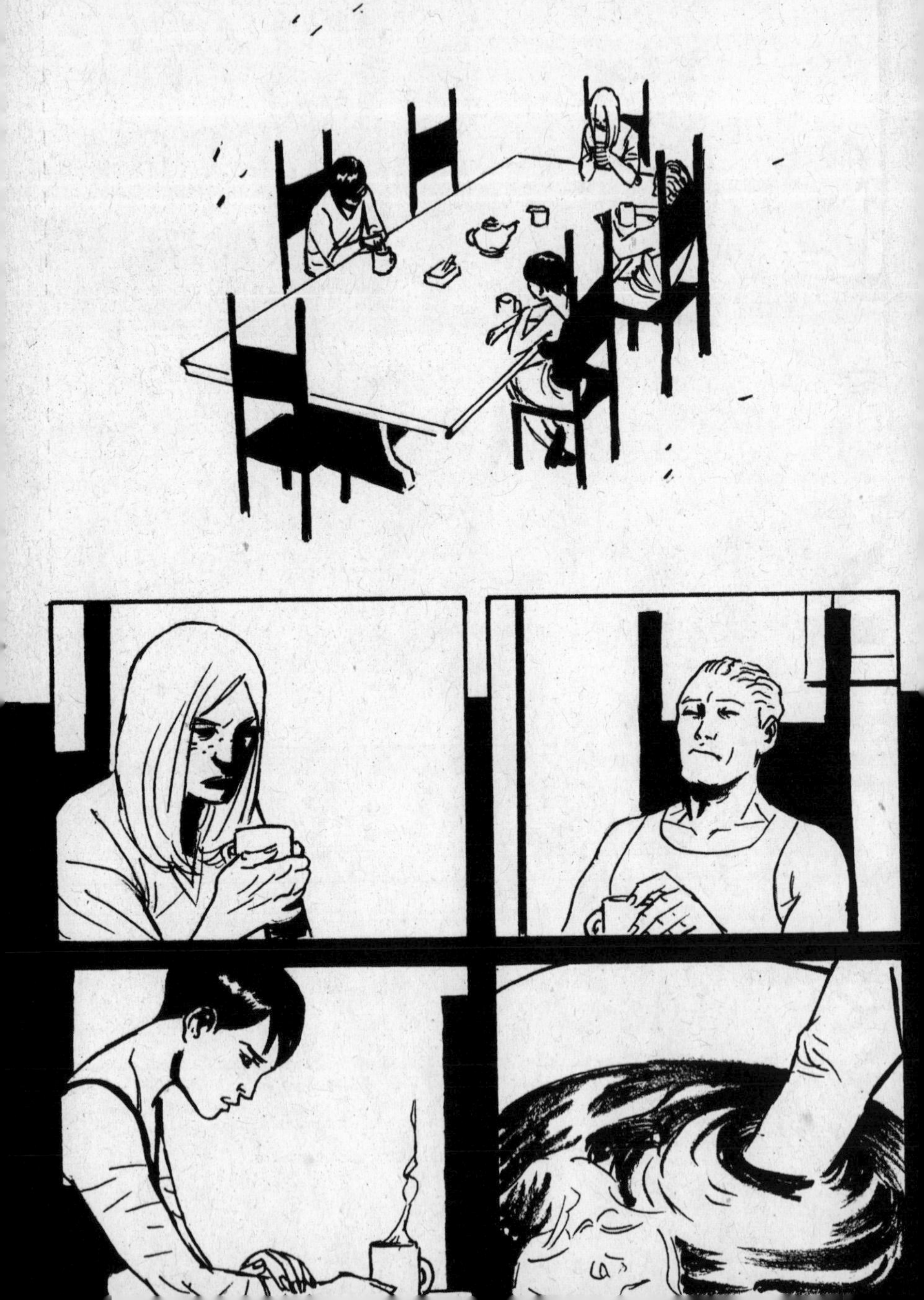

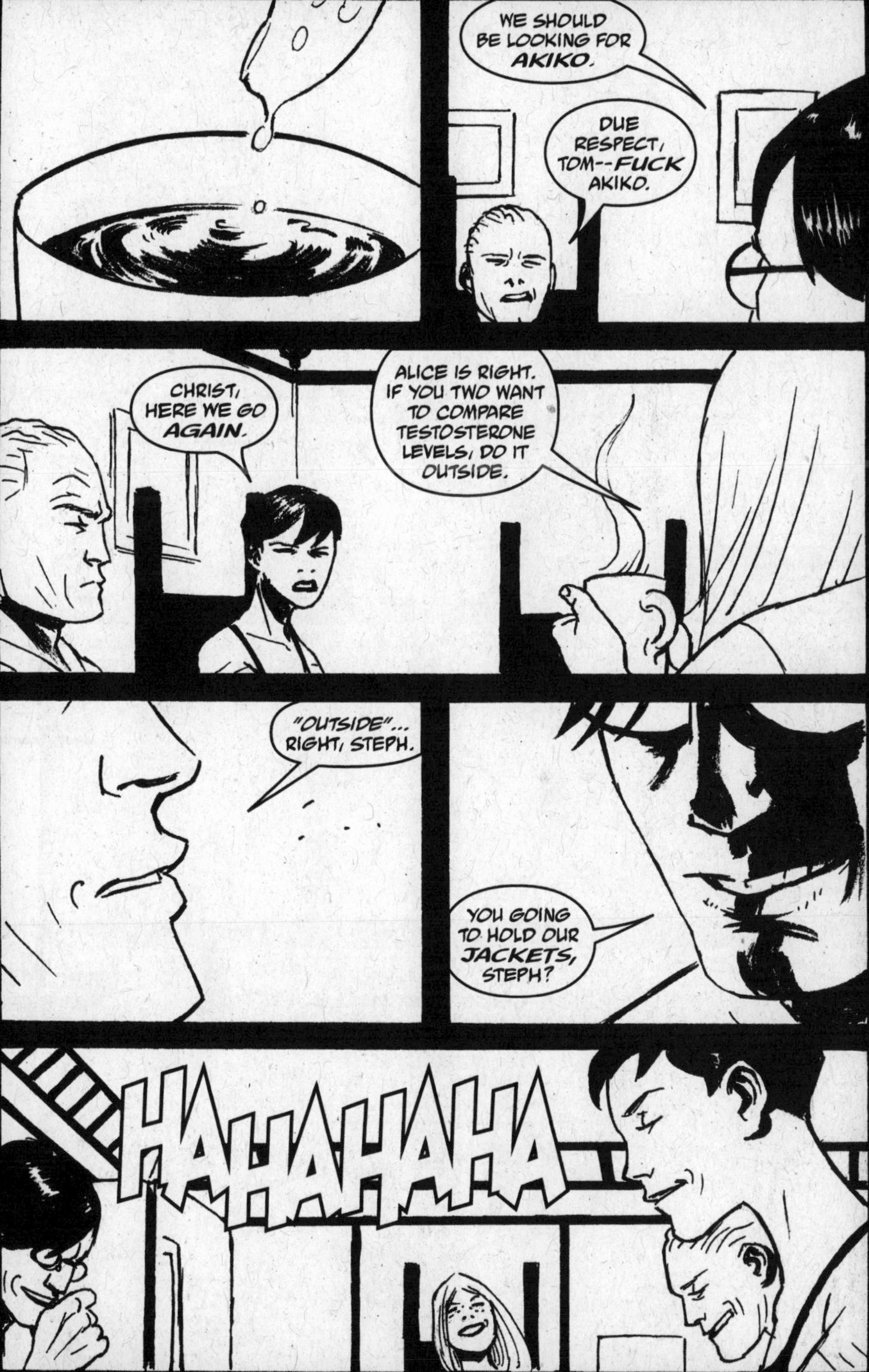
WE SHOULD BE LOOKING FOR AKIKO.
DUE RESPECT, TOM--FUCK AKIKO.
CHRIST, HERE WE GO AGAIN.
ALICE IS RIGHT. IF YOU TWO WANT TO COMPARE TESTOSTERONE LEVELS, DO IT OUTSIDE.
"OUTSIDE"... RIGHT, STEPH.
YOU GOING TO HOLD OUR JACKETS, STEPH?
HAHAHAHA

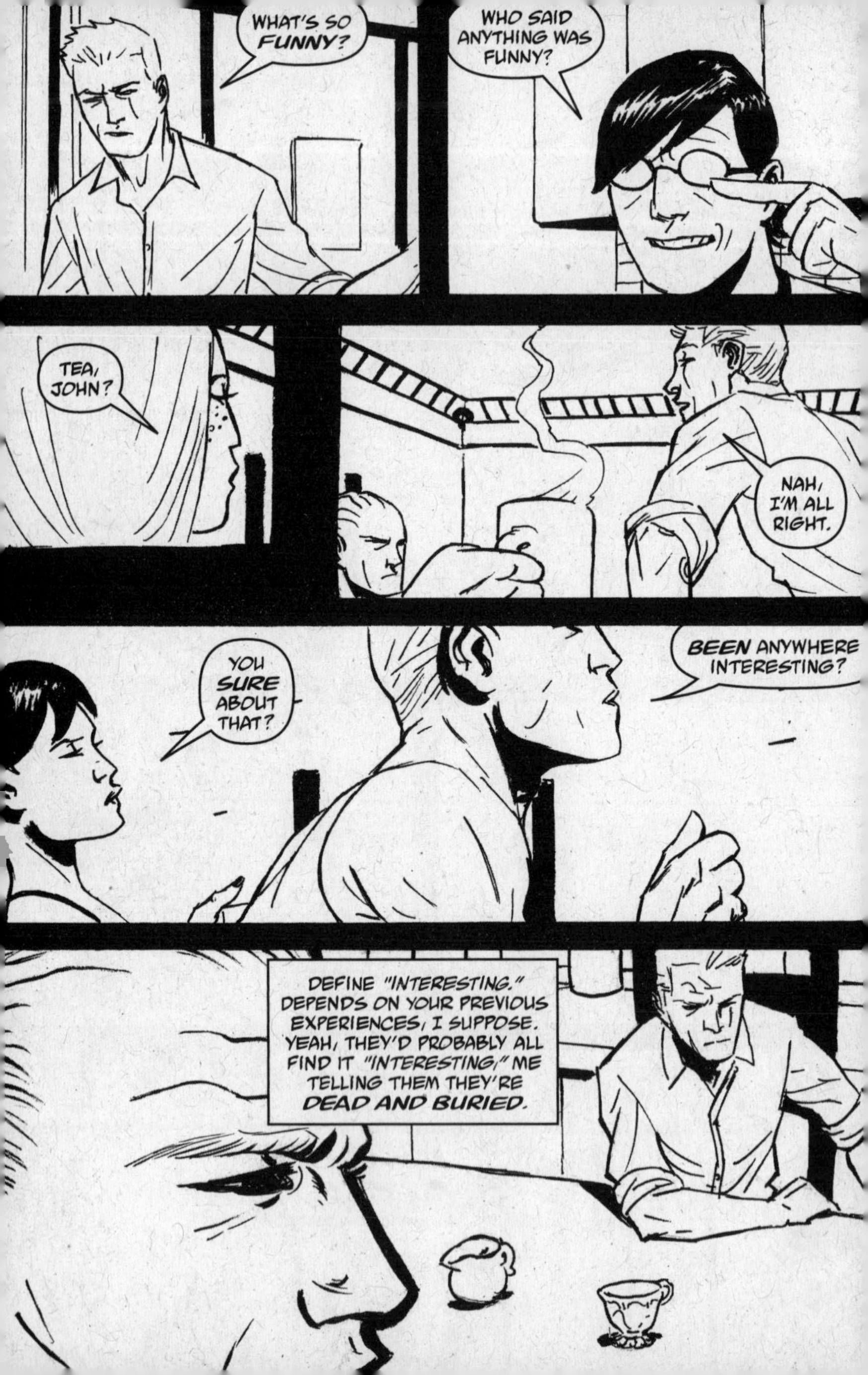
WHAT'S SO FUNNY?
WHO SAID ANYTHING WAS FUNNY?
TEA, JOHN?
NAH, I'M ALL RIGHT.
YOU SURE ABOUT THAT?
BEEN ANYWHERE INTERESTING?
DEFINE "INTERESTING." DEPENDS ON YOUR PREVIOUS EXPERIENCES, I SUPPOSE. YEAH, THEY'D PROBABLY ALL FIND IT "INTERESTING," ME TELLING THEM THEY'RE DEAD AND BURIED.

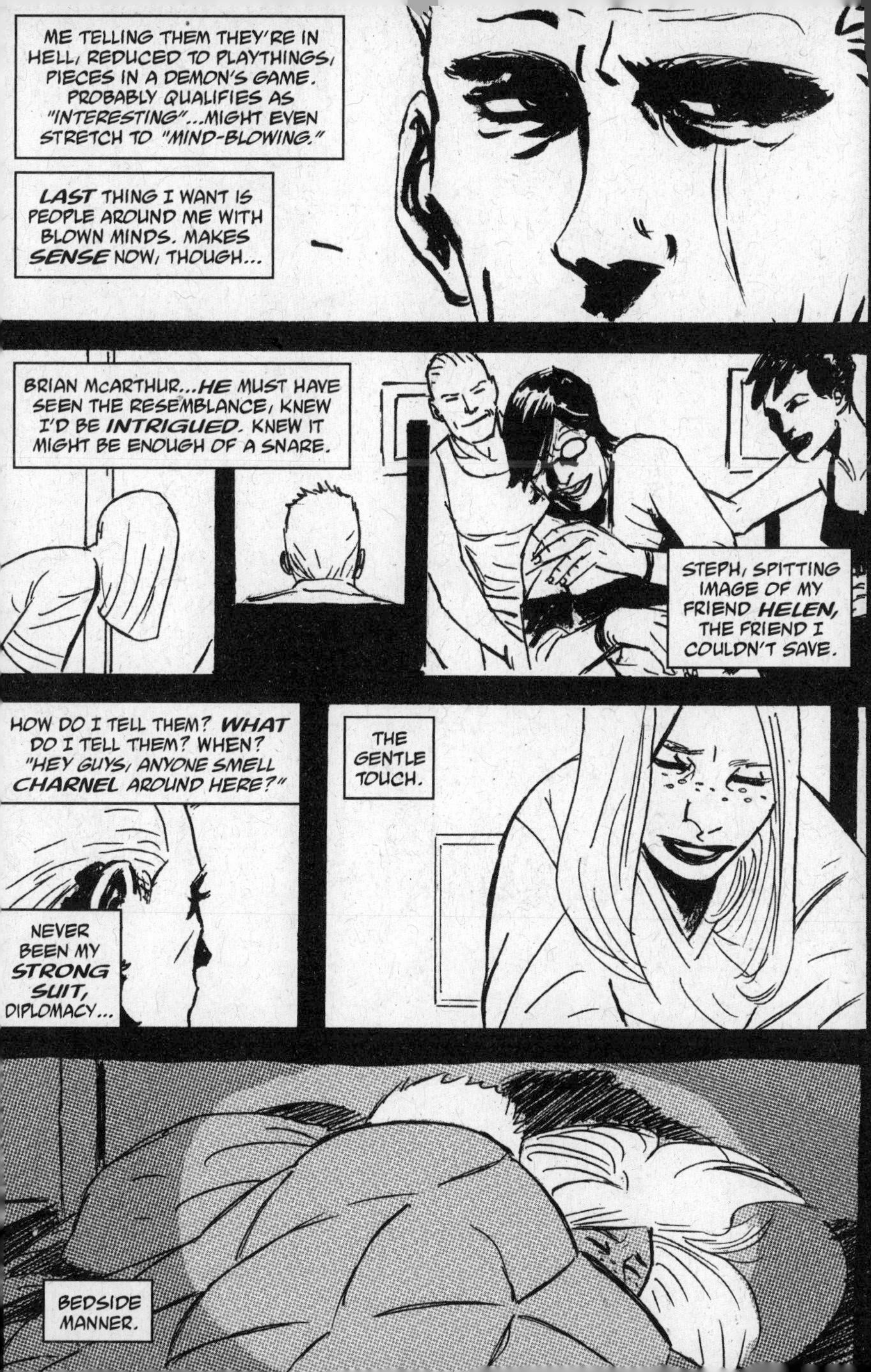
ME TELLING THEM THEY'RE IN HELL, REDUCED TO PLAYTHINGS, PIECES IN A DEMON'S GAME. PROBABLY QUALIFIES AS "INTERESTING"...MIGHT EVEN STRETCH TO "MIND-BLOWING."
LAST THING I WANT IS PEOPLE AROUND ME WITH BLOWN MINDS. MAKES SENSE NOW, THOUGH...
BRIAN McARTHUR...HE MUST HAVE SEEN THE RESEMBLANCE, KNEW I'D BE INTRIGUED. KNEW IT MIGHT BE ENOUGH OF A SNARE.
STEPH, SPITTING IMAGE OF MY FRIEND HELEN, THE FRIEND I COULDN'T SAVE.
HOW DO I TELL THEM? WHAT DO I TELL THEM? WHEN? "HEY GUYS, ANYONE SMELL CHARNEL AROUND HERE?"
NEVER BEEN MY STRONG SUIT, DIPLOMACY...
THE GENTLE TOUCH.
BEDSIDE MANNER.

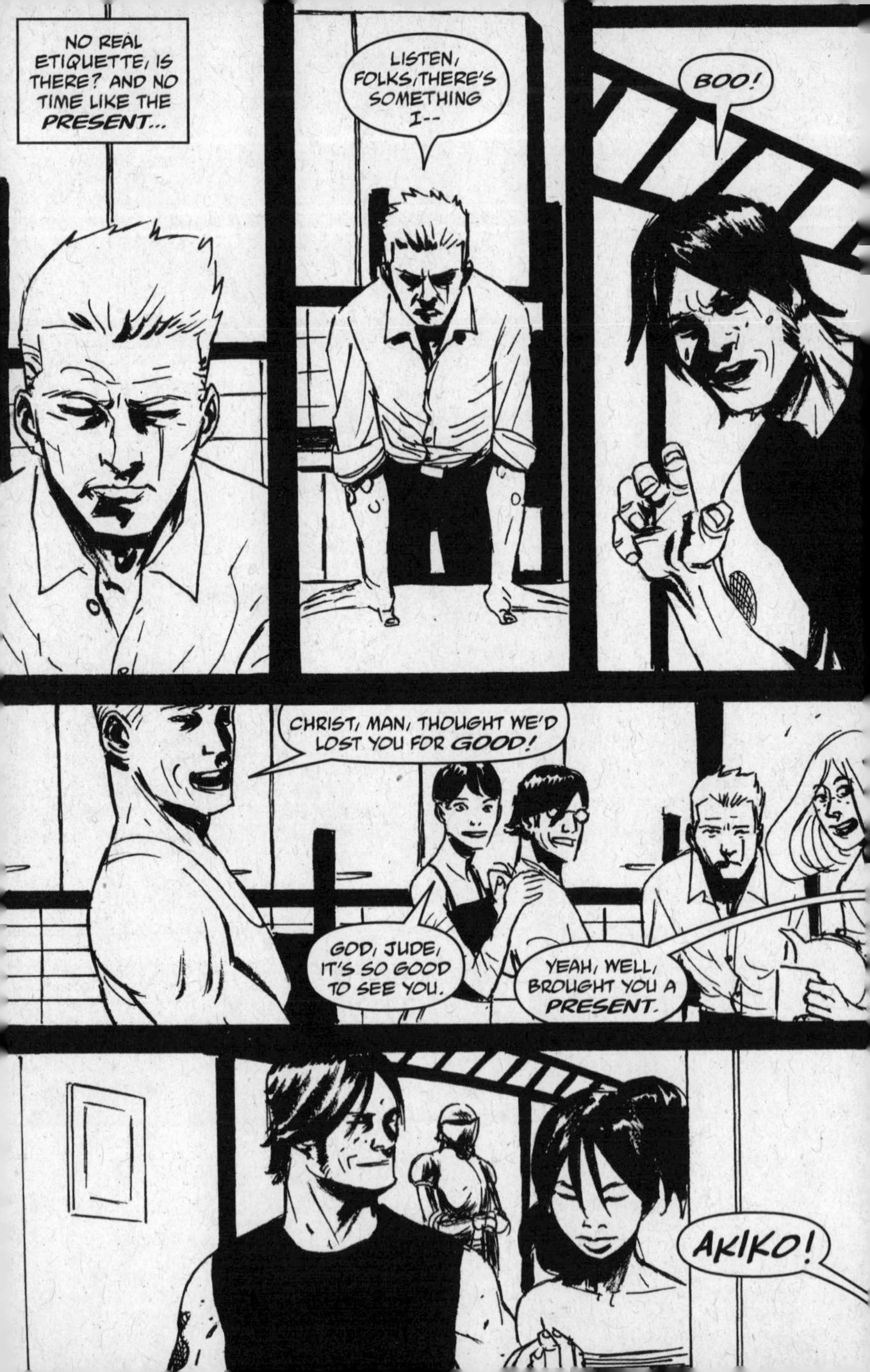
NO REAL ETIQUETTE, IS THERE? AND NO TIME LIKE THE PRESENT...
LISTEN, FOLKS, THERE'S SOMETHING I--
BOO!
CHRIST, MAN, THOUGHT WE'D LOST YOU FOR GOOD!
GOD, JUDE, IT'S SO GOOD TO SEE YOU.
YEAH, WELL, BROUGHT YOU A PRESENT.
AKIKO!

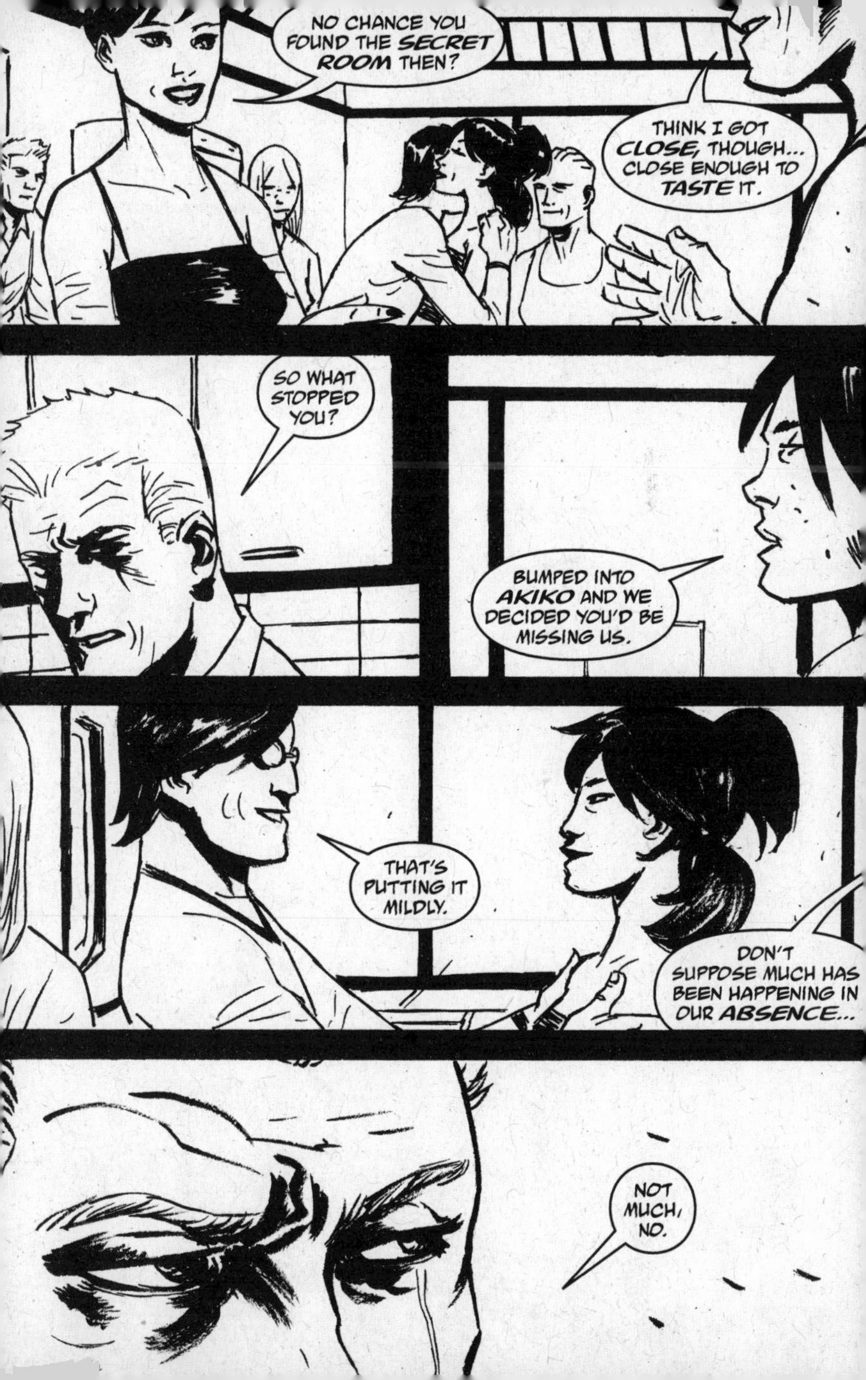
NO CHANCE YOU FOUND THE SECRET ROOM THEN?
THINK I GOT CLOSE, THOUGH... CLOSE ENOUGH TO TASTE IT.
SO WHAT STOPPED YOU?
BUMPED INTO AKIKO AND WE DECIDED YOU'D BE MISSING US.
THAT'S PUTTING IT MILDLY.
DON'T SUPPOSE MUCH HAS BEEN HAPPENING IN OUR ABSENCE...
NOT MUCH, NO.

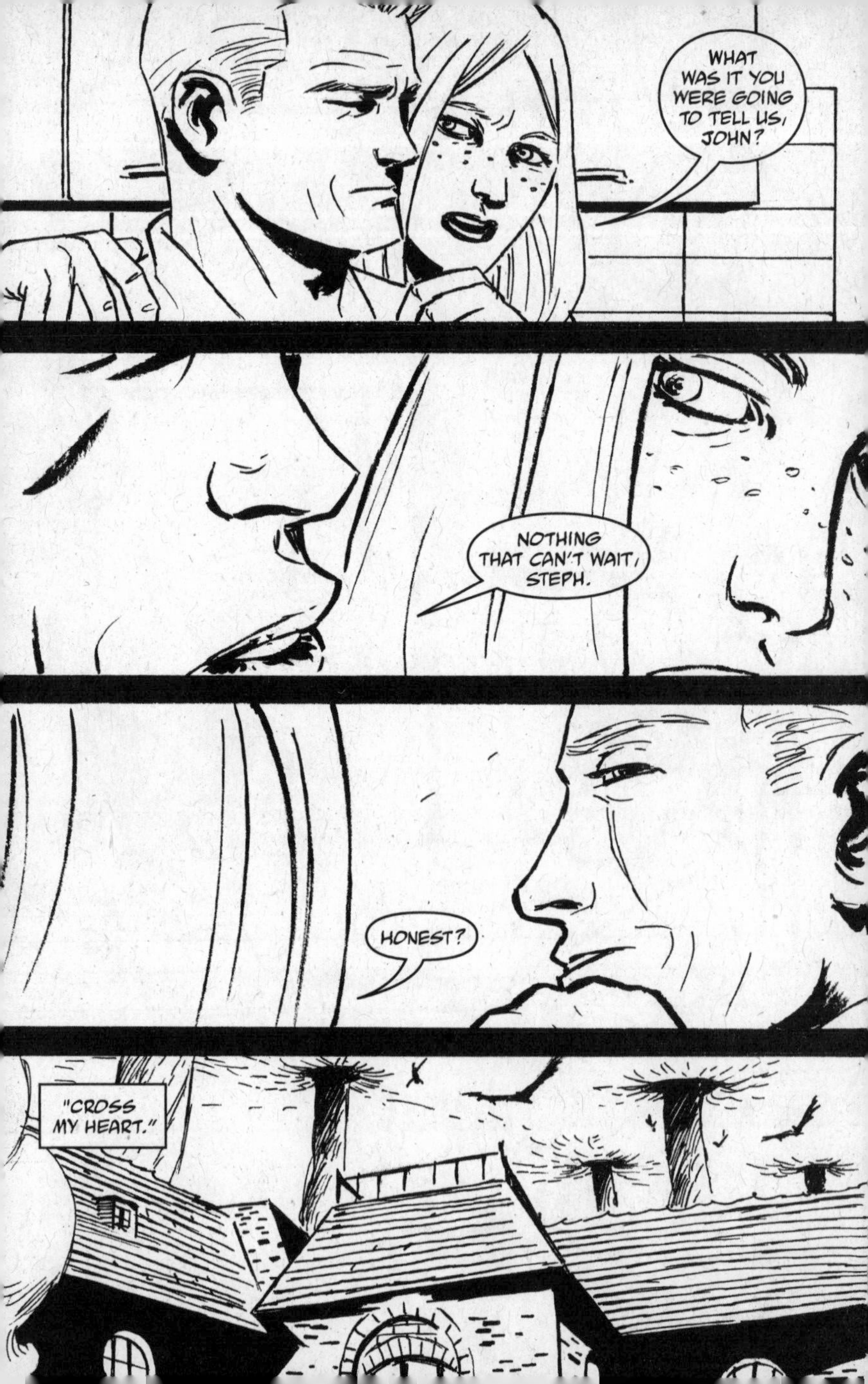
WHAT WAS IT YOU WERE GOING TO TELL US, JOHN?
NOTHING THAT CAN'T WAIT, STEPH.
HONEST?
"CROSS MY HEART."

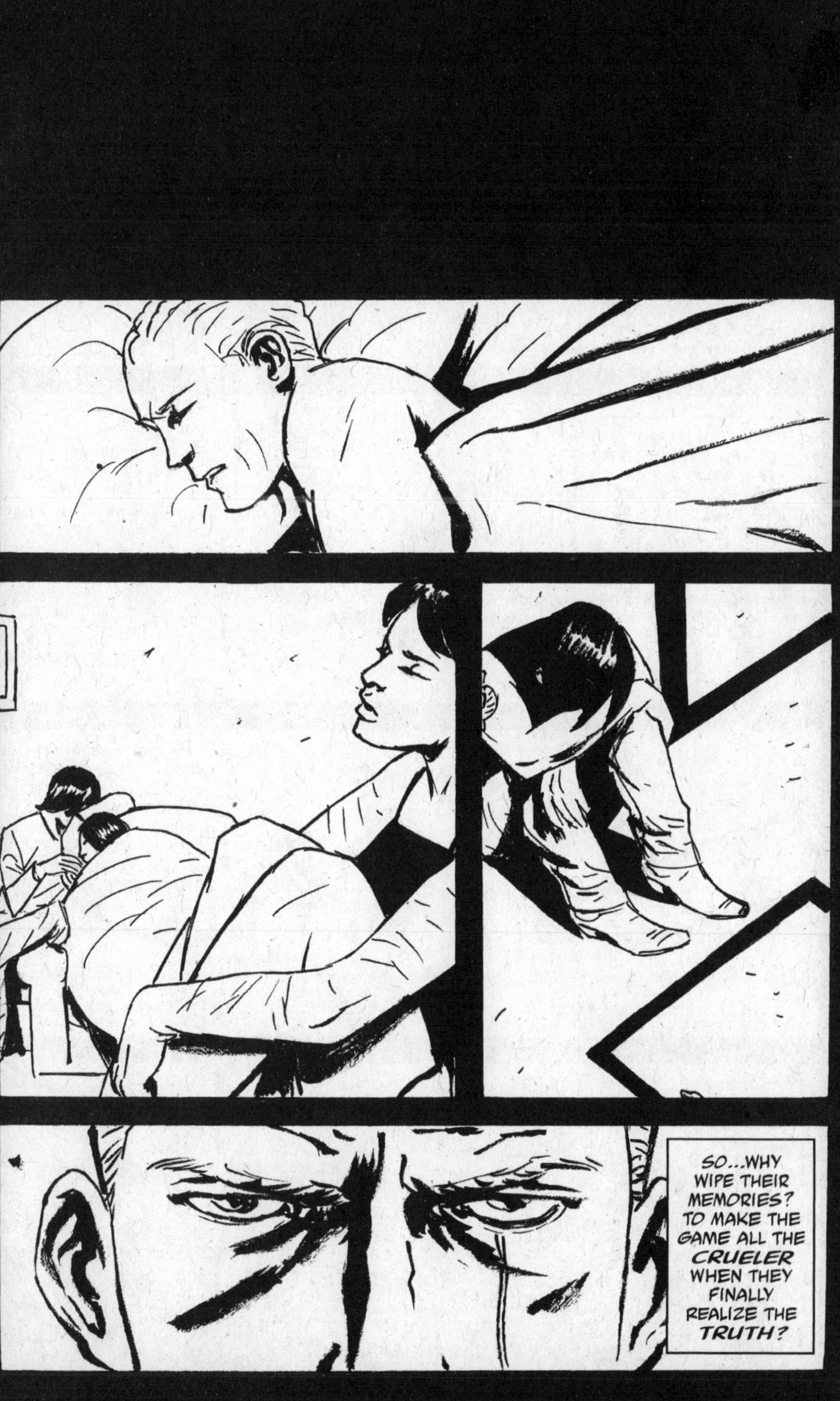

SO...WHY WIPE THEIR MEMORIES? TO MAKE THE GAME ALL THE CRUELER WHEN THEY FINALLY REALIZE THE TRUTH?

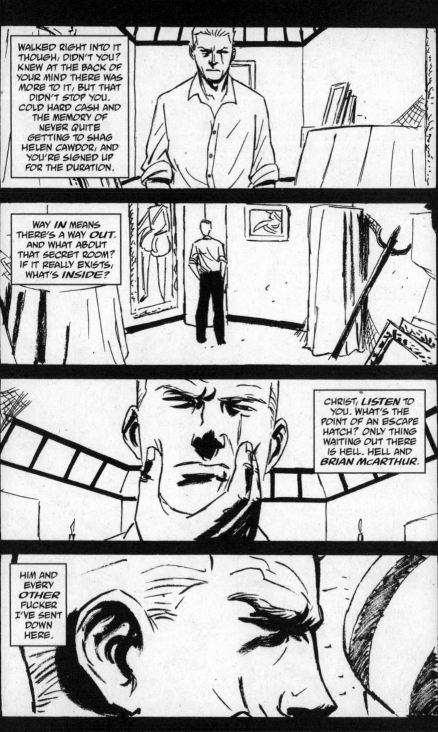

WALKED RIGHT INTO IT THOUGH, DIDN'T YOU? KNEW AT THE BACK OF YOUR MIND THERE WAS MORE TO IT, BUT THAT DIDN'T STOP YOU. COLD HARD CASH AND THE MEMORY OF NEVER QUITE GETTING TO SHAG HELEN CAWDOR, AND YOU'RE SIGNED UP FOR THE DURATION.

WAY *IN* MEANS THERE'S A WAY *OUT*. AND WHAT ABOUT THAT SECRET ROOM? IF IT REALLY EXISTS, WHAT'S *INSIDE*?

CHRIST, *LISTEN* TO YOU. WHAT'S THE POINT OF AN ESCAPE HATCH? ONLY THING WAITING OUT THERE IS HELL. HELL AND *BRIAN McARTHUR*.

HIM AND EVERY *OTHER* FUCKER I'VE SENT DOWN HERE.

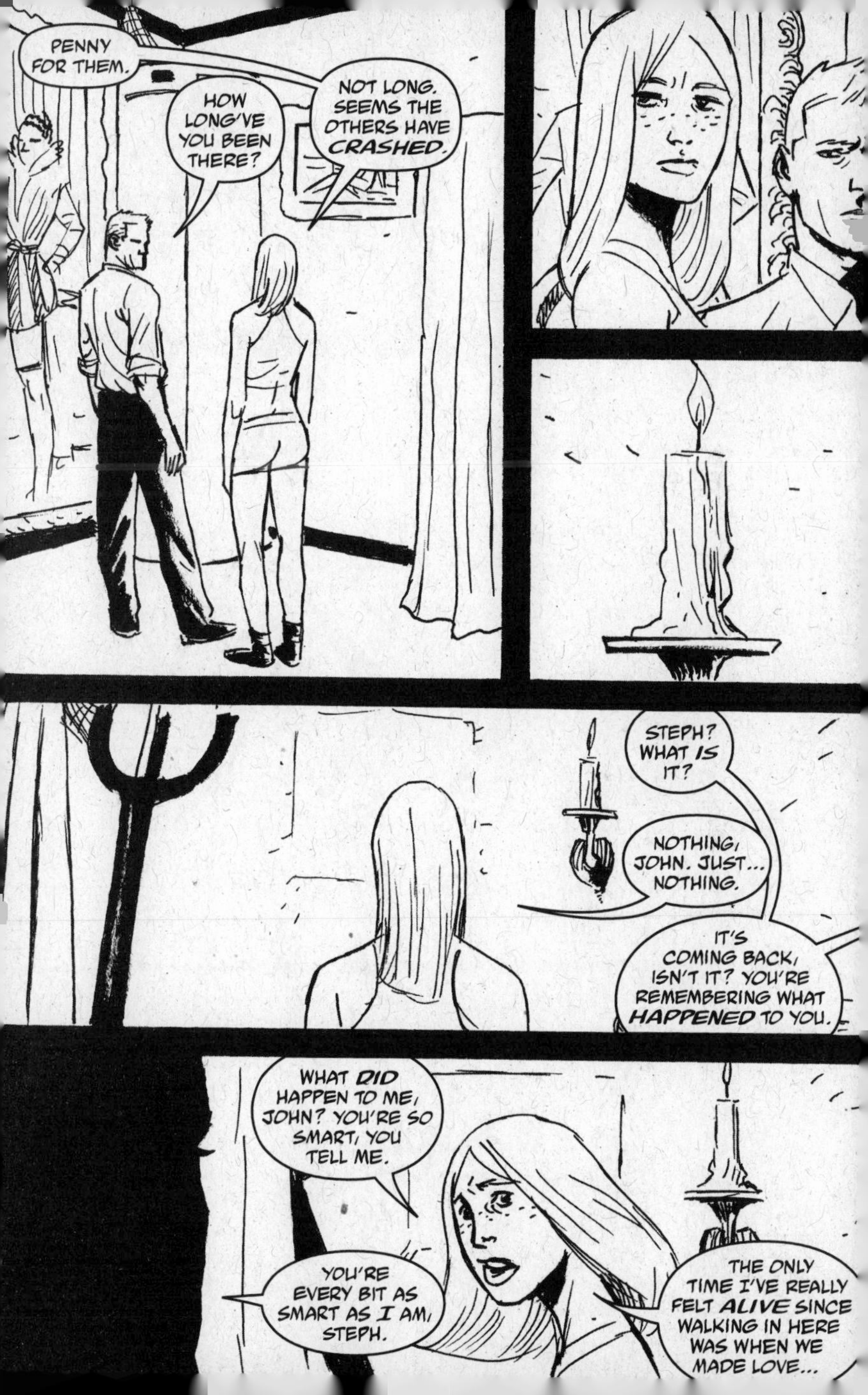
PENNY FOR THEM.
HOW LONG'VE YOU BEEN THERE?
NOT LONG. SEEMS THE OTHERS HAVE CRASHED.
STEPH? WHAT IS IT?
NOTHING, JOHN. JUST... NOTHING.
IT'S COMING BACK, ISN'T IT? YOU'RE REMEMBERING WHAT HAPPENED TO YOU.
WHAT DID HAPPEN TO ME, JOHN? YOU'RE SO SMART, YOU TELL ME.
YOU'RE EVERY BIT AS SMART AS I AM, STEPH.
THE ONLY TIME I'VE REALLY FELT ALIVE SINCE WALKING IN HERE WAS WHEN WE MADE LOVE...

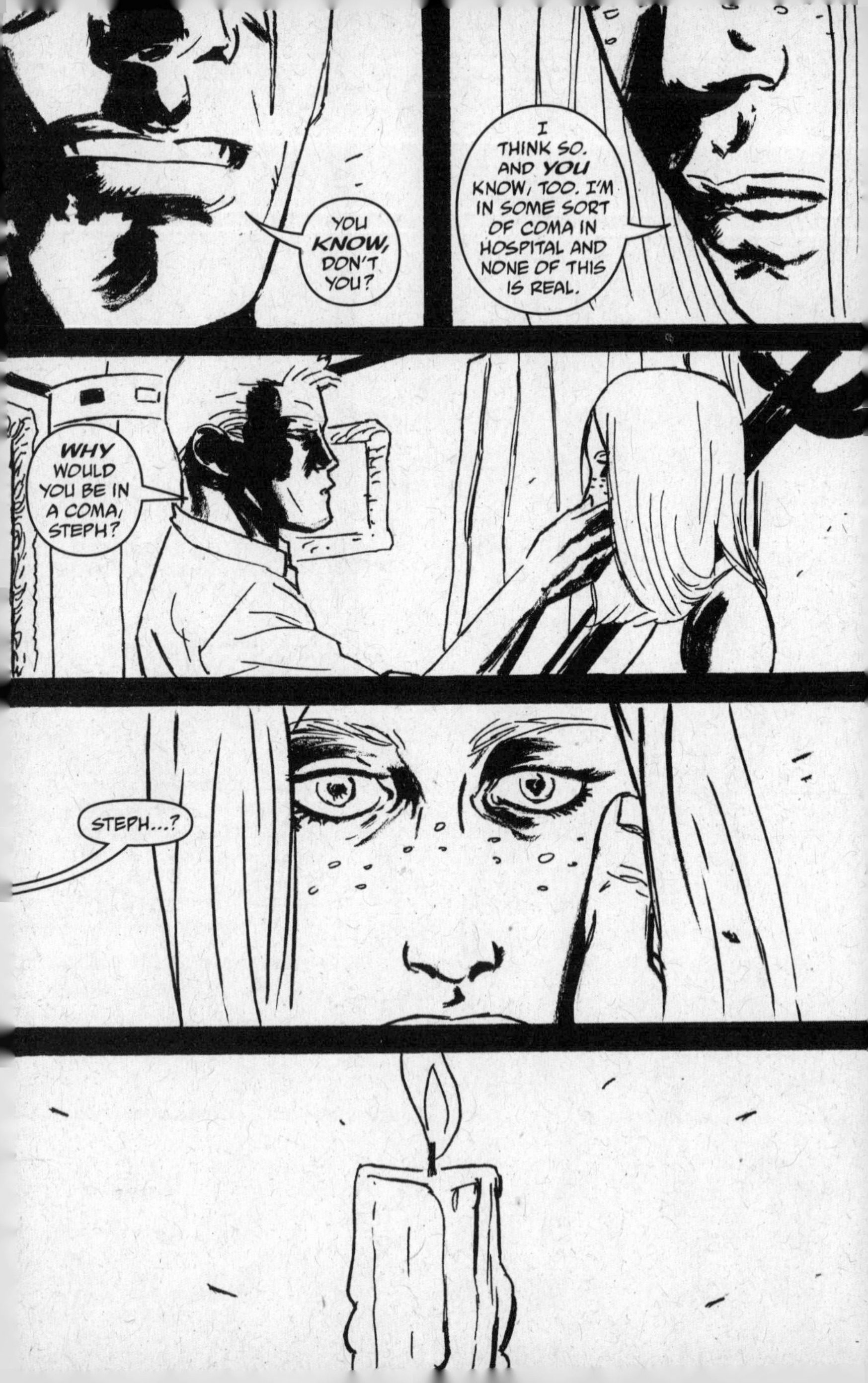
YOU KNOW, DON'T YOU?
I THINK SO. AND YOU KNOW, TOO. I'M IN SOME SORT OF COMA IN HOSPITAL AND NONE OF THIS IS REAL.
WHY WOULD YOU BE IN A COMA, STEPH?
STEPH...?

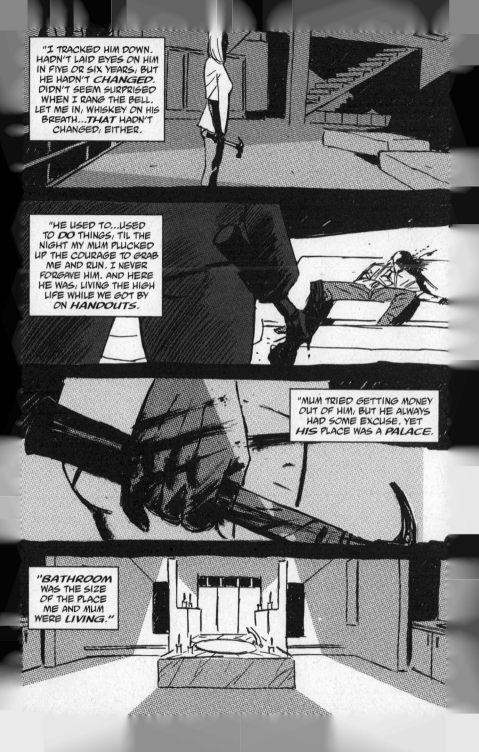

"I TRACKED HIM DOWN. HADN'T LAID EYES ON HIM IN FIVE OR SIX YEARS, BUT HE HADN'T *CHANGED.* DIDN'T SEEM SURPRISED WHEN I RANG THE BELL. LET ME IN, WHISKEY ON HIS BREATH...*THAT* HADN'T CHANGED, EITHER.

"HE USED TO...USED TO *DO* THINGS, TIL THE NIGHT MY MUM PLUCKED UP THE COURAGE TO GRAB ME AND RUN. I NEVER FORGAVE HIM. AND HERE HE WAS, LIVING THE HIGH LIFE WHILE WE GOT BY ON *HANDOUTS.*

"MUM TRIED GETTING MONEY OUT OF HIM, BUT HE ALWAYS HAD SOME EXCUSE. YET *HIS* PLACE WAS A *PALACE.*

"*BATHROOM* WAS THE SIZE OF THE PLACE ME AND MUM WERE *LIVING.*"

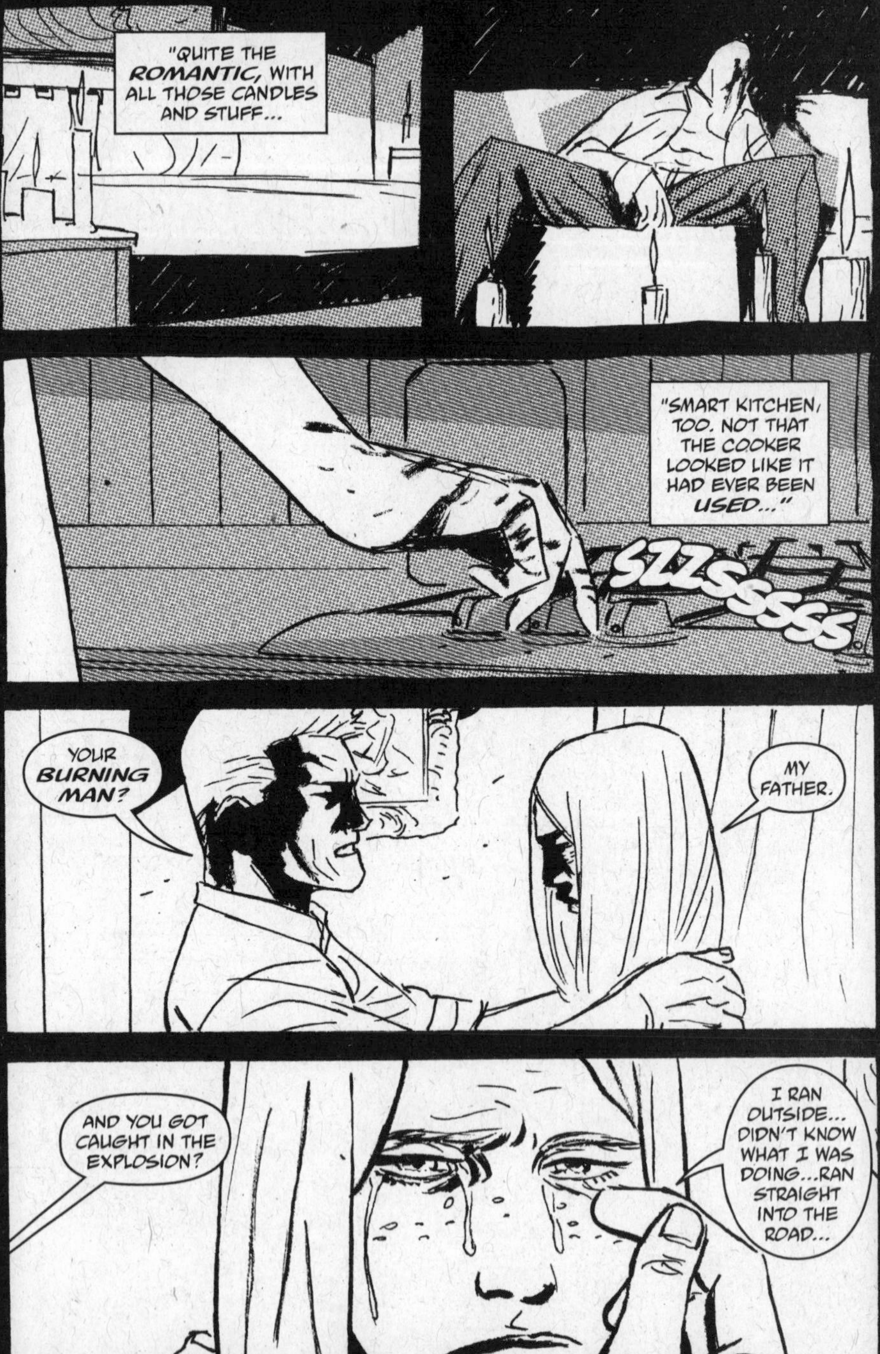
"QUITE THE ROMANTIC, WITH ALL THOSE CANDLES AND STUFF...
"SMART KITCHEN, TOO. NOT THAT THE COOKER LOOKED LIKE IT HAD EVER BEEN USED..."
SZZSSSSSS
YOUR BURNING MAN?
MY FATHER.
AND YOU GOT CAUGHT IN THE EXPLOSION?
I RAN OUTSIDE... DIDN'T KNOW WHAT I WAS DOING...RAN STRAIGHT INTO THE ROAD...

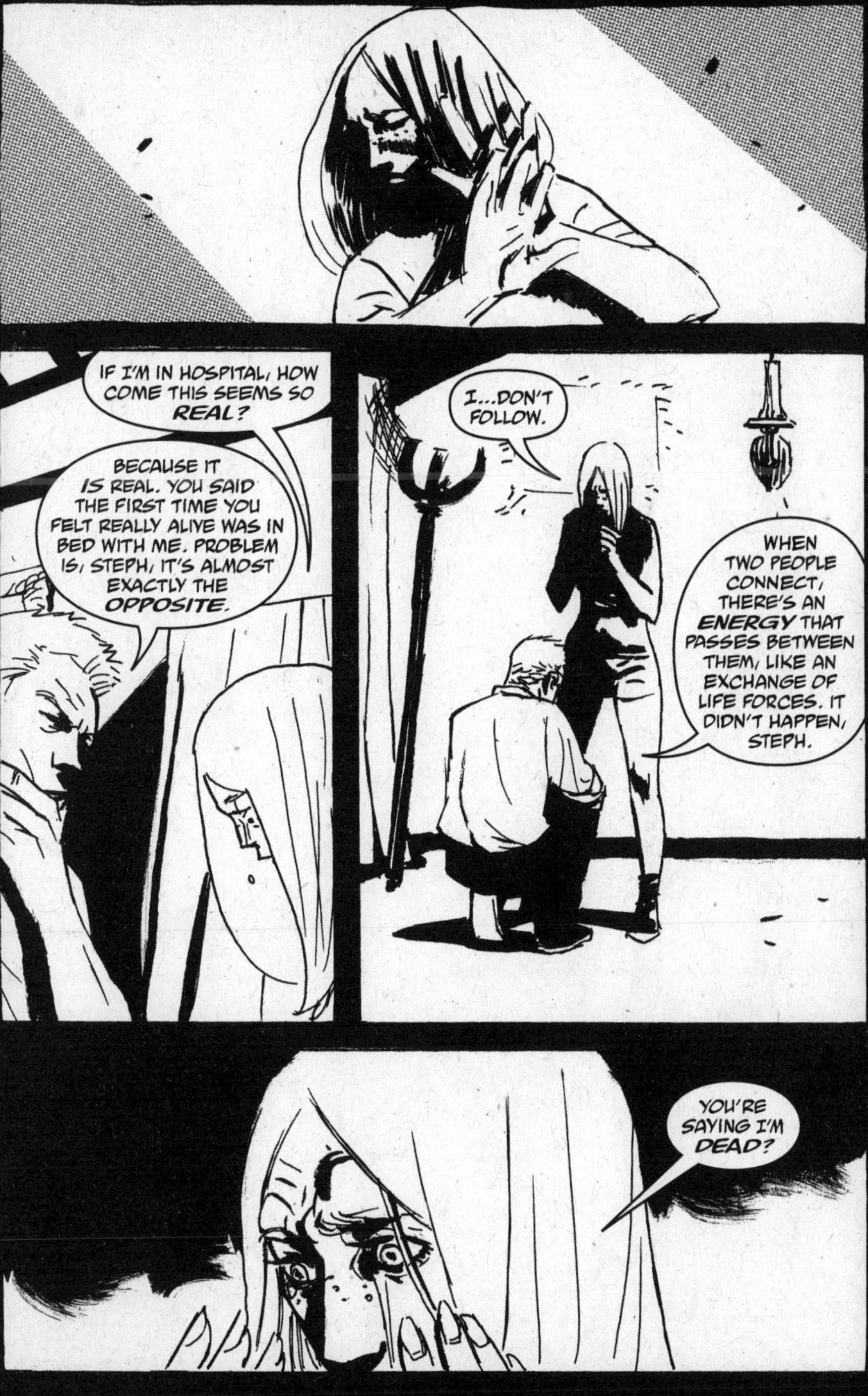
IF I'M IN HOSPITAL, HOW COME THIS SEEMS SO REAL?
BECAUSE IT IS REAL. YOU SAID THE FIRST TIME YOU FELT REALLY ALIVE WAS IN BED WITH ME. PROBLEM IS, STEPH, IT'S ALMOST EXACTLY THE OPPOSITE.
I...DON'T FOLLOW.
WHEN TWO PEOPLE CONNECT, THERE'S AN ENERGY THAT PASSES BETWEEN THEM, LIKE AN EXCHANGE OF LIFE FORCES. IT DIDN'T HAPPEN, STEPH.
YOU'RE SAYING I'M DEAD?

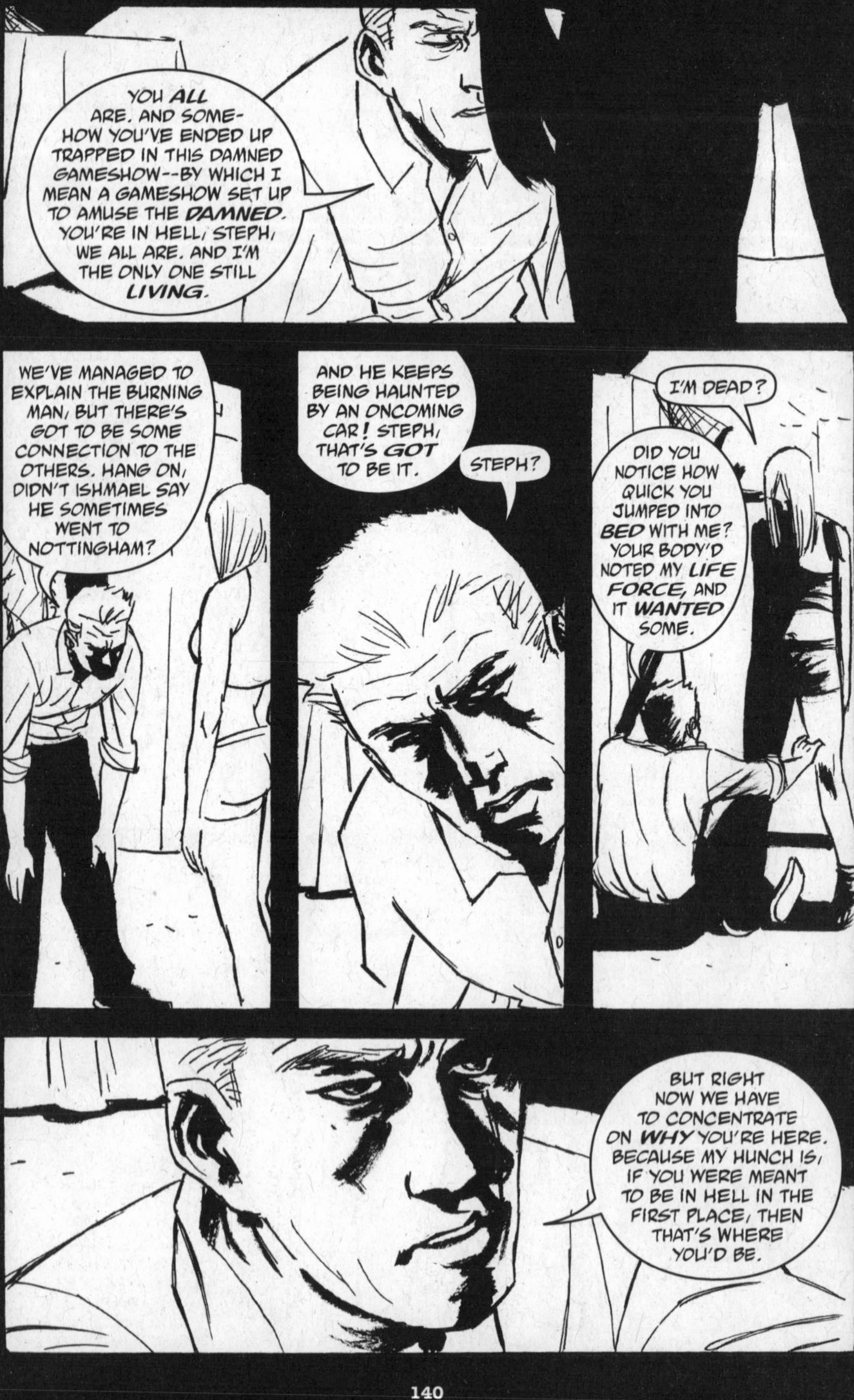
YOU ALL ARE. AND SOMEHOW YOU'VE ENDED UP TRAPPED IN THIS DAMNED GAMESHOW--BY WHICH I MEAN A GAMESHOW SET UP TO AMUSE THE DAMNED. YOU'RE IN HELL, STEPH, WE ALL ARE. AND I'M THE ONLY ONE STILL LIVING.
WE'VE MANAGED TO EXPLAIN THE BURNING MAN, BUT THERE'S GOT TO BE SOME CONNECTION TO THE OTHERS. HANG ON, DIDN'T ISHMAEL SAY HE SOMETIMES WENT TO NOTTINGHAM?
AND HE KEEPS BEING HAUNTED BY AN ONCOMING CAR! STEPH, THAT'S GOT TO BE IT.
STEPH?
I'M DEAD?
DID YOU NOTICE HOW QUICK YOU JUMPED INTO BED WITH ME? YOUR BODY'D NOTED MY LIFE FORCE, AND IT WANTED SOME.
BUT RIGHT NOW WE HAVE TO CONCENTRATE ON WHY YOU'RE HERE. BECAUSE MY HUNCH IS, IF YOU WERE MEANT TO BE IN HELL IN THE FIRST PLACE, THEN THAT'S WHERE YOU'D BE.

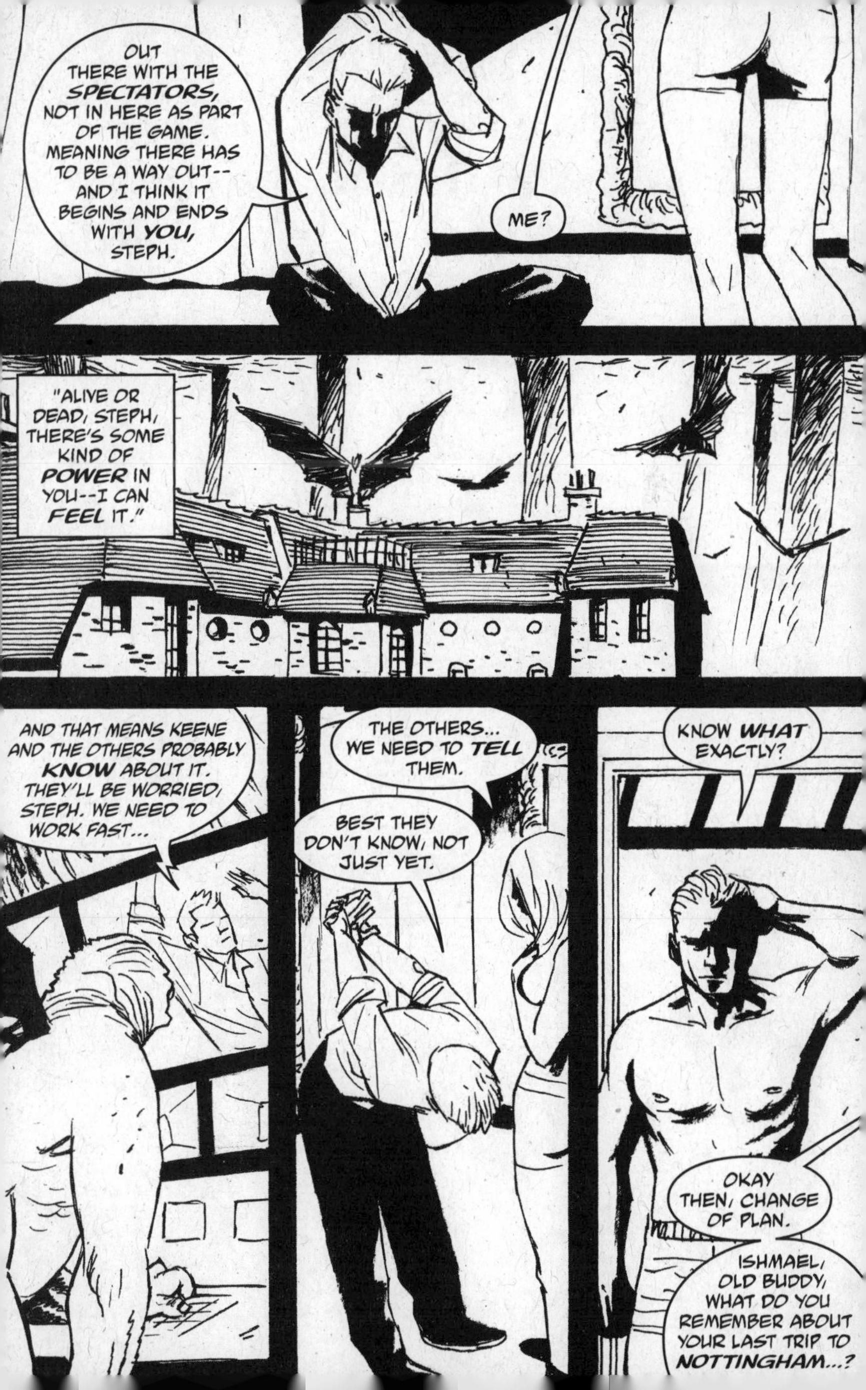
OUT THERE WITH THE SPECTATORS, NOT IN HERE AS PART OF THE GAME. MEANING THERE HAS TO BE A WAY OUT-- AND I THINK IT BEGINS AND ENDS WITH YOU, STEPH.
ME?
"ALIVE OR DEAD, STEPH, THERE'S SOME KIND OF POWER IN YOU--I CAN FEEL IT."
AND THAT MEANS KEENE AND THE OTHERS PROBABLY KNOW ABOUT IT. THEY'LL BE WORRIED, STEPH. WE NEED TO WORK FAST...
THE OTHERS... WE NEED TO TELL THEM.
BEST THEY DON'T KNOW, NOT JUST YET.
KNOW WHAT EXACTLY?
OKAY THEN, CHANGE OF PLAN.
ISHMAEL, OLD BUDDY, WHAT DO YOU REMEMBER ABOUT YOUR LAST TRIP TO NOTTINGHAM...?

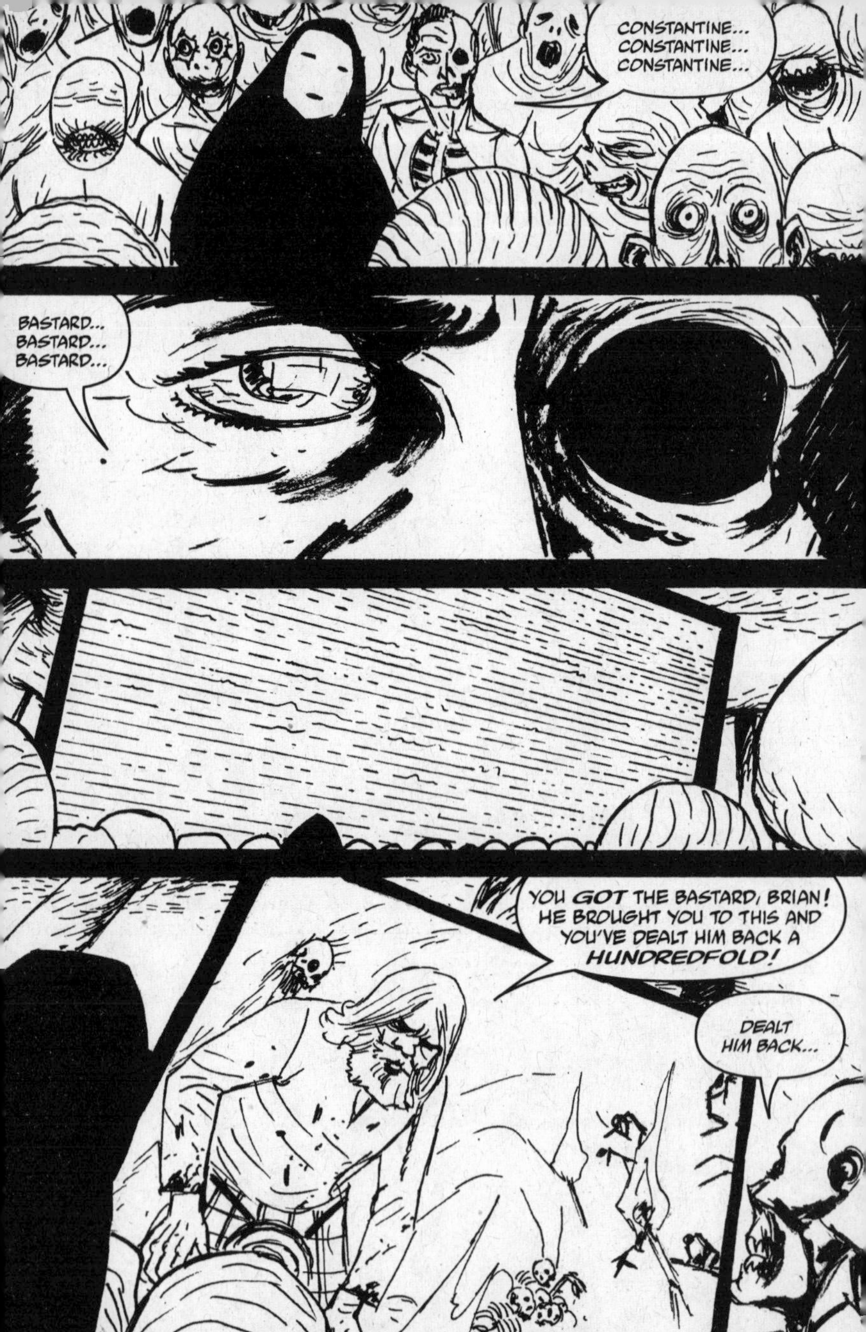
CONSTANTINE...
CONSTANTINE...
CONSTANTINE...
BASTARD...
BASTARD...
BASTARD...
YOU GOT THE BASTARD, BRIAN! HE BROUGHT YOU TO THIS AND YOU'VE DEALT HIM BACK A HUNDREDFOLD!
DEALT HIM BACK...

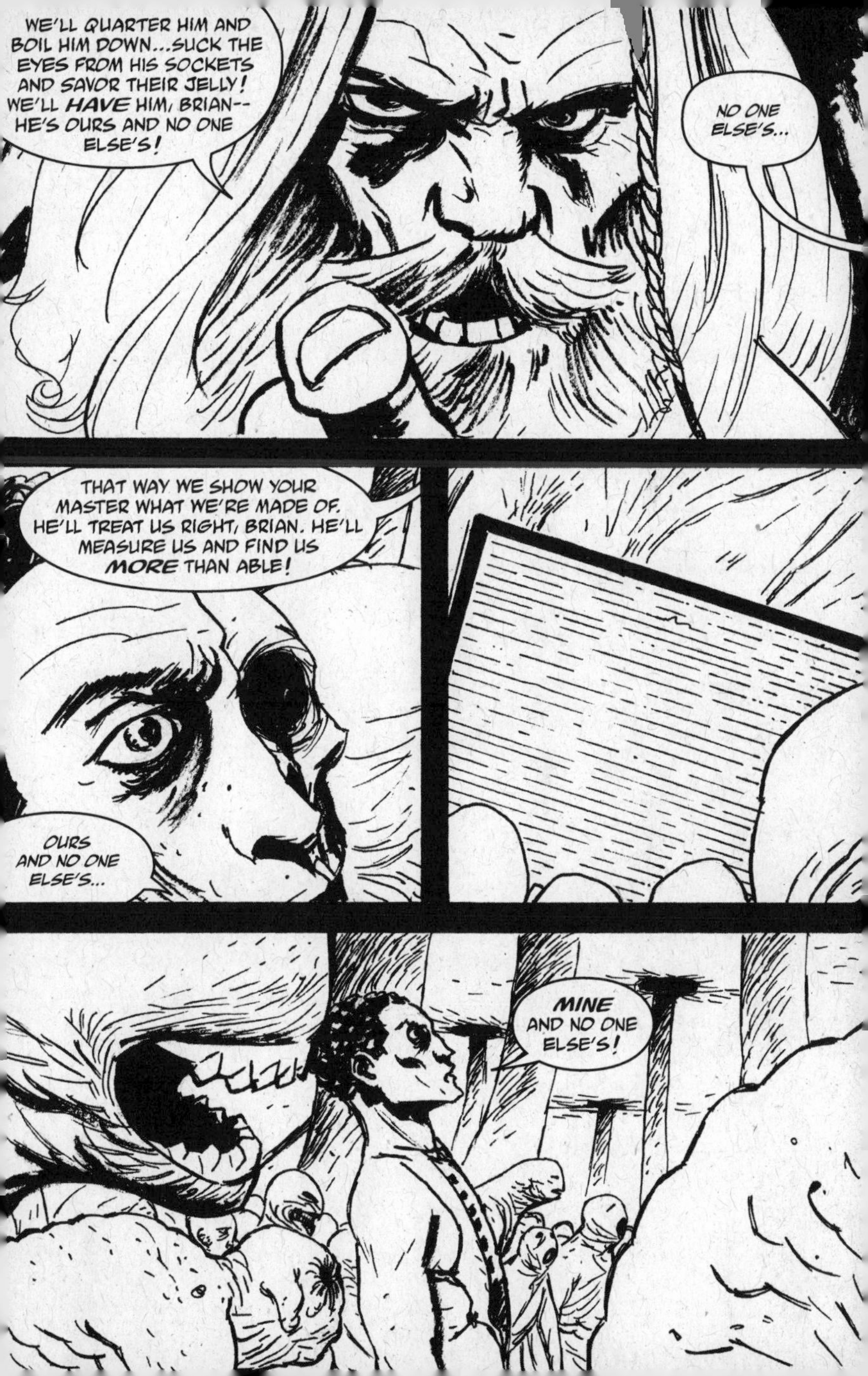
WE'LL QUARTER HIM AND BOIL HIM DOWN...SUCK THE EYES FROM HIS SOCKETS AND SAVOR THEIR JELLY! WE'LL HAVE HIM, BRIAN--HE'S OURS AND NO ONE ELSE'S!
NO ONE ELSE'S...
THAT WAY WE SHOW YOUR MASTER WHAT WE'RE MADE OF. HE'LL TREAT US RIGHT, BRIAN. HE'LL MEASURE US AND FIND US MORE THAN ABLE!
OURS AND NO ONE ELSE'S...
MINE AND NO ONE ELSE'S!

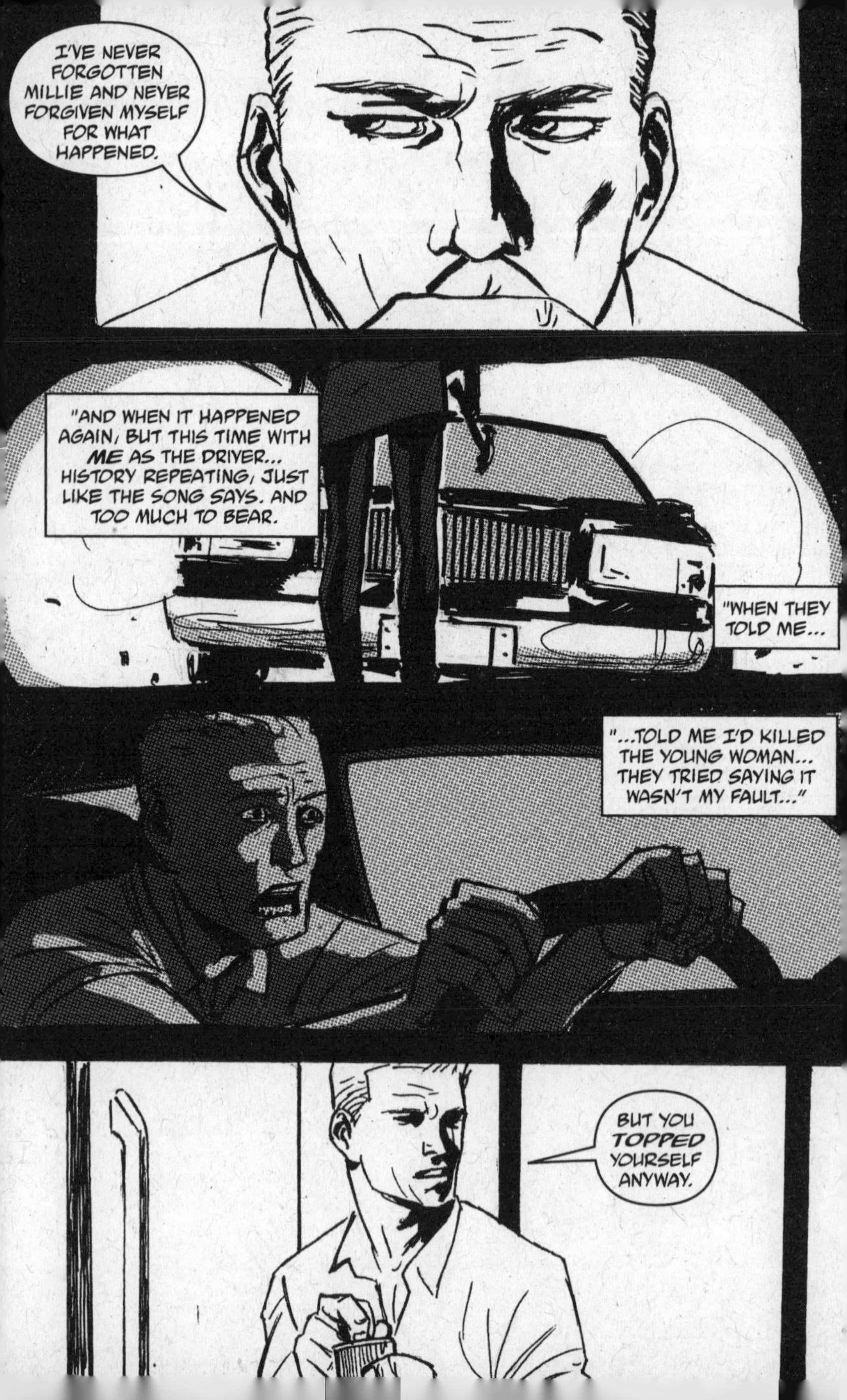
I'VE NEVER FORGOTTEN MILLIE AND NEVER FORGIVEN MYSELF FOR WHAT HAPPENED.
"AND WHEN IT HAPPENED AGAIN, BUT THIS TIME WITH *ME* AS THE DRIVER... HISTORY REPEATING, JUST LIKE THE SONG SAYS. AND TOO MUCH TO BEAR.
"WHEN THEY TOLD ME...
"...TOLD ME I'D KILLED THE YOUNG WOMAN... THEY TRIED SAYING IT WASN'T MY FAULT..."
BUT YOU *TOPPED* YOURSELF ANYWAY.

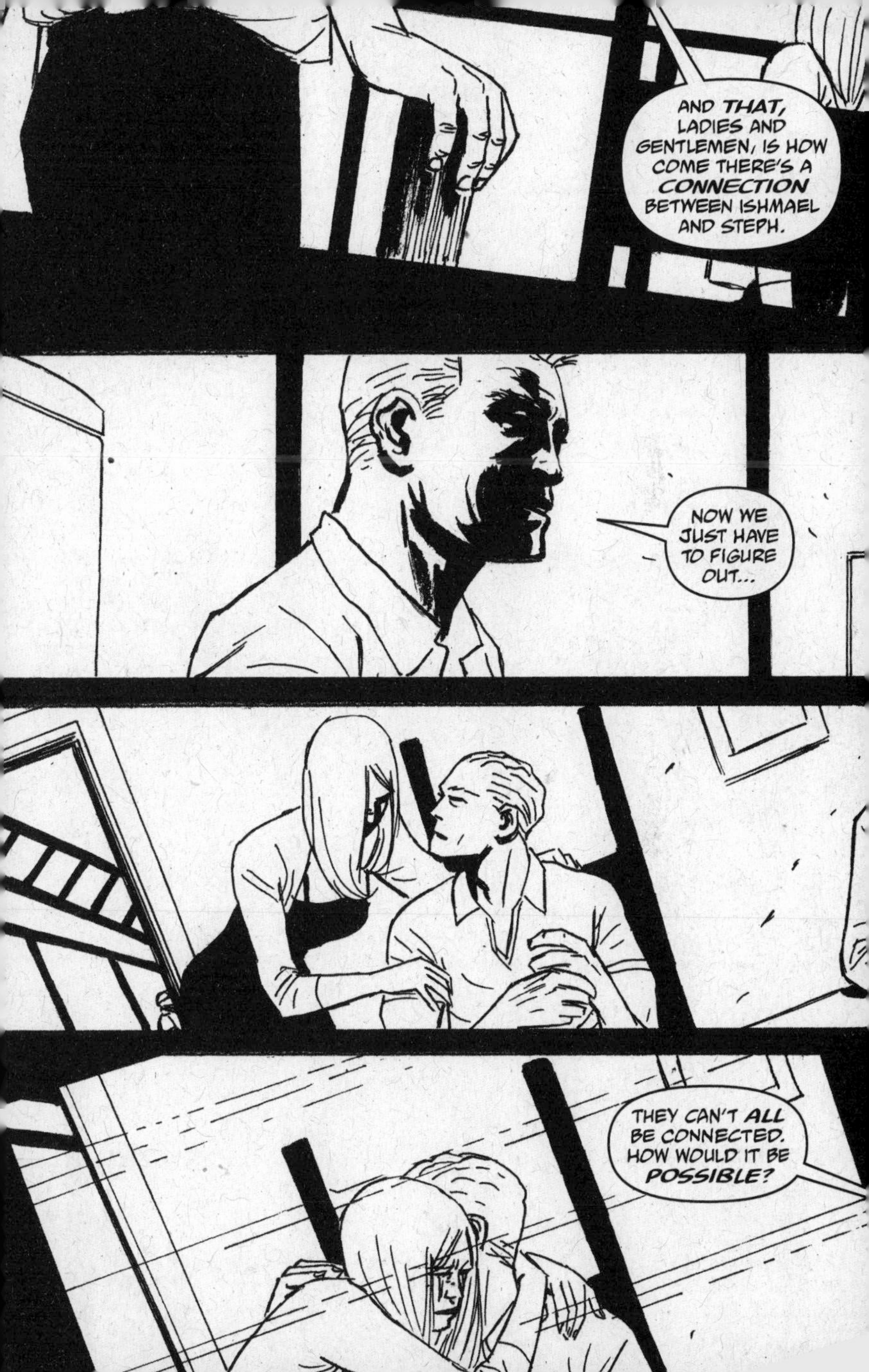
AND THAT, LADIES AND GENTLEMEN, IS HOW COME THERE'S A CONNECTION BETWEEN ISHMAEL AND STEPH.
NOW WE JUST HAVE TO FIGURE OUT...
THEY CAN'T ALL BE CONNECTED. HOW WOULD IT BE POSSIBLE?

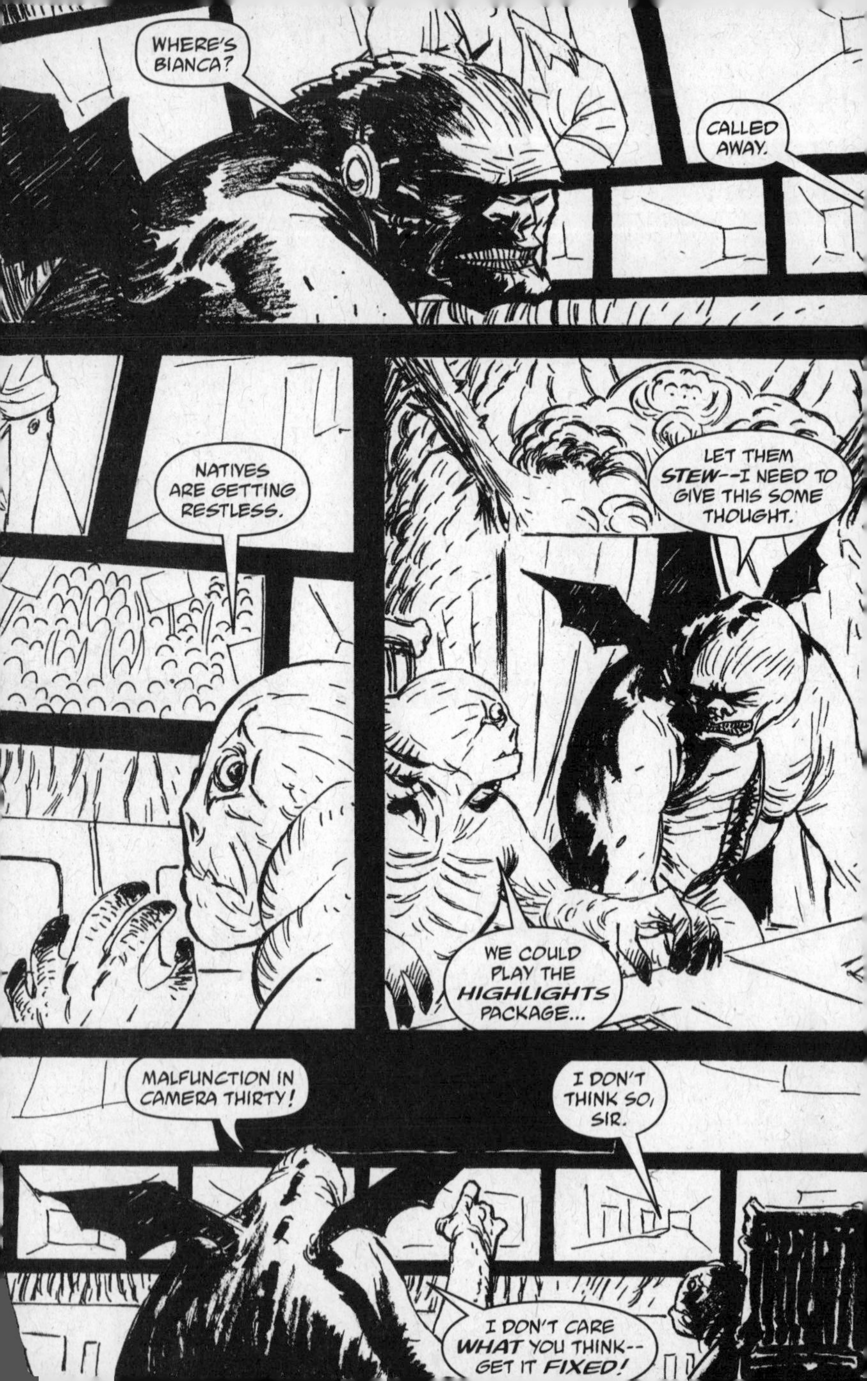
WHERE'S BIANCA?
CALLED AWAY.
NATIVES ARE GETTING RESTLESS.
LET THEM STEW--I NEED TO GIVE THIS SOME THOUGHT.
WE COULD PLAY THE HIGHLIGHTS PACKAGE...
MALFUNCTION IN CAMERA THIRTY!
I DON'T THINK SO, SIR.
I DON'T CARE WHAT YOU THINK--GET IT FIXED!

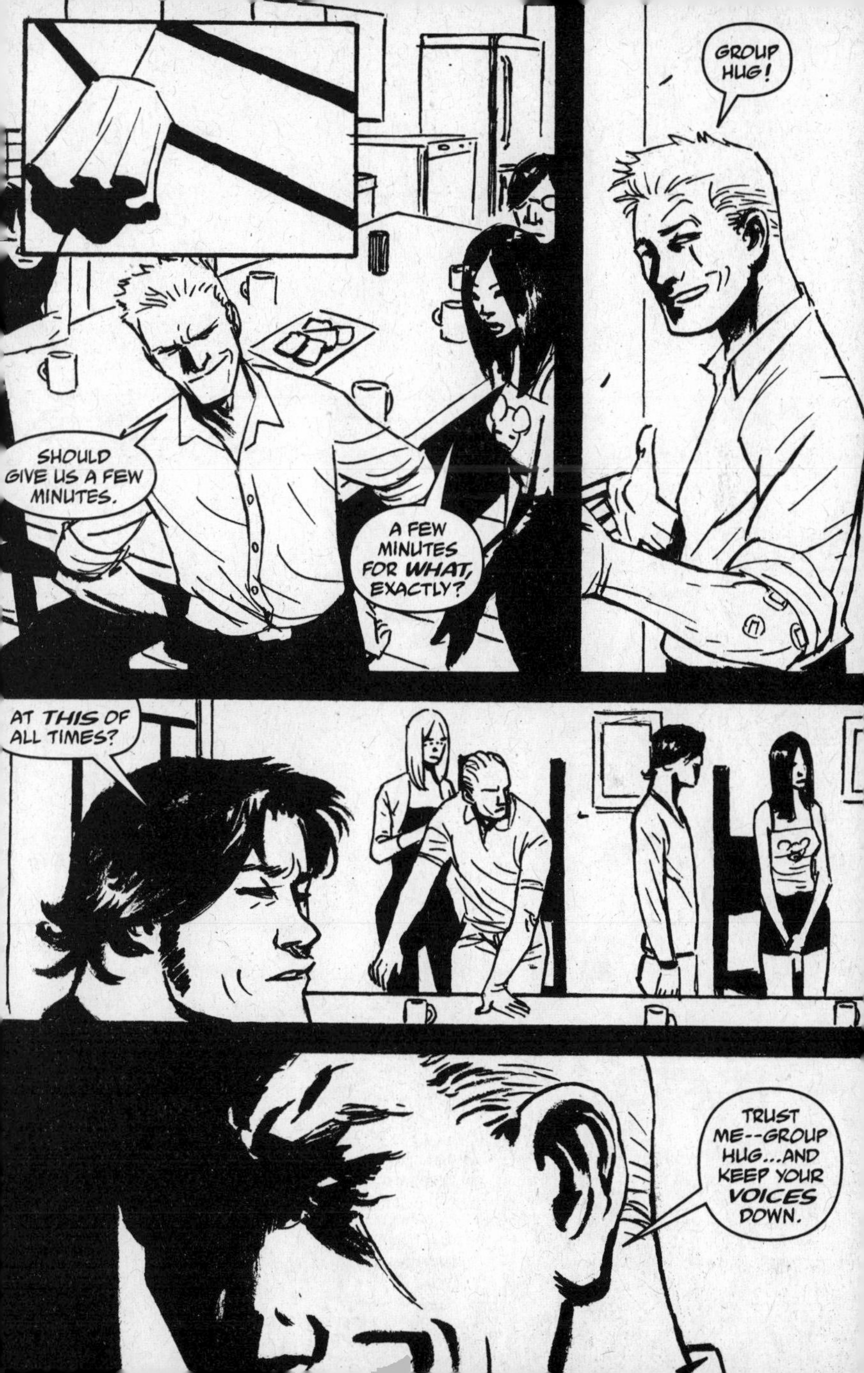
GROUP HUG!
SHOULD GIVE US A FEW MINUTES.
A FEW MINUTES FOR **WHAT**, EXACTLY?
AT **THIS** OF ALL TIMES?
TRUST ME--GROUP HUG...AND KEEP YOUR **VOICES** DOWN.

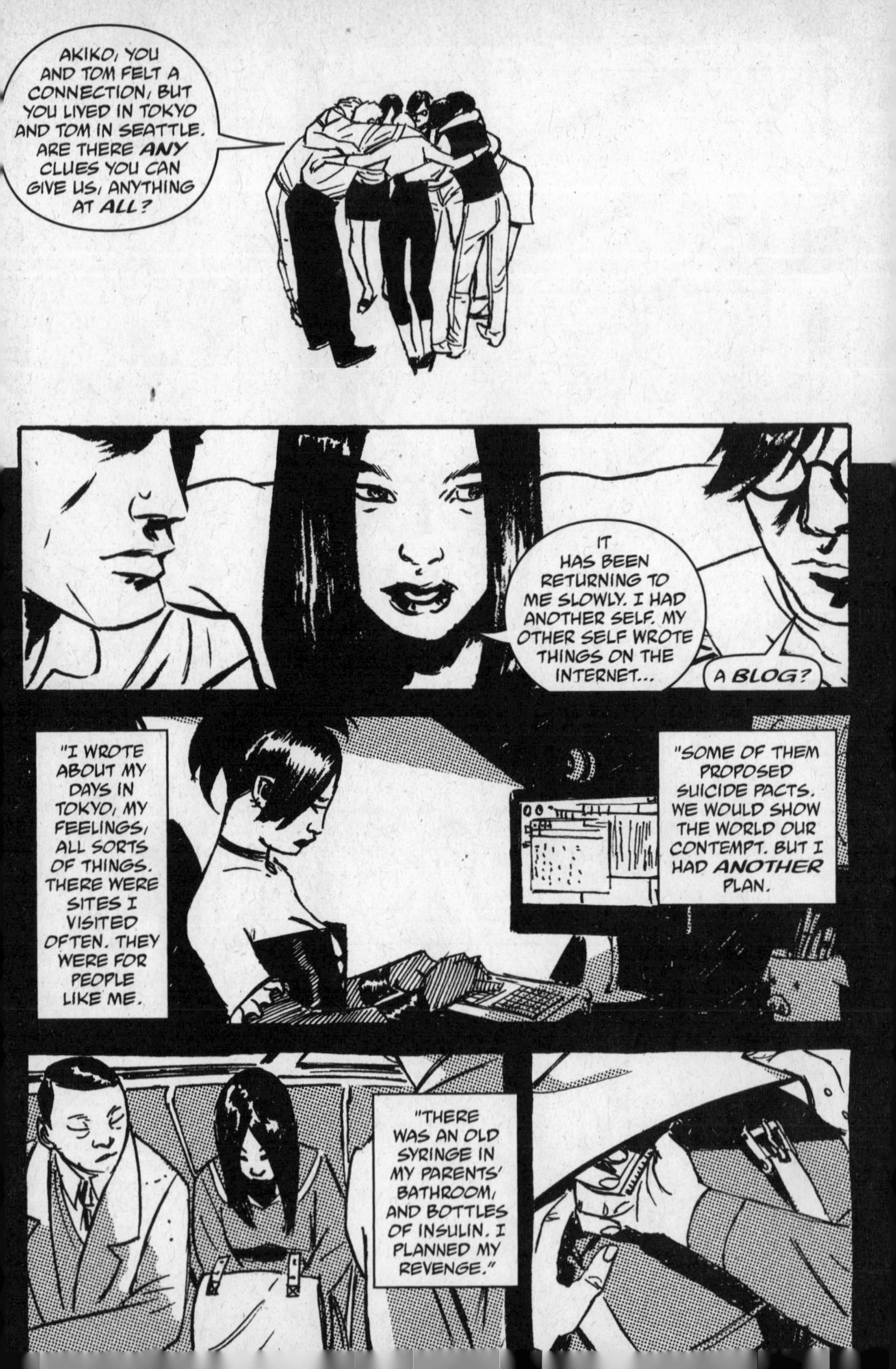
AKIKO, YOU AND TOM FELT A CONNECTION, BUT YOU LIVED IN TOKYO AND TOM IN SEATTLE. ARE THERE ANY CLUES YOU CAN GIVE US, ANYTHING AT ALL?
IT HAS BEEN RETURNING TO ME SLOWLY. I HAD ANOTHER SELF. MY OTHER SELF WROTE THINGS ON THE INTERNET...
A BLOG?
"I WROTE ABOUT MY DAYS IN TOKYO, MY FEELINGS, ALL SORTS OF THINGS. THERE WERE SITES I VISITED OFTEN. THEY WERE FOR PEOPLE LIKE ME.
"SOME OF THEM PROPOSED SUICIDE PACTS. WE WOULD SHOW THE WORLD OUR CONTEMPT. BUT I HAD ANOTHER PLAN.
"THERE WAS AN OLD SYRINGE IN MY PARENTS' BATHROOM, AND BOTTLES OF INSULIN. I PLANNED MY REVENGE."

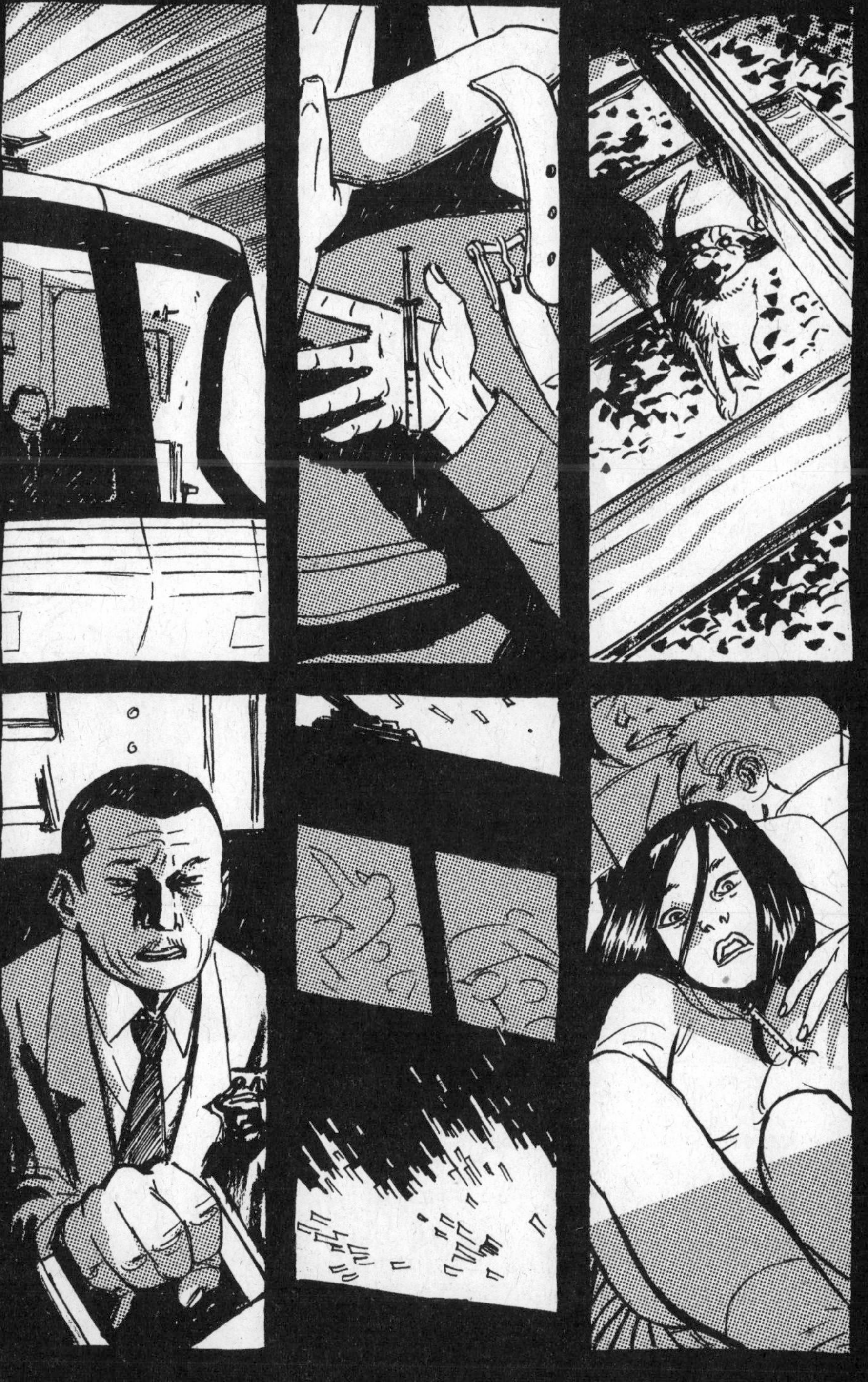

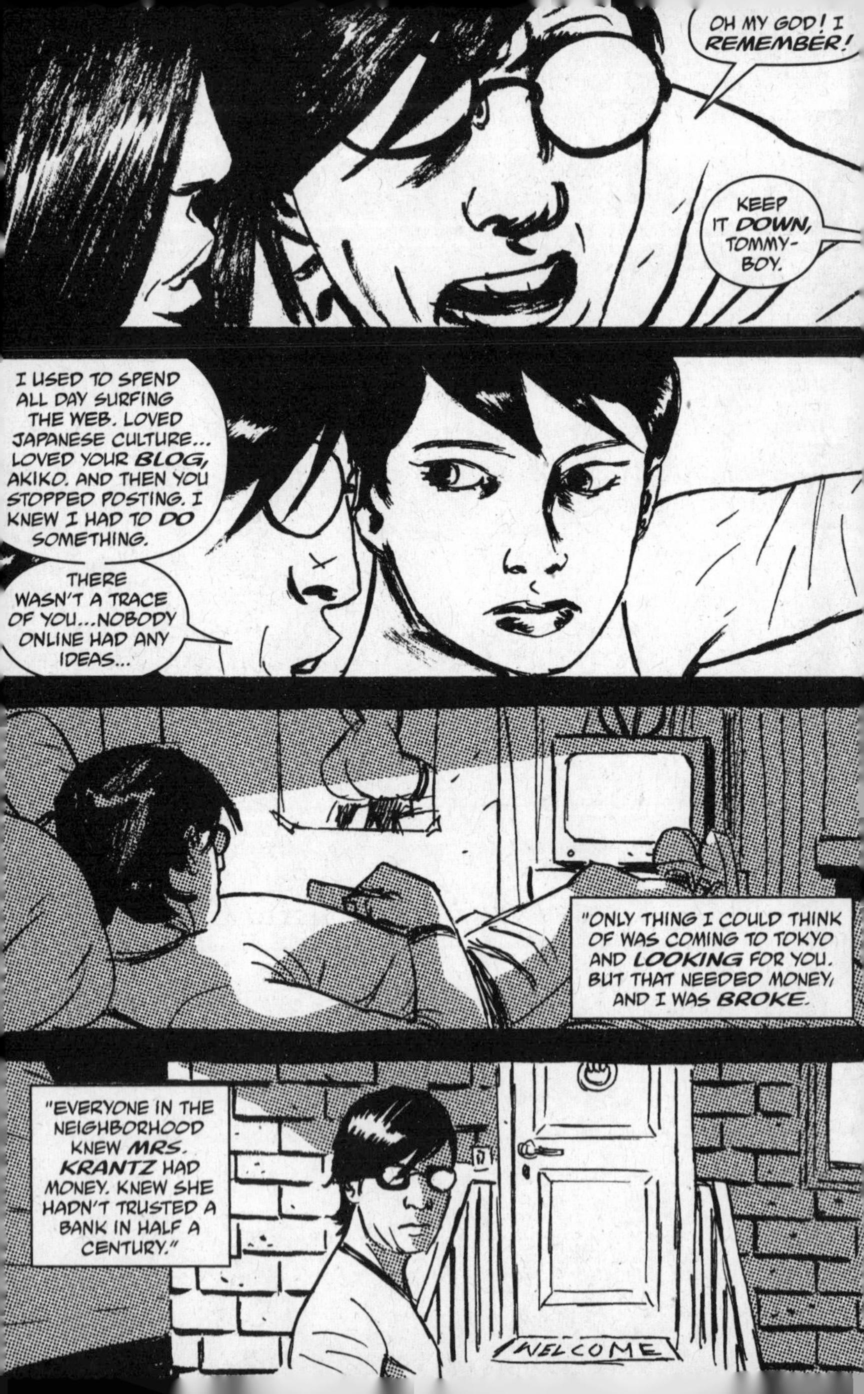
OH MY GOD! I REMEMBER!
KEEP IT DOWN, TOMMY-BOY.
I USED TO SPEND ALL DAY SURFING THE WEB. LOVED JAPANESE CULTURE... LOVED YOUR BLOG, AKIKO. AND THEN YOU STOPPED POSTING. I KNEW I HAD TO DO SOMETHING.
THERE WASN'T A TRACE OF YOU...NOBODY ONLINE HAD ANY IDEAS...
"ONLY THING I COULD THINK OF WAS COMING TO TOKYO AND LOOKING FOR YOU. BUT THAT NEEDED MONEY, AND I WAS BROKE.
"EVERYONE IN THE NEIGHBORHOOD KNEW MRS. KRANTZ HAD MONEY. KNEW SHE HADN'T TRUSTED A BANK IN HALF A CENTURY."
WELCOME

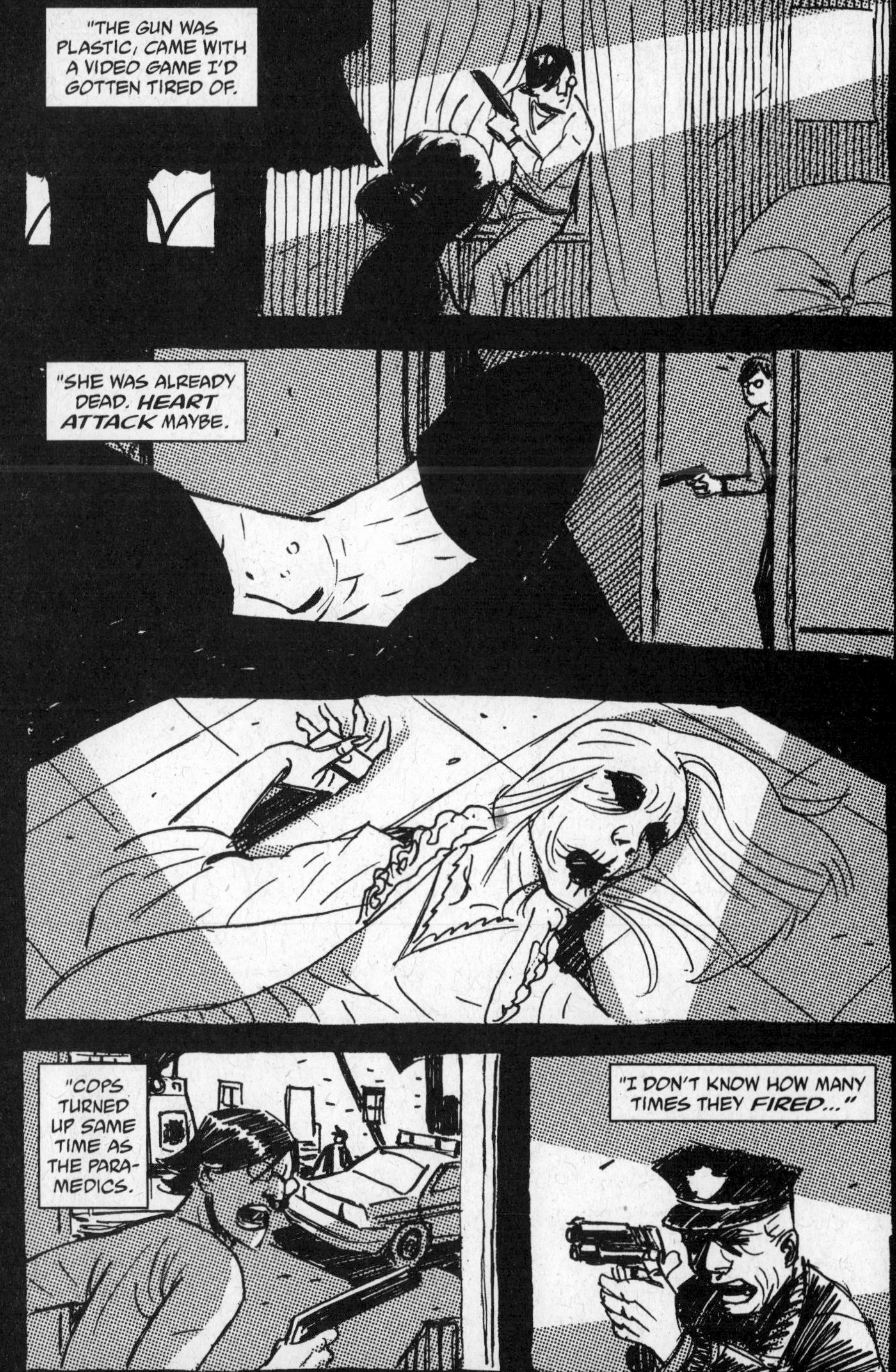
"THE GUN WAS PLASTIC, CAME WITH A VIDEO GAME I'D GOTTEN TIRED OF.
"SHE WAS ALREADY DEAD. HEART ATTACK MAYBE.
"COPS TURNED UP SAME TIME AS THE PARA-MEDICS.
"I DON'T KNOW HOW MANY TIMES THEY FIRED..."

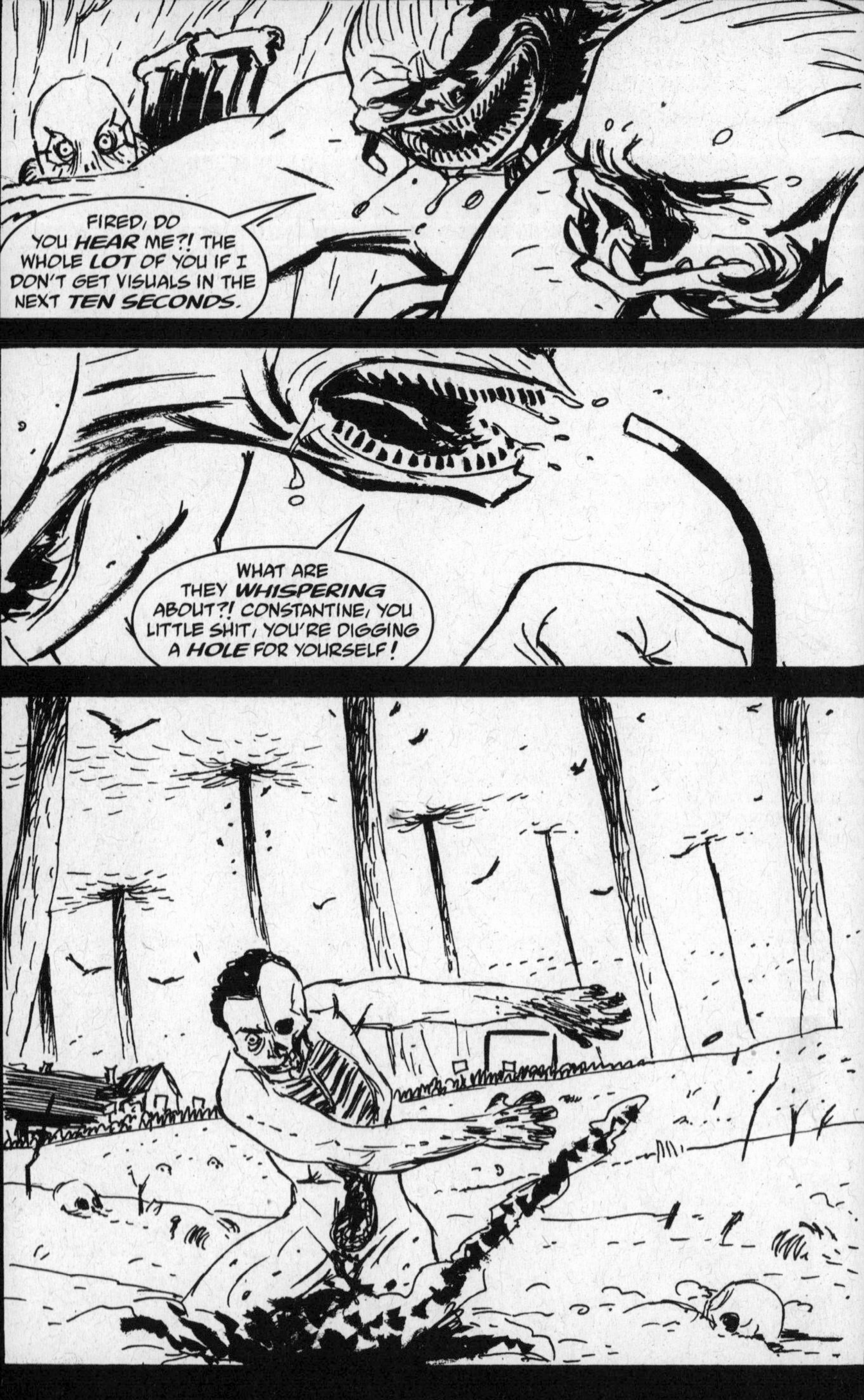
FIRED, DO YOU HEAR ME?! THE WHOLE LOT OF YOU IF I DON'T GET VISUALS IN THE NEXT TEN SECONDS.
WHAT ARE THEY WHISPERING ABOUT?! CONSTANTINE, YOU LITTLE SHIT, YOU'RE DIGGING A HOLE FOR YOURSELF!

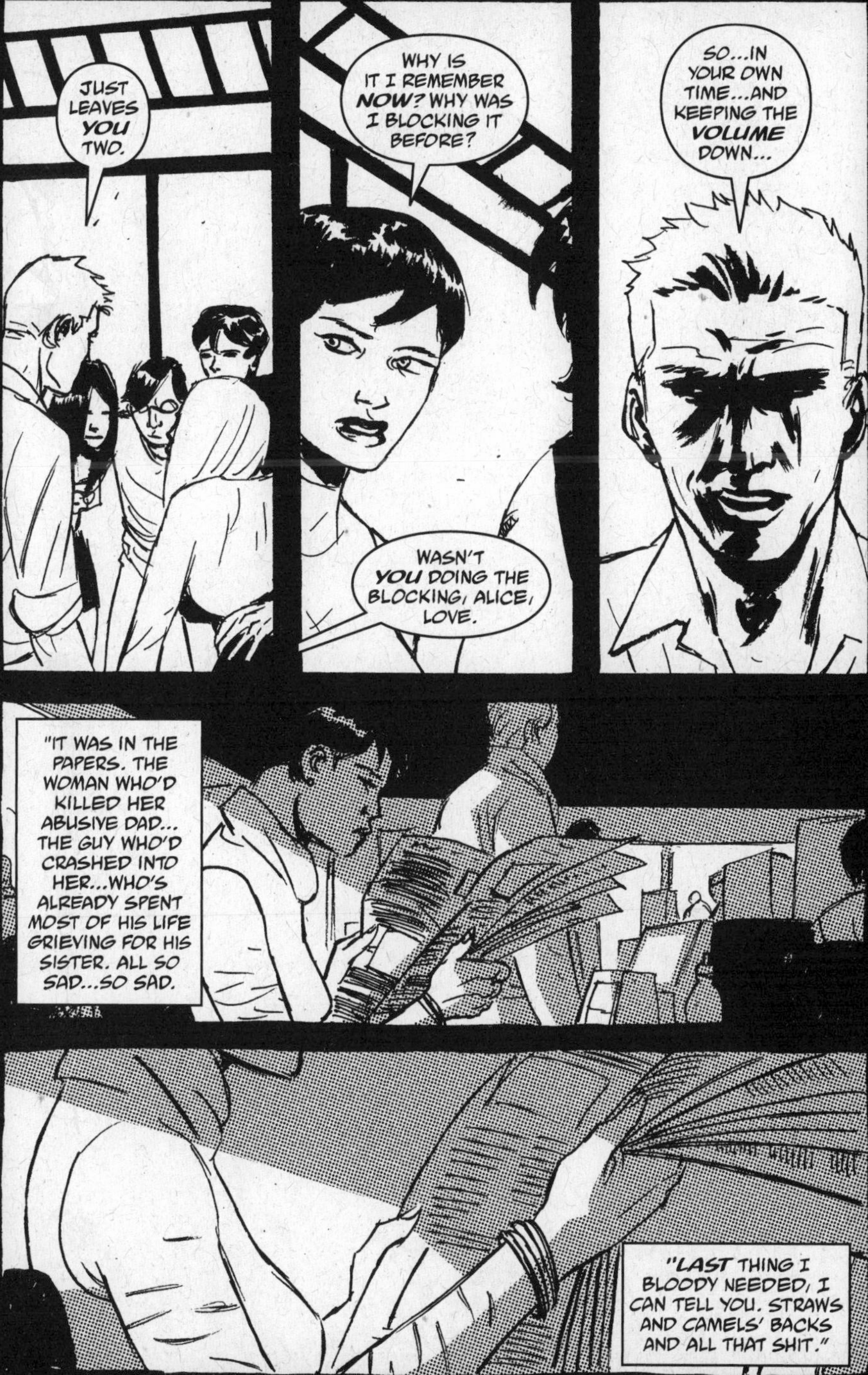
JUST LEAVES *YOU* TWO.
WHY IS IT I REMEMBER *NOW?* WHY WAS I BLOCKING IT BEFORE?
WASN'T *YOU* DOING THE BLOCKING, ALICE, LOVE.
SO...IN YOUR OWN TIME...AND KEEPING THE *VOLUME* DOWN...
"IT WAS IN THE PAPERS. THE WOMAN WHO'D KILLED HER ABUSIVE DAD... THE GUY WHO'D CRASHED INTO HER...WHO'S ALREADY SPENT MOST OF HIS LIFE GRIEVING FOR HIS SISTER. ALL SO SAD...SO SAD.
"*LAST* THING I BLOODY NEEDED, I CAN TELL YOU. STRAWS AND CAMELS' BACKS AND ALL THAT SHIT."

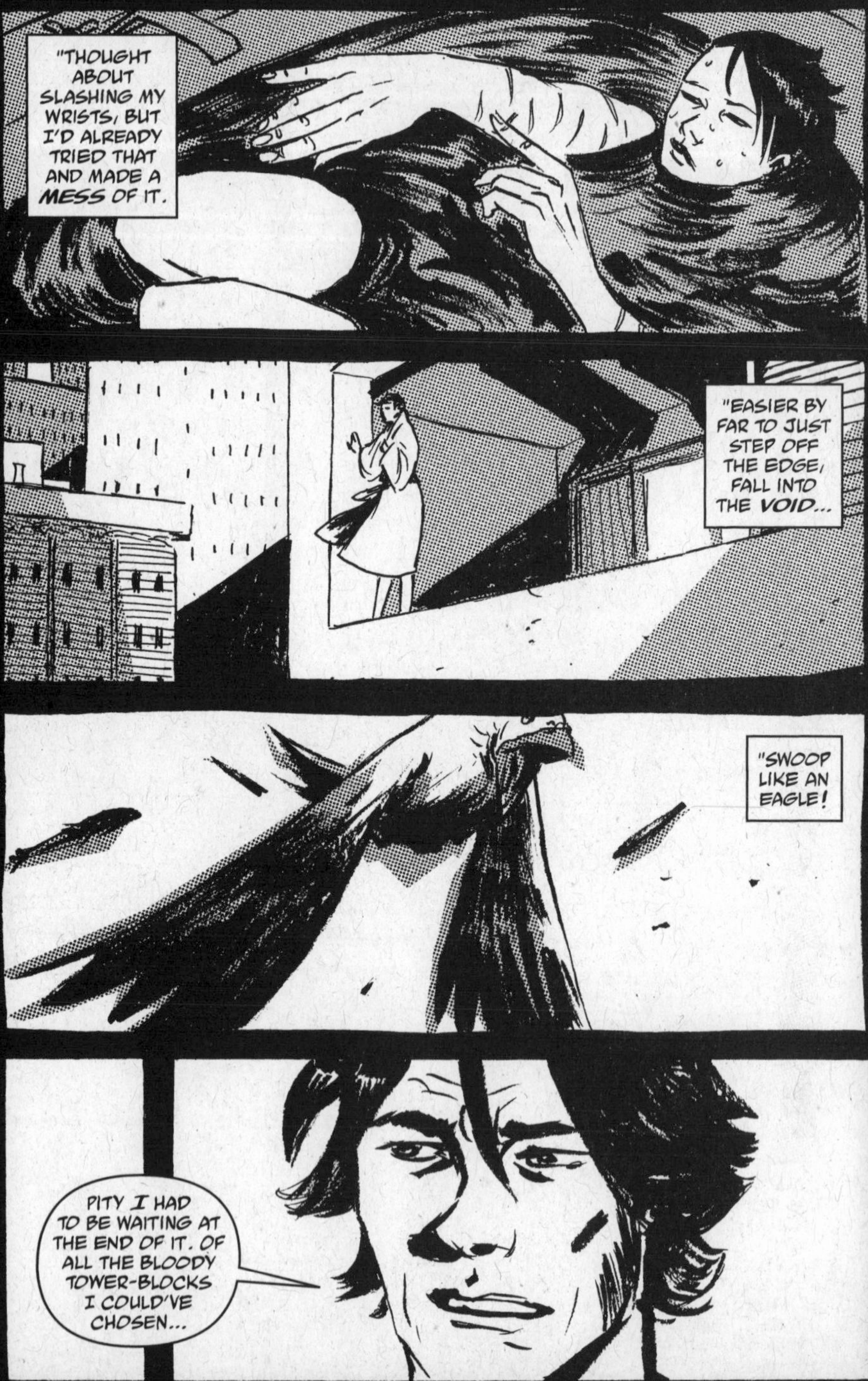
"THOUGHT ABOUT SLASHING MY WRISTS, BUT I'D ALREADY TRIED THAT AND MADE A *MESS* OF IT.
"EASIER BY FAR TO JUST STEP OFF THE EDGE, FALL INTO THE *VOID*...
"SWOOP LIKE AN EAGLE!
PITY *I* HAD TO BE WAITING AT THE END OF IT. OF ALL THE BLOODY TOWER-BLOCKS I COULD'VE CHOSEN...

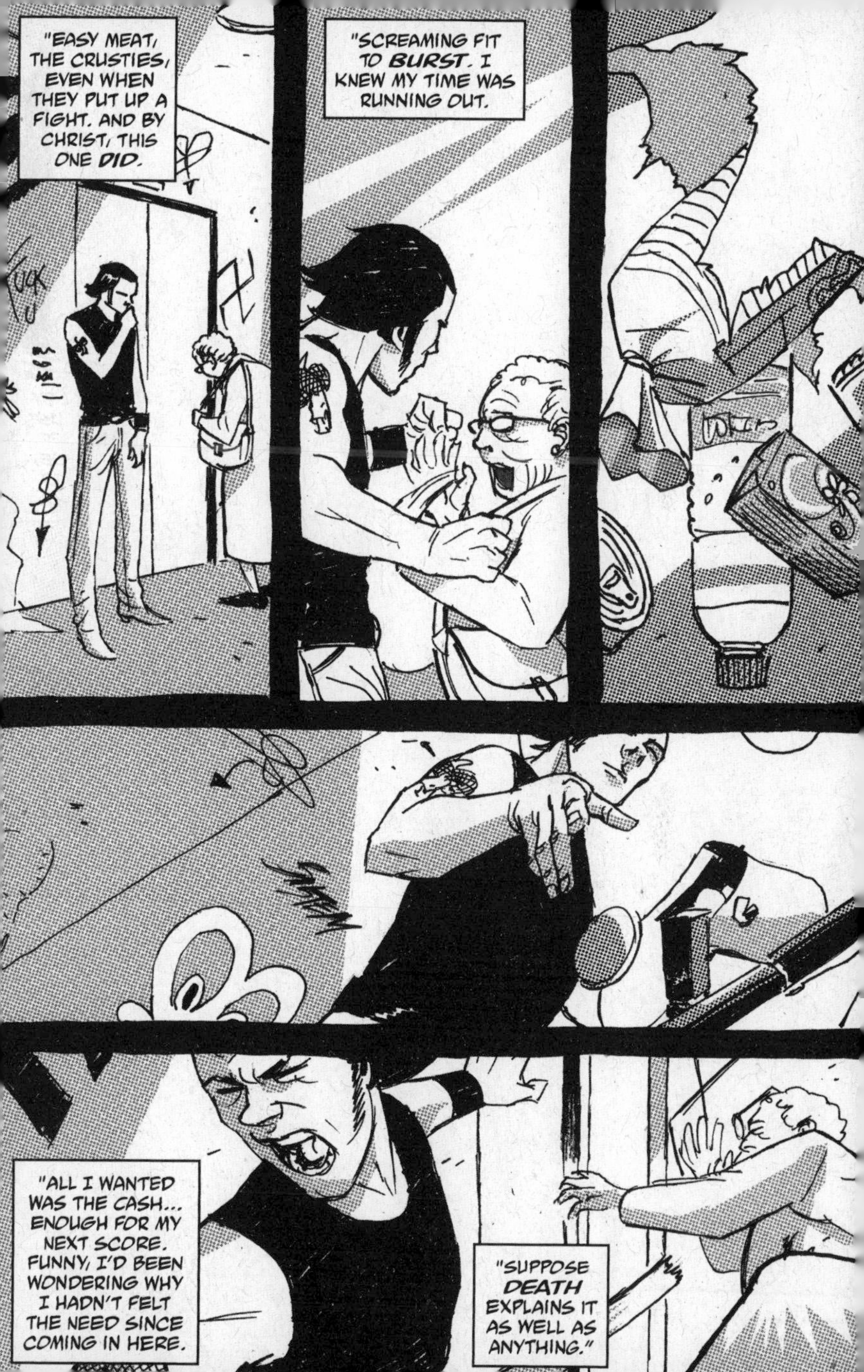
"EASY MEAT, THE CRUSTIES, EVEN WHEN THEY PUT UP A FIGHT. AND BY CHRIST, THIS ONE DID.
"SCREAMING FIT TO BURST. I KNEW MY TIME WAS RUNNING OUT.
"ALL I WANTED WAS THE CASH... ENOUGH FOR MY NEXT SCORE. FUNNY, I'D BEEN WONDERING WHY I HADN'T FELT THE NEED SINCE COMING IN HERE.
"SUPPOSE DEATH EXPLAINS IT AS WELL AS ANYTHING."

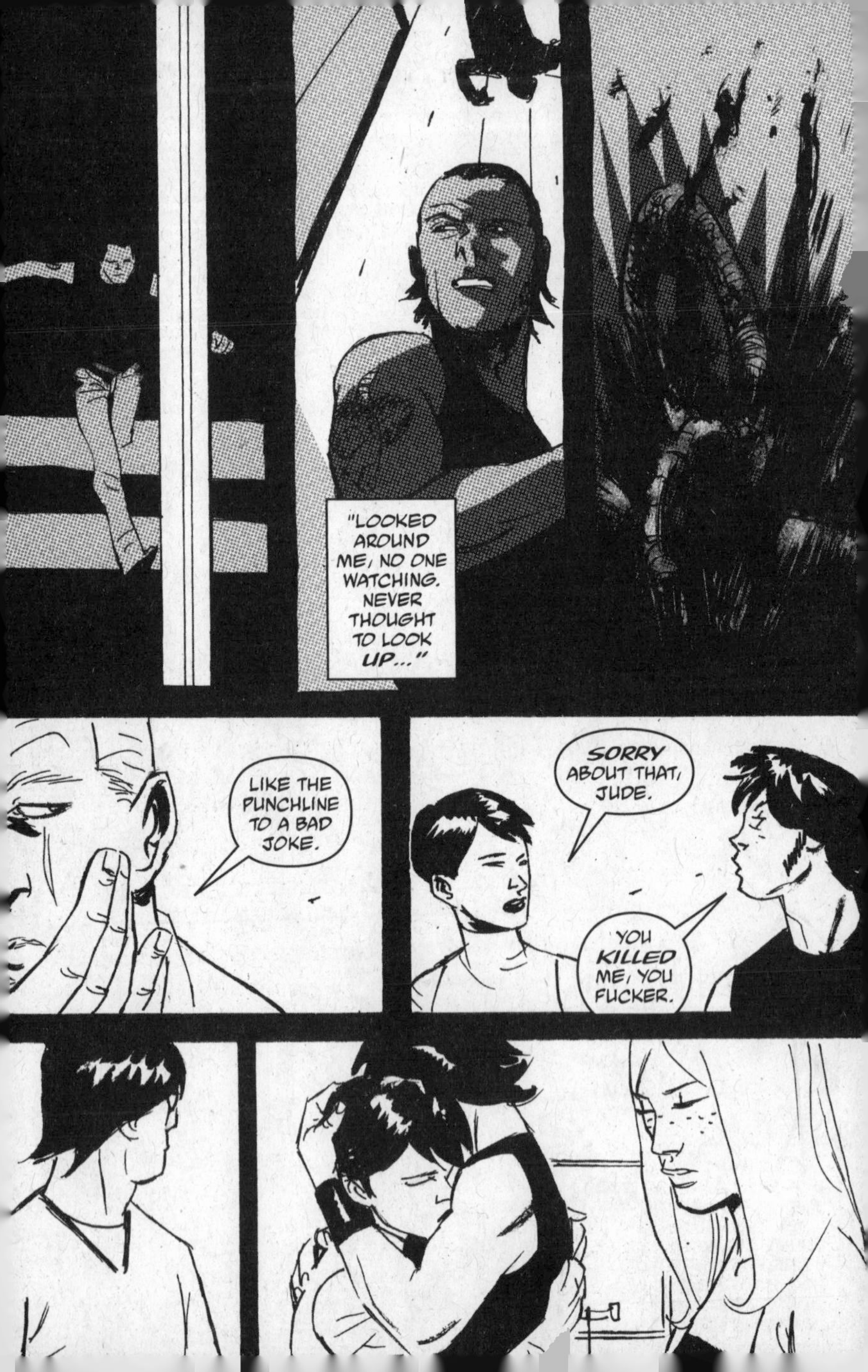
"LOOKED AROUND ME, NO ONE WATCHING. NEVER THOUGHT TO LOOK *UP*..."
LIKE THE PUNCHLINE TO A BAD JOKE.
SORRY ABOUT THAT, JUDE.
YOU *KILLED* ME, YOU FUCKER.

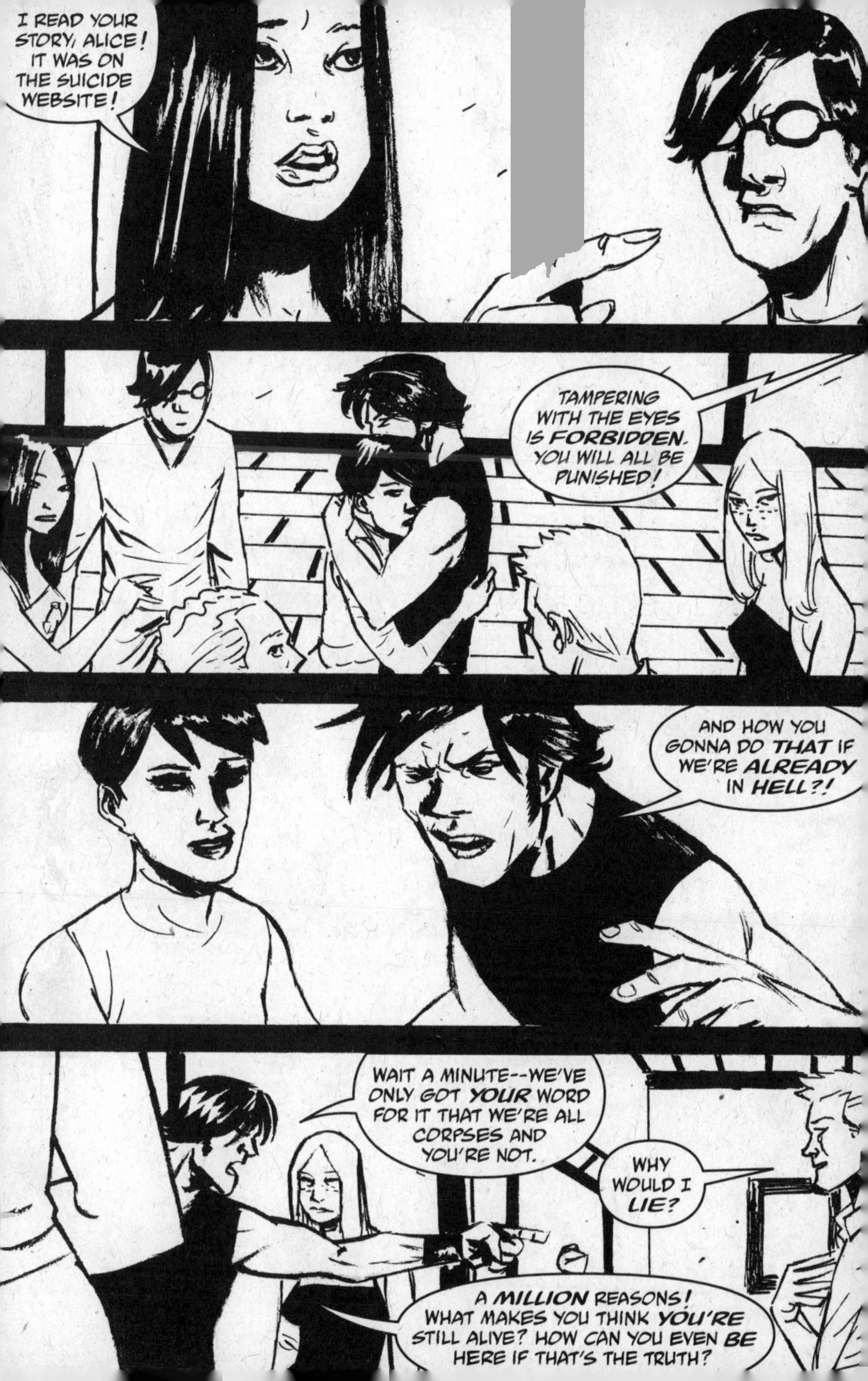
I READ YOUR STORY, ALICE! IT WAS ON THE SUICIDE WEBSITE!
TAMPERING WITH THE EYES IS FORBIDDEN. YOU WILL ALL BE PUNISHED!
AND HOW YOU GONNA DO THAT IF WE'RE ALREADY IN HELL?!
WAIT A MINUTE--WE'VE ONLY GOT YOUR WORD FOR IT THAT WE'RE ALL CORPSES AND YOU'RE NOT.
WHY WOULD I LIE?
A MILLION REASONS! WHAT MAKES YOU THINK YOU'RE STILL ALIVE? HOW CAN YOU EVEN BE HERE IF THAT'S THE TRUTH?

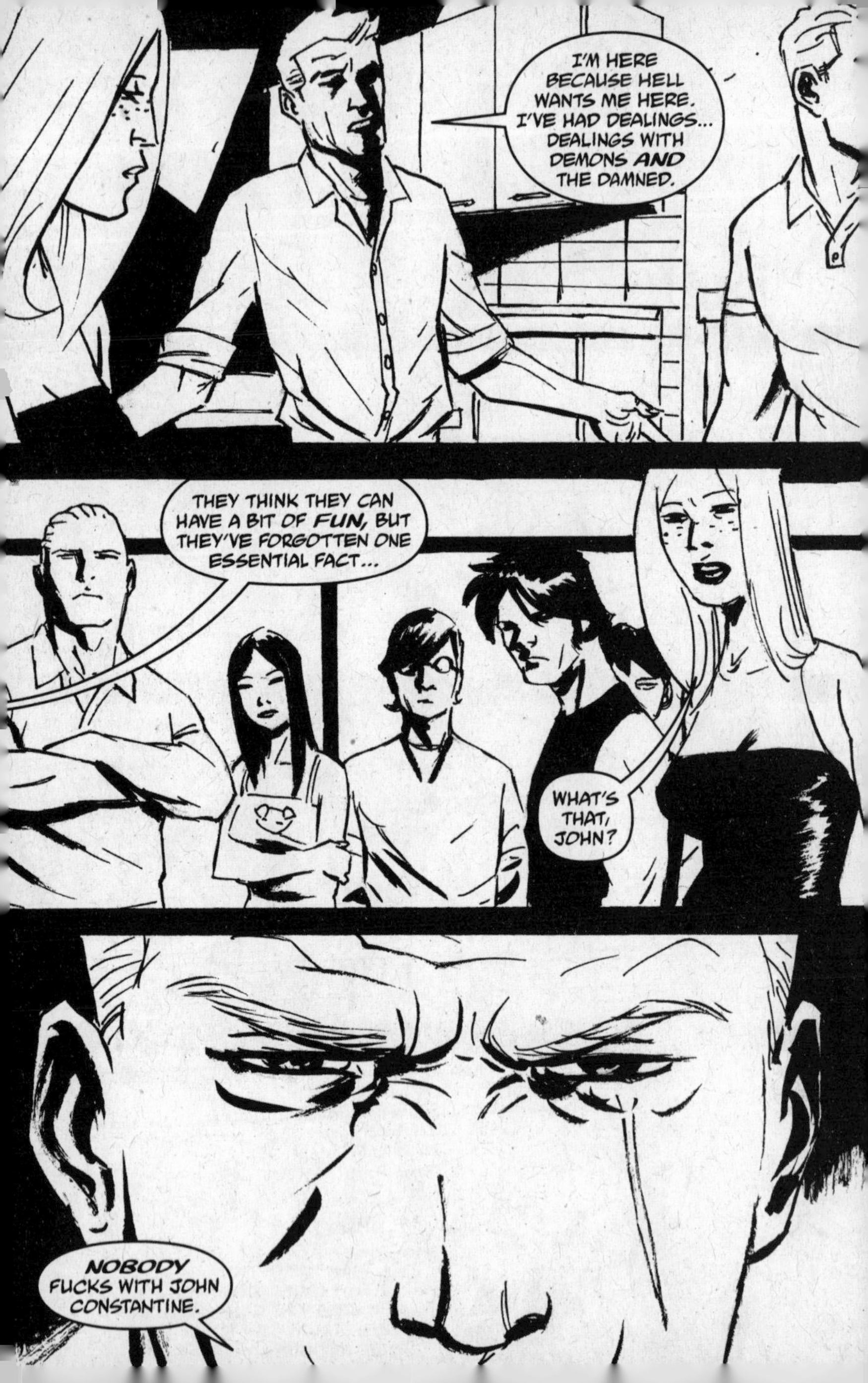
I'M HERE BECAUSE HELL WANTS ME HERE. I'VE HAD DEALINGS... DEALINGS WITH DEMONS AND THE DAMNED.
THEY THINK THEY CAN HAVE A BIT OF FUN, BUT THEY'VE FORGOTTEN ONE ESSENTIAL FACT...
WHAT'S THAT, JOHN?
NOBODY FUCKS WITH JOHN CONSTANTINE.

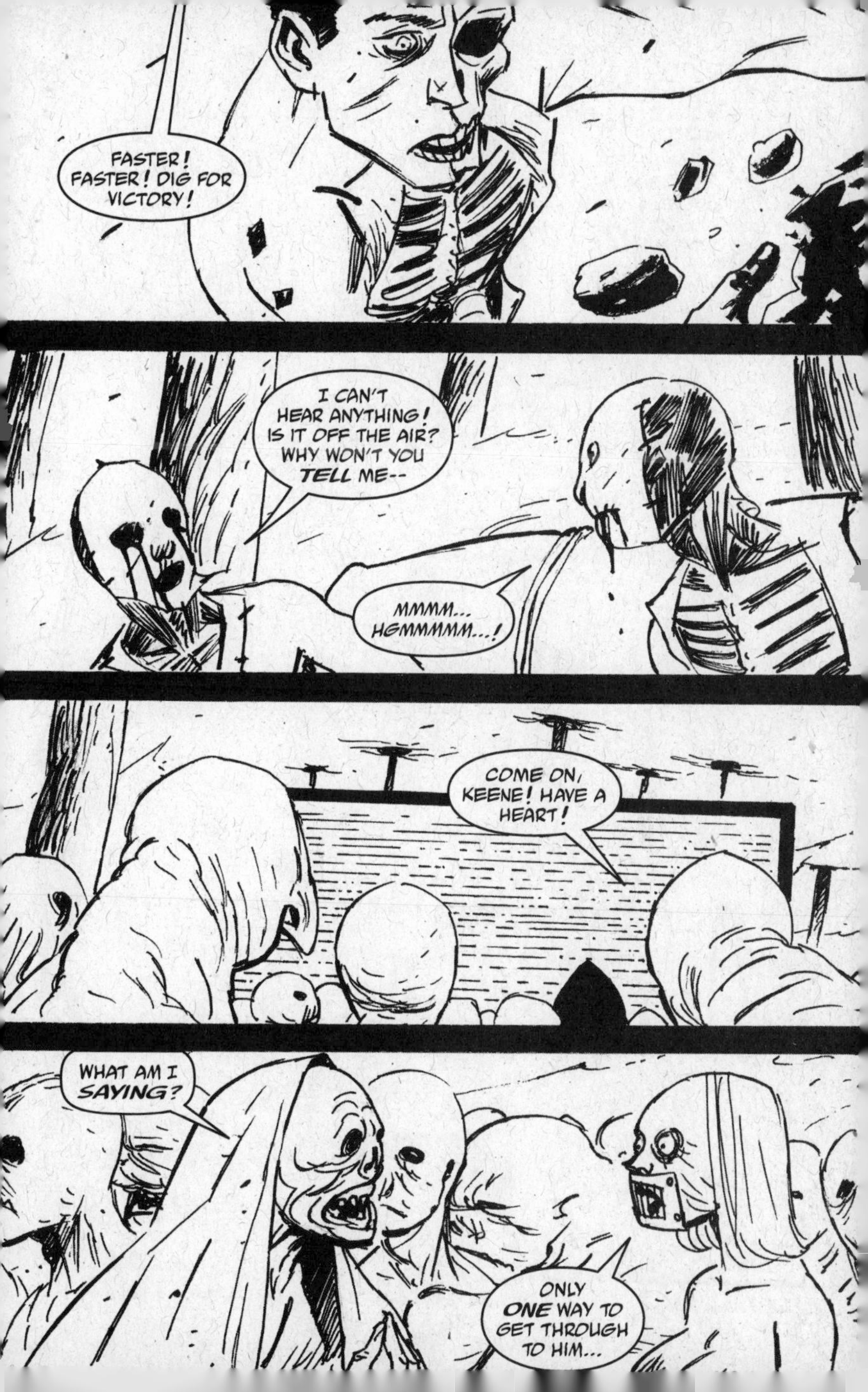
FASTER! FASTER! DIG FOR VICTORY!
I CAN'T HEAR ANYTHING! IS IT OFF THE AIR? WHY WON'T YOU TELL ME--
MMMM... HGMMMMM...!
COME ON, KEENE! HAVE A HEART!
WHAT AM I SAYING?
ONLY ONE WAY TO GET THROUGH TO HIM...

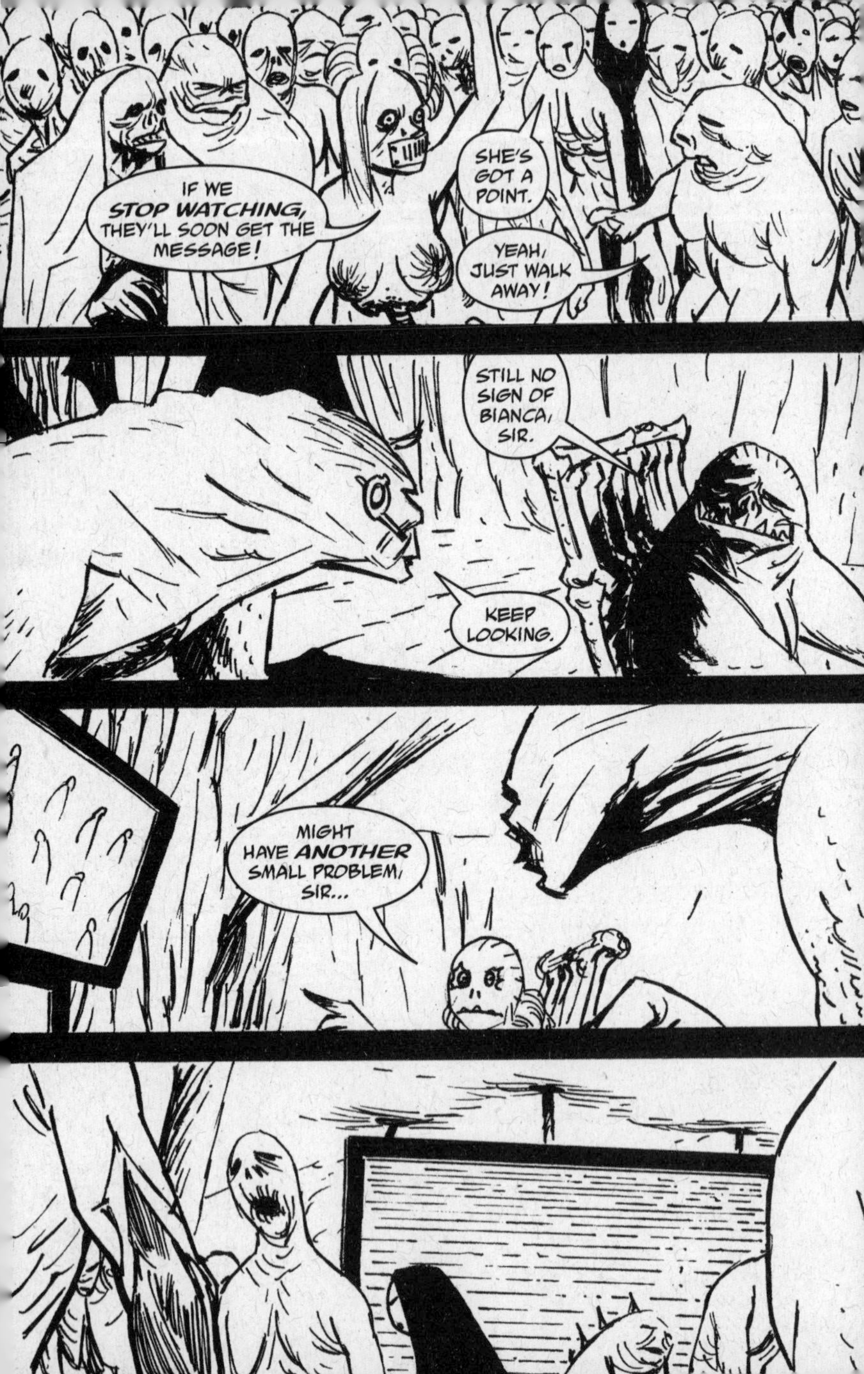
IF WE STOP WATCHING, THEY'LL SOON GET THE MESSAGE!
SHE'S GOT A POINT.
YEAH, JUST WALK AWAY!
STILL NO SIGN OF BIANCA, SIR.
KEEP LOOKING.
MIGHT HAVE ANOTHER SMALL PROBLEM, SIR...

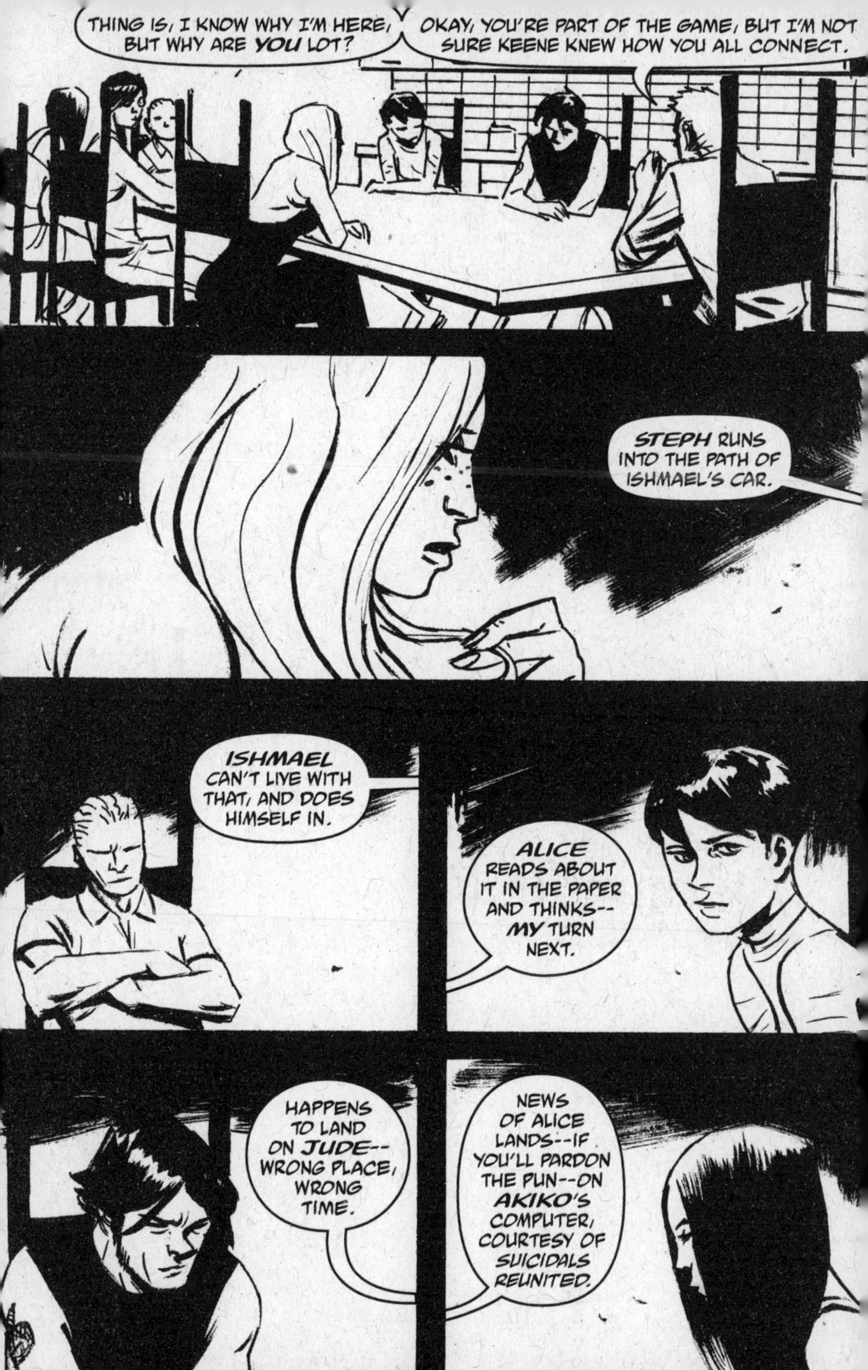
THING IS, I KNOW WHY I'M HERE, BUT WHY ARE YOU LOT?
OKAY, YOU'RE PART OF THE GAME, BUT I'M NOT SURE KEENE KNEW HOW YOU ALL CONNECT.
STEPH RUNS INTO THE PATH OF ISHMAEL'S CAR.
ISHMAEL CAN'T LIVE WITH THAT, AND DOES HIMSELF IN.
ALICE READS ABOUT IT IN THE PAPER AND THINKS--MY TURN NEXT.
HAPPENS TO LAND ON JUDE--WRONG PLACE, WRONG TIME.
NEWS OF ALICE LANDS--IF YOU'LL PARDON THE PUN--ON AKIKO'S COMPUTER, COURTESY OF SUICIDALS REUNITED.

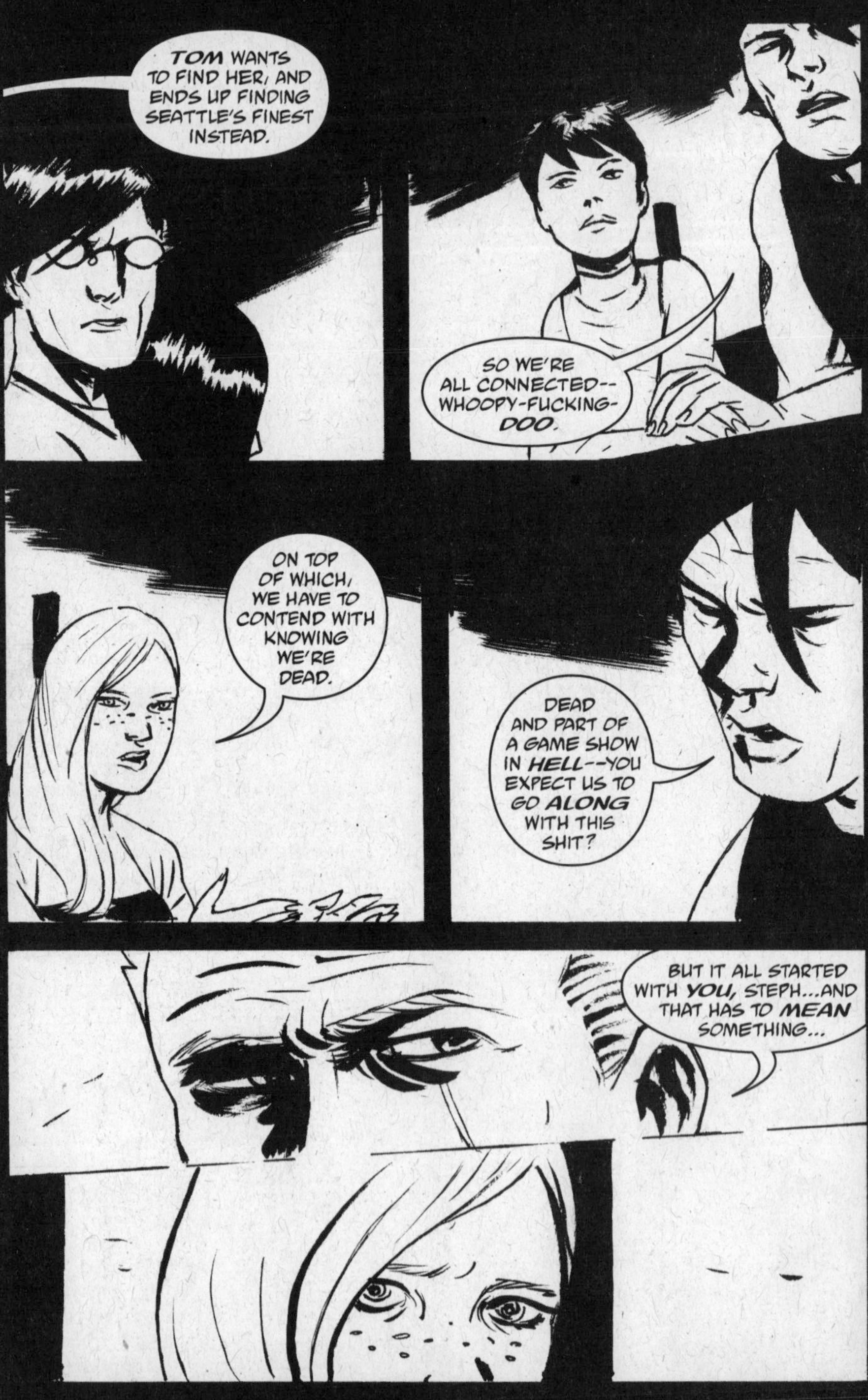
TOM WANTS TO FIND HER, AND ENDS UP FINDING SEATTLE'S FINEST INSTEAD.
SO WE'RE ALL CONNECTED-- WHOOPY-FUCKING-DOO.
ON TOP OF WHICH, WE HAVE TO CONTEND WITH KNOWING WE'RE DEAD.
DEAD AND PART OF A GAME SHOW IN HELL--YOU EXPECT US TO GO ALONG WITH THIS SHIT?
BUT IT ALL STARTED WITH YOU, STEPH...AND THAT HAS TO MEAN SOMETHING...

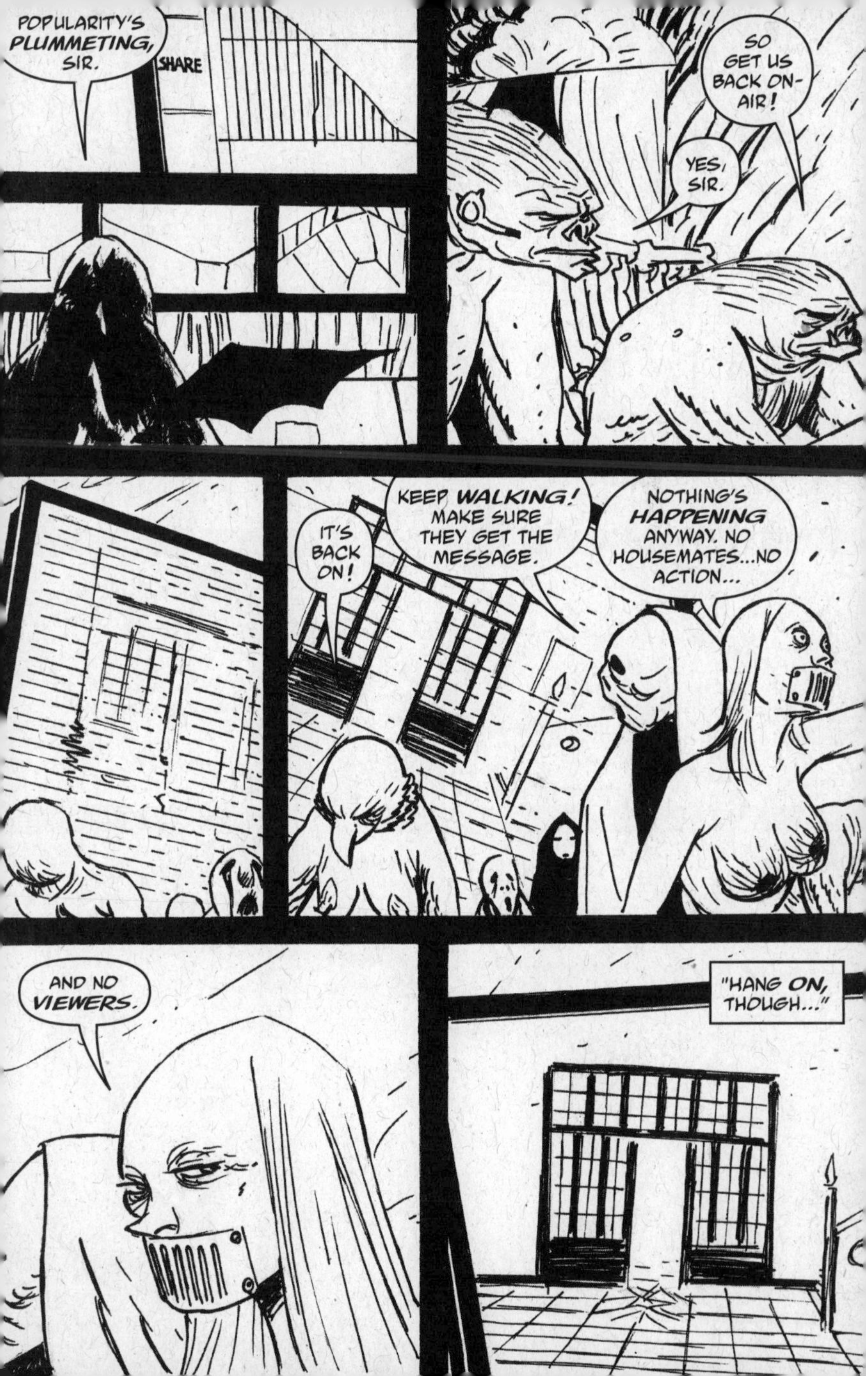
POPULARITY'S PLUMMETING, SIR.
SHARE
SO GET US BACK ON-AIR!
YES, SIR.
IT'S BACK ON!
KEEP WALKING! MAKE SURE THEY GET THE MESSAGE.
NOTHING'S HAPPENING ANYWAY. NO HOUSEMATES...NO ACTION...
AND NO VIEWERS.
"HANG ON, THOUGH..."

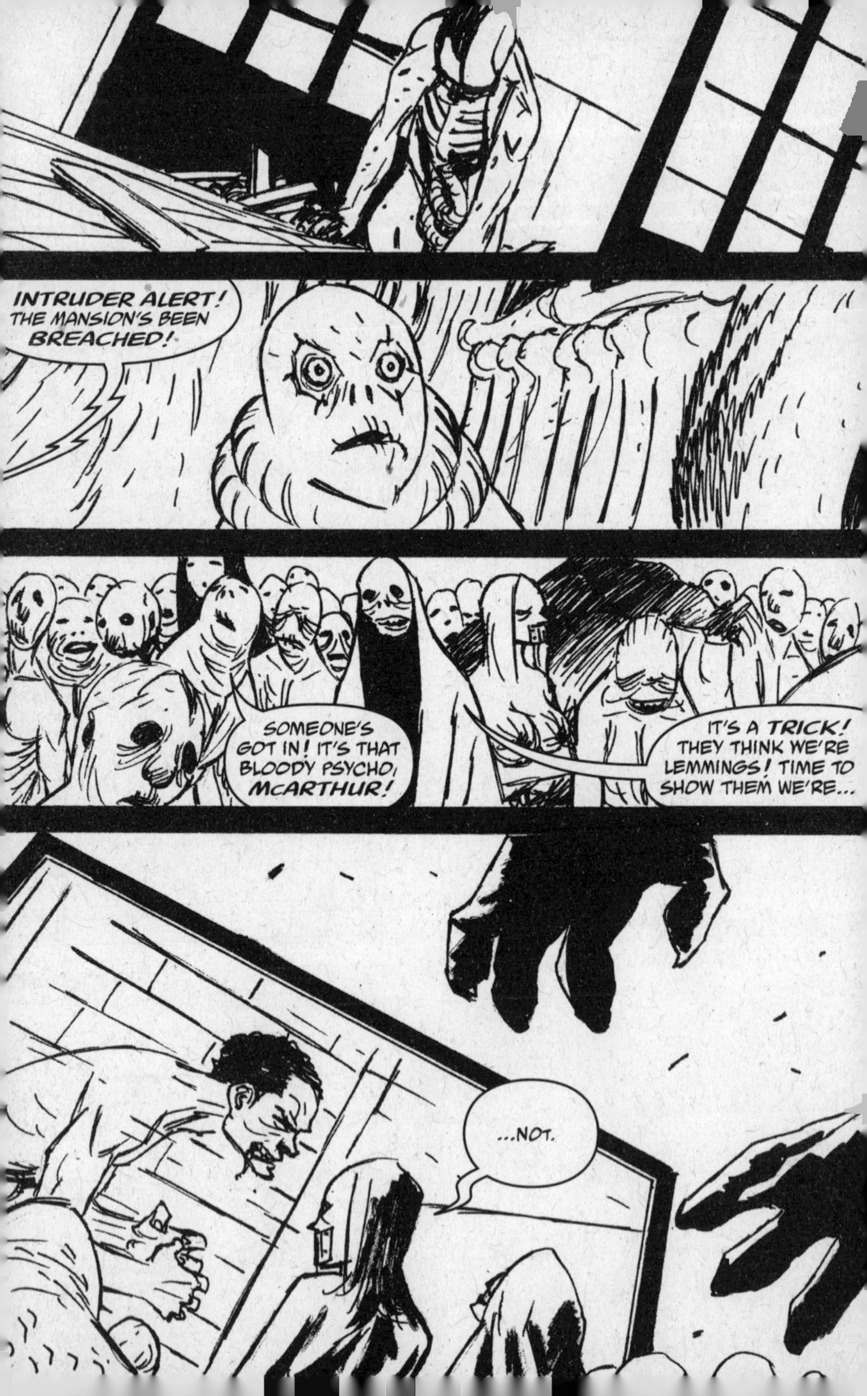
INTRUDER ALERT! THE MANSION'S BEEN BREACHED!
SOMEONE'S GOT IN! IT'S THAT BLOODY PSYCHO, McARTHUR!
IT'S A TRICK! THEY THINK WE'RE LEMMINGS! TIME TO SHOW THEM WE'RE...
...NOT.

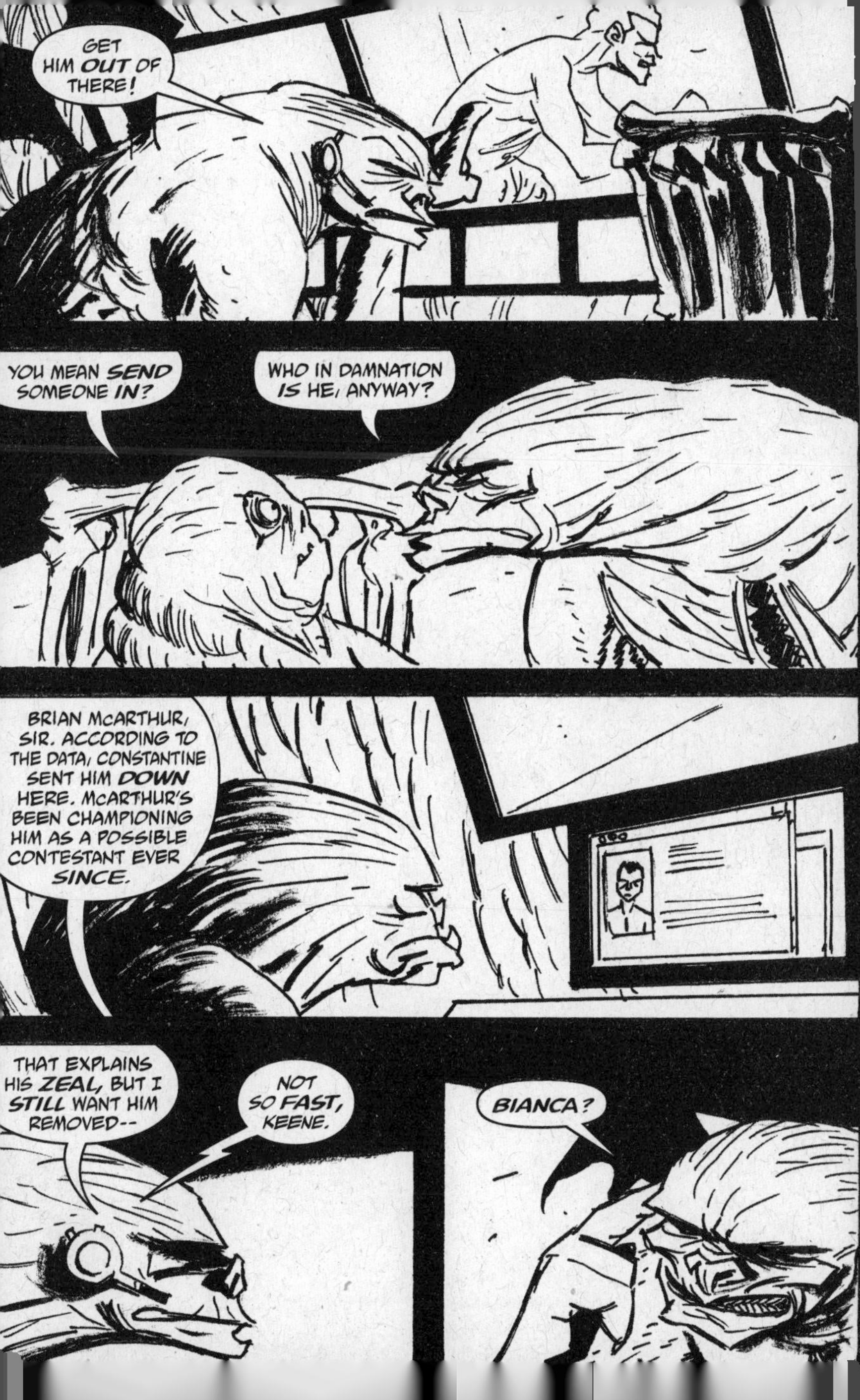

GET HIM OUT OF THERE!
YOU MEAN SEND SOMEONE IN?
WHO IN DAMNATION IS HE, ANYWAY?
BRIAN McARTHUR, SIR. ACCORDING TO THE DATA, CONSTANTINE SENT HIM DOWN HERE. McARTHUR'S BEEN CHAMPIONING HIM AS A POSSIBLE CONTESTANT EVER SINCE.
THAT EXPLAINS HIS ZEAL, BUT I STILL WANT HIM REMOVED--
NOT SO FAST, KEENE.
BIANCA?

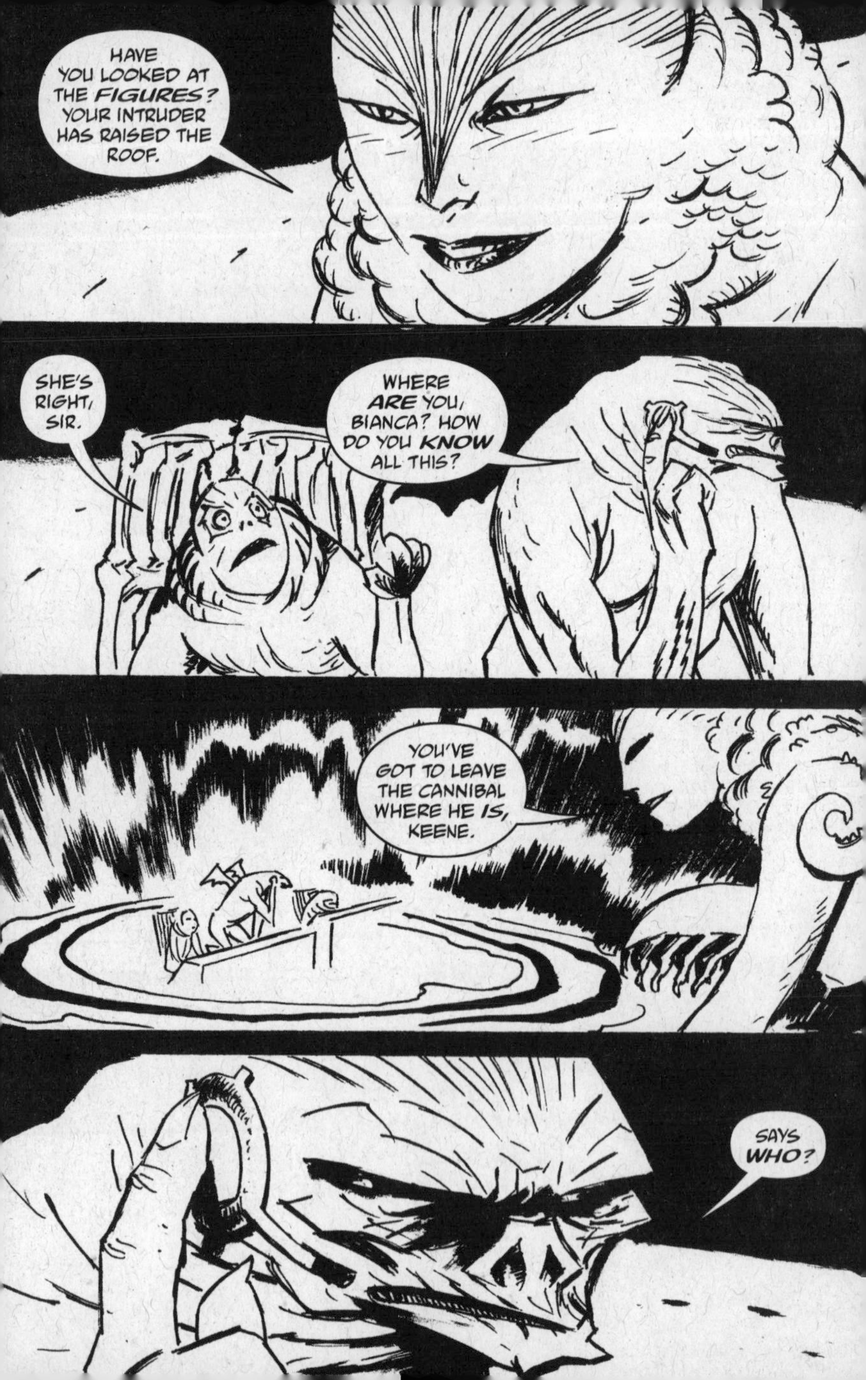
HAVE YOU LOOKED AT THE FIGURES? YOUR INTRUDER HAS RAISED THE ROOF.
SHE'S RIGHT, SIR.
WHERE ARE YOU, BIANCA? HOW DO YOU KNOW ALL THIS?
YOU'VE GOT TO LEAVE THE CANNIBAL WHERE HE IS, KEENE.
SAYS WHO?

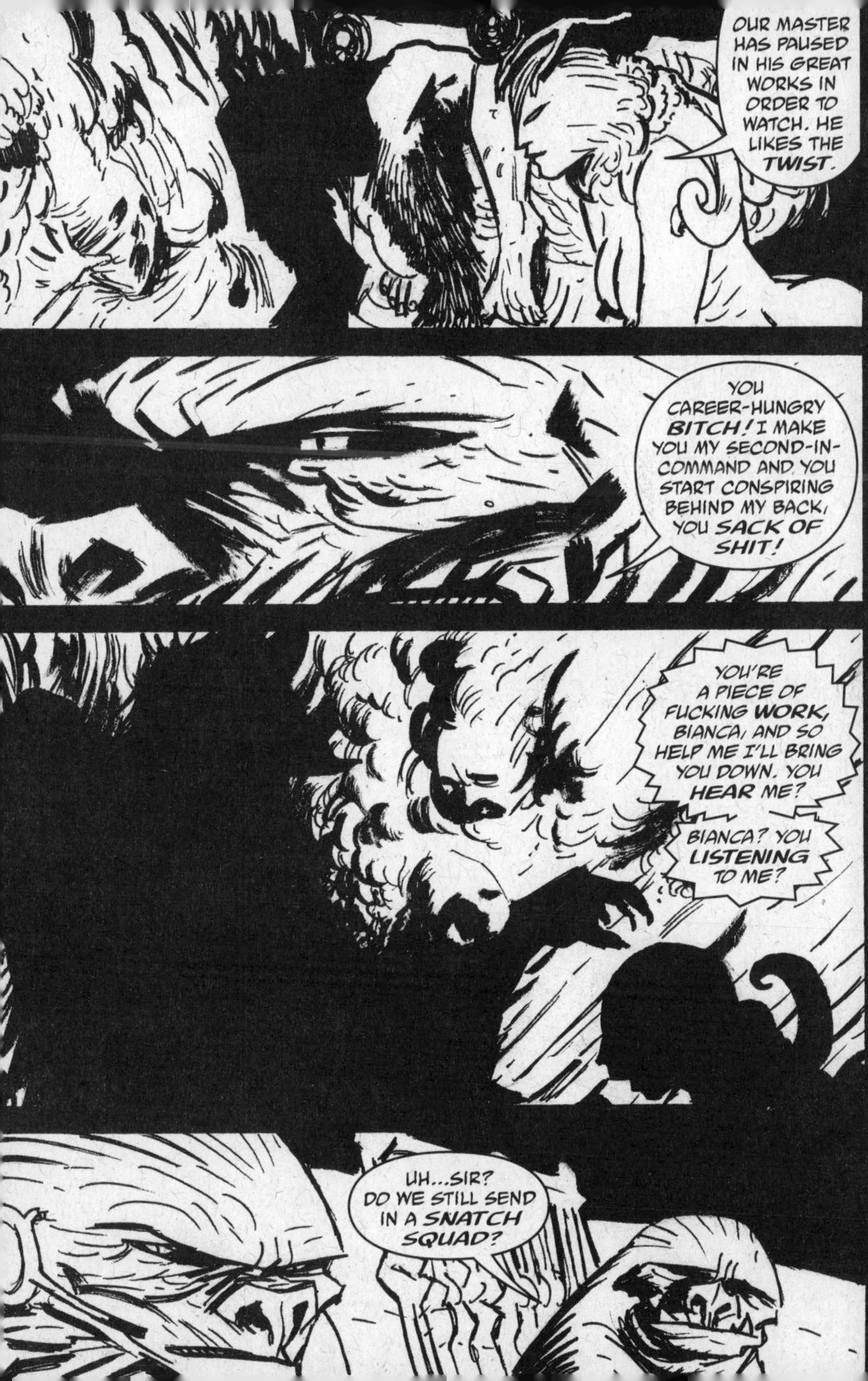
OUR MASTER HAS PAUSED IN HIS GREAT WORKS IN ORDER TO WATCH. HE LIKES THE TWIST.
YOU CAREER-HUNGRY BITCH! I MAKE YOU MY SECOND-IN-COMMAND AND YOU START CONSPIRING BEHIND MY BACK, YOU SACK OF SHIT!
YOU'RE A PIECE OF FUCKING WORK, BIANCA, AND SO HELP ME I'LL BRING YOU DOWN. YOU HEAR ME?
BIANCA? YOU LISTENING TO ME?
UH...SIR? DO WE STILL SEND IN A SNATCH SQUAD?

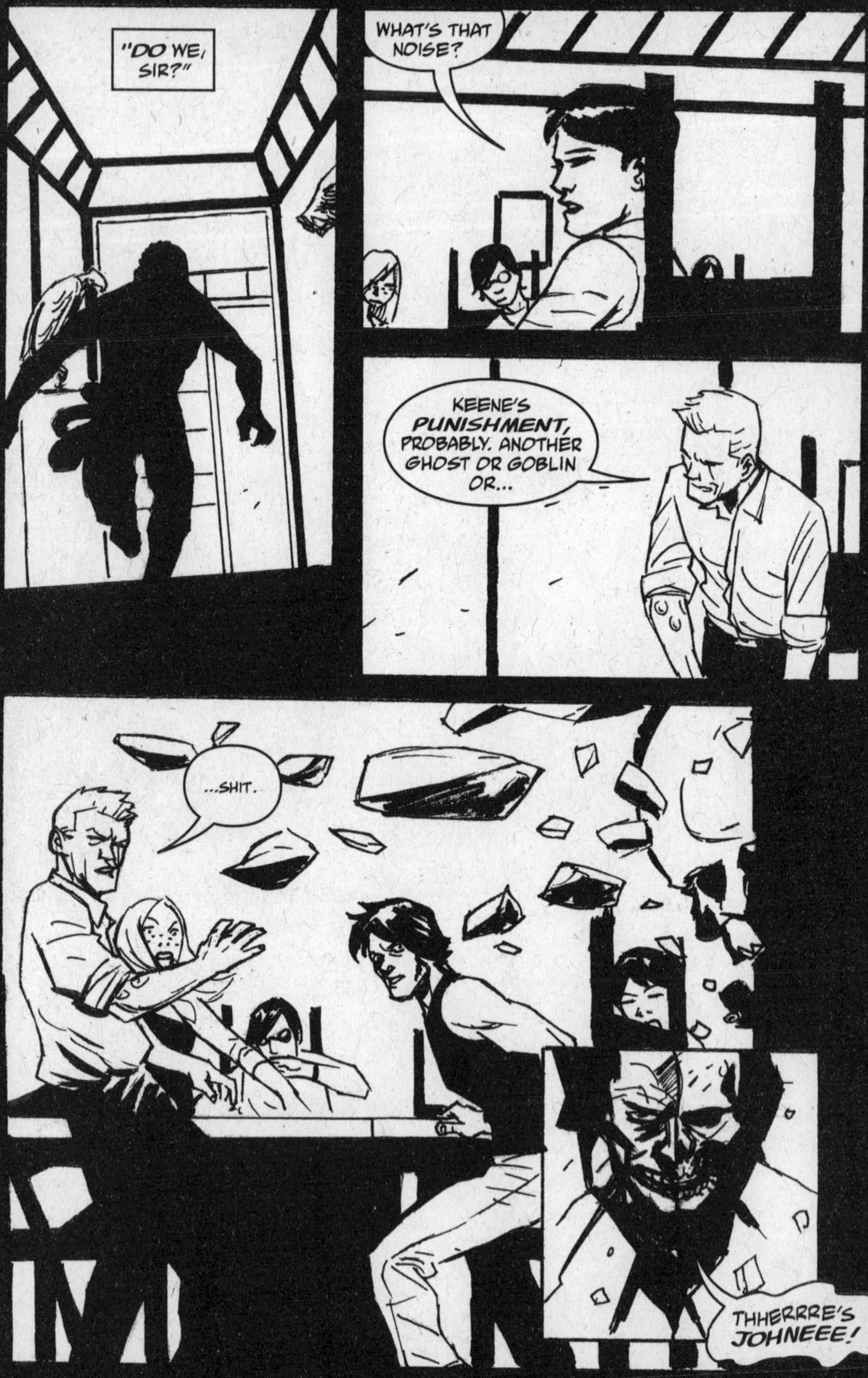
"DO WE, SIR?"
WHAT'S THAT NOISE?
KEENE'S PUNISHMENT, PROBABLY. ANOTHER GHOST OR GOBLIN OR...
...SHIT.
THHERRRE'S JOHNEEE!

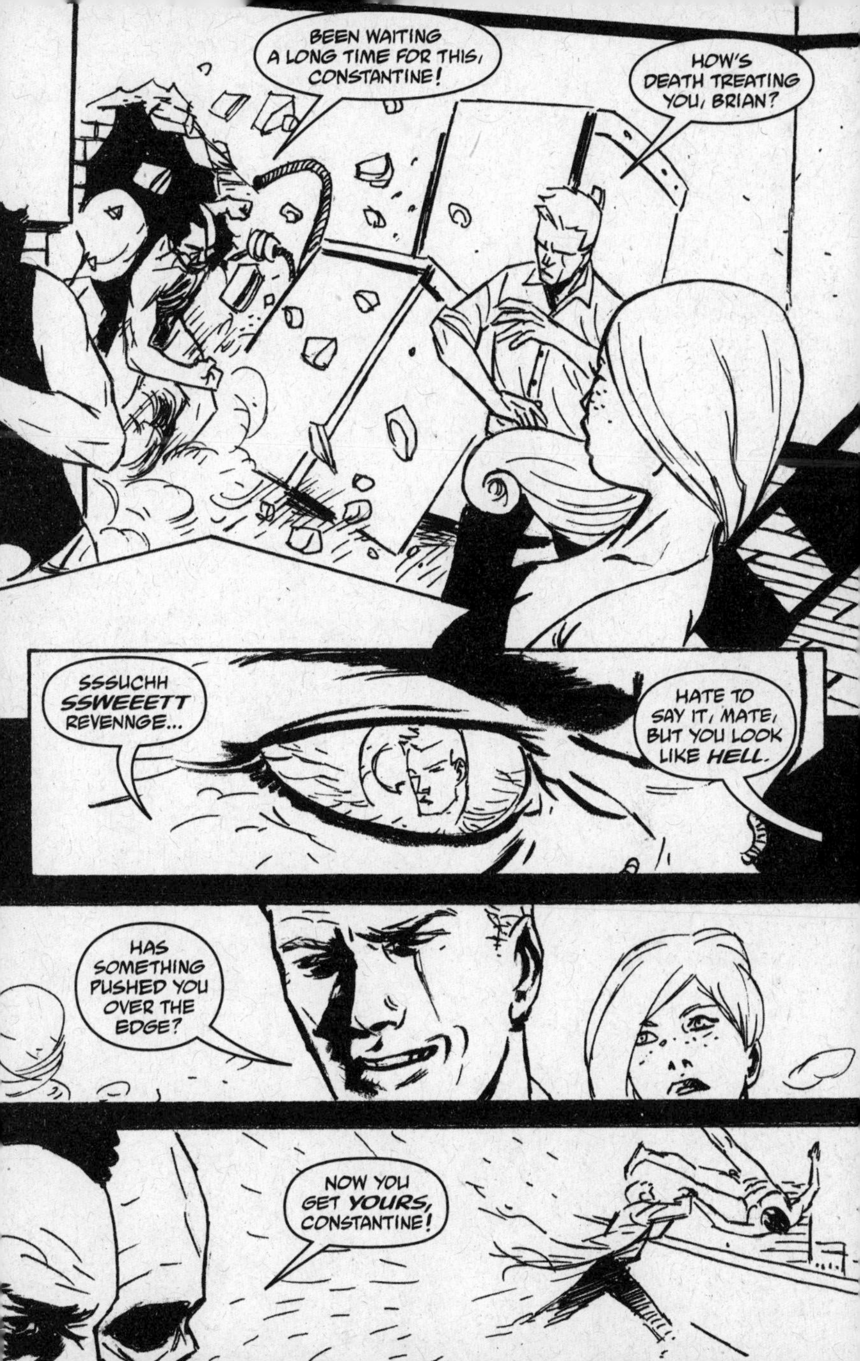
BEEN WAITING A LONG TIME FOR THIS, CONSTANTINE!
HOW'S DEATH TREATING YOU, BRIAN?
SSSUCHH SSWEEETT REVENNGE...
HATE TO SAY IT, MATE, BUT YOU LOOK LIKE HELL.
HAS SOMETHING PUSHED YOU OVER THE EDGE?
NOW YOU GET YOURS, CONSTANTINE!

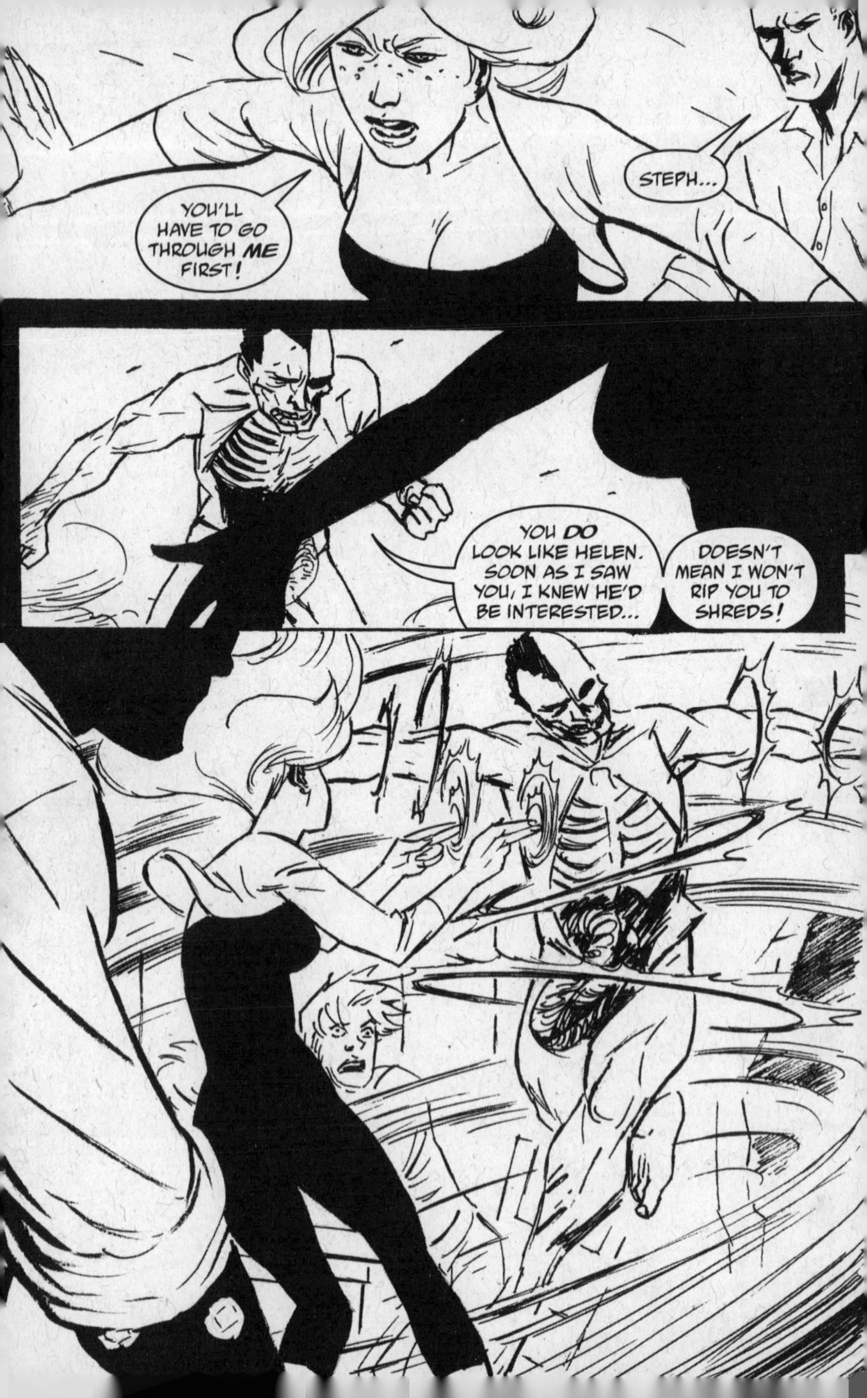
YOU'LL HAVE TO GO THROUGH ME FIRST!
STEPH...
YOU DO LOOK LIKE HELEN. SOON AS I SAW YOU, I KNEW HE'D BE INTERESTED...
DOESN'T MEAN I WON'T RIP YOU TO SHREDS!

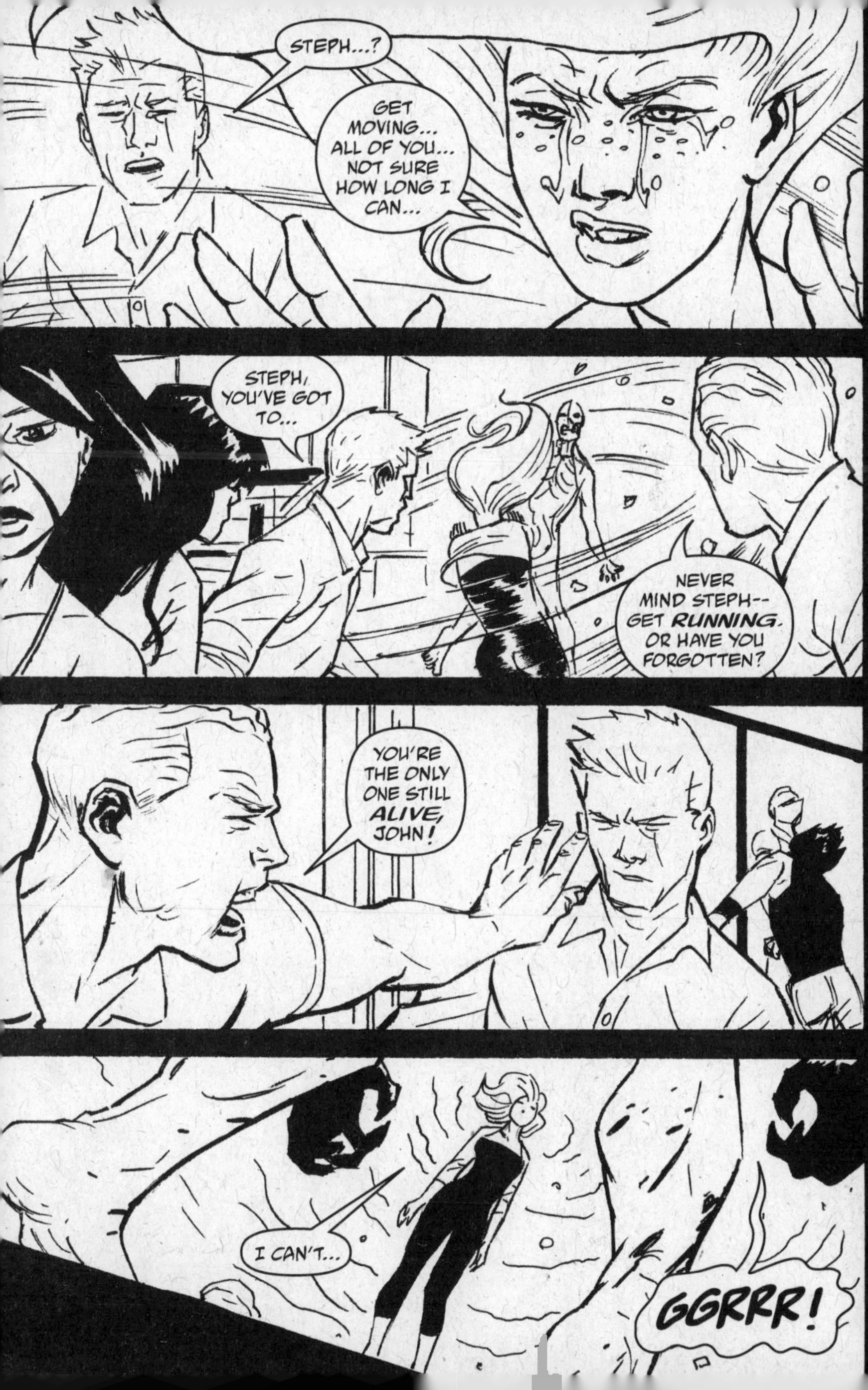
STEPH...?
GET MOVING... ALL OF YOU... NOT SURE HOW LONG I CAN...
STEPH, YOU'VE GOT TO...
NEVER MIND STEPH-- GET RUNNING. OR HAVE YOU FORGOTTEN?
YOU'RE THE ONLY ONE STILL ALIVE, JOHN!
I CAN'T...
GGRRR!

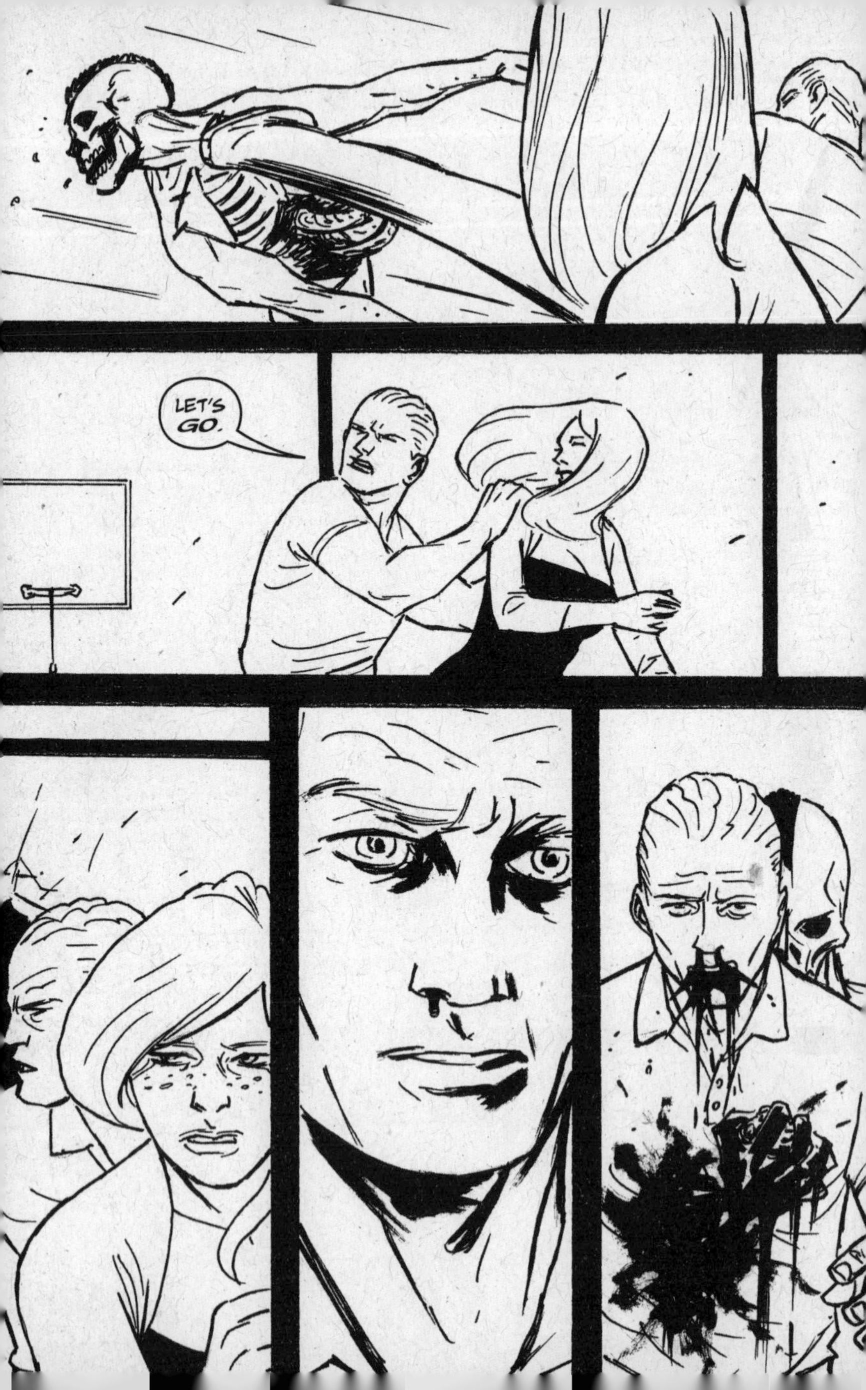
LET'S GO.

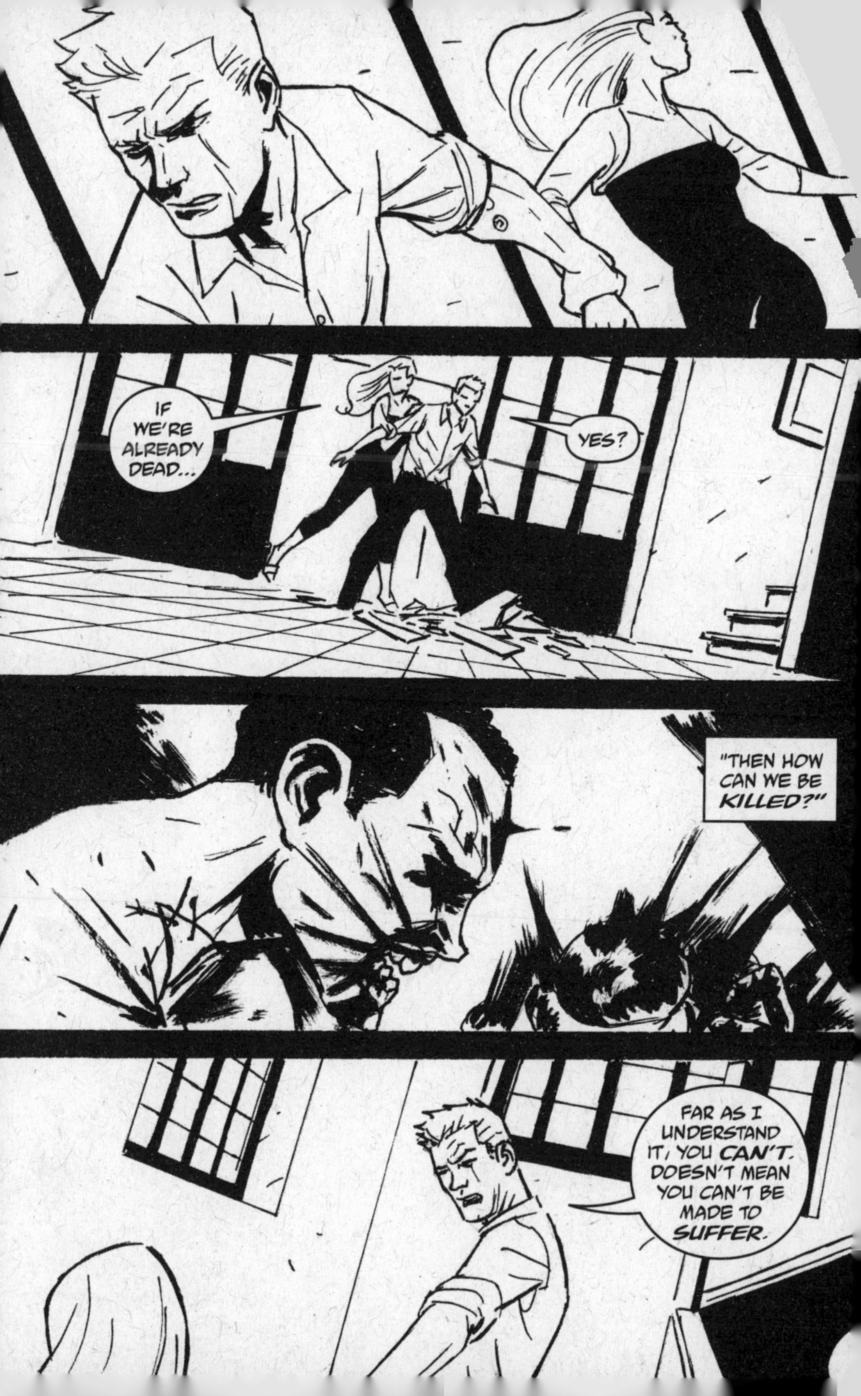
IF WE'RE ALREADY DEAD...
YES?
"THEN HOW CAN WE BE KILLED?"
FAR AS I UNDERSTAND IT, YOU CAN'T. DOESN'T MEAN YOU CAN'T BE MADE TO SUFFER.

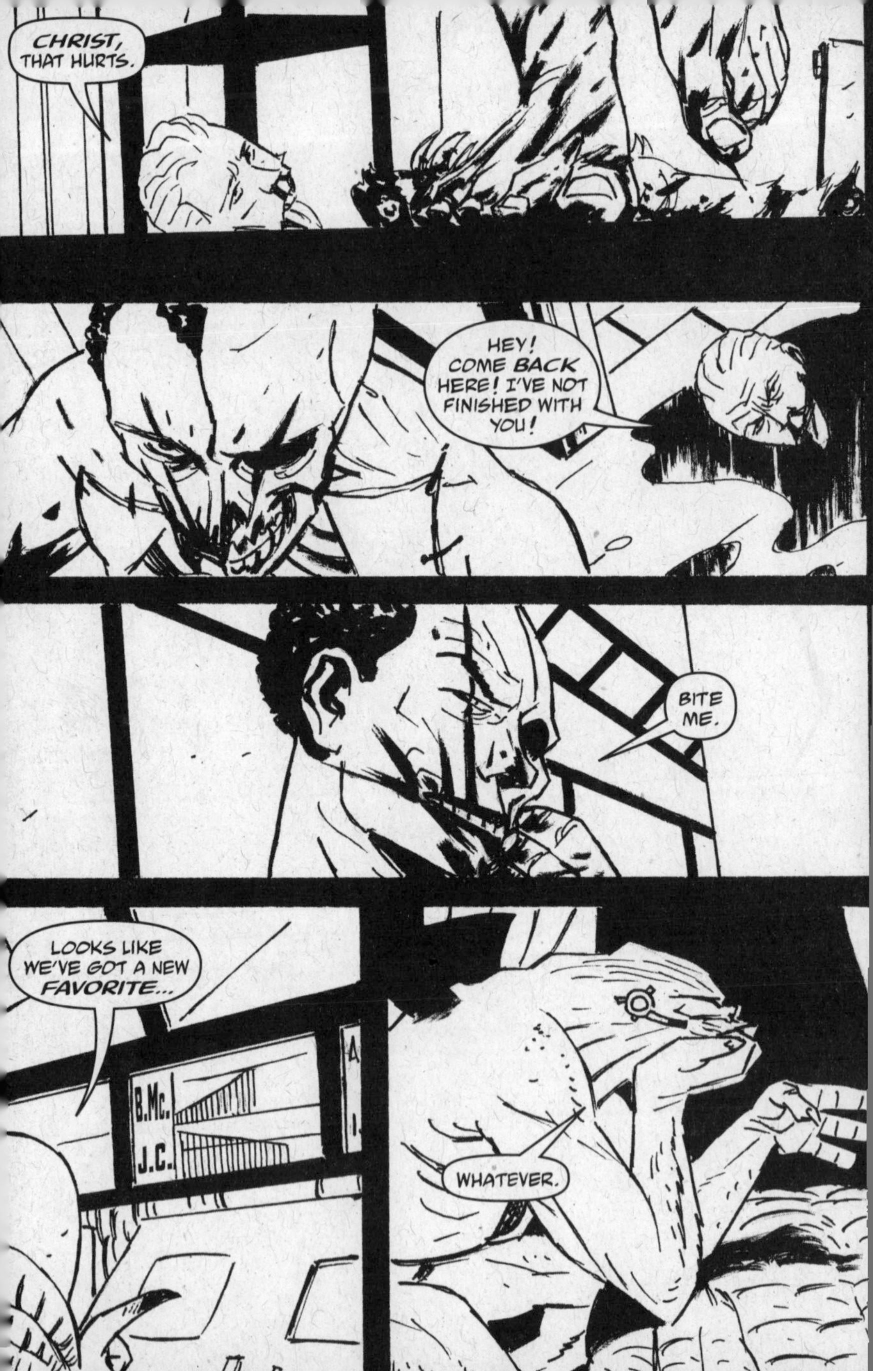
CHRIST, THAT HURTS.
HEY! COME BACK HERE! I'VE NOT FINISHED WITH YOU!
BITE ME.
LOOKS LIKE WE'VE GOT A NEW FAVORITE...
B.Mc.
J.C.
WHATEVER.

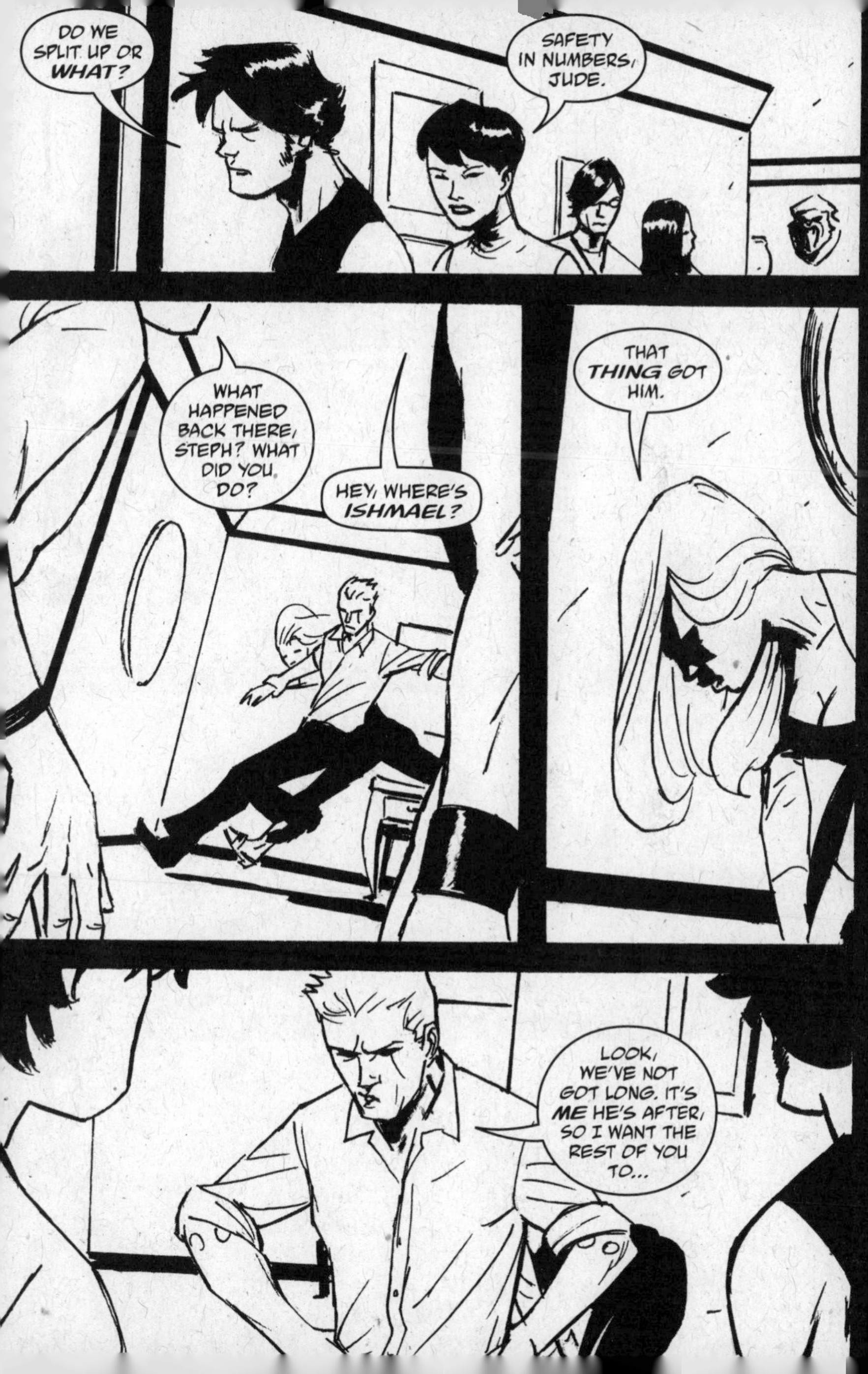
DO WE SPLIT UP OR WHAT?
SAFETY IN NUMBERS, JUDE.
WHAT HAPPENED BACK THERE, STEPH? WHAT DID YOU DO?
HEY, WHERE'S ISHMAEL?
THAT THING GOT HIM.
LOOK, WE'VE NOT GOT LONG. IT'S ME HE'S AFTER, SO I WANT THE REST OF YOU TO...

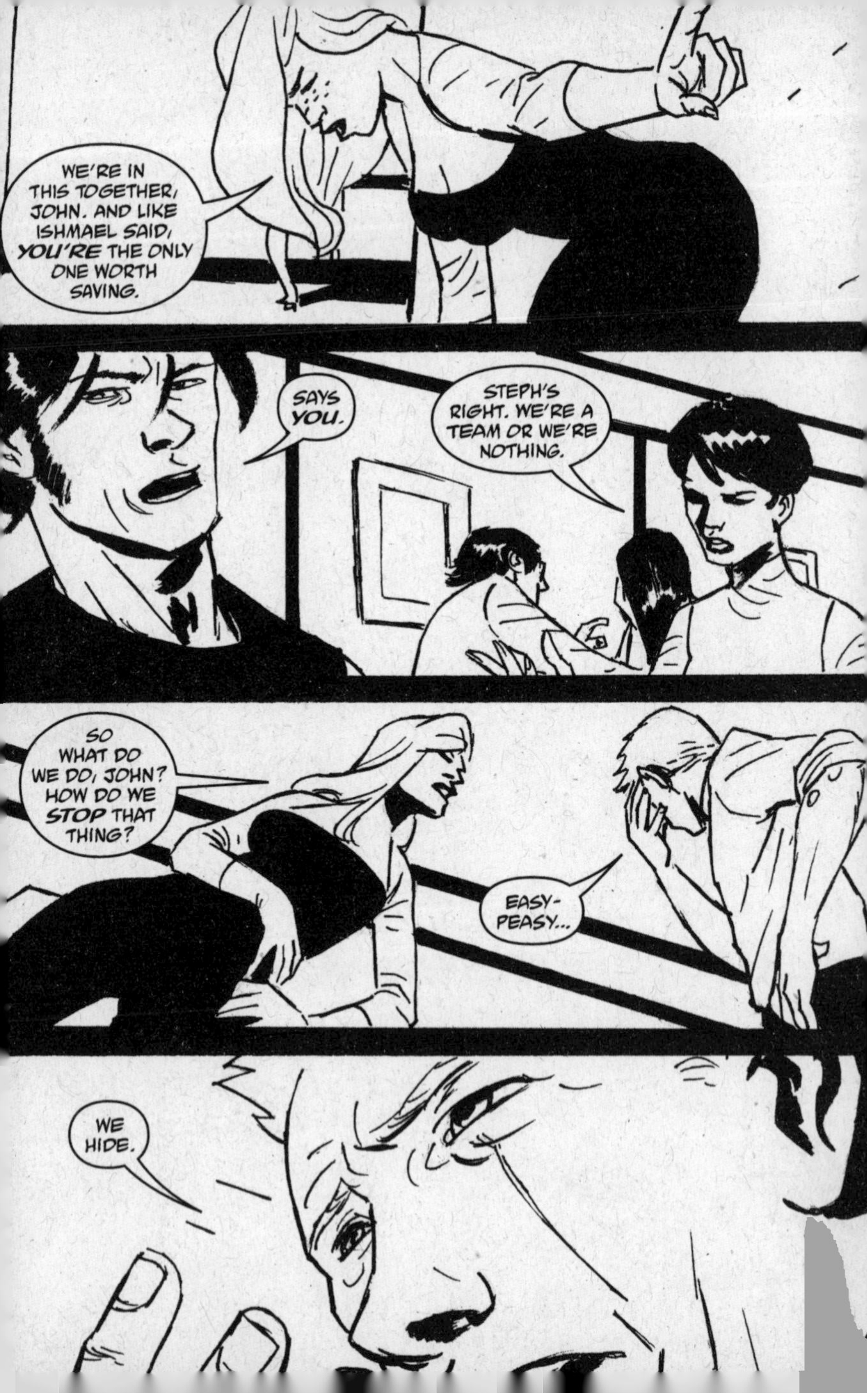
WE'RE IN THIS TOGETHER, JOHN. AND LIKE ISHMAEL SAID, YOU'RE THE ONLY ONE WORTH SAVING.
SAYS YOU.
STEPH'S RIGHT. WE'RE A TEAM OR WE'RE NOTHING.
SO WHAT DO WE DO, JOHN? HOW DO WE STOP THAT THING?
EASY-PEASY...
WE HIDE.

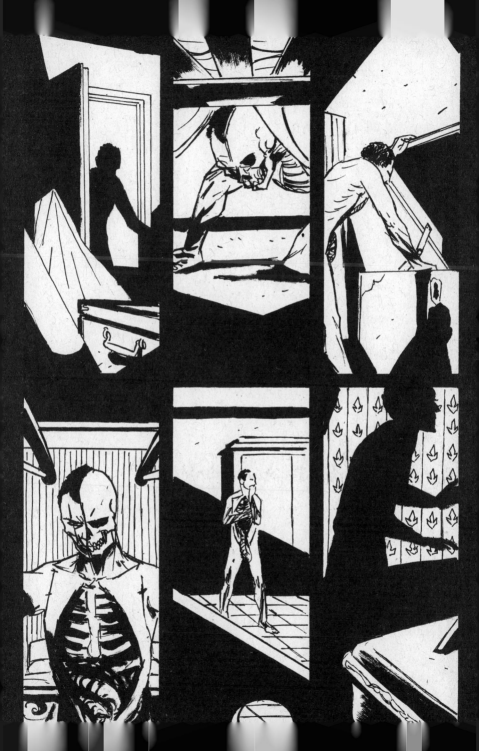

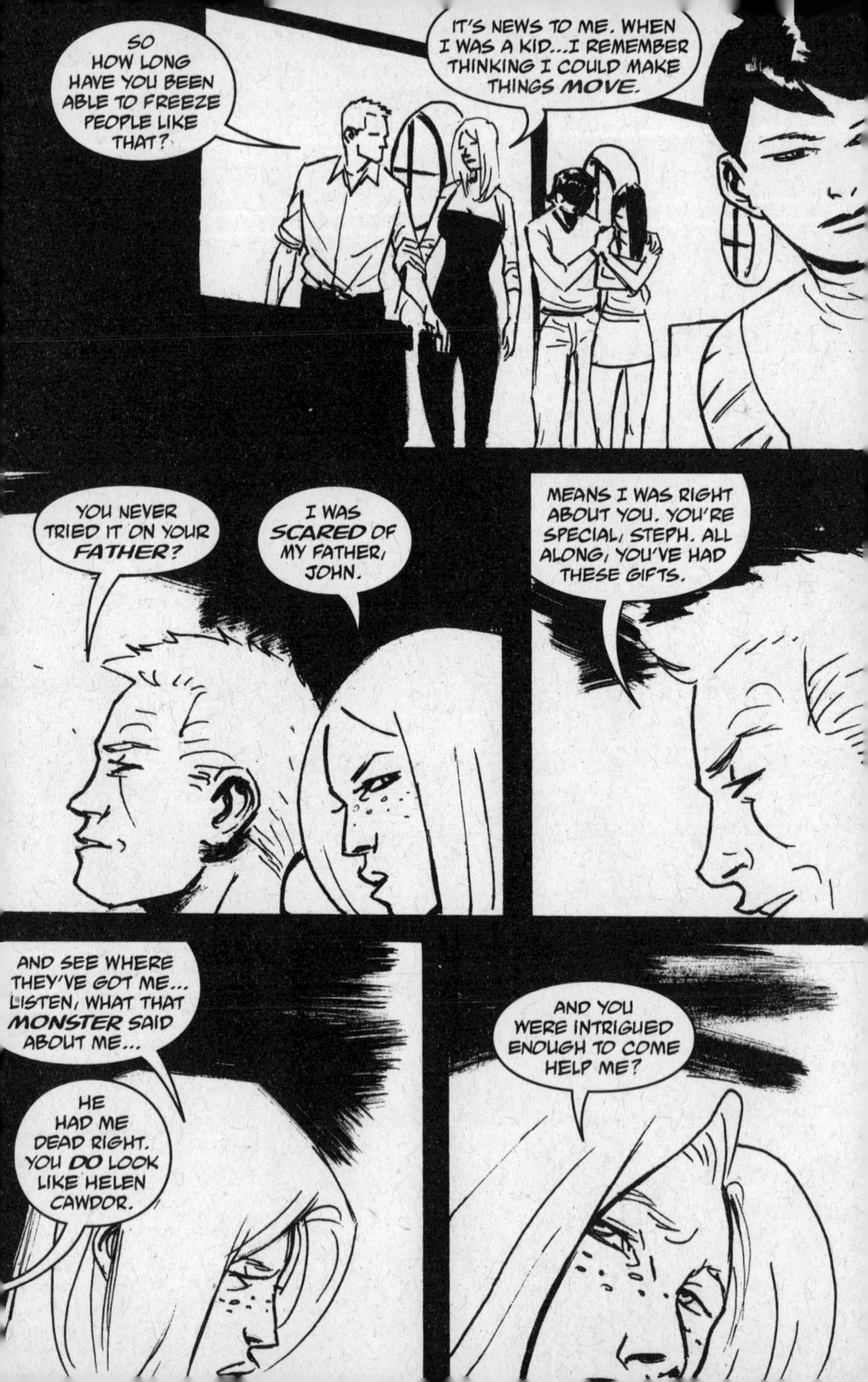
SO HOW LONG HAVE YOU BEEN ABLE TO FREEZE PEOPLE LIKE THAT?
IT'S NEWS TO ME. WHEN I WAS A KID...I REMEMBER THINKING I COULD MAKE THINGS MOVE.
YOU NEVER TRIED IT ON YOUR FATHER?
I WAS SCARED OF MY FATHER, JOHN.
MEANS I WAS RIGHT ABOUT YOU. YOU'RE SPECIAL, STEPH. ALL ALONG, YOU'VE HAD THESE GIFTS.
AND SEE WHERE THEY'VE GOT ME... LISTEN, WHAT THAT MONSTER SAID ABOUT ME...
HE HAD ME DEAD RIGHT. YOU DO LOOK LIKE HELEN CAWDOR.
AND YOU WERE INTRIGUED ENOUGH TO COME HELP ME?

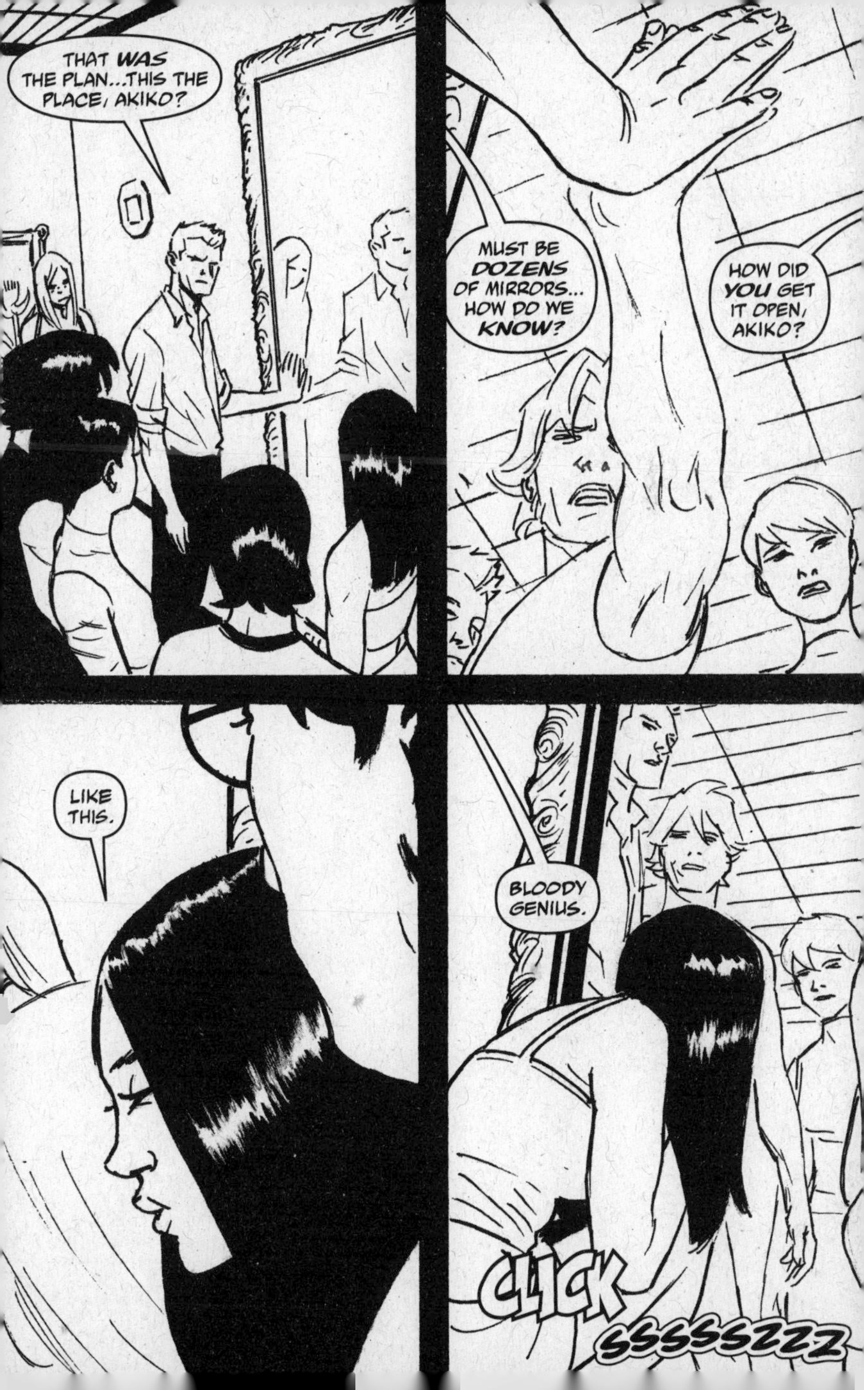
THAT WAS THE PLAN...THIS THE PLACE, AKIKO?
MUST BE DOZENS OF MIRRORS... HOW DO WE KNOW?
HOW DID YOU GET IT OPEN, AKIKO?
LIKE THIS.
BLOODY GENIUS.
CLICK
SSSSSZZZ

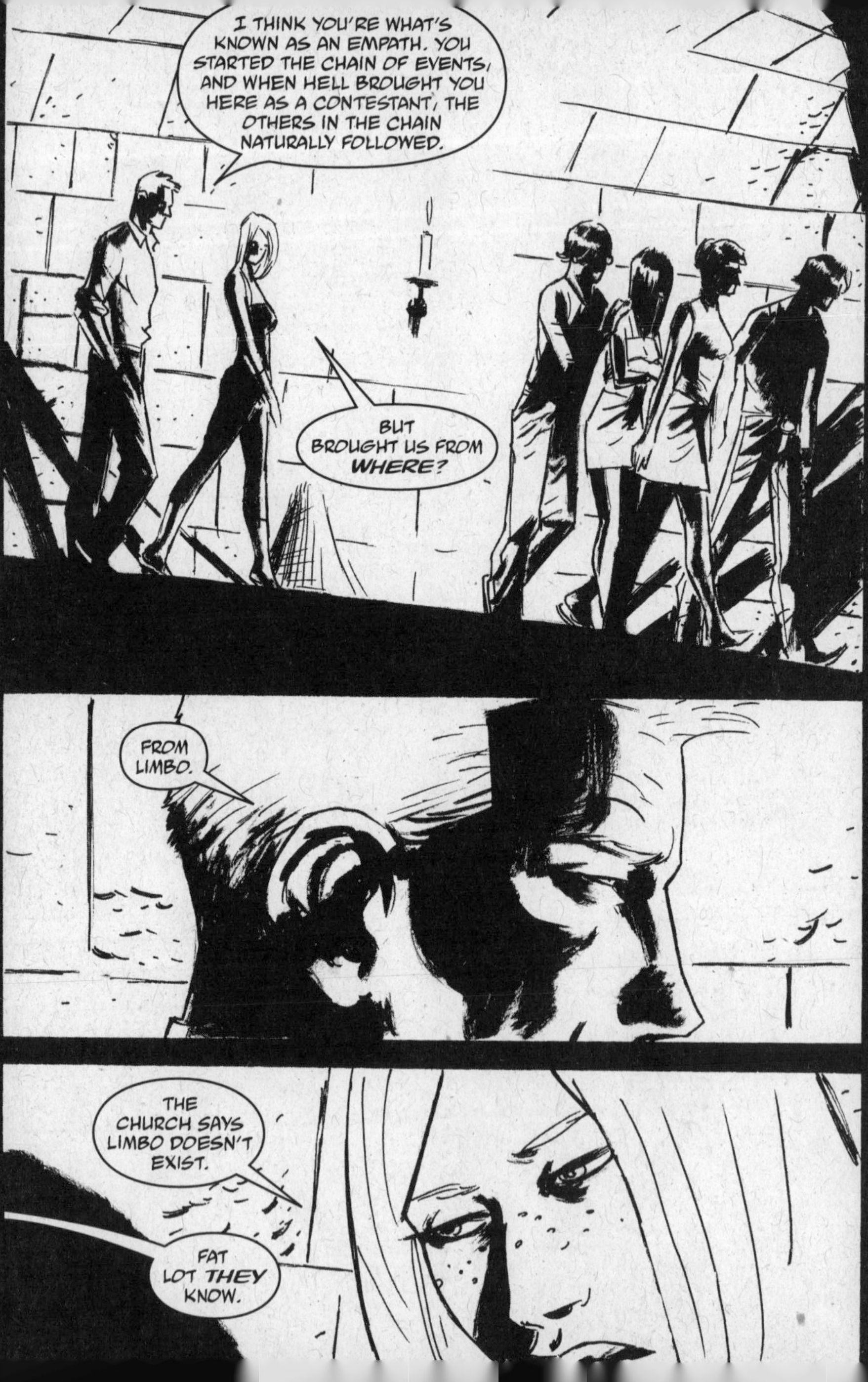
I THINK YOU'RE WHAT'S KNOWN AS AN EMPATH. YOU STARTED THE CHAIN OF EVENTS, AND WHEN HELL BROUGHT YOU HERE AS A CONTESTANT, THE OTHERS IN THE CHAIN NATURALLY FOLLOWED.
BUT BROUGHT US FROM *WHERE?*
FROM LIMBO.
THE CHURCH SAYS LIMBO DOESN'T EXIST.
FAT LOT *THEY* KNOW.

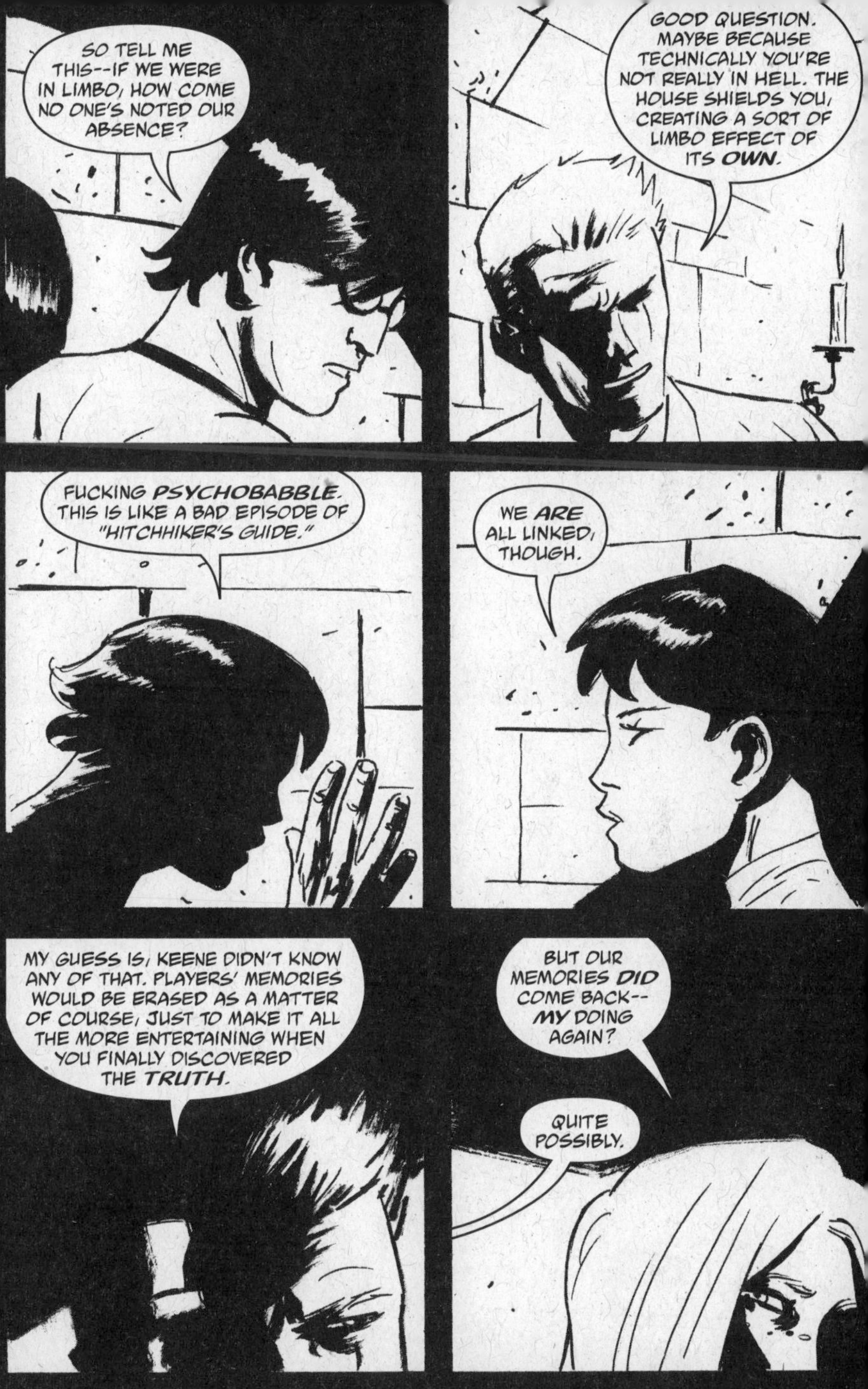
SO TELL ME THIS--IF WE WERE IN LIMBO, HOW COME NO ONE'S NOTED OUR ABSENCE?
GOOD QUESTION. MAYBE BECAUSE TECHNICALLY YOU'RE NOT REALLY IN HELL. THE HOUSE SHIELDS YOU, CREATING A SORT OF LIMBO EFFECT OF ITS OWN.
FUCKING PSYCHOBABBLE. THIS IS LIKE A BAD EPISODE OF "HITCHHIKER'S GUIDE."
WE ARE ALL LINKED, THOUGH.
MY GUESS IS, KEENE DIDN'T KNOW ANY OF THAT. PLAYERS' MEMORIES WOULD BE ERASED AS A MATTER OF COURSE, JUST TO MAKE IT ALL THE MORE ENTERTAINING WHEN YOU FINALLY DISCOVERED THE TRUTH.
BUT OUR MEMORIES DID COME BACK--MY DOING AGAIN?
QUITE POSSIBLY.

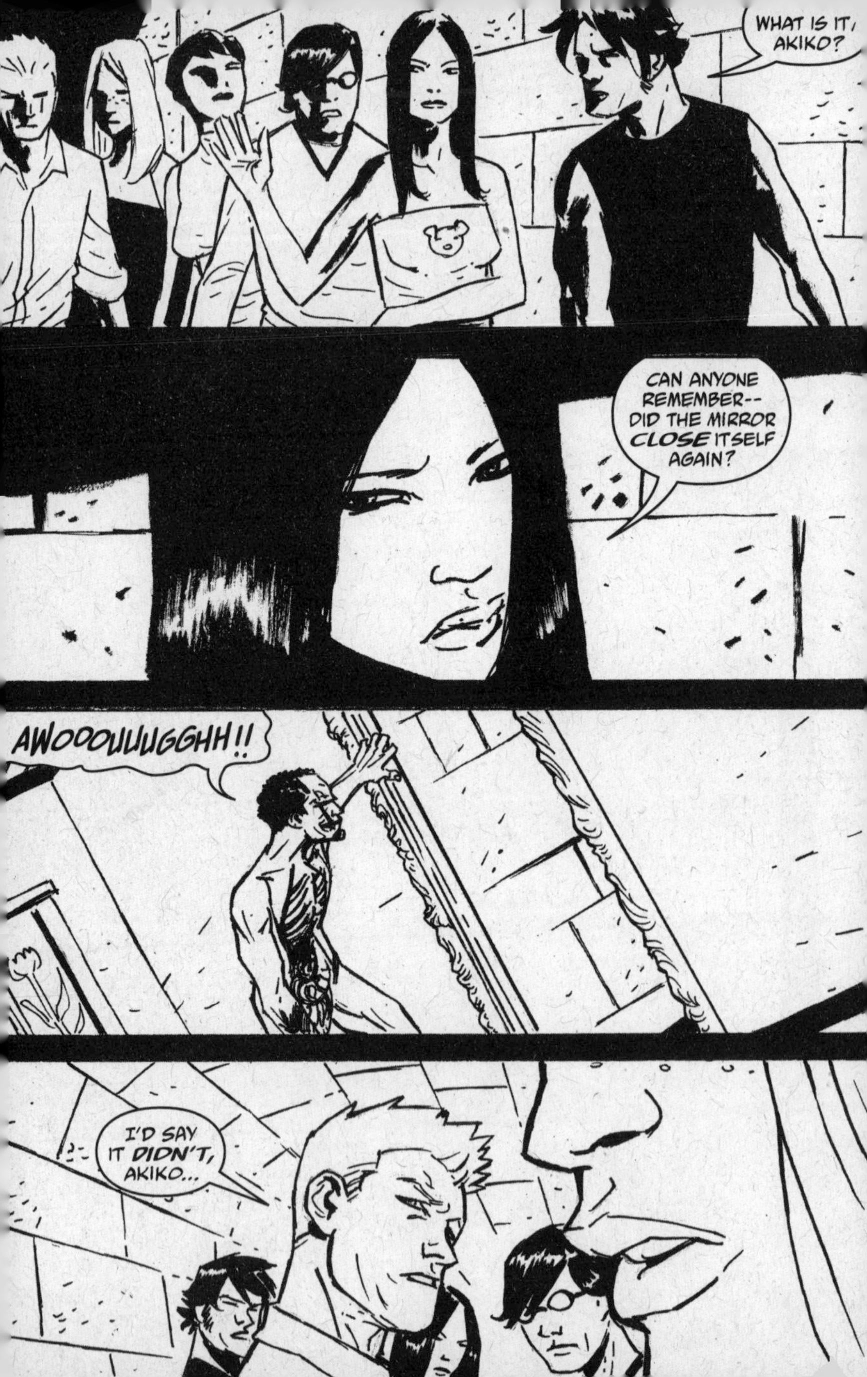
WHAT IS IT, AKIKO?
CAN ANYONE REMEMBER-- DID THE MIRROR CLOSE ITSELF AGAIN?
AWOOOUUUGGHH!!
I'D SAY IT DIDN'T, AKIKO...

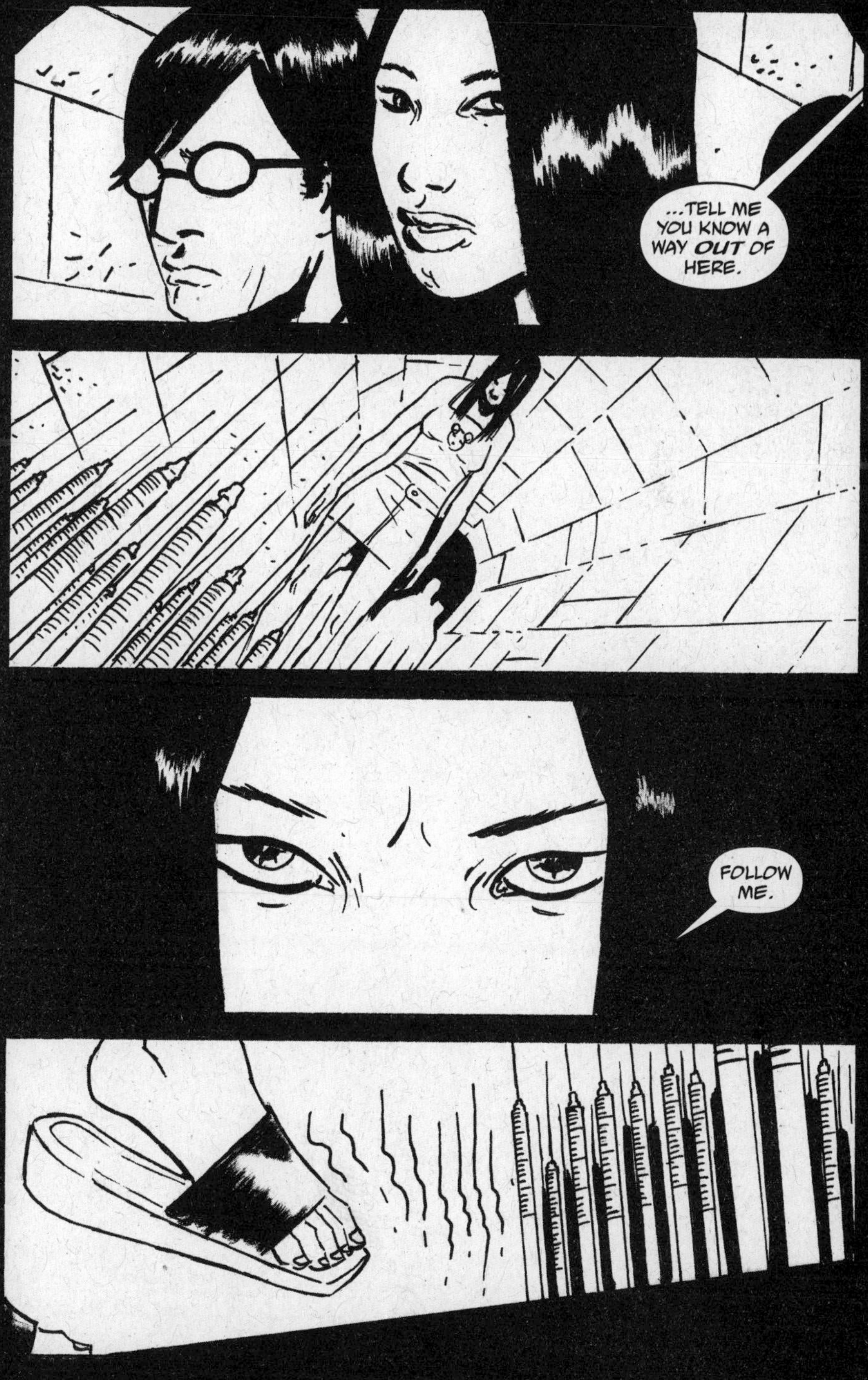
...TELL ME YOU KNOW A WAY OUT OF HERE.
FOLLOW ME.

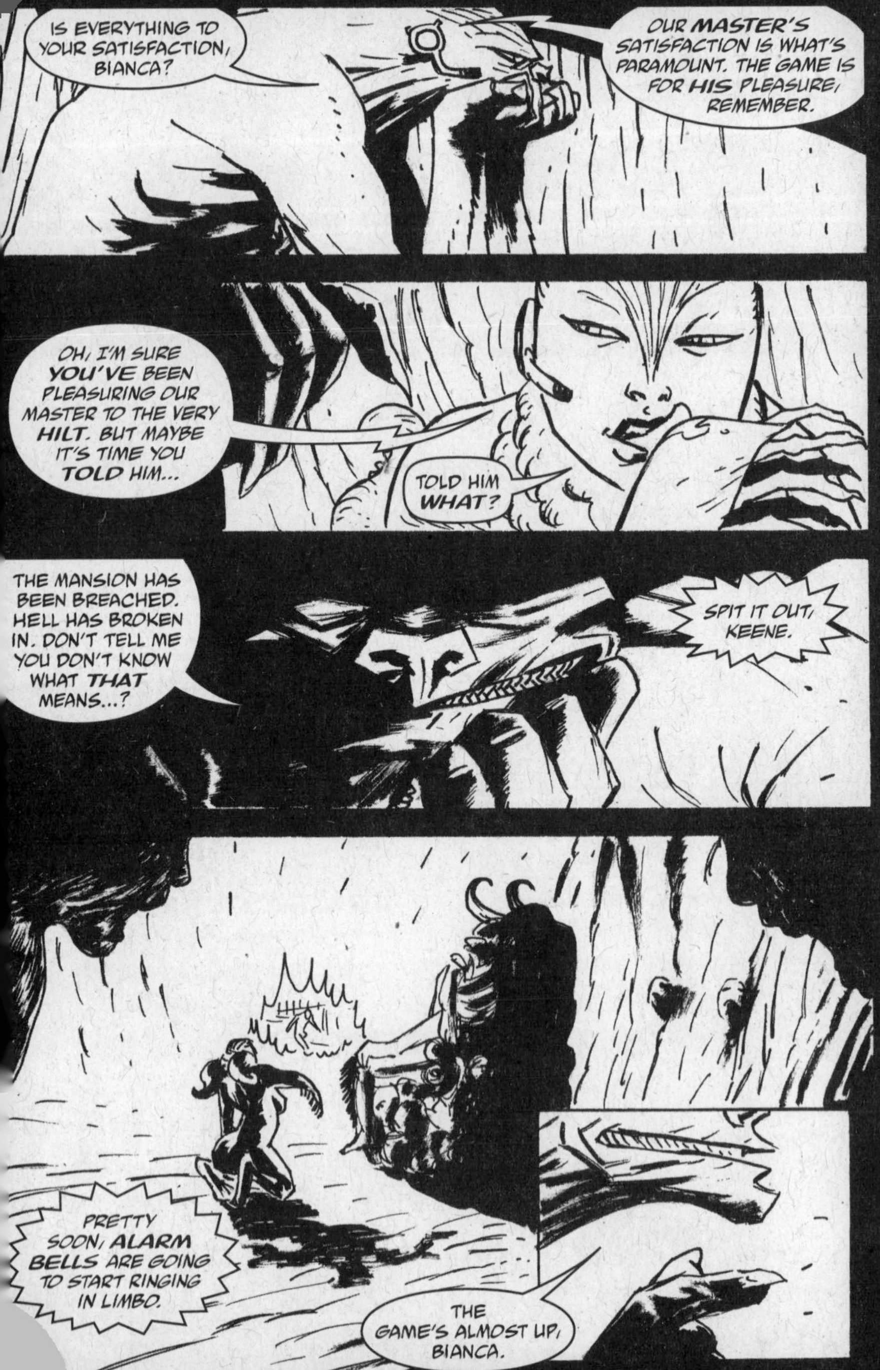

IS EVERYTHING TO YOUR SATISFACTION, BIANCA?
OUR MASTER'S SATISFACTION IS WHAT'S PARAMOUNT. THE GAME IS FOR HIS PLEASURE, REMEMBER.
OH, I'M SURE YOU'VE BEEN PLEASURING OUR MASTER TO THE VERY HILT. BUT MAYBE IT'S TIME YOU TOLD HIM...
TOLD HIM WHAT?
THE MANSION HAS BEEN BREACHED. HELL HAS BROKEN IN. DON'T TELL ME YOU DON'T KNOW WHAT THAT MEANS...?
SPIT IT OUT, KEENE.
PRETTY SOON, ALARM BELLS ARE GOING TO START RINGING IN LIMBO.
THE GAME'S ALMOST UP, BIANCA.

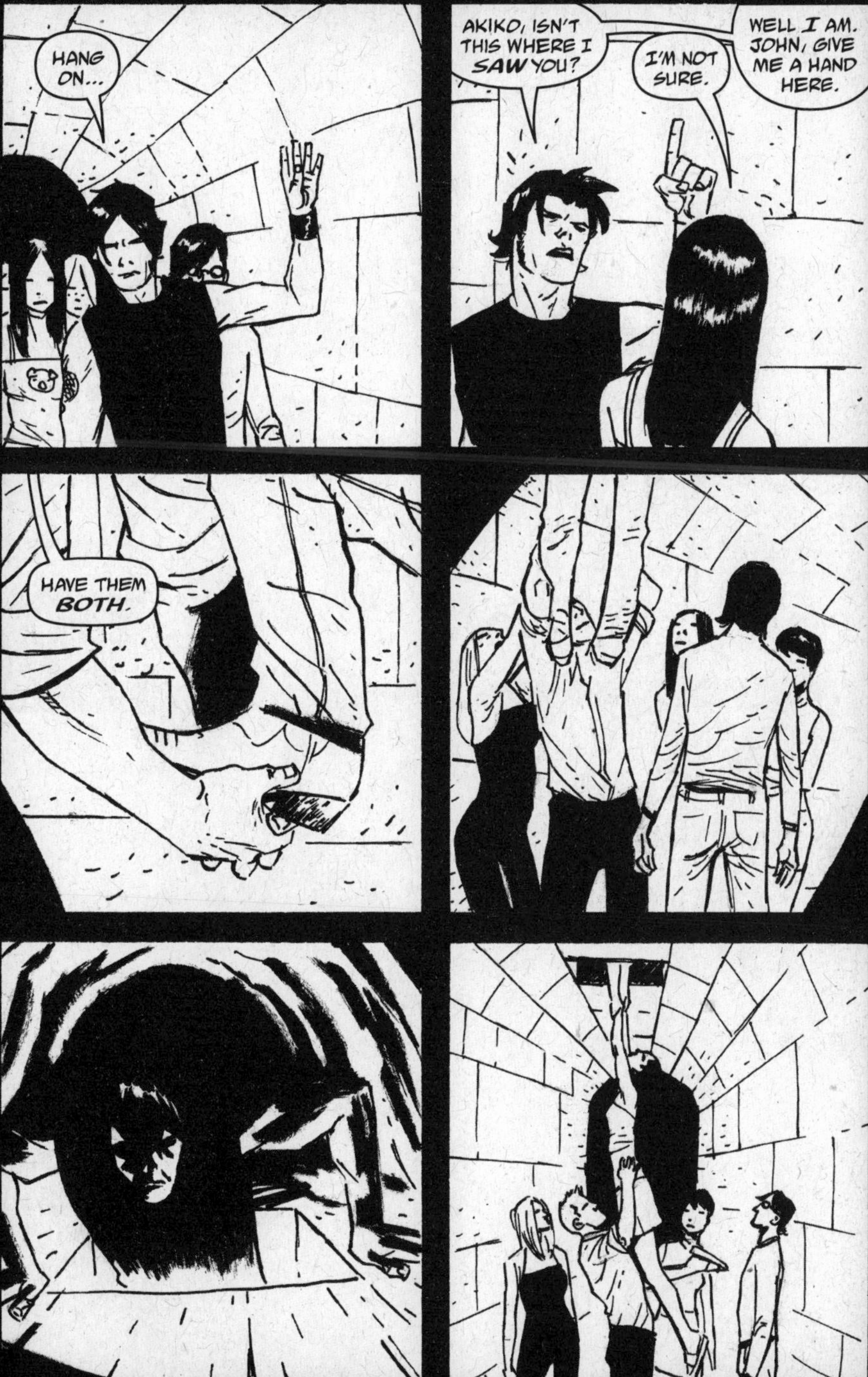
HANG ON...
AKIKO, ISN'T THIS WHERE I SAW YOU?
I'M NOT SURE.
WELL I AM. JOHN, GIVE ME A HAND HERE.
HAVE THEM BOTH.

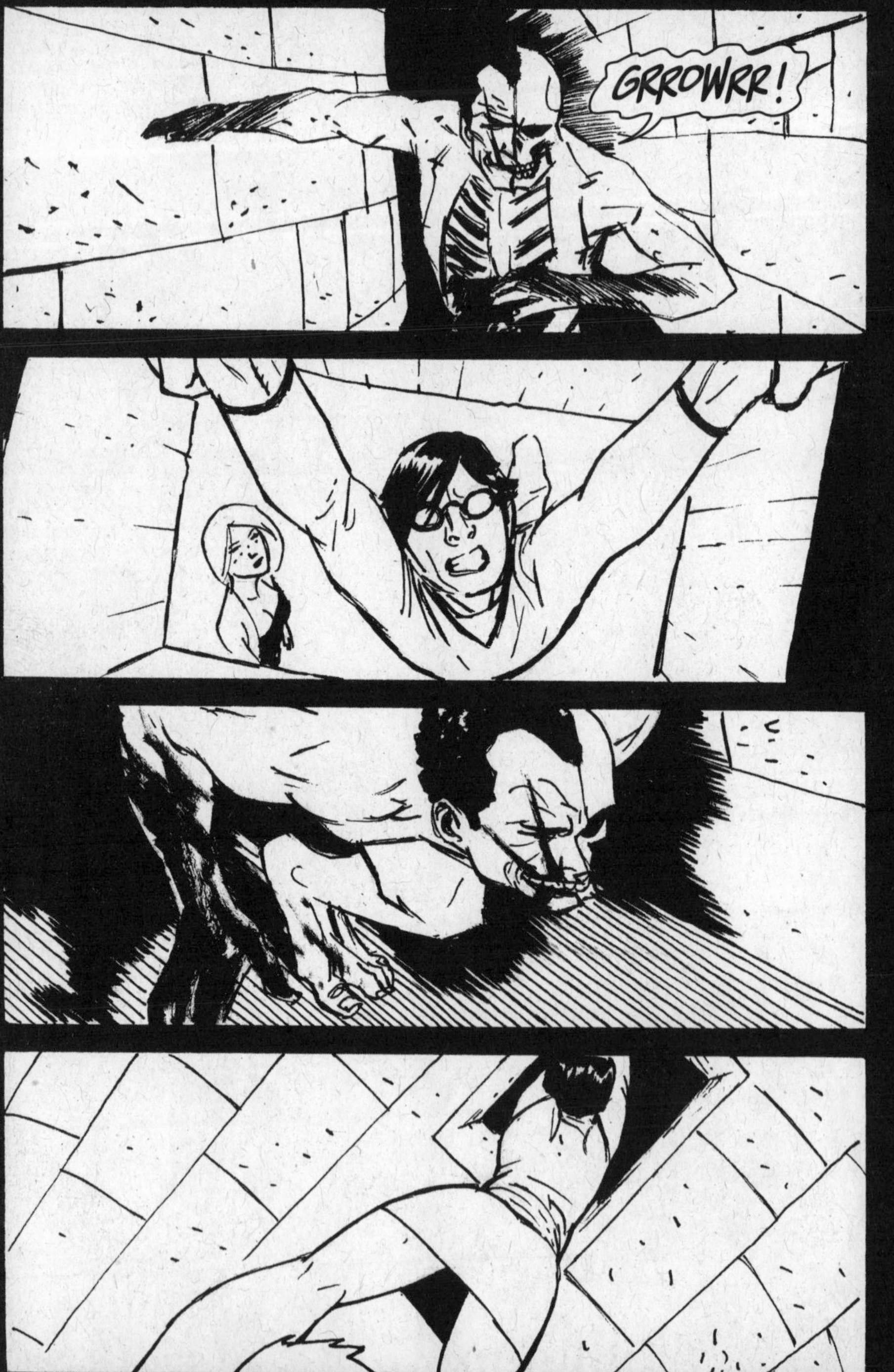
GRROWRR!

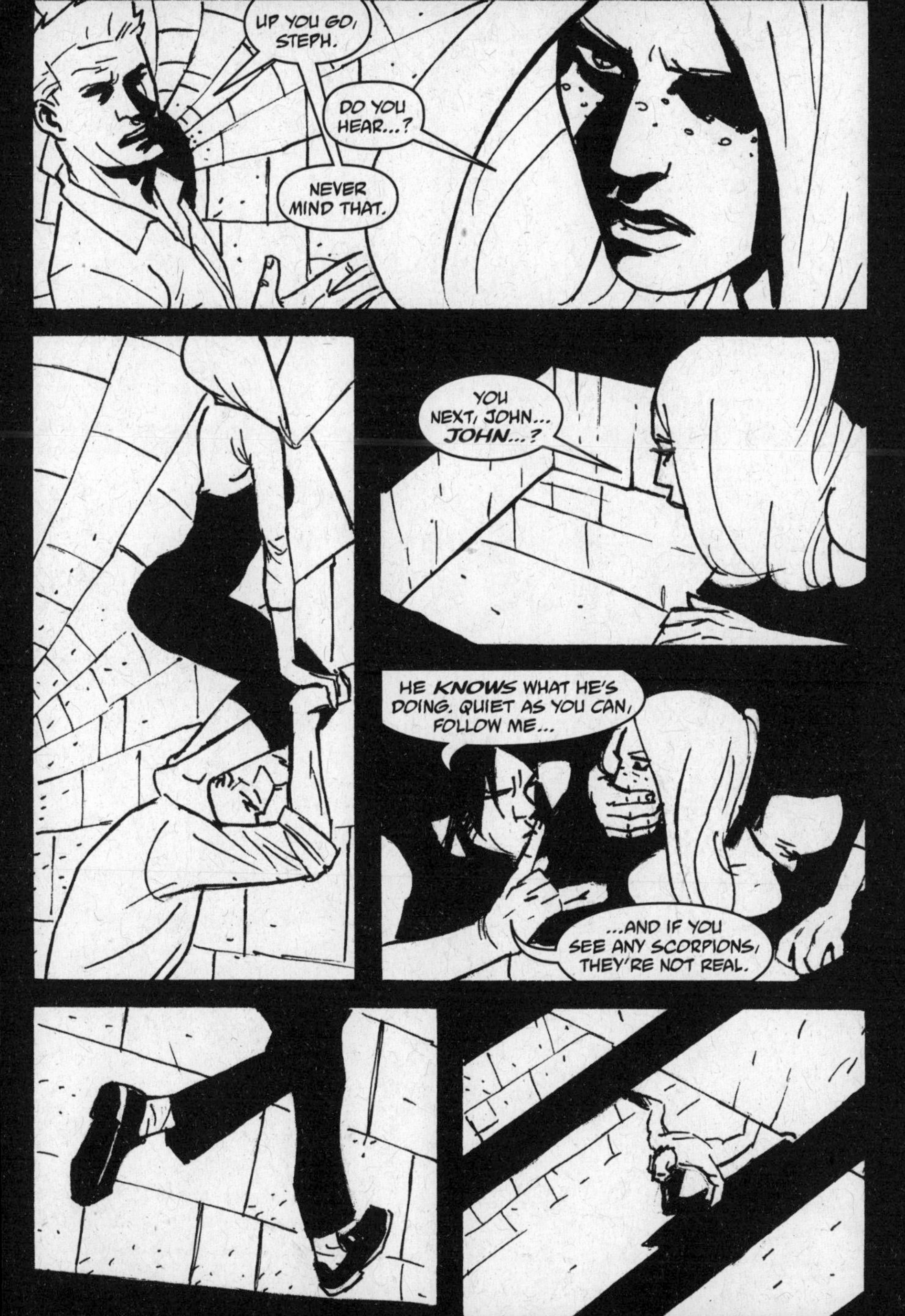
UP YOU GO, STEPH.
DO YOU HEAR...?
NEVER MIND THAT.
YOU NEXT, JOHN... JOHN...?
HE KNOWS WHAT HE'S DOING. QUIET AS YOU CAN, FOLLOW ME...
...AND IF YOU SEE ANY SCORPIONS, THEY'RE NOT REAL.

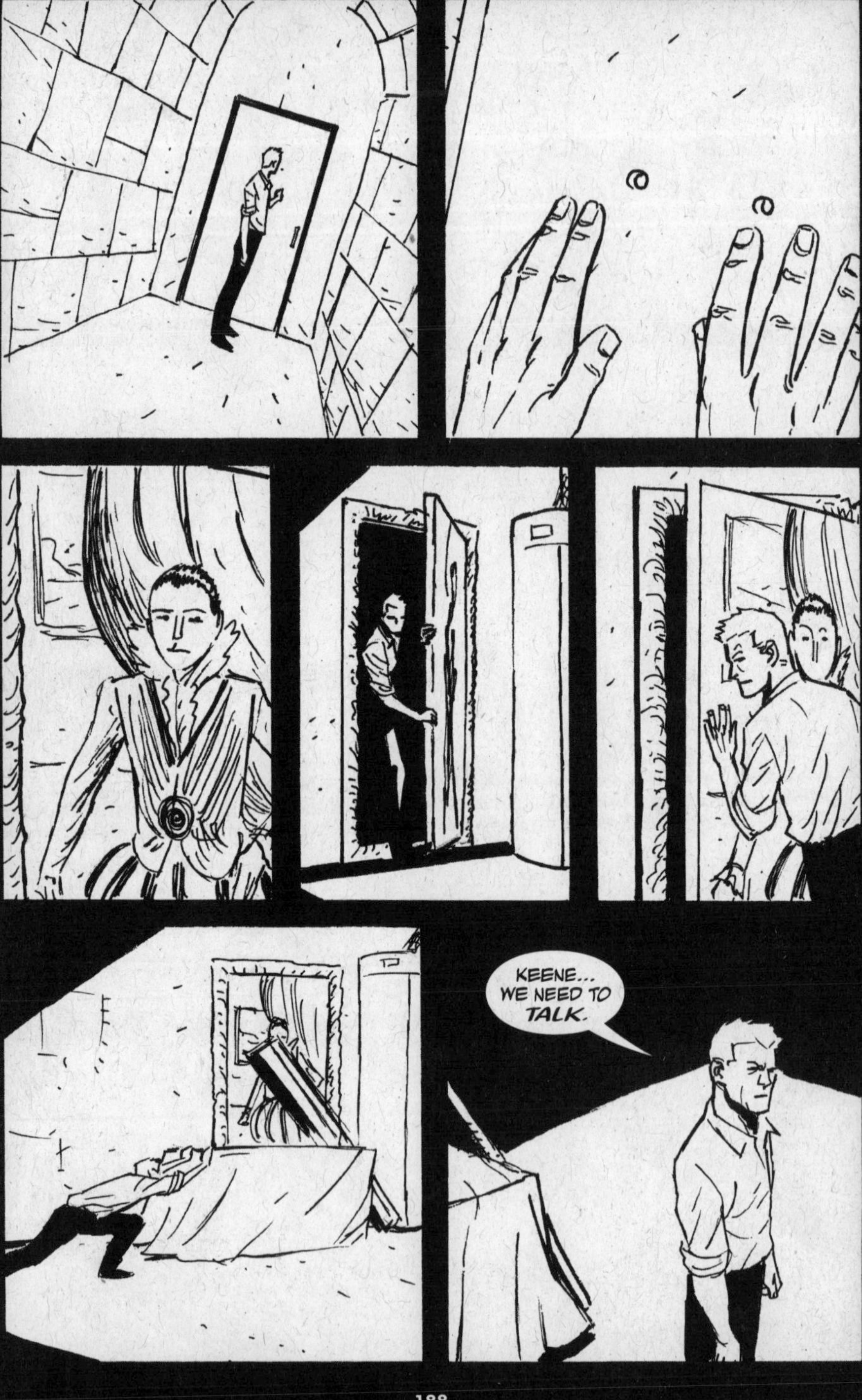
KEENE... WE NEED TO TALK.

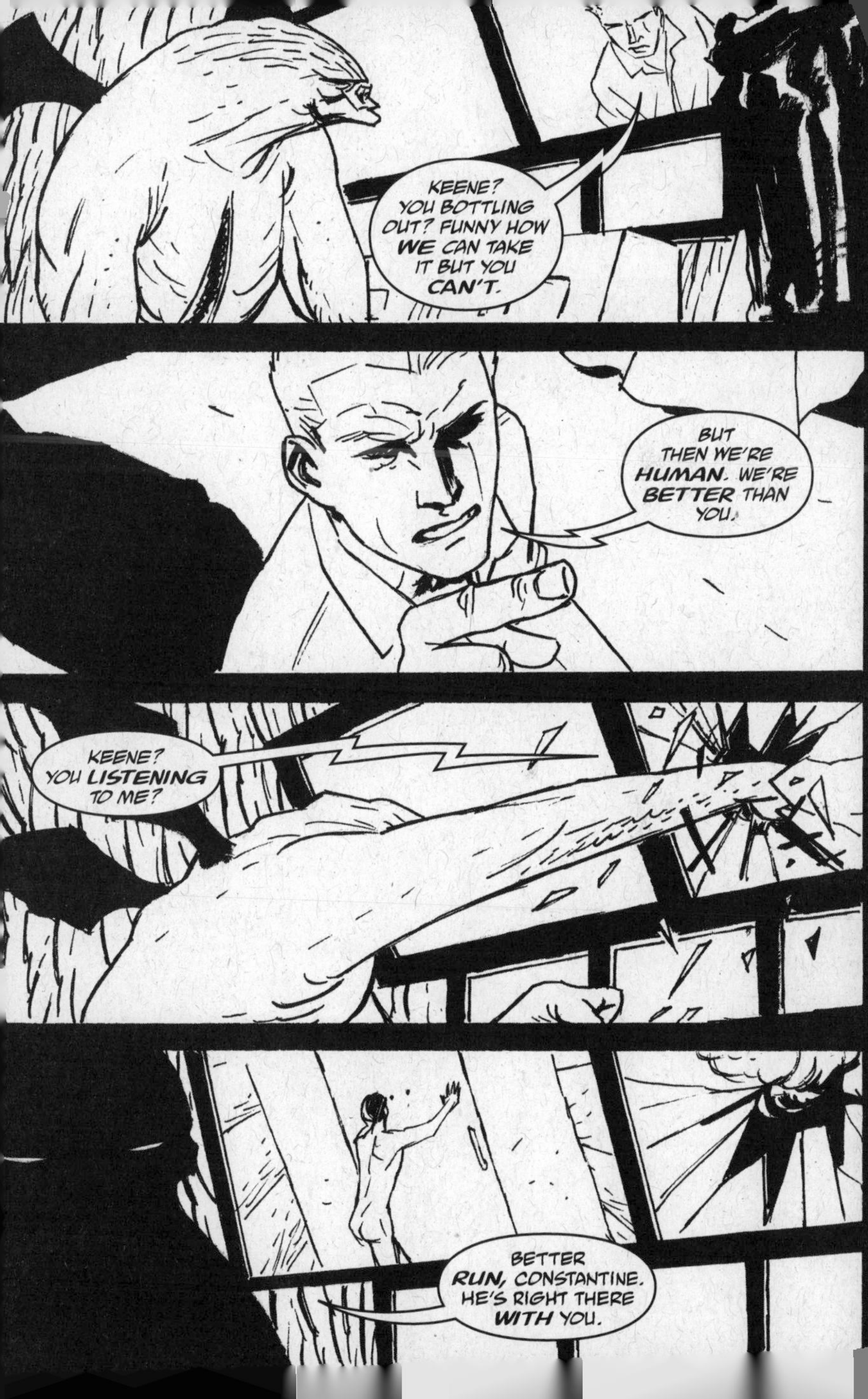
KEENE? YOU BOTTLING OUT? FUNNY HOW WE CAN TAKE IT BUT YOU CAN'T.
BUT THEN WE'RE HUMAN. WE'RE BETTER THAN YOU.
KEENE? YOU LISTENING TO ME?
BETTER RUN, CONSTANTINE. HE'S RIGHT THERE WITH YOU.

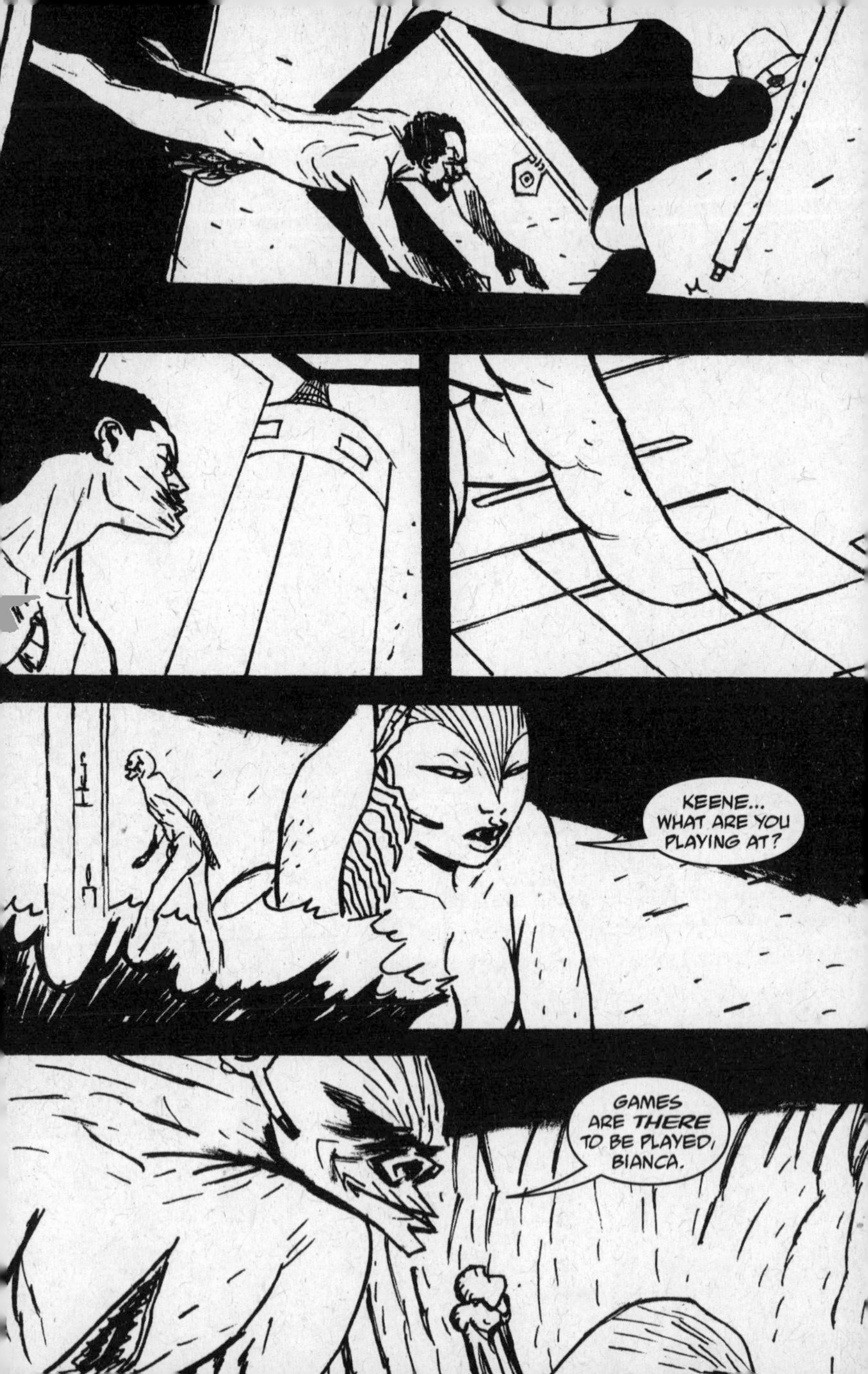
KEENE... WHAT ARE YOU PLAYING AT?
GAMES ARE THERE TO BE PLAYED, BIANCA.

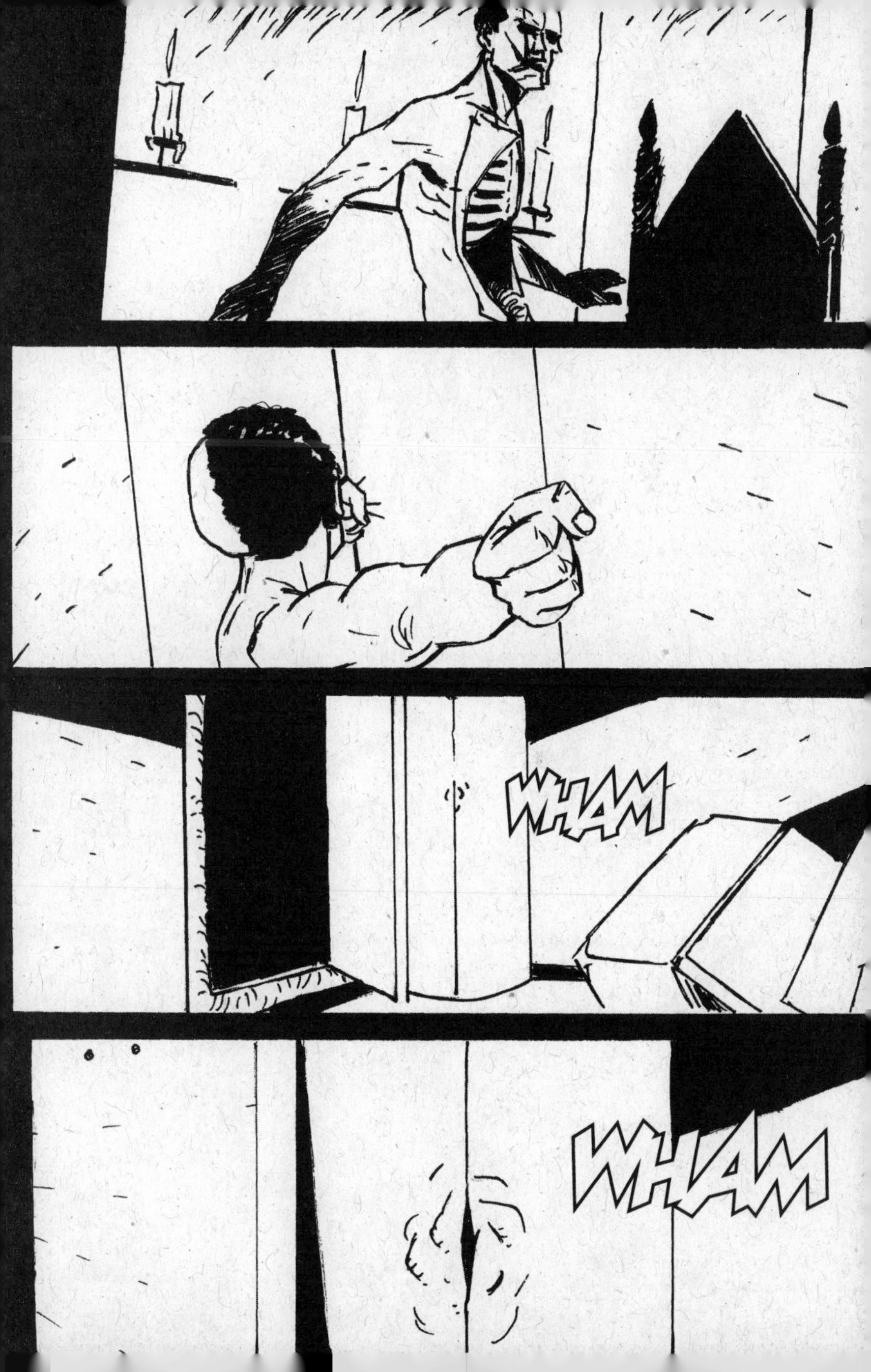
WHAM
WHAM

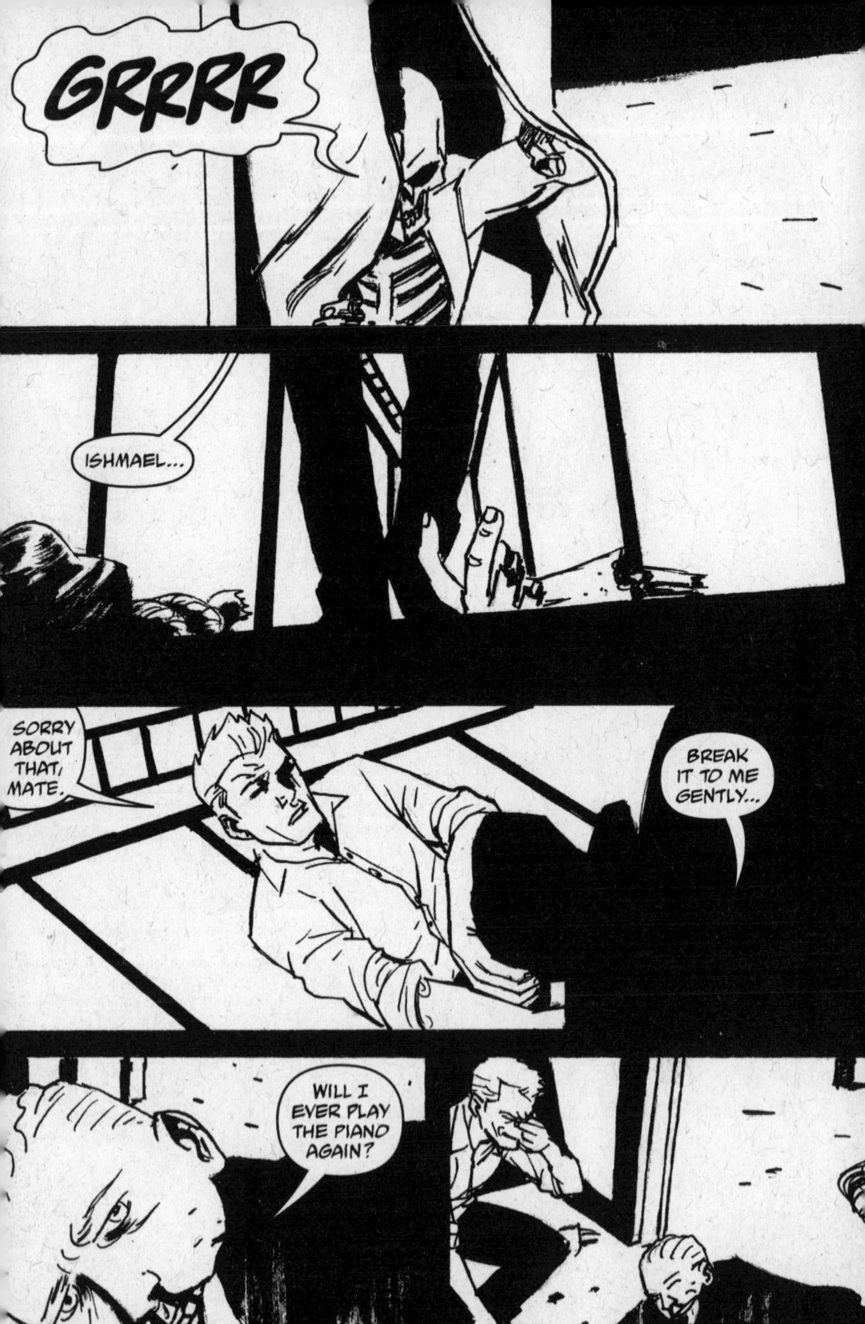
GRRRR
ISHMAEL...
SORRY ABOUT THAT, MATE.
BREAK IT TO ME GENTLY...
WILL I EVER PLAY THE PIANO AGAIN?

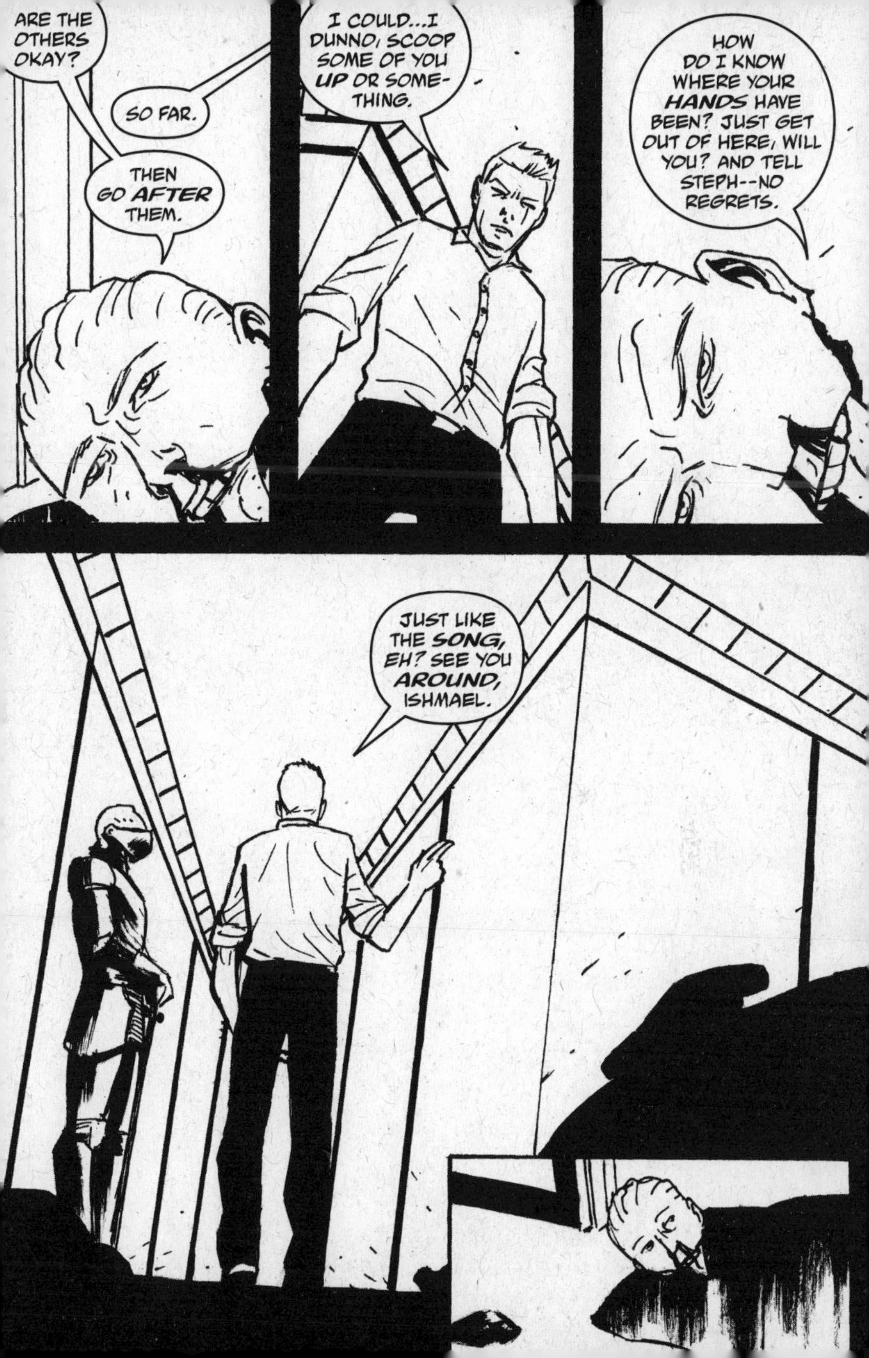
ARE THE OTHERS OKAY?
SO FAR.
THEN GO AFTER THEM.
I COULD...I DUNNO, SCOOP SOME OF YOU UP OR SOME-THING.
HOW DO I KNOW WHERE YOUR HANDS HAVE BEEN? JUST GET OUT OF HERE, WILL YOU? AND TELL STEPH--NO REGRETS.
JUST LIKE THE SONG, EH? SEE YOU AROUND, ISHMAEL.

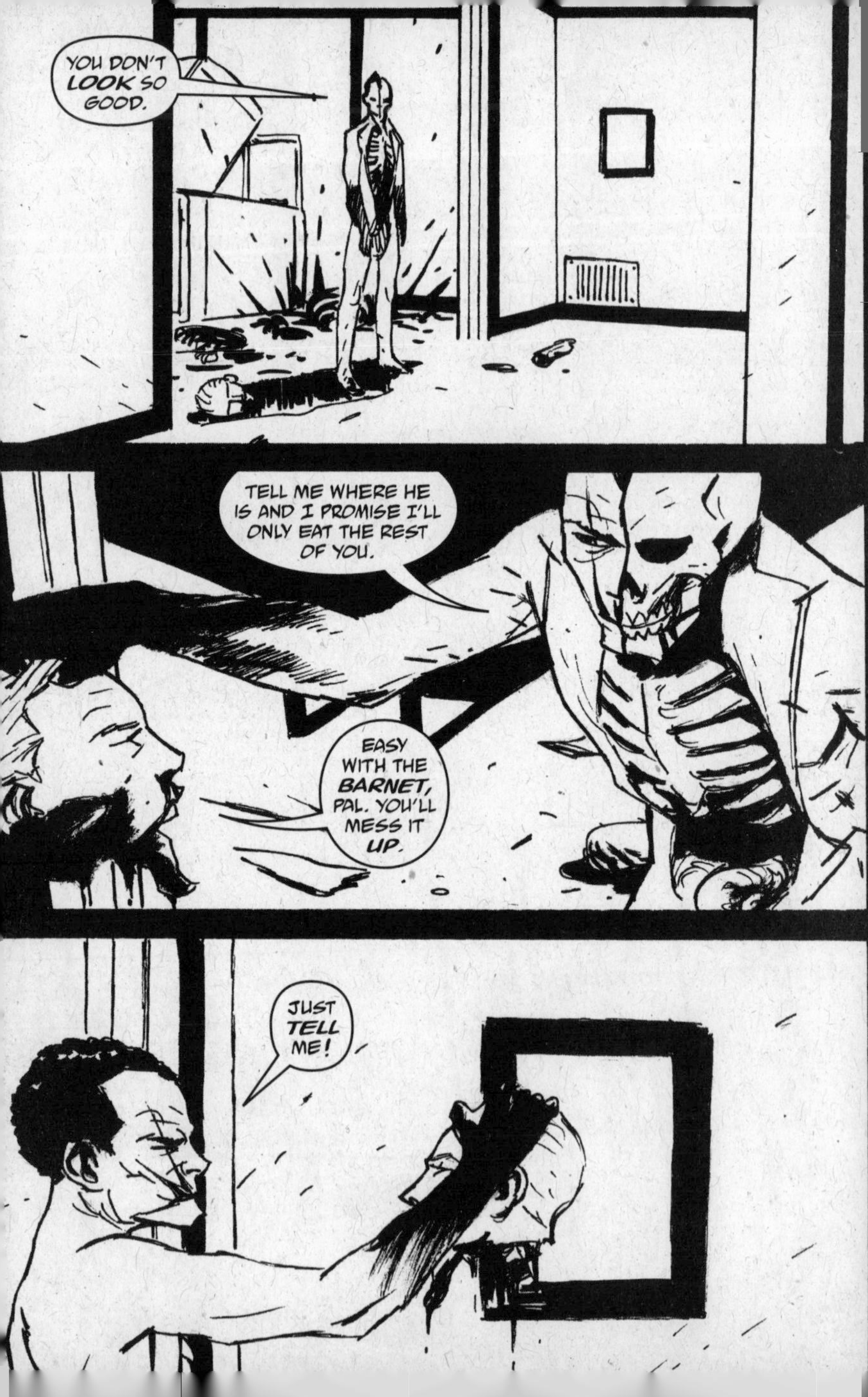

YOU DON'T LOOK SO GOOD.
TELL ME WHERE HE IS AND I PROMISE I'LL ONLY EAT THE REST OF YOU.
EASY WITH THE BARNET, PAL. YOU'LL MESS IT UP.
JUST TELL ME!

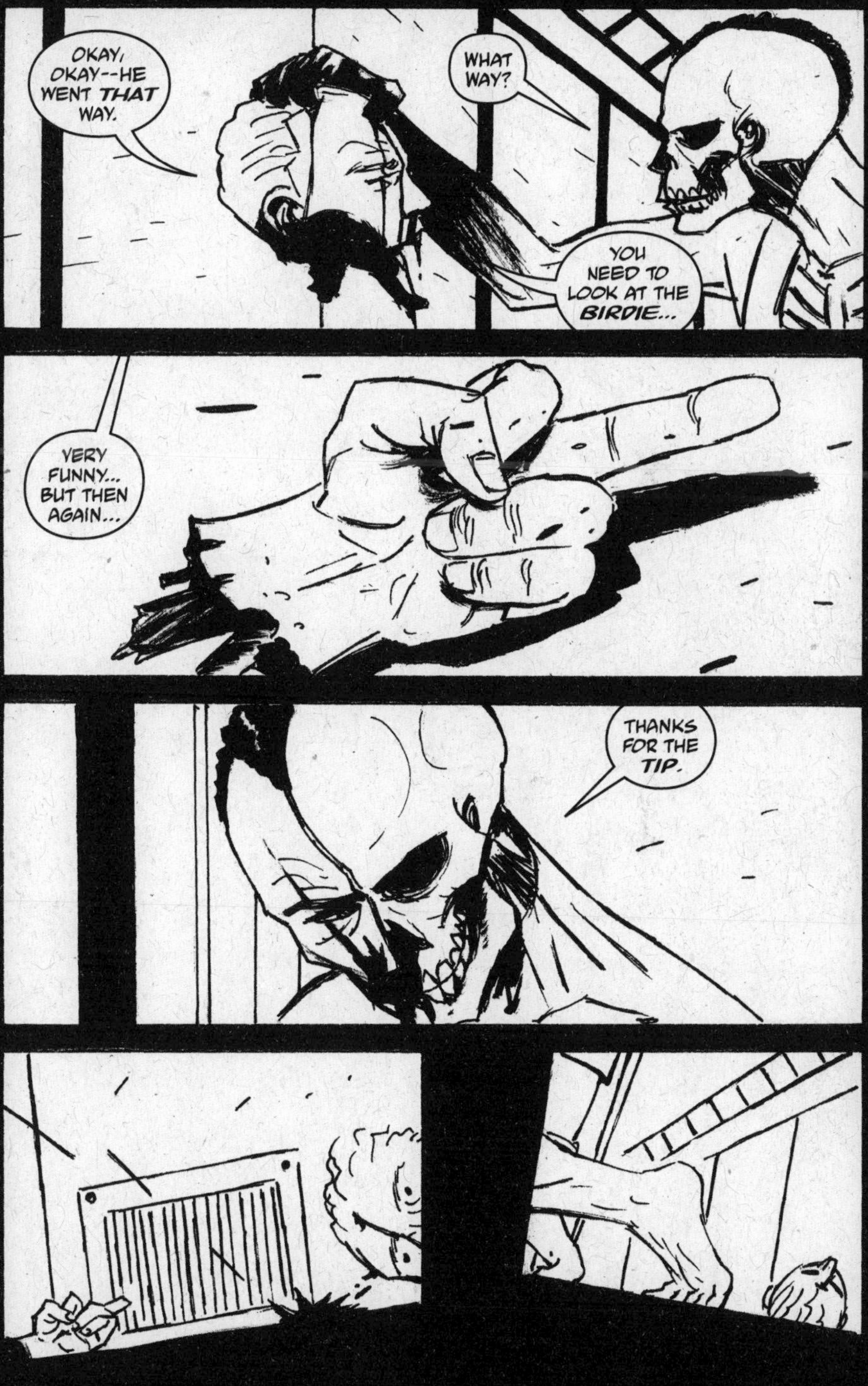
OKAY, OKAY--HE WENT THAT WAY.
WHAT WAY?
YOU NEED TO LOOK AT THE BIRDIE...
VERY FUNNY... BUT THEN AGAIN...
THANKS FOR THE TIP.

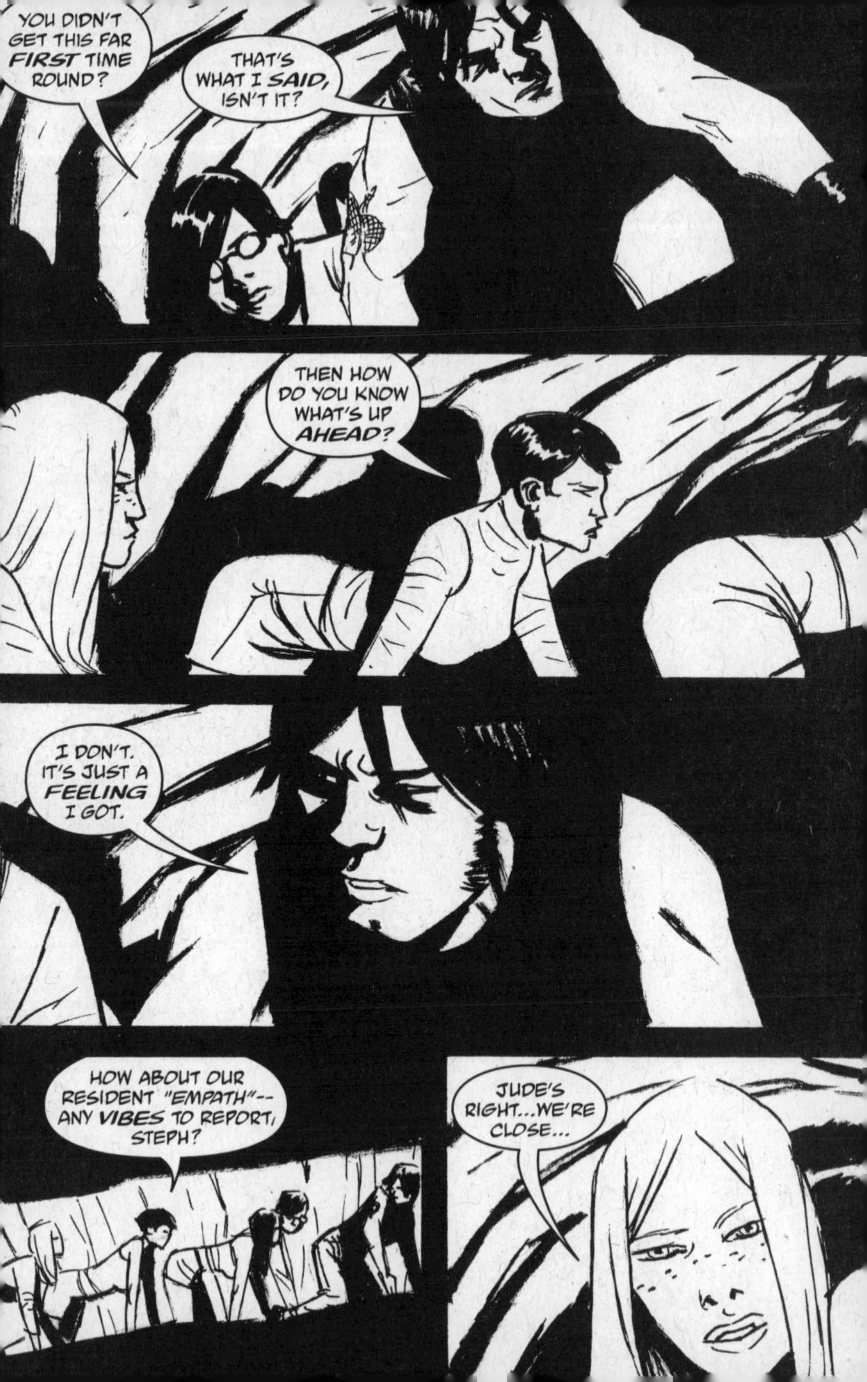
YOU DIDN'T GET THIS FAR FIRST TIME ROUND?
THAT'S WHAT I SAID, ISN'T IT?
THEN HOW DO YOU KNOW WHAT'S UP AHEAD?
I DON'T. IT'S JUST A FEELING I GOT.
HOW ABOUT OUR RESIDENT "EMPATH"-- ANY VIBES TO REPORT, STEPH?
JUDE'S RIGHT...WE'RE CLOSE...

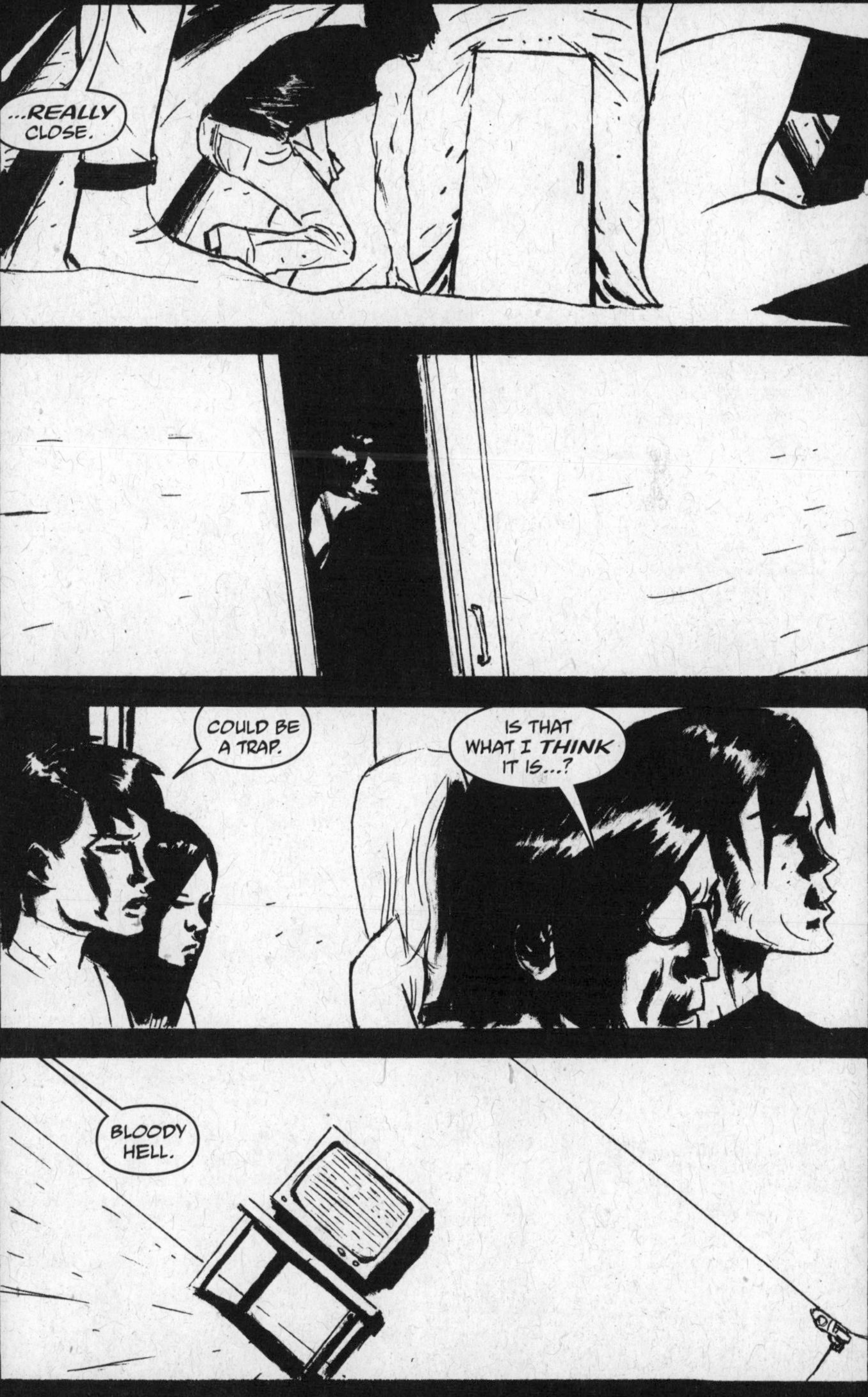
...REALLY CLOSE.
COULD BE A TRAP.
IS THAT WHAT I THINK IT IS...?
BLOODY HELL.

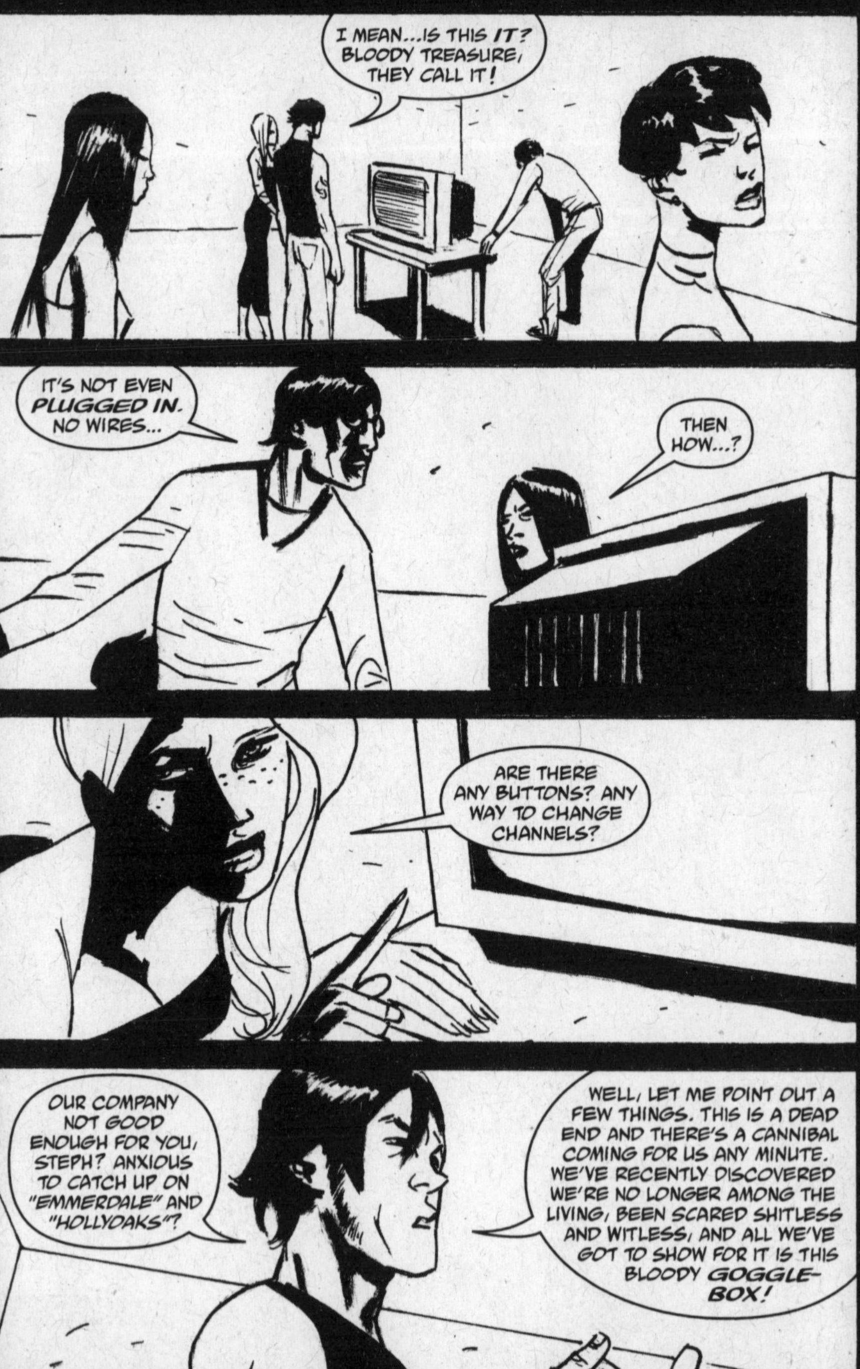
I MEAN...IS THIS *IT?* BLOODY TREASURE, THEY CALL IT!
IT'S NOT EVEN *PLUGGED IN.* NO WIRES...
THEN HOW...?
ARE THERE ANY BUTTONS? ANY WAY TO CHANGE CHANNELS?
OUR COMPANY NOT GOOD ENOUGH FOR YOU, STEPH? ANXIOUS TO CATCH UP ON "EMMERDALE" AND "HOLLYOAKS"?
WELL, LET ME POINT OUT A FEW THINGS. THIS IS A DEAD END AND THERE'S A CANNIBAL COMING FOR US ANY MINUTE. WE'VE RECENTLY DISCOVERED WE'RE NO LONGER AMONG THE LIVING, BEEN SCARED SHITLESS AND WITLESS, AND ALL WE'VE GOT TO SHOW FOR IT IS THIS BLOODY *GOGGLE-BOX!*

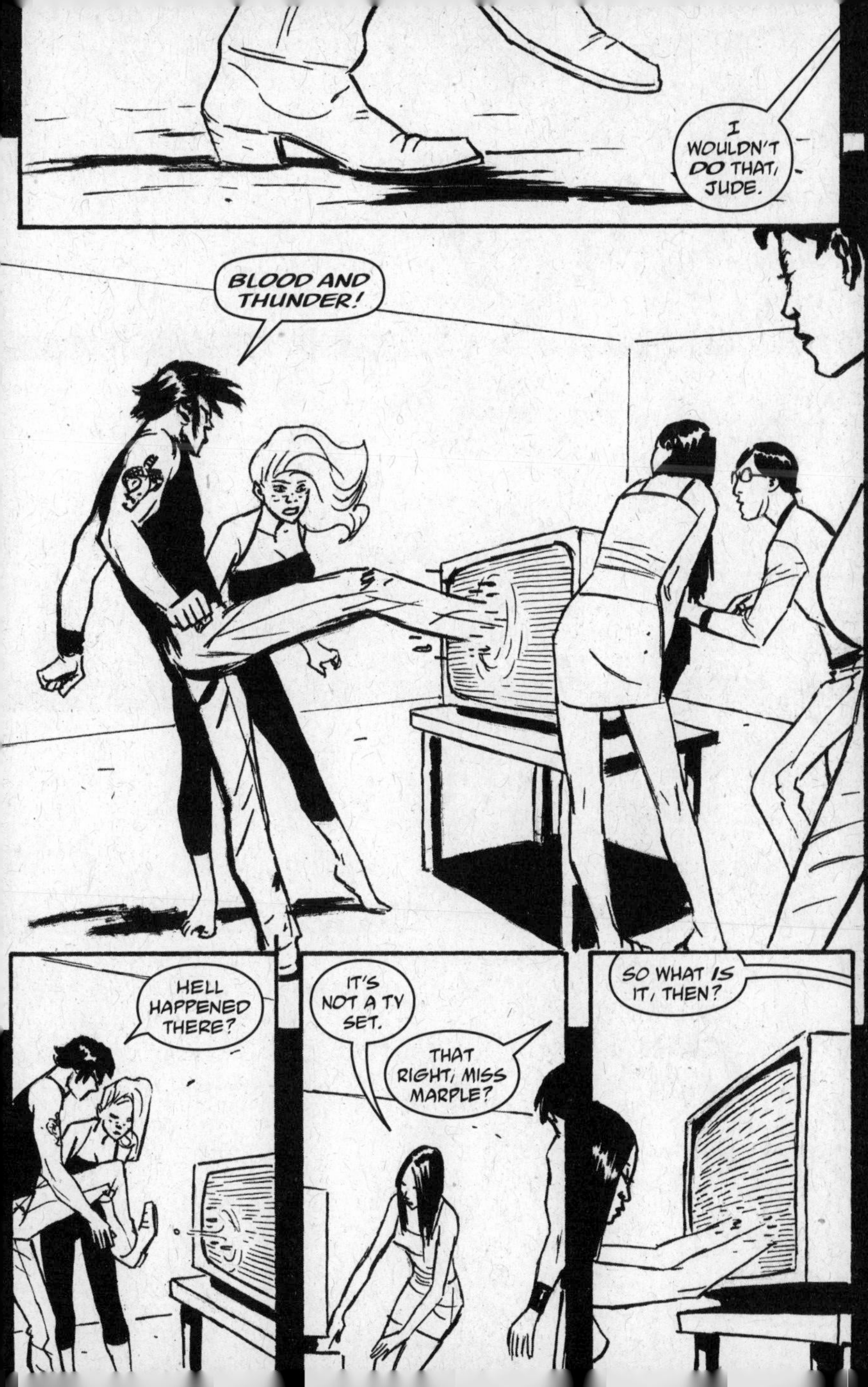
I WOULDN'T DO THAT, JUDE.
BLOOD AND THUNDER!
HELL HAPPENED THERE?
IT'S NOT A TV SET.
THAT RIGHT, MISS MARPLE?
SO WHAT IS IT, THEN?

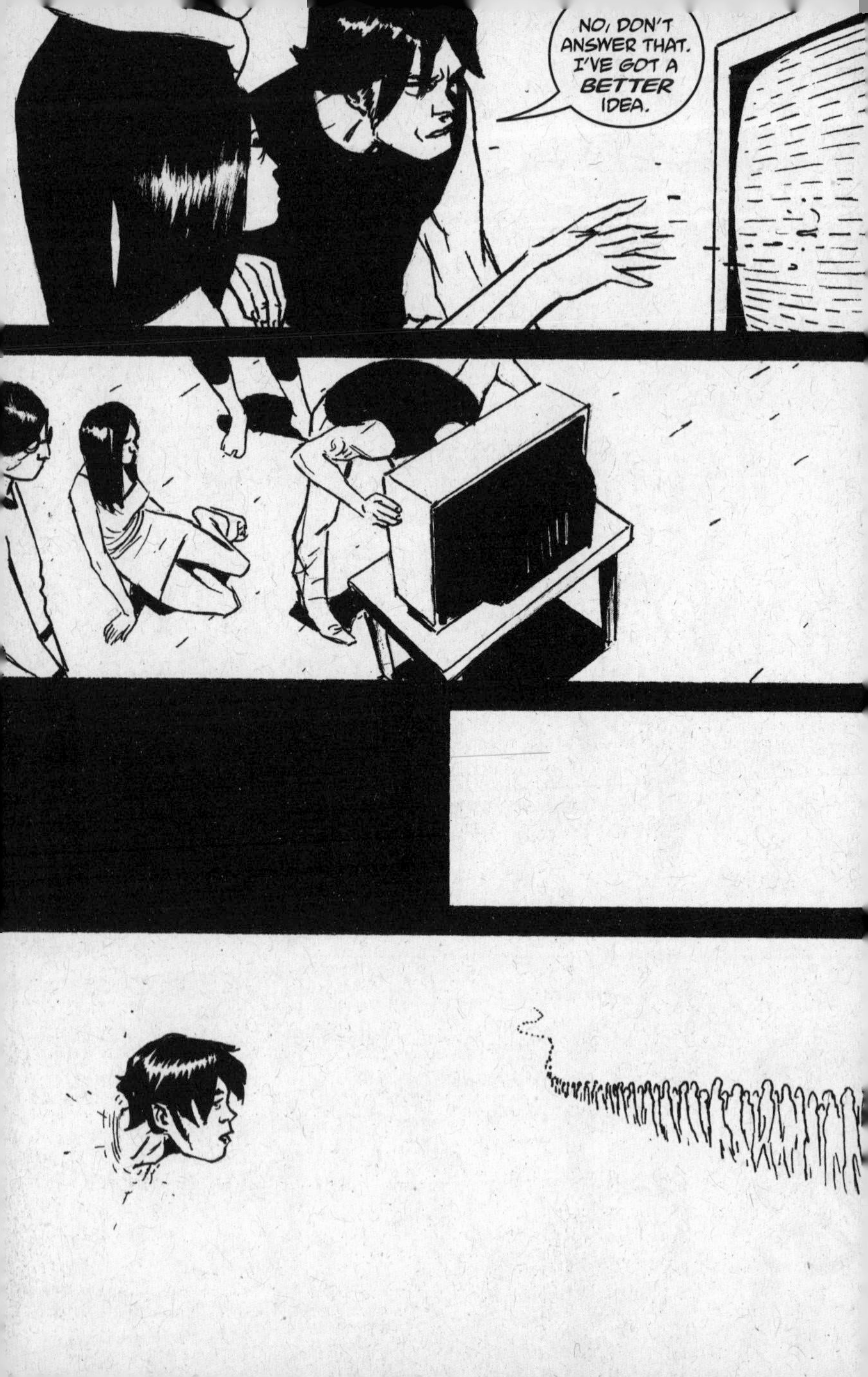
NO, DON'T ANSWER THAT. I'VE GOT A BETTER IDEA.

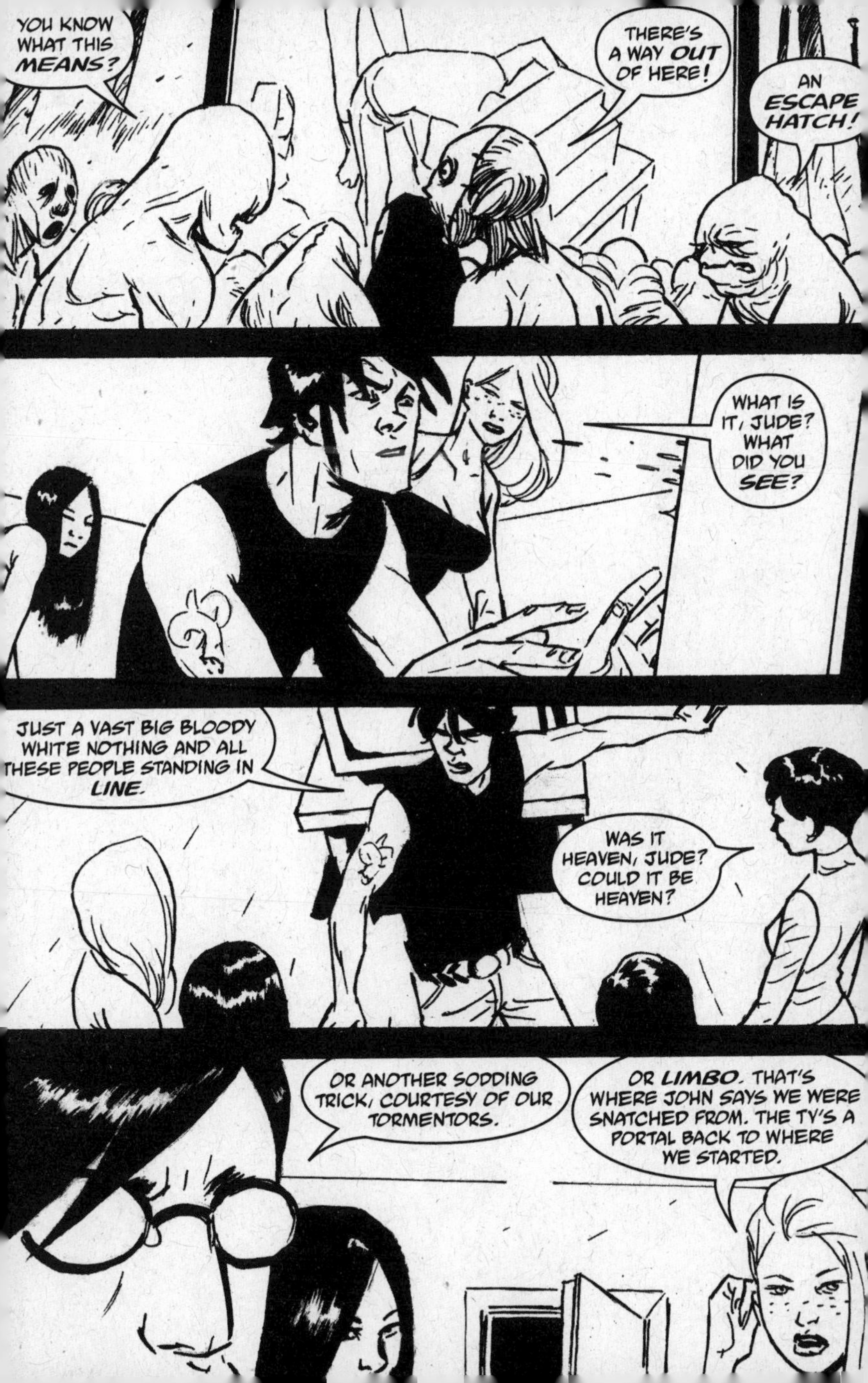
YOU KNOW WHAT THIS MEANS?
THERE'S A WAY OUT OF HERE!
AN ESCAPE HATCH!
WHAT IS IT, JUDE? WHAT DID YOU SEE?
JUST A VAST BIG BLOODY WHITE NOTHING AND ALL THESE PEOPLE STANDING IN LINE.
WAS IT HEAVEN, JUDE? COULD IT BE HEAVEN?
OR ANOTHER SODDING TRICK, COURTESY OF OUR TORMENTORS.
OR LIMBO. THAT'S WHERE JOHN SAYS WE WERE SNATCHED FROM. THE TV'S A PORTAL BACK TO WHERE WE STARTED.

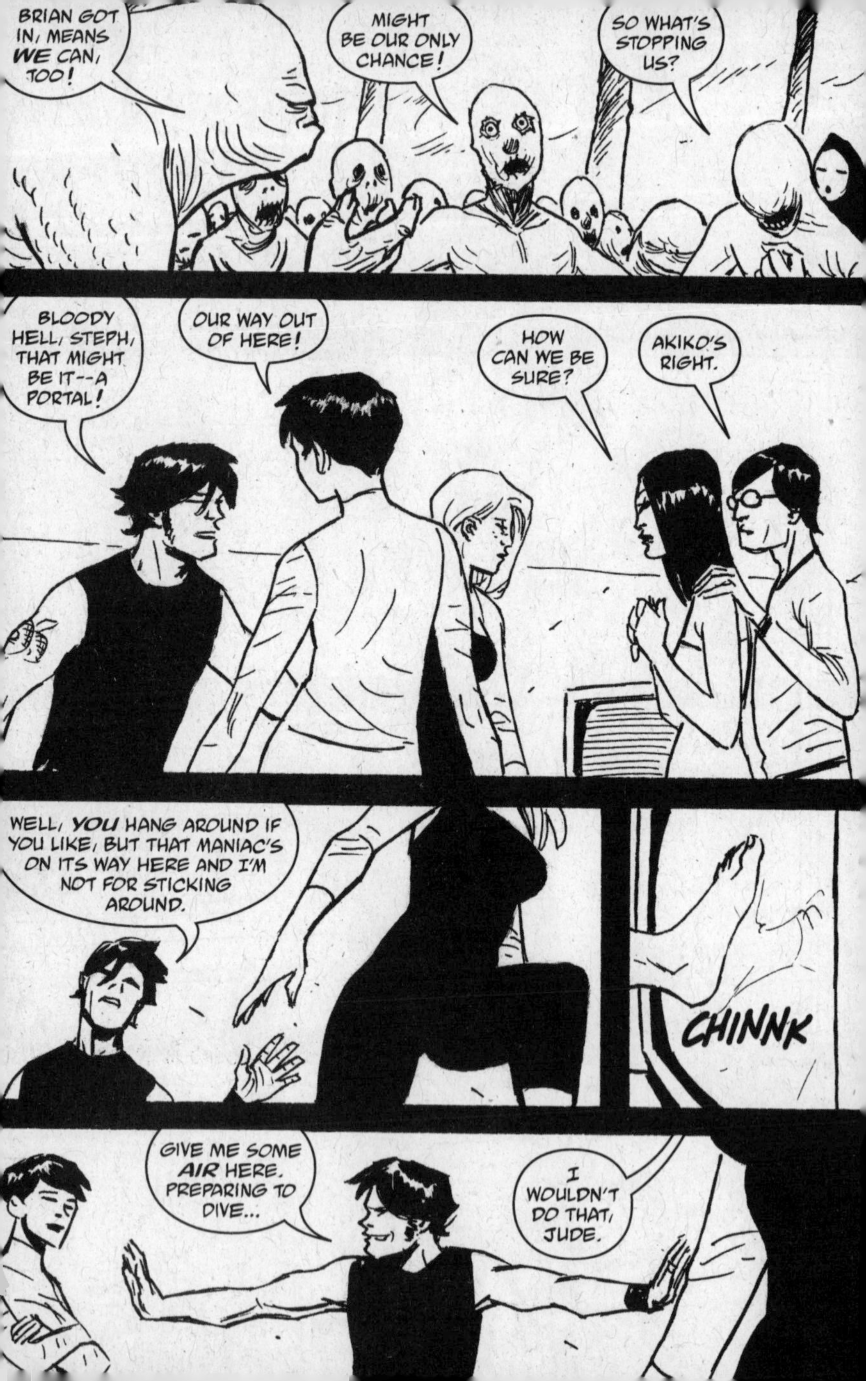
BRIAN GOT IN, MEANS WE CAN, TOO!
MIGHT BE OUR ONLY CHANCE!
SO WHAT'S STOPPING US?
BLOODY HELL, STEPH, THAT MIGHT BE IT--A PORTAL!
OUR WAY OUT OF HERE!
HOW CAN WE BE SURE?
AKIKO'S RIGHT.
WELL, YOU HANG AROUND IF YOU LIKE, BUT THAT MANIAC'S ON ITS WAY HERE AND I'M NOT FOR STICKING AROUND.
CHINNK
GIVE ME SOME AIR HERE. PREPARING TO DIVE...
I WOULDN'T DO THAT, JUDE.

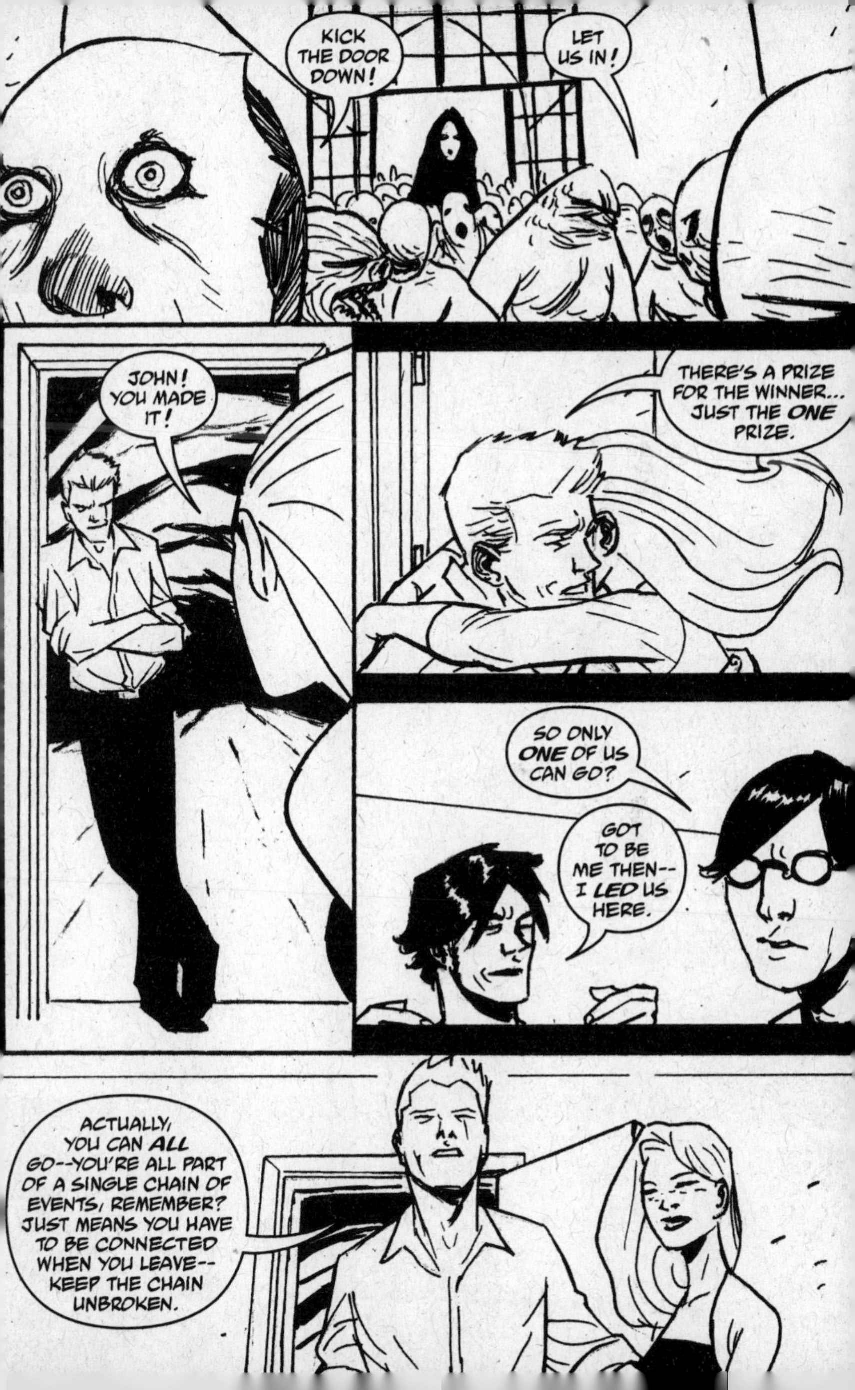
KICK THE DOOR DOWN!
LET US IN!
JOHN! YOU MADE IT!
THERE'S A PRIZE FOR THE WINNER... JUST THE ONE PRIZE.
SO ONLY ONE OF US CAN GO?
GOT TO BE ME THEN-- I LED US HERE.
ACTUALLY, YOU CAN ALL GO--YOU'RE ALL PART OF A SINGLE CHAIN OF EVENTS, REMEMBER? JUST MEANS YOU HAVE TO BE CONNECTED WHEN YOU LEAVE-- KEEP THE CHAIN UNBROKEN.

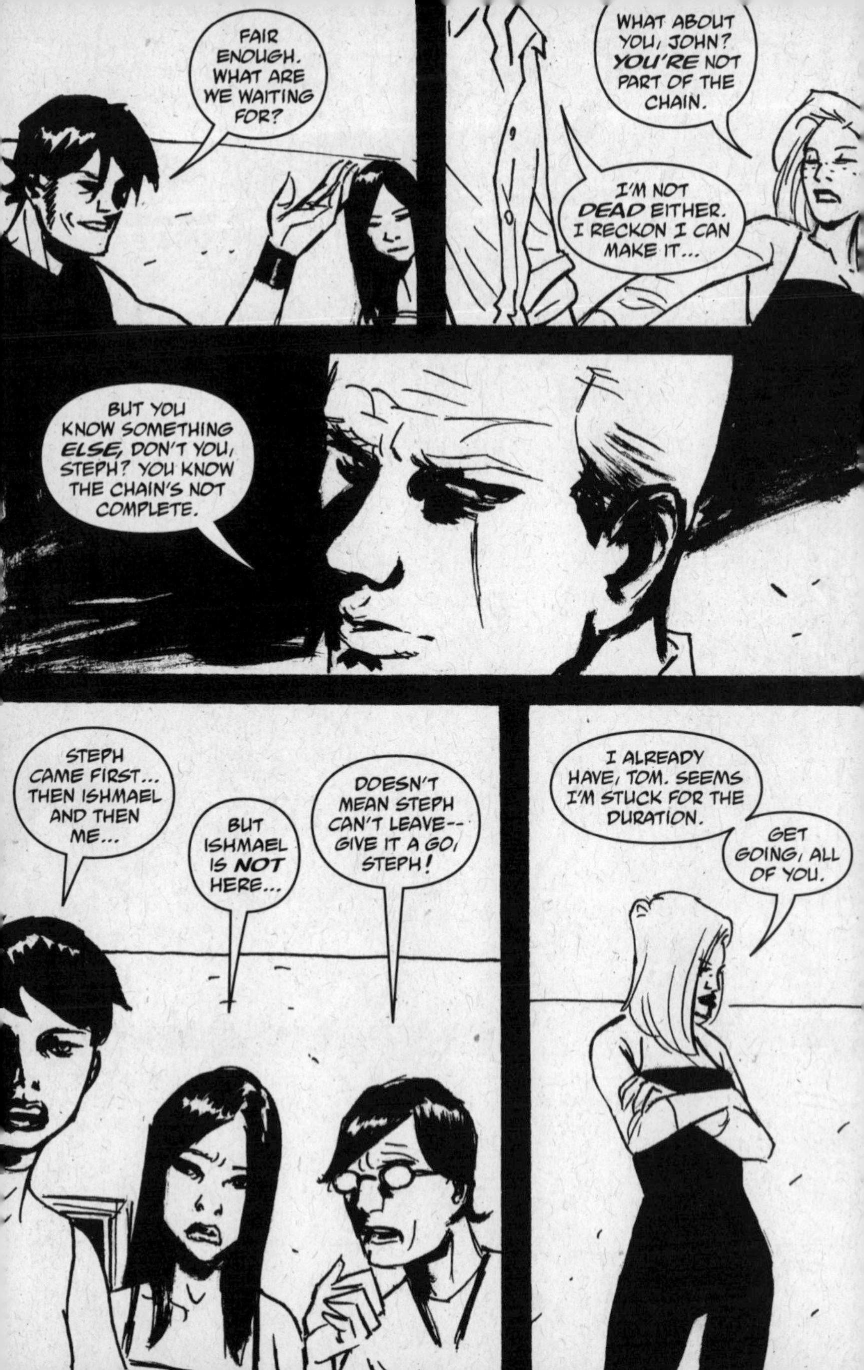
FAIR ENOUGH. WHAT ARE WE WAITING FOR?
WHAT ABOUT YOU, JOHN? YOU'RE NOT PART OF THE CHAIN.
I'M NOT DEAD EITHER. I RECKON I CAN MAKE IT...
BUT YOU KNOW SOMETHING ELSE, DON'T YOU, STEPH? YOU KNOW THE CHAIN'S NOT COMPLETE.
STEPH CAME FIRST... THEN ISHMAEL AND THEN ME...
BUT ISHMAEL IS NOT HERE...
DOESN'T MEAN STEPH CAN'T LEAVE--GIVE IT A GO, STEPH!
I ALREADY HAVE, TOM. SEEMS I'M STUCK FOR THE DURATION.
GET GOING, ALL OF YOU.

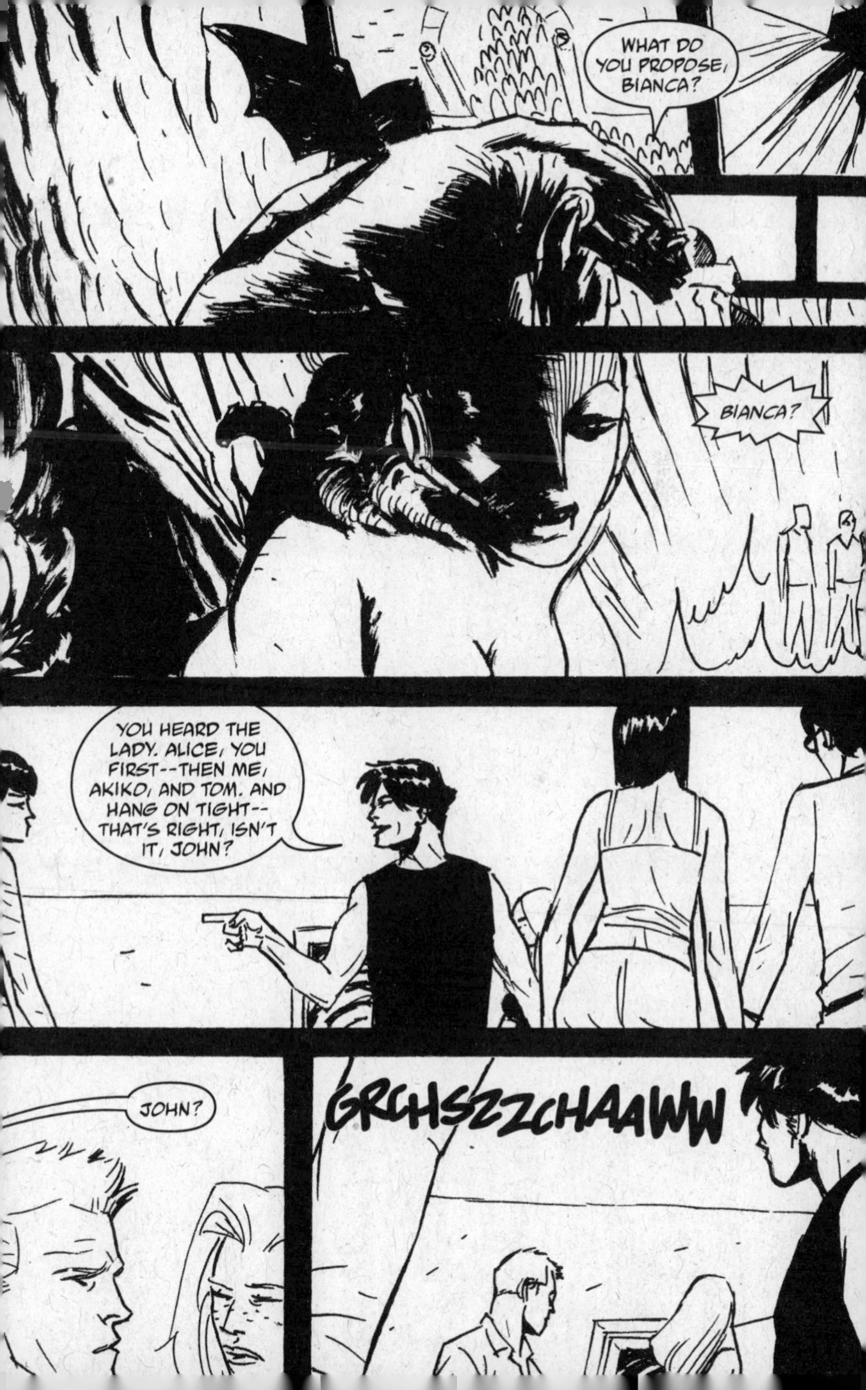
WHAT DO YOU PROPOSE, BIANCA?
BIANCA?
YOU HEARD THE LADY. ALICE, YOU FIRST--THEN ME, AKIKO, AND TOM. AND HANG ON TIGHT--THAT'S RIGHT, ISN'T IT, JOHN?
JOHN?
GRCHSZZCHAAWW

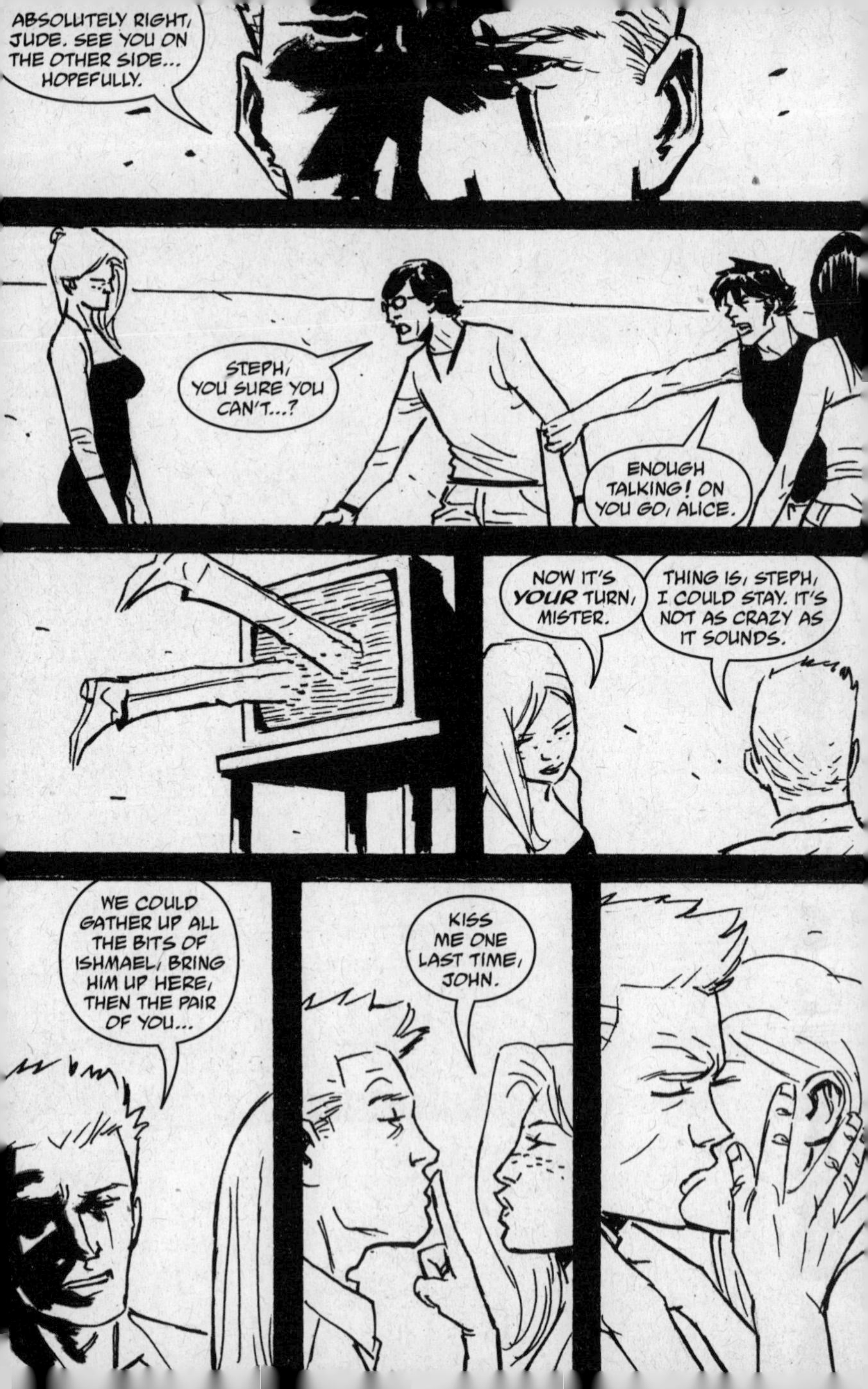
ABSOLUTELY RIGHT, JUDE. SEE YOU ON THE OTHER SIDE... HOPEFULLY.
STEPH, YOU SURE YOU CAN'T...?
ENOUGH TALKING! ON YOU GO, ALICE.
NOW IT'S YOUR TURN, MISTER.
THING IS, STEPH, I COULD STAY. IT'S NOT AS CRAZY AS IT SOUNDS.
WE COULD GATHER UP ALL THE BITS OF ISHMAEL, BRING HIM UP HERE, THEN THE PAIR OF YOU...
KISS ME ONE LAST TIME, JOHN.

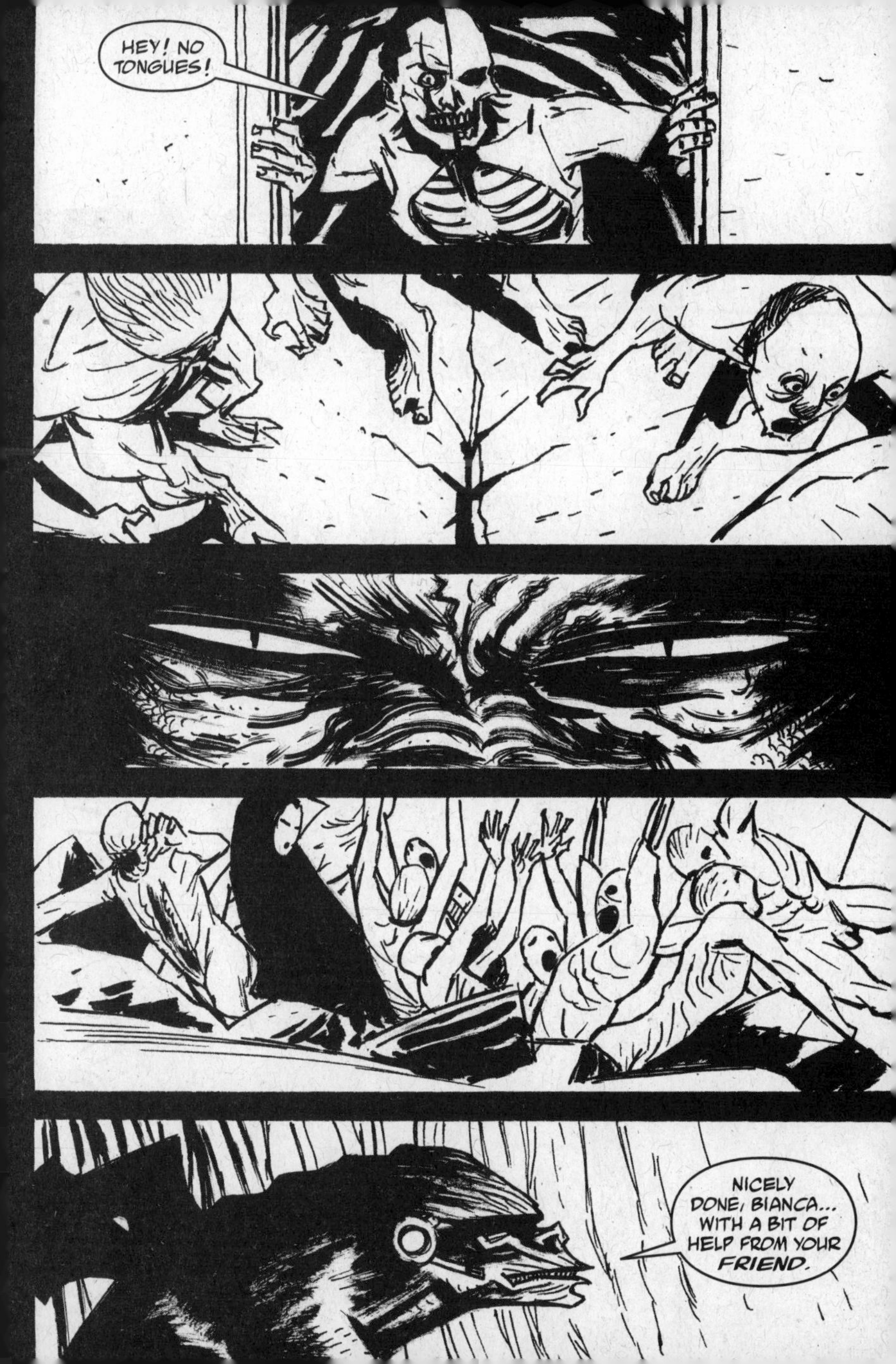
HEY! NO TONGUES!
NICELY DONE, BIANCA... WITH A BIT OF HELP FROM YOUR FRIEND.

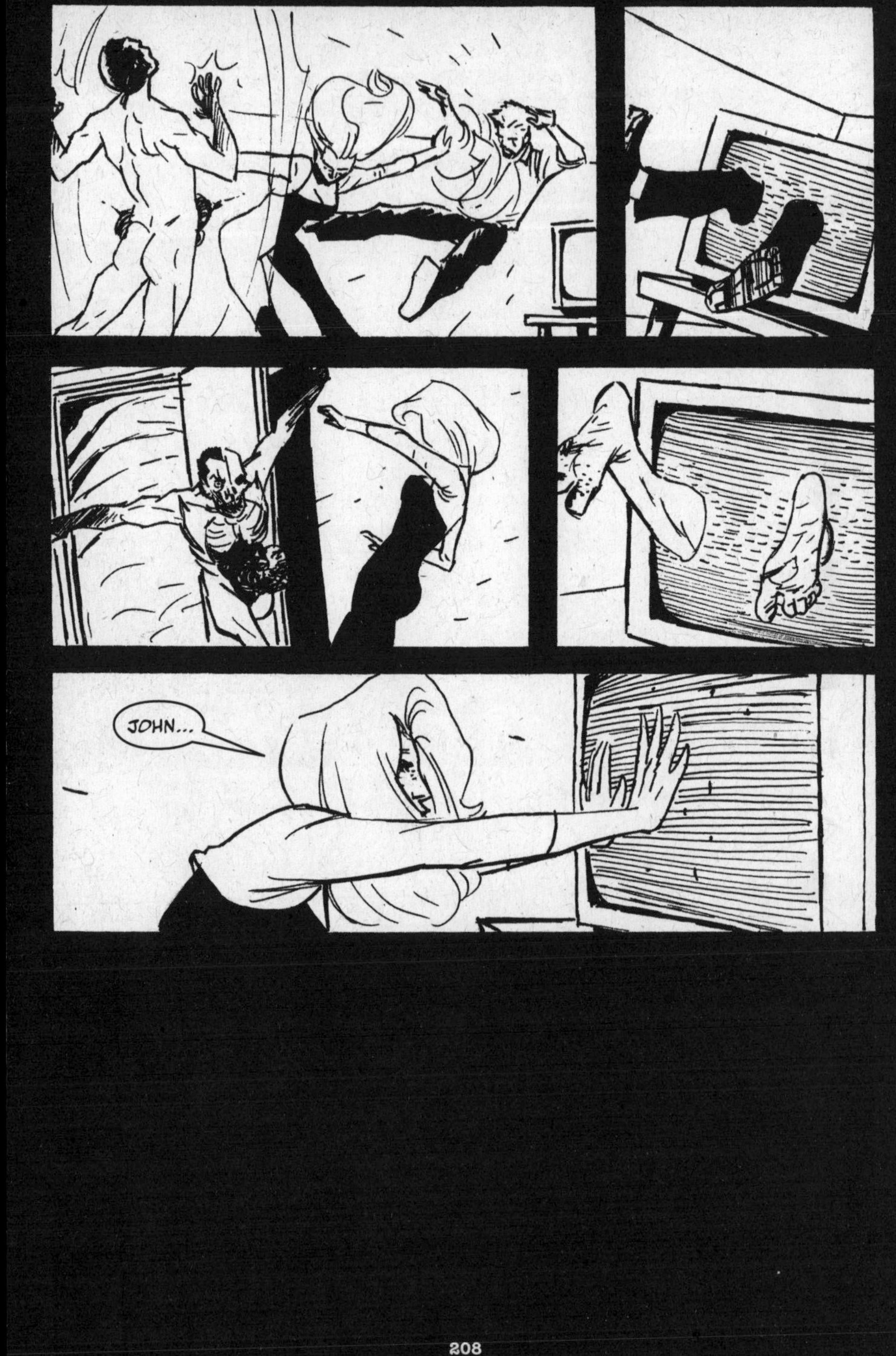
JOHN...

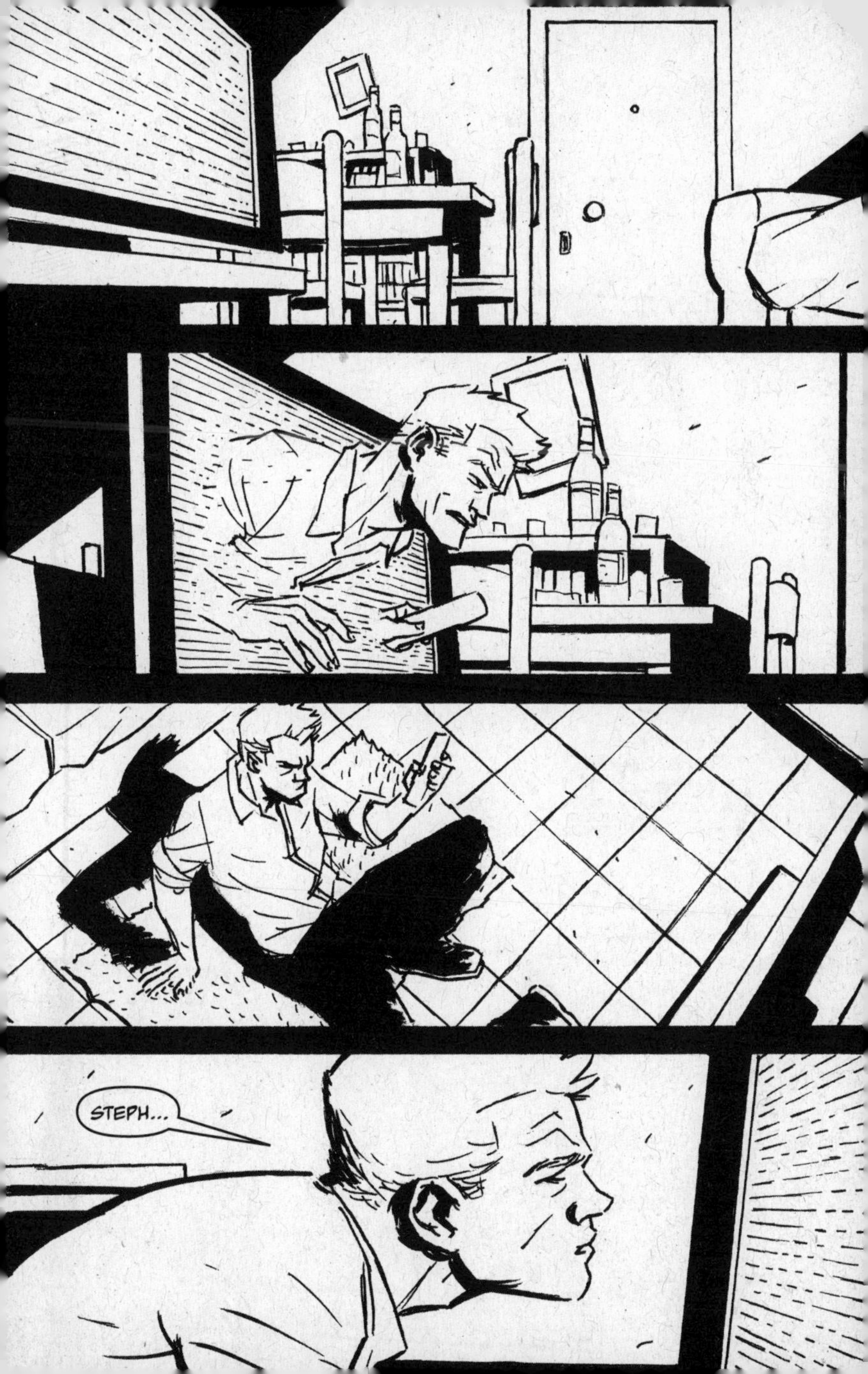
STEPH...

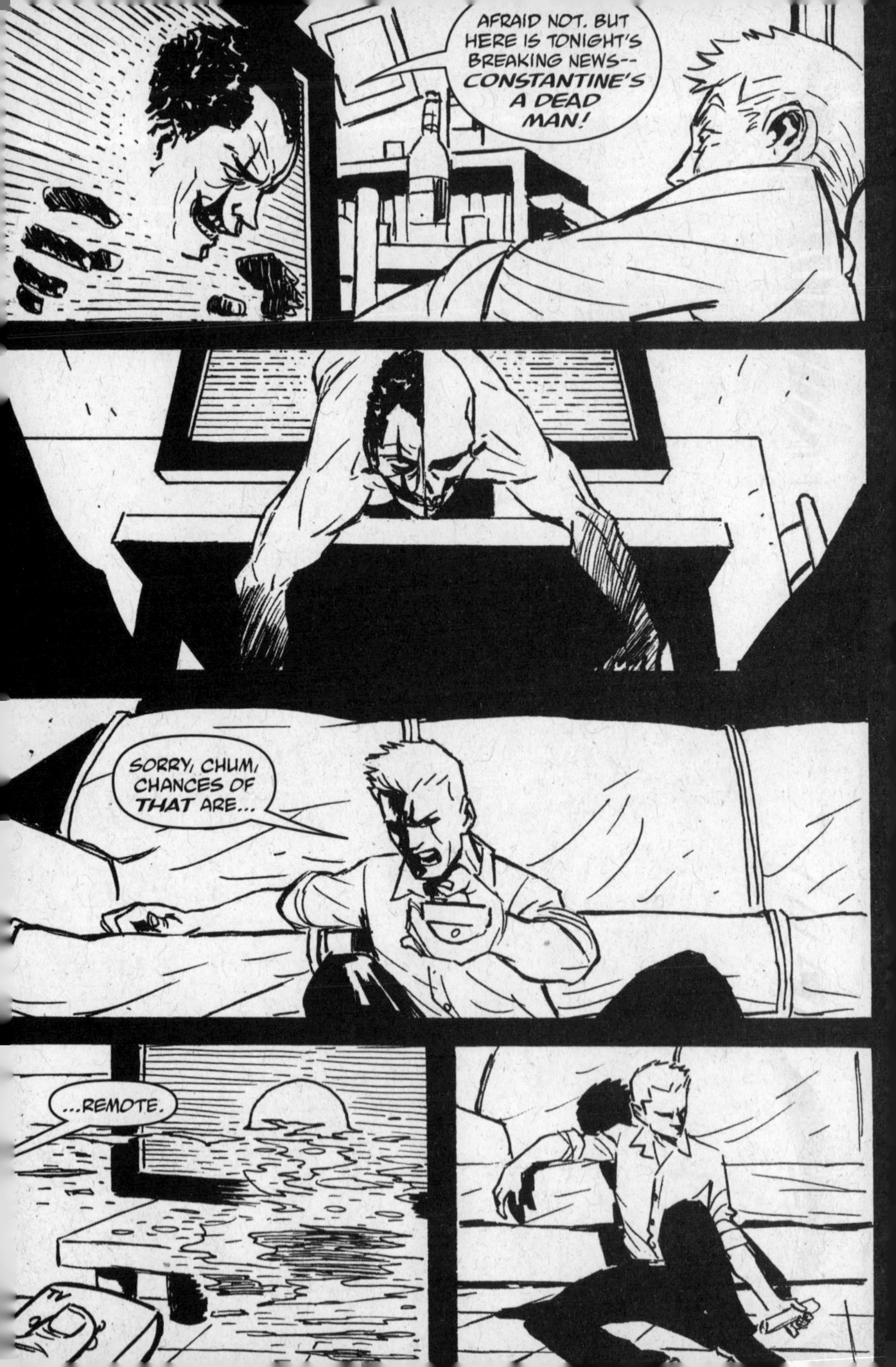
AFRAID NOT. BUT HERE IS TONIGHT'S BREAKING NEWS-- CONSTANTINE'S A DEAD MAN!
SORRY, CHUM, CHANCES OF THAT ARE...
...REMOTE.
TV

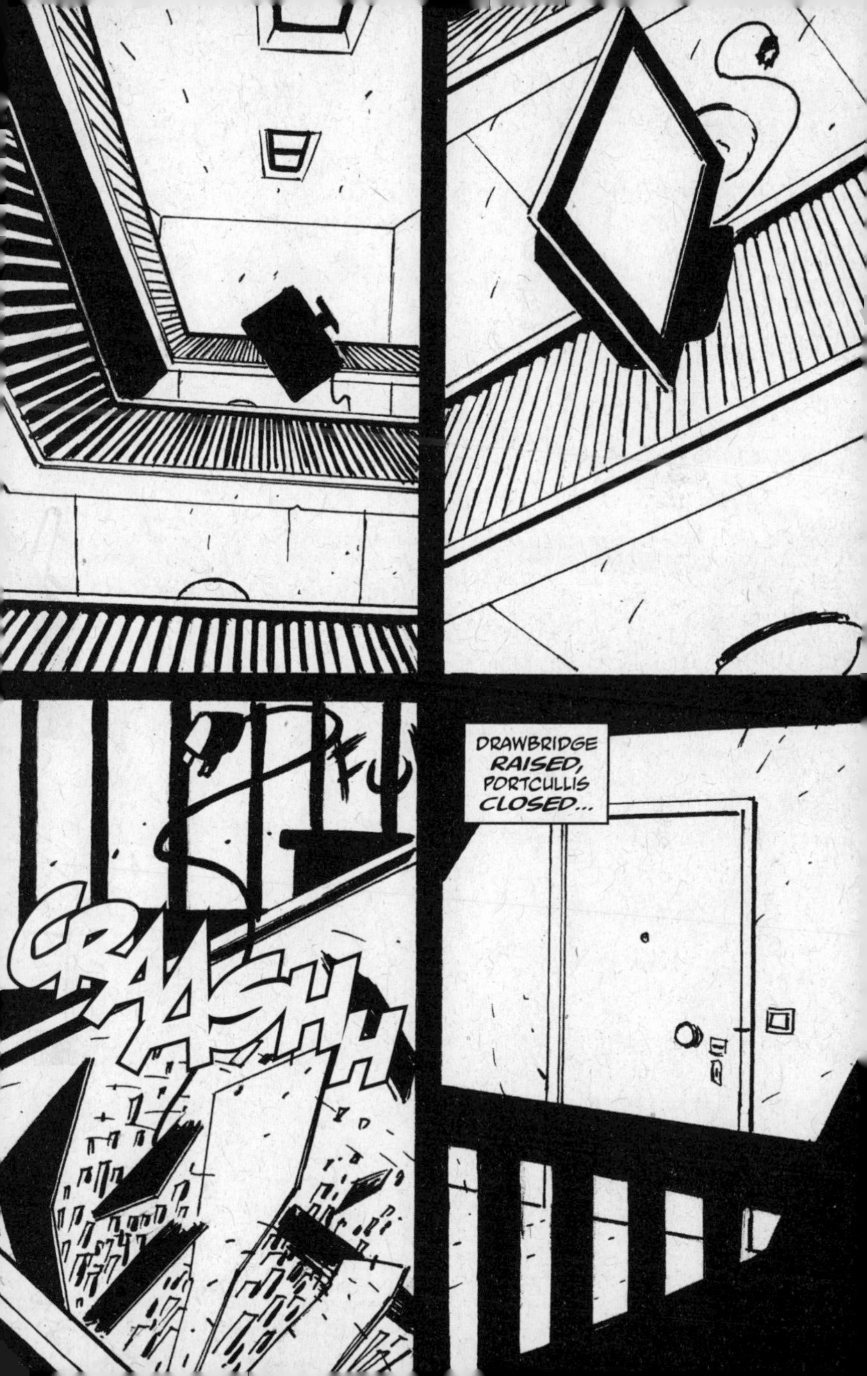
CRASH
DRAWBRIDGE RAISED, PORTCULLIS CLOSED...

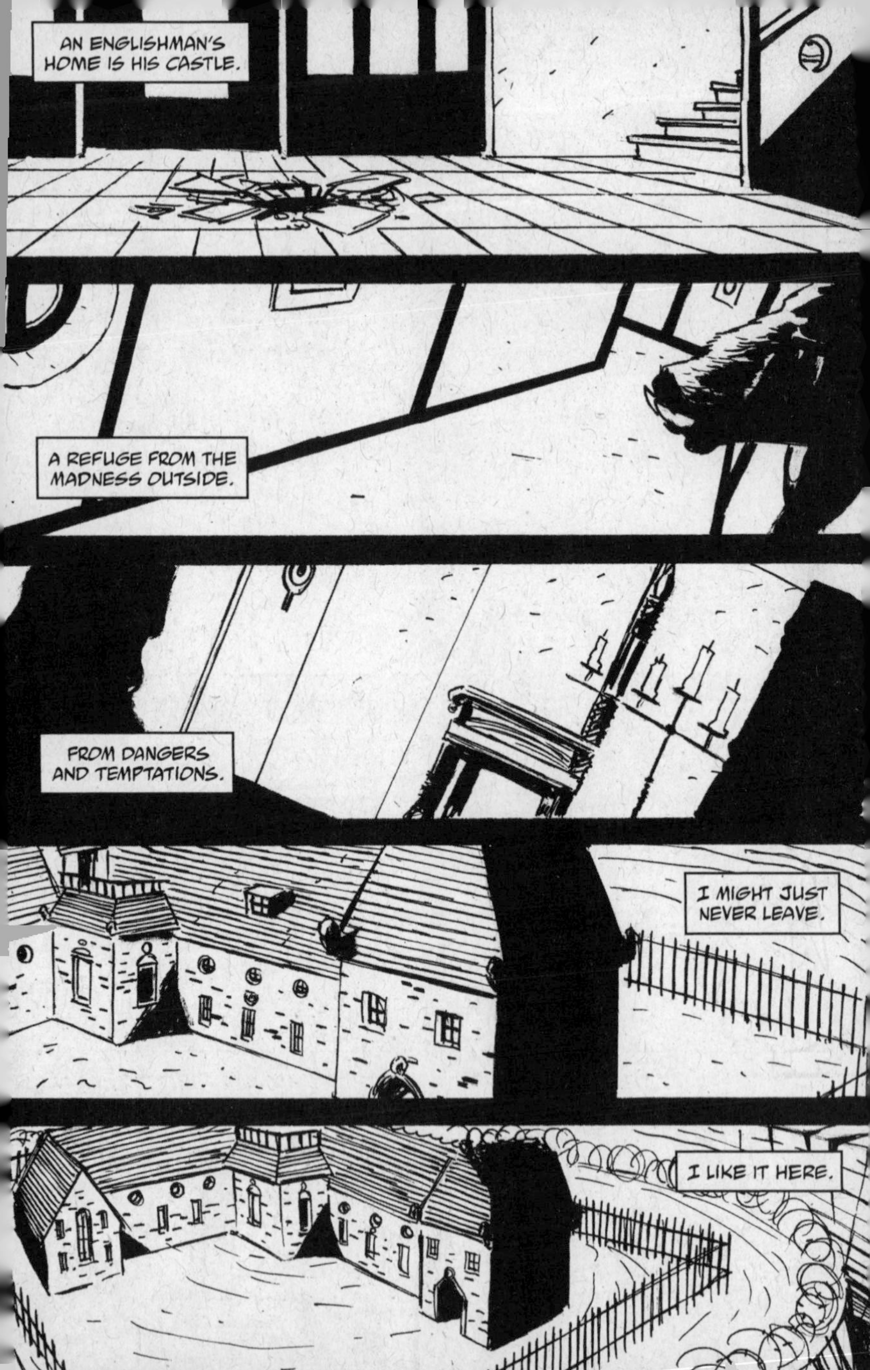
AN ENGLISHMAN'S HOME IS HIS CASTLE.
A REFUGE FROM THE MADNESS OUTSIDE.
FROM DANGERS AND TEMPTATIONS.
I MIGHT JUST NEVER LEAVE.
I LIKE IT HERE.

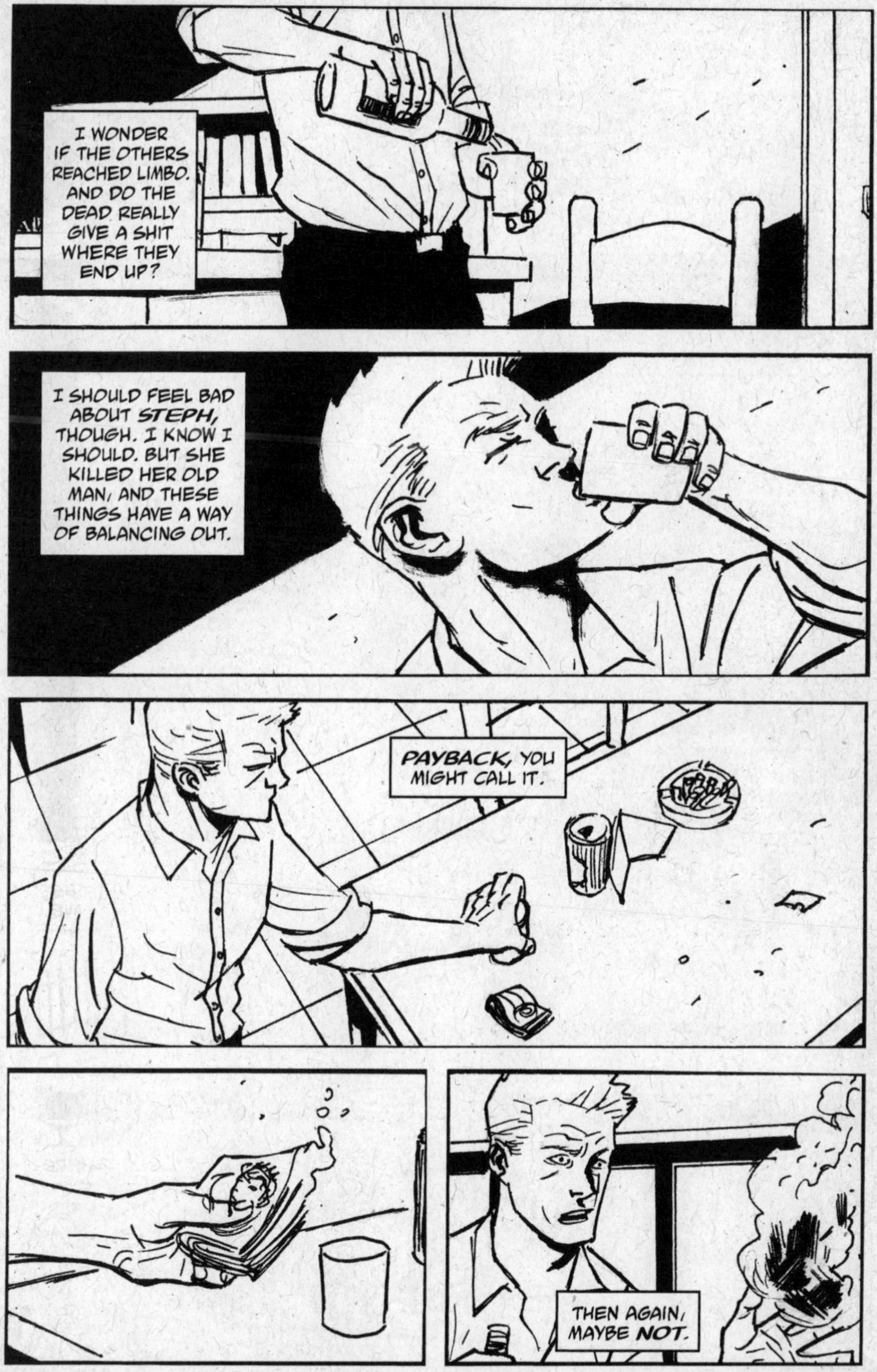
I WONDER IF THE OTHERS REACHED LIMBO. AND DO THE DEAD REALLY GIVE A SHIT WHERE THEY END UP?
I SHOULD FEEL BAD ABOUT STEPH, THOUGH. I KNOW I SHOULD. BUT SHE KILLED HER OLD MAN, AND THESE THINGS HAVE A WAY OF BALANCING OUT.
PAYBACK, YOU MIGHT CALL IT.
THEN AGAIN, MAYBE NOT.

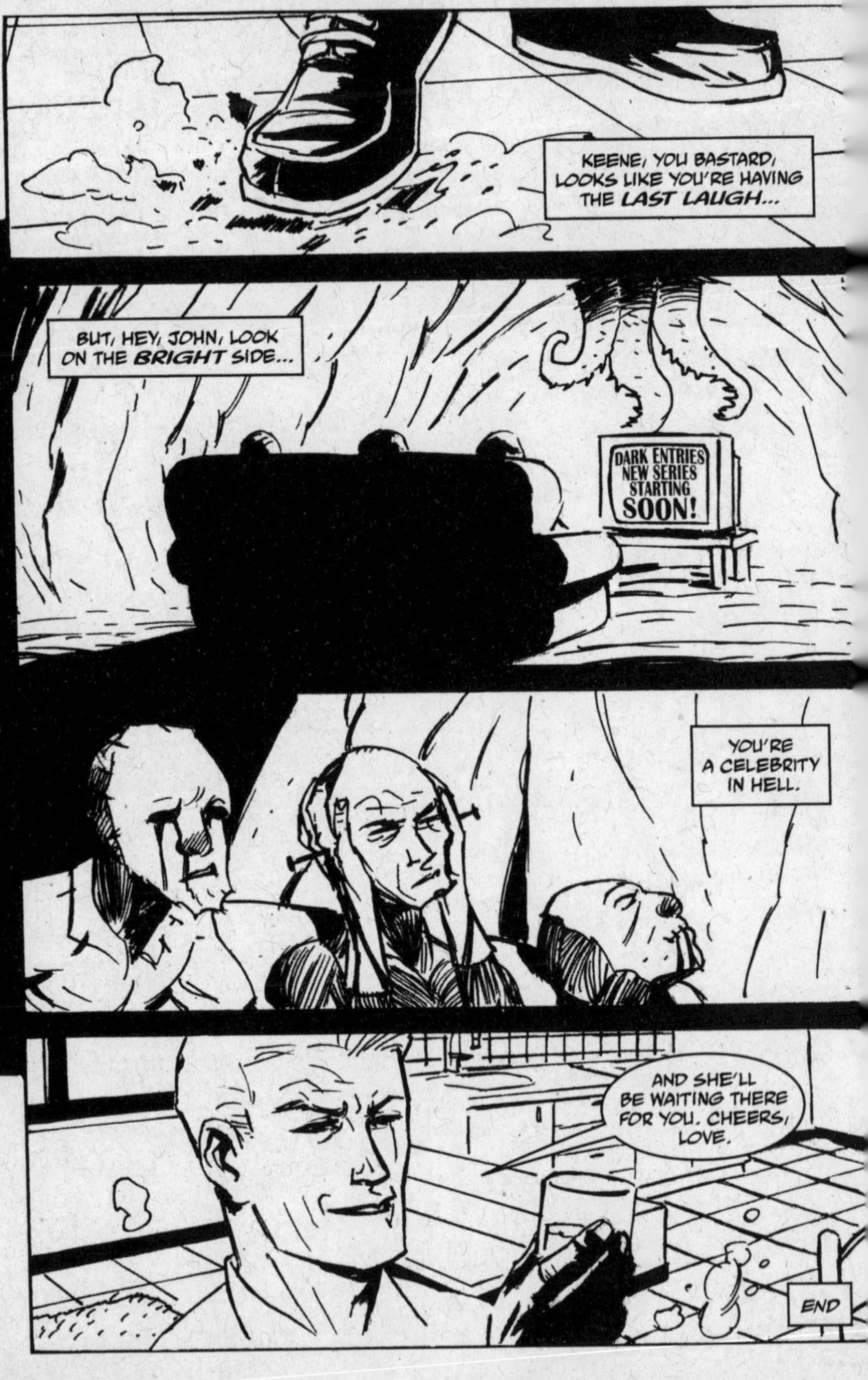
KEENE, YOU BASTARD, LOOKS LIKE YOU'RE HAVING THE LAST LAUGH...
BUT, HEY, JOHN, LOOK ON THE BRIGHT SIDE...
DARK ENTRIES NEW SERIES STARTING SOON!
YOU'RE A CELEBRITY IN HELL.
AND SHE'LL BE WAITING THERE FOR YOU. CHEERS, LOVE.
END

MORE VERTIGO CRIME

JASON
STARR
Art by
MICK
THE CHILL

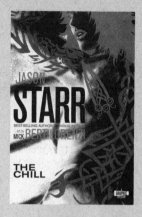

THE CHILL
AVAILABLE NOW

Written by **JASON STARR**
(Best-selling author of *Panic Attack* and *The Follower*)

Art by **MICK BERTILORENZI**

A modern thriller steeped in Celtic mythology – a broken-down cop tracks a seductive killer who possesses the supernatural power known as "the chill." Can he stop her before her next victim dies horribly... but with a smile on his face?

PETER
MILLIGAN
JAMES
ROMBERGER
THE BRONX KILL
VERTIGO CRIME

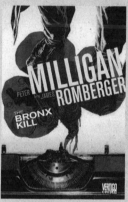

THE BRONX KILL
AVAILABLE NOW

Written by **PETER MILLIGAN**
(GREEK STREET)

Art by **JAMES ROMBERGER**

A struggling writer is investigating his Irish cop roots for his next novel. When he returns home from a research trip, his wife is missing and finding her will lead him to a dark secret buried deep in his family's past.

VERTIGO CRIME
THE EXECUTOR
JON
EVANS
Art by ANDREA MUTTI
Hockey 1-4, Captain 4

THE EXECUTOR
AVAILABLE NOW

Written by **JON EVANS**
(Author of *Dark Places* and *Invisible Armies*)

Art by **ANDREA MUTTI**

When a washed-up ex-hockey player is mysteriously named executor of an old girlfriend's will, he must return to the small town he left years earlier. There, he finds a deadly secret from his past that could hold the key to his girlfriend's murder... if it doesn't kill him first.

VERTIGO CRIME

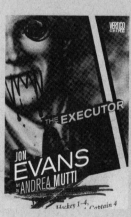